American Bed & Breakfast Association's

Inspected, Rated & Approved

Bed & Breakfasts

♛♛♛

Country Inns

Fourth Edition

Publisher: Sarah W. Sonke
Chief Editor: Beth Burgreen Stuhlman

ISBN: 0-934473-26-9

Manufactured in the United States of America
Printed by Bookcrafters
Fourth Edition/First Printing

The cover story: Our cover painting "Stafford's Roselawn Porch" from original watercolor (30x22"), by Jan Vandenbrink, overlooks the pristine waters and sunsets of Little Traverse Bay on Michigan's Northwest shoreline near her Petoskey home. This gracious Victorian country inn is in the Bay View Association, a registered landmark founded in 1875.

Jan's watercolor and pastel paintings include natural and structural landmarks, wetlands, woodlands, waterfronts and figures. She states, "As lifestyles are rapidly changing and our lives become too fleeting, we seek natural elements to slow us down and provide peace, solitude, reflection and discovery. Therefore, the images in my work are an impressionistic response to that need... considerations of positive and sustaining harmonies in my environment and life experiences."

This cover artwork is available in a limited edition offset lithograph. For information contact: Jan Vandenbrink Studio, 505 Cherry Street, Petoskey, MI 49770.

Contents

How to travel B&B successfully

Personal hospitality, delicious home-made breakfasts, and uniquely decorated rooms are a few of the reasons B&Bs nationwide continue to gain favor with travelers and those looking for a special getaway. But now, more and more experienced travelers are looking for an assurance that "they get what they pay for." This guidebook is a first in that it incorporates evaluations and ratings of its members throughout North America on a consistent <u>nation-wide</u> standard for quality.

Bed & breakfast has come a long way in North America since its humble beginnings a little over a decade ago. With an estimated 20,000 accommodations now available throughout the United States and Canada, there is a B&B for everyone's taste and budget.

The wide variety of accommodations can range from a lobsterman's island home off the coast of Maine to a beach house in California. From an elegant high-rise apartment in New York City to an Alaskan farm with a trout stream where the host promises, "if you catch 'em and clean 'em, I'll cook 'em for breakfast." For the adventurous, there's B&B on a tugboat. If you're a history buff, you'll enjoy the many restored antique homes available, from Southern ante-bellum mansions to quaint New England sea captains' homes. Nature lovers might enjoy staying at a working cattle ranch out West or visiting a new cedar lodge overlooking a pure mountain river in West Virginia which is a ninety minute trip from the nearest paved road by four-wheel drive.

Keys to an enjoyable B&B stay

The key to an enjoyable stay at a bed and breakfast is to choose one that matches your individuality, style, and pocketbook. As a potential guest, you should let your specific desires be known. Some of the questions you should ask before making a reservation include:

♕ Consider the location. Is parking available if you are arriving by car? Is the neighborhood safe for your morning jog? Do you need public transportation? What activities and restaurants are nearby?

♕ What is the purpose of your visit? If the purpose of your visit is a week-end getaway, be sure to mention this, especially if you'd like privacy, a romantic room with a fireplace, whirlpool tub, and a bottle of chilled wine waiting. If you are traveling on business you may want to request a quiet room with a private bath, private telephone, television, desk with good lighting, and a corporate rate.

♔ Do you prefer a large guest room? Would you prefer a private bath? Check whether the room is air-conditioned if this is important to you. If you are traveling to a scenic location check to see if there is a room with a good view. If climbing steps is a problem be sure to ask for a first-floor guest room.

♔ What price range do you have in mind? Would spending an additional $10 get you an upgraded room? Does the B&B accept credit cards? What is their cancellation policy? What happens if you arrive and don't like your guest room?

♔ The host family at a B&B may include small children as well as pets. Check on this in advance if you are trying to get a quiet weekend away from your children, or if you have allergies to pets.

♔ Most B&B homes and inns will not allow smoking in guest rooms or common areas. If the inn's non-smoking policy is a concern to you check in advance. A number of non-smoking inns will charge a hefty cleaning fee if guests smoke in non-smoking rooms.

♔ All B&Bs must include a full or continental breakfast in the overnight room rate. These breakfasts can really vary from a pastry and coffee to five-course meal. Ask what time breakfast is served and be sure it fits into your travel schedule. After all, you don't want to miss breakfast when you've already paid for it. Be certain to discuss any special dietary needs you may have with your hosts in advance.

♔ Special considerations: If you are traveling with children or pets be sure to mention this on the telephone. Some bed and breakfast do have handi-capped facilities but many do not have this provision so be sure to check in advance if you have special needs.

♔ Is the B&B inspected by a national organization such as the American Bed & Breakfast Association, American Automobile Association, or Mobil Travel Guide? Only about 10% of all bed and breakfasts agree to open their doors for an annual inspection from an organization that sets consistent standards for every state. This number will naturally increase though as more and more travelers insist on inspected properties and B&B owners understand the credibility of passing an annual inspection can bring to their establish-ment.

How to be a good guest

Once you have made reservations, here are some pointers to help ensure a happy stay at a bed and breakfast:

♕ Call you host and give the approximate time of arrival. Get specific directions from the host that will aid you in finding the B&B, especially in the dark.

♕ When there's an unexpected delay and you're going to arrive late, telephone your hosts in advance so that they are prepared to stay up late or make arrangements to leave a key for you.

♕ Adhere to your host's policies regarding smoking, children, and pets.

♕ If you must cancel your stay, contact your host immediately. Cancellation policies differ from one B&B to the next. Be sure to cancel within the time period of their cancellation policy to ensure a full refund of your deposit.

♕ After your visit provide feedback to your host or the reservation agency handling your accommodations.

Which type of B&B suits you?

When planning your B&B stay, it is important to determine which type best suits your individuality, style, and pocketbook. The large number of bed & breakfast accommodations now available can be divided into several distinct categories: private B&B homes, B&B inns, and country inns with restaurants.

B&B homes are the traditional style of B&B in a private home whose hosts are individuals who enjoy meeting other people, sharing their homes and communities, and perhaps even showing off in the kitchen with their favorite breakfast recipes. Hosts generally have jobs outside the home during the day but enjoy taking occasional guests when their schedules allow. Guests are made to feel part of the family in this people-to-people hospitality concept which has thrived in Europe for decades. Reservations at most B&B homes are made in advance through B&B reservation agencies as the names and addresses of B&B homes are not published and these hosts prefer advance reservations. Rates for two range from $45 to 75 per night, depending upon location and amenities offered.

B&B inns and country inns are commercial lodgings that pride themselves on providing personal attention and clean, comfortable accommodations. A wide variety of inns are available, from historic homes to contemporary mansions, each having established their own unique individuality and charm. Rates for inns generally range from $75 to well over $100, depending upon location and amenities offered. Reservations are usually made directly with the inn.

B&B Reservation Agencies

Many travelers use the services of a B&B reservation agency to help choose the perfect B&B. B&B reservation agencies are businesses that are similar to a travel agency whose specialty is B&Bs. They will arrange all of the details of a B&B stay for guests who wish to choose from a variety of accommodations but prefer to make only one phone call. Look for names and telephone numbers of the American Bed & Breakfast Association member B&B reservation agencies at the beginning page of each state as well as as in the back of this book.

How to use this guide

Each B&B is listed alphabetically by state, city, and business name. The description provides an overview of the property. Rates were accurate at press time but are subject to change.

About the AB&BA inspection and rating system

The American Bed & Breakfast Association is the only organization within the bed and breakfast industry that has established national standards and a consumer rating system for every property. Meeting minimum standards is verified by an annual on-site inspection performed by trained AB&BA evaluators. The ratings that appear in this book are intended to give readers a true feel for the overall quality of the property, the level of guest services, cleanliness, and how well the building and its contents are maintained.

The ratings in this book are very similar to grades awarded in schools throughout the United States. The rating appears as a crown symbol and is accompanied by a letter grade which sometimes shows a plus or minus sign.

♔ or a rating of of C means "Acceptable, meets basic requirements."

♔♔ or rating of B means "Good, exceeds basic requirements."

♔♔♔ or a rating of A means "Excellent, far exceeds basic requirements."

♔♔♔♔ or a rating of AA means "Outstanding."

Guest comments

All guest comments which appear in this book are verified and an affidavit signed by the guest is on file with the association.

What is the American Bed & Breakfast Association?

The American Bed & Breakfast Association (AB&BA) has been a trusted name in B&B travel since it was founded in 1981. Objectives of the association are:

♛ To encourage and support B&B travel in North America.

♛ To gather and distribute reliable B&B travel information.

♛ To encourage public and private sector efforts to promote B&B.

♛ To unite the diverse components of the B&B industry and implement programs that support common goals.

♛ To provide a forum for addressing industry-wide issues.

♛ To provide services, conduct studies, disseminate information, and provide networking opportunities for the benefit of its membership.

AB&BA Code of Ethics

1. We acknowledge ethics and morality as inseparable elements of doing business and will test every decision against the highest standards of honesty, legality, fairness, impunity, and conscience.

2. We will conduct ourselves personally and collectively at all times such as to bring credit to the service and tourism industry at large.

3. We will concentrate our time, energy, and resources on the improvement of our own product and services and we will not denigrate our competition in the pursuit of our own success.

4. We will treat all guests equally regardless of race, religion, nationality, creed, or sex.

5. We will deliver standards of service and product with total consistency to every guest.

6. We will provide a safe and sanitary environment at all times for every guest and employee.

7. We will strive constantly, in words, actions, and deeds, to develop and maintain the highest level of trust, honesty and understanding among guests, clients, employees, employers and the public at large.

8. We will provide every employee at every level all of the knowledge, training, equipment, and motivation required to perform his or her own tasks according to our standards.

9. We will guarantee that every employee at every level will have the same opportunity to perform, advance, and will be evaluated against the same standard as all employees engaged in the same or similar tasks.

10. We will actively and consciously work to protect and preserve our natural environment and natural resources in all that we do.

11. We will seek a fair and honest profit.

Your comments invited

The American Bed & Breakfast Association hears from B&B travelers every day and would enjoy hearing from you too! What do you like about B&B travel? What could B&B owners do to make your travel more enjoyable? Is there a B&B you highly recommend that is not in this book? Written comments should be sent to:

American Bed & Breakfast Association
P.O. Box 1387
Midlothian, VA 23113-1387
U.S.A.

Additional information about B&Bs in Alabama is available through the following B&B reservation agency: Lincoln Ltd. B&B (601) 482-5483.

Greenville/Forest Home

Pine Flat Plantation Bed & Breakfast
P.O. Box 33, Hwy. 10 West
Forest Home, AL 36030
(334) 471-8024 or (334) 346-2739
(Use area code 205 before 1/15/95)
Innkeeper: Jane Inge

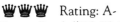 Rating: A-
Rates: Single/$65-85; Double/$70-90
Auto club discount

Joined by a 5,000 acre wildlife management area and hunting club, this 1825 Greek Revival home is 50 miles southwest of Montgomery. Heart pine floors, walls, and ceilings are found throughout the inn which offers five guest rooms, each with private bath. The whole house is furnished with antiques, fresh flowers, Oriental rugs, and watercolors by local artists. Explore the surrounding acreage with its rustic log cabin (available for rental with advance notice). Visit the on-site fishing pond as well as the two-story smoke house, country store, horse barn, hen house, cook's house, and pump house. Hike the trails along the 1,100 acres of family timberland, go hunting, fishing, horseback riding, or take a hay ride with pre-arranged guides on the property. Antique shopping and golf are available. A full country breakfast is offered which often includes eggs, grits, biscuits, and ham. A large entrance foyer with living and dining areas offers suitable space for weddings and parties. No smoking. Families welcome.

Guests write: *"This is without exception the most charming country retreat imaginable. The house itself is impeccably clean and decorated with attractive fabrics with fresh colors of yellow, blues, greens and corals. The owners retained the original style of the period while incorporating every needed comfort of the 90s. It is a trip back in time to a life of Southern ladies and gentlemen. The porches are romantic, the bathrooms large and wonderfully equipped, the breakfast grand and delicious, and the grounds are dreamy. I have travelled the world and have experienced B&Bs from London to Mississippi, and this one is more of the distinction of a country inn. Absolutely a divine get-a-way."* (S. Ashurst)

Montgomery

Red Bluff Cottage
551 Clay Street
Montgomery, AL 36104
(205) 264-0056
Innkeepers: Mark and Anne Waldo

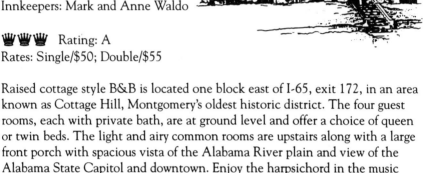

♛♛♛ Rating: A
Rates: Single/$50; Double/$55

Raised cottage style B&B is located one block east of I-65, exit 172, in an area known as Cottage Hill, Montgomery's oldest historic district. The four guest rooms, each with private bath, are at ground level and offer a choice of queen or twin beds. The light and airy common rooms are upstairs along with a large front porch with spacious vista of the Alabama River plain and view of the Alabama State Capitol and downtown. Enjoy the harpsichord in the music room and collection of good books. Interesting sites nearby include Montgomery's magnificent Shakespeare Festival Theater, Museum of Fine Arts, and the newly expanded zoo. Well-lit, off-street parking is available. Full breakfast served. No smoking. Families welcome.

Guests write: *"This is our third stay at Red Bluff Cottage and it was wonderful as were two previous visits. Breakfast was great - a real treat! Very clean with charming hosts. I think the rating in your book should have been higher. The Waldo's are wonderful hosts and make our visits very enjoyable."* (M. Alvarez)

"After visiting the First White House of the Confederacy we mentioned to Anne at Red Bluff Cottage the beautiful white rose we had seen there and that we would like to purchase such a rose plant. Anne contacted the director of the foundation and was told that that particular rose was not available, however, if we would like to get some cuttings we could. We returned to Red Bluff Cottage where Anne had the proper materials to provide a start for the clippings. The hospitality provided was above and beyond even what one comes to expect as Southern hospitality. The accommodations are excellent." (A. James)

Additional information on B&Bs in Alaska is available from the following B&B reservation agency: Alaska Private Lodgings, Stay with a Friend (907) 258-1717.

Anchorage

Arctic Loon B&B
P.O. Box 110333
Anchorage, AK 99511
(907) 345-4935
Innkeepers: Jane and Lee Johnson

♔♔♔   Rating: A
Rates: Single/$60-75; Double/$75-90
Credit Cards: MC, V

Contemporary Swedish Long House with bay windows is located twelve miles from the airport and situated high above the city with "million-dollar" panoramic views. Choose from three guest rooms, one with private bath. All are decorated with an emphasis on light and open space. One room offers a private entrance, microwave, separate seating area, TV with VCR, and extensive movie collection. There is a lower level recreation room for guest use with Jacuzzi, sauna, and exercise room. The second-floor music room offers a grand piano. Full breakfast includes fresh fruit, special egg dishes, and regional specialties such as smoked salmon or caribou. Two night minimum stay.

Guests write: *"We stayed at the Arctic Loon B&B and recommend it very highly. The Johnsons are nice people. The accommodations are outstanding and breakfast yummy (don't miss the poppy seed muffins). You will need a car to get there, it is about 20 minutes to downtown or the airport."* (Tom Wadsworth)

Anchorage

Snowline Bed and Breakfast
11101 Snowline Drive
Anchorage, Alaska 99516
(907) 346-1631
Innkeepers: Ed and Dana Klinkhart

♔♔♔   Rating: A
Rates: Single or Double/$85-105

Alpine A-frame home is located in the quiet hillside just 20 minutes from the airport and downtown Anchorage. Two guest rooms are available. One is a two-room suite with a king-size bed and private bath. A second room offers over 500 square feet of living space with a magnificent view, private entrance, queen-size bed and six-person Jacuzzi. Enjoy a panoramic view of Anchorage, Cook Inlet, and Mount McKinley from the living room or sun deck. Chugach State Park, hiking trails, golf course, and the Alaska Zoo are just minutes away. Continental breakfast features homemade pastries and fresh-ground coffee. Families welcome. No smoking.

Guests write: *"There was a moose on the beautiful lawn two different nights when we returned to Snowline. Dana and Ed are very pleasant and informative about the state and city. Breakfasts of homemade goodies were a delicious start for the day."* (W. Graham)

"Alaskan hospitality is alive and well at the Snowline B&B. The hosts, Ed and Dana, were friendly and informative. The inn was immaculate and comfortable. A great place to start or finish a trip to Alaska. We did both there." (S. Davison)

"They treated me to moose, smoked salmon, homemade muffins, biscuits and lots of coffee and conversation. I took beautiful photos of sunsets and the twinkling lights of Anchorage - all from my room. Ed & Dana had lots of videos and magazines on Anchorage." (C. Wilde)

Chugiak

Peters Creek Inn
22635 Davidson Road
Chugiak, AK 99567
(907) 688-2776 or Fax: (907) 688-2080
Innkeepers: Pamela and Douglas Buyse

♛♛   Rating: B+
Rates: Single/$55; Double/$65
Credit Cards: MC, V

Located 18 miles from Anchorage, just north of Anchorage's bedroom community of Eagle River, this contemporary home provides guests with a private entrance, dining room, and living room facilities. Each of the five guest rooms with private baths have been decorated with an Alaskan theme: the Angler, the Prospector, the Musher, the Trapper, and the Sourdough. The inn is close enough to Anchorage to enjoy the local attractions found there yet still offer a secluded retreat in a rural setting. Nearby attractions include Eklutna Village Historical Park, Thunderbird Falls, Chugach State Park, Independence Mine State Historical Park, and the Knick Glaciers. Farm-fresh eggs and sourdough pancakes are accompanied with freshly ground coffee and fresh fruit. Small meeting facilities available. Families welcome. No smoking.

Fairbanks

Alaska's 7 Gables Bed & Breakfast
4312 Birch Lane
Fairbanks, AK 99708
(907) 479-0751
Fax: (907) 479-2229
Innkeepers: Paul and Leicha Welton

♛♛   Rating: B+
Rates: Single/$45-75; Double/$50-95
Credit Cards: AE, MC, V

Modern Tudor home built near the river boasts a two-story sun space with floral solarium and is located one mile west of Fairbanks, between the airport and the university. Choose from ten guest rooms with cable television, VCR, private phones; eight offer a private bath. Several of the rooms are suites and six have Jacuzzis. Relax in the garden or solarium, use one of the inn's canoes to explore the river, or borrow a bike to tour the area. Many of Alaska's unique points of interest are nearby such as the Pipeline, the Sternwheeler river boat, University of Alaska Museum, the Alaskaland Theme Park, or Santa Claus' House in the North Pole. Pan for gold at the Gold Dredge #8 or visit the Musk Ox and Reindeer Farm. Gourmet full breakfast often includes homemade bran or berry muffins, egg dishes, fruit, and herbal teas. Wedding and meeting facilities. Restricted smoking. Families welcome.

Guests write: *"The exterior belies the quite lovely and spacious interior with a homey atmosphere in the common areas. The suites still allow you to escape to noise-free seclusion. The private Jacuzzi was a nice treat. Walking through the solarium filled with fragrant flowers and vegetables was the highlight of our stay."* (A&M Sheppard)

"I spent only 7 days, but had a very happy time. Hosts are very kind, even for foreigners. I'm not good at English but with his help, I am gradually getting the ability to understand English." (T. Ojio)

"I loved the Green room with the slanted roof from the gable, Kermit the Frog door stop, Miss Piggy dressed in green. The gourmet breakfast included yogurt frappe drink, crab souffle, baked eggs with asparagus and hollaindaise sauce, and tasty muffins." (R. Moore)

Juneau

Pearson's Pond Luxury Inn & Travel Service
4541 Sawa Circle
Juneau, AK 99801
(907) 789-3772; Fax: (907) 789-6722
Innkeepers: Diane and Steve Pearson

♛♛♛ Rating: A-
Rates: Single/$64-145; Double/$74-149
Corporate & weekly off-season discounts
Credit Cards: MC, V

A view of the Mendenhall Glacier is the scenic backdrop for this modern cedar inn located in Alaska's capital city of Juneau. Three guest rooms, one with private bath, offer private entries, queen sized beds, and VCR with stereo and tapes. Relax in the hot tub on the banks of a wilderness lily pond with its view of the glacier. Sit in front of the fire in the fireside room or in the living room. Go biking, skiing, hiking, fishing, or boating. This is a convenient location near the river, airport, ferry, and shopping as well as to Glacier Bay National Monument. A flexible, self-serve, full variety breakfast is offered, featuring cappucino and fresh, homemade bread. No smoking.

Guests write: *"The spectacular view of the Mendenhall Glacier from my hot tub will be imprinted in my mind forever. The peaceful beauty of nature abounds everywhere. Diane's love and enthusiasm for her land is evident in her warm personality. The yard is a palate of color from her master gardening skills."* (K&C Fink)

"We enjoyed the large room, the great homemade bread and the Jacuzzi. We will highly recommend it to others." (F. Barton)

"Great hospitality. They have a beautiful home and I enjoyed every minute that I was there. Whether it be relaxing in the hot tub, feeding the ducks, or just sitting on the porch with a cup of coffee, the peacefulness that exudes from there is very special." (P. Coolidge)

"We arrived in the city late in the evening. Much to our disappointment, our reserved hotel room was nothing like the advertisement. In our search to find appropriate accommodations for honeymooners, we called Diane at Pearson's Pond. This contact not only salvaged our vacation, but offered us an exceptional environment for an intimate hide away. Great place!" (C. Sumrall)

Wasilla

Yukon Don's B&B Inn
2221 Yukon Circle
Wasilla, AK 99654
(907) 376-7472 or (800) 478-7472
Innkeepers: Don and Kristan Tanner

♛♛♛   Rating: A-
Rates: Single/$55; Double/$65; Suite/$75-105
Gold dust, cash, personal checks, or traveler's checks accepted
Senior and corporate discounts

Historic Alaskan homestead barn with views of the Talkeetna Mountains is now a unique inn located 35 miles north of Anchorage and 4 miles south of Wasilla. Five guest rooms are available, two with private bath. All rooms are spacious, have interesting Alaskan decor, and feature a vast collection of Alaskan memorabilia. A large recreation room offers a TV with VCR, pool table and library of books and videos on Alaska. Arrangements can be made for guided tour groups. Continental breakfast. Families welcome. No smoking.

Guests write: *"I just love walking through the B&B because it is like a walk through the best that Alaska has to offer...with memorabilia and artifacts at every turn. We are so confident with the service and hospitality here at Yukon Don's that we also have our guests stay here at the beginning of their journey to spend time with us in "bush Alaska". It is a tremendous way to begin their trip...they get to see a little of the past, present and future Alaska at Yukon Don's Bed and Breakfast."* (J&C Chadd)

Arizona

Additional information about B&Bs throughout Arizona is available through the following reservation agency: Mi Casa, Su Casa (800) 456-0682.

Flagstaff

The Inn at 410
410 North Leroux Street
Flagstaff, AZ 86001
(800) 774-2008 or (602) 774-0088
Innkeepers: Howard & Sally Krueger

Rating: B+
Rates: Single or Double/$70-110
Credit Cards: AE, MC, V

1907 Craftsman two-story inn is located north of Phoenix on I-17 at the cross roads of I-17 and I-40. The inn has a recent addition with front porch and gazebo, landscaped patio with perennial gardens, and a rock wall accenting the front yard. Choose from nine guest rooms, seven with private bath and six serving as suites. Each room has been individually decorated with special features such as bent twig furniture, iron fence headboard, mahogany wood-work, stained glass, and antiques. Relax on the front porch swing and enjoy a sunset view or sit in the large living room with board games, CD player, and conversation seating. Round tables fashioned from old sewing machine bases are arranged near the living room fireplace. Walk to restaurants, antique shops, and Native American galleries. Area attractions: Sedona & Oak Creek Canyon, Wupatki National Park, Sunset Crater National Monument, Walnut Canyon National Monument. Enjoy nearby Grand Canyon National Park, Northern Arizona University, and the museum of Northern Arizona. A full breakfast is served on china with silver service and linens. Sample menu includes fruit cup, peach melba bread pudding with raspberry sauce, fresh muffins and a juice blend. Entrees are healthy and low-fat whenever possible. Facilities for small weddings. Wheelchair accessible. Families welcome. No smoking.

Guests write: *"The rooms at the inn are tastefully appointed, a delight to the eye. Breakfast is an experience of homemade delectables that are different each morning. Soft, classical music floats through the cozy breakfast room to enhance the flavors. From the moment I encountered the graciousness of our hosts, I knew that their business was hospitality. This B&B even turned out to be an ideal location for a small workshop."* (M. McCormack)

Sedona

A Touch of Sedona
595 Jordan Road
Sedona, AZ 86336
(602) 282-6462; Fax: (602) 282-1534
Innkeepers: Bill & Sharon Larsen

♛♛♛   Rating: A
Rates: Single or Double/$85-125
Credit Cards: MC, V

California Spanish inn with a red tile roof is situated 27 miles south of
Flagstaff at the south end of Oak Creek Canyon. The surrounding desert
landscape accents the property and Red Rock, Steamboat Rock, and Mount
Wilson are just at the end of the road, affording quite a view from the deck.
There are five rooms from which to choose, each with a private bath, and one
new studio apartment with a gas fireplace and full kitchen. Guests can gather
in the spacious great room furnished with comfortable seating, antique tables
perfect for playing cards or board games, and huge picture windows with views
of Snoopy Rock. There are shops and restaurants nearby in the Jordan Road
Historic area and plenty of photo opportunities including Native American
sacred sites. Other attractions include hiking, fishing, skiing, swimming, golf,
horseback riding, and jeep tours. Full breakfast includes fresh-baked muffins.
Meeting facilities available. No smoking.

Guests write: *"Outstanding contemporary Southwestern decor! Rooms are
comfortable, spacious with privacy but with easy access to the central kitchen and
common room. Close to shopping, yet set in a quiet residential area. Hosts were
friendly and extremely helpful providing information on the Sedona area, yet were
respectful and non-intrusive."* (R. Guest)

*"Bill and Sharon made our stay in Sedona really wonderful with their hospitality and
knowledge of the area. Bill makes a filling hiker's breakfast. This was our first
experience in a B&B and from now on this is how we will travel."* (T. Pesta)

*"Beautifully decorated suite with a king-size lodge-pole bed. The full kitchen was well
outfitted. Fantastic breakfasts — blintzes, French toast, eggs Florentine —
wonderful! We stayed four nights."* (S. Purnell)

*"Upon arriving at A Touch of Sedona, Bill and Sharon made us feel more like family
than guests. The atmosphere and hospitality had a real make-yourself-at-home
quality. It was a wonderful experience."* (W.T. Workman)

Sedona

Canyon Villa Bed & Breakfast Inn
125 Canyon Circle Drive
Sedona, AZ 86351
(602) 284-1226 or (800) 453-1166
Fax: (602) 284-2114
Innkeepers: Chuck & Marion Yadon

♛♛♛♛ Rating: AA-
Rates: Single:$95-165; Double:$105-175
Credit Cards: MC, V

Canyon Villa Bed & Breakfast is located 117 miles north of Phoenix, Arizona via I-17 to SR 179 exit. This Southwest Spanish Mission style stucco inn, featuring arches, stained glass windows, and spectacular Red Rock views, sits adjacent to Coconino National Forest. The grounds provide a desert landscape in front, and swimming pool, patio area, fish pond, fountain, and lush garden area adjacent to guest rooms in the back. Each of the eleven guest rooms offers a private bath and decor ranging from country charm and Western romance to Victorian elegance. Room amenities include television, bathrobes, and telephone. Enjoy complimentary soft drinks, juices, and fresh fruit in the common rooms, which boast large windows and 20-foot high beamed ceilings with skylights. The living room and dining room are divided by a see-through fireplace and furnished with family heirlooms, antiques, and fine art. Quiet reading areas are found in the well-stocked library. Within walking distance is the National Forest, two 18-hole championship golf courses, one 9-hole golf course, and tennis courts. Area attractions: Sedona's scenic Red Rocks, hiking in Coconino National Forest, Southwestern artists and galleries, jeep rides, hot-air ballooning, tennis, biking, fishing, ancient Indian ruins, Red Rock State Park, Slide Rock State Park, Jerome (ghost town), Oak Creek Canyon, Boynton Canyon, Schnebly Hill Road, and Flagstaff. Full breakfast served on china includes juice, fresh fruit, yeast breads and a hot entree such as French toast, pancakes, ham and egg casserole, Southwestern omelet, or scrambled eggs in potato boats. Wheelchair access. No smoking.

Guests write: *"My wife and I have stayed in perhaps a hundred or so B&Bs throughout Europe and England. Each one was selected based on some remarkable attribute such as location, view, food, and amenities. We were overwhelmed by the stunning combination of all these features at Canyon Villa."* (R. Dalton)

"The owners, Chuck & Marion Yadan, have thought of every detail from the decor of each room to the presentation of afternoon snacks, to the Sweet Dreams surprises

awaiting you in the living room before you settle in at night. Unsurpassed in all ways, definitely a must for all. You can fill your days with great sights or relax by the pool with the latest best-seller. Either way, you won't be disappointed." (J. West)

"Canyon Villa has amenities above other B&Bs that we've visited such as: the view, the Jacuzzi in the bathroom, fresh fruit and cold drinks available all the time, afternoon snacks, cookies at bed time... we note that this is a far above the average B&B." (B. Feshel)

"We have only praise for Canyon Villa: beautiful decor, good breakfast, friendly staff, spectacular view, attractive landscaping. We'll alert our Arizona relatives about this B&B." (N. Rourke)

Sedona

Casa Sedona
55 Hozoni Drive
Sedona, AZ 86336
(800) 525-3756 or (602) 282-2938
Innkeeper: Misty Zitko

♔♔♔   Rating: A
Rates: Single/$85-140; Double/$95-150
Credit Cards: MC, V

Southwest Spanish hacienda was designed by a Frank Lloyd Wright architect to blend into the surrounding desert beauty. It has outstanding views of the surrounding natural rock formations and is located 120 miles north of Phoenix; 35 miles south of Flagstaff. Each of the eleven guest rooms offers a Red Rock view, terrace, private bath, whirlpool tub, and fireplace. Sit and watch a desert sunrise in the Sunrise Alcove or relax in the library with its fireplace and comfortable furniture. Watch television or listen to music in the Sierra Room. Area attractions: Native American ruins, jeep touring, hiking, and hot air ballooning. Take a van tour to the Grand Canyon or a scenic airplane ride to view the Red Rocks from the sky. Sedona's resorts offer live entertainment and the town is known for its artist colony and numerous galleries. A full breakfast is served in the dining room or Sunrise Room and often includes Eggs Benedict or bread pudding. Wheelchair access. No smoking.

Eureka Springs

The Heartstone Inn and Cottages
35 Kings Highway
Eureka Springs, AR 72632
(501) 253-8916
Innkeepers: Iris and Bill Simantel

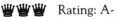 Rating: A-
Rates: Single or Double/$63-118
Credit Cards: AE, MC, V

1903 Victorian inn with cottage built in 1882 is set along a tree lined street
just four blocks away from the historic downtown of Eureka Springs and 50
miles from Fayetteville. Eleven guest rooms offer private baths, antique
furnishings, color cable television, and king or queen sized beds. Two cottages
are also available and offer complete privacy. The Victoria House features two
bedrooms, fully equipped kitchen, and a front porch perfect for relaxing in a
rocker. Take advantage of the on-site massage therapy/reflexology studio.
Enjoy the terraced gardens, porches, and gazebo or walk to downtown shops,
galleries, parks, and restaurants. Take horseback or carriage rides, see the local
Passion Play or music shows, and explore the many lakes nearby. A full
breakfast offers crepes or souffles. The gazebo is used for small weddings and
meetings are held in the breakfast room. Restricted smoking.

Guests write: *"One of the finest B&Bs in the state. Iris and Bill are a one-of-a-kind
couple; a definite asset to the industry and to the state of Arkansas." (K. Kraus)*

*"Outstanding! The best of the eight inns I have stayed at in the past year. Really top-
of-the-line breakfast. Very comfortable and outstanding decor. The deck overlooking
the trees and forest was beautiful. Parking was very good even though the inn was
located on the historic loop. We would stay there again anytime." (D. Dryer)*

*"The Heartstone is still our favorite. Why? Iris and Bill-always friendly and helpful;
the rooms-beautifully decorated and clean; the food always special and delicious;
convenience of being on the trolley route. The Heartstone is a jewel. From the
beautifully restored rooms to the bountiful and delicious breakfasts, every detail was
perfect." (S. Hardy)*

Hardy

Olde Stonehouse B&B Inn
511 Main Street
Hardy, AR 72542
(501) 856-2983
Innkeepers: Peggy and David Johnson

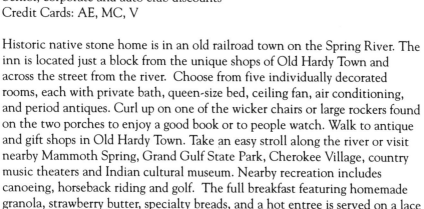

♛♛   Rating: B
Rates: Single/$50-80; Double/$55-85
Senior, corporate and auto club discounts
Credit Cards: AE, MC, V

Historic native stone home is in an old railroad town on the Spring River. The inn is located just a block from the unique shops of Old Hardy Town and across the street from the river. Choose from five individually decorated rooms, each with private bath, queen-size bed, ceiling fan, air conditioning, and period antiques. Curl up on one of the wicker chairs or large rockers found on the two porches to enjoy a good book or to people watch. Walk to antique and gift shops in Old Hardy Town. Take an easy stroll along the river or visit nearby Mammoth Spring, Grand Gulf State Park, Cherokee Village, country music theaters and Indian cultural museum. Nearby recreation includes canoeing, horseback riding and golf. The full breakfast featuring homemade granola, strawberry butter, specialty breads, and a hot entree is served on a lace tablecloth set with Grandma's china and silver. Special occasion packages, murder mystery weekends, dinner parties, and gift certificates available. No smoking.

Guests write: *"I had a wonderful time. The home is lovely, everything was so clean and decorated so lovely, we truly felt at home here. The hostess really went out of her way to leave dessert and coffee for us each night and the food was delicious!"* (L. Hall)

"The breakfast served was wonderful and elegant. We had homebaked bread, German pancakes, cereal, juice, fresh fruit - best I've ever had." (J. Reagan)

"All I can say is that we've been twice and already are talking about when we are going again! They say there is no place like home but this would have to be as close as you can get." (J. Clifton)

"The history and character of the house and furnishings, the delicious food, and the beauty of the Ozarks were only surpassed by the gracious hospitality of our hosts." (S. Payne)

Additional information about B&Bs throughout California is available through the following reservation agency: Eye Openers B&B Reservations (213) 684-4428 or (818) 798-3640.

Alameda

Garratt Mansion
900 Union Street
Alameda, CA 94501
(510) 521-4779 or Fax: (510) 521-6796
Innkeepers: Royce and Betty Gladden

♕♕♕ Rating: A-
Rates: Single/$65-100; Double/$75-125
Credit Cards: AE, MC, V
Corporate discount

Victorian inn built in the Colonial Revival style was the home of a turn-of-the-century industrialist and is located just 20 miles east of San Francisco. Choose from seven distinctive guest rooms, five of which offer a private bath. Enjoy the local examples of fine architecture or travel to nearby San Francisco, Berkeley, and the beach. A guest parlor and pantry on the second floor offer cold drinks and snacks any hour of the day. Full breakfast specialties of the inn include treats such as Dutch babies which are low-fat giant popovers filled with fresh fruit. Fresh squeezed juice and fresh ground coffee are served each day. All food is prepared with an accent on health using fresh herbs grown on the property and low-fat or non-fat dishes except the fresh baked chocolate chip cookies served each afternoon. Wedding and meeting facilities available. Families welcome. No smoking.

Aptos

Bayview Hotel B&B Inn
8041 Soquel Drive
Aptos, CA 95003
(408) 688-8654; Fax: (408) 688-5128
Innkeepers: Barry Hooper and Sue Parker

♕♕ Rating: B+
Rates: Single/$80-130; Double/$90-155
Credit Cards: AE, MC, V

Historic Victorian inn built in 1878 is a landmark building located in Aptos

Village, less than a mile from the Seacliff exit off Route 1; 35 miles south of San Jose. Choose from eleven guest rooms, some with fireplaces. Each offers a private bath, phone, and antique furnishings. Area attractions include antique shops, fine restaurants, state beaches, redwood parks, hiking and bicycle trails, golf, and tennis. Buffet-style breakfast is served in the restaurant on the lower level of the inn and includes fresh squeezed juice, seasonal fruit, egg dish, muesli, pastries, and gourmet coffee. No smoking.

Aptos

Mangels House
570 Aptos Creek Road
P.O. Box 302
Aptos, CA 95001
(408) 688-7982
Innkeeper: Jacqueline Fisher

♛♛♛   Rating: A
Rates: Single or Double/$98-125
Credit Cards: AE, MC, V

Four acres of orchards and woodlands near Monterey Bay's sailing and surfing is the setting for this Southern-style Colonial inn built circa 1880. The five guest rooms feature high ceilings and double-hung windows; three have a private bath. The downstairs parlor room is spacious and features a large grand piano, huge fireplace, and comfortable seating. Stroll through the formal gardens on the premises. The location is ideal as a retreat from city life and is known for the local summer music and theater festivals. Excellent restaurants can be found nearby as well as the North Monterey Bay's forests and beaches. Full breakfast and an evening sherry are offered. Restricted smoking.

Guests write: *"The Mangels house provided us the perfect romantic escape. The beautiful mauve room with its high ceilings, large old fashioned windows and second floor view of the front lane made me feel we'd gone back in time. Jackie's English upbringing was apparent at her scrumptious breakfasts. We discovered coddled eggs, scones, crumpets and tea with milk to be as delicious as they've always sounded. I have fond memories of Jackie trying to teach my husband how to properly hold an English tea cup."* (V. Holmes)

   "We arrived in the rain and were right away offered tea which appeared on a teacart with little tarts fresh out of the oven, plus a most welcome decanter of Dubonnet. The beauty of the place and the warmth of the host and hostess made a cozy evening in the flooding storm." (G. Wheeler)   (Continued)

"*Claus Mangel's soul may grace this home but the hosts are its heart. Because of Mr. Mangel, I was able to give my wife the tranquillity of a redwood forest, but the hosts provided the lovely garden to walk through. Mr. Mangel constructed the high ceilings, redwood floor and grand fireplace, but it was the hosts who lit the hearth whenever we returned from an outing. I mentioned my wife's birthday, then magically found three dozen roses in our room with a card signed by me. Was it my hosts or the Mangel's ghost that pulled that one off?*" (C. Accardi)

Baywood Park

Baywood Bed & Breakfast Inn
1370 2nd Street
Baywood Park, CA 93402
(805) 528-8888
Innkeepers: Alex and Pat Benson

♛♛♛   Rating: A
Rates: Single or Double/$80-140

Newly constructed contemporary inn sits on Morro Bay overlooking the coastal mountains near the San Luis Obispo area of Southern California. Fifteen guest rooms are available with individual decor and theme. Each offers a private bath, queen-size bed, sitting area, wood-burning fireplace, and kitchenette stocked with snacks and beverages. Eleven rooms offer a bay view. Visit nearby San Luis Obispo, Hearst Castle, and Montano De Oro Park. Continental breakfast and afternoon wine and cheese offered. Additional meals are available in the restaurant on the lower level. Families welcome. Wheelchair access. No smoking.

Guests write: "*Our room, the Appalachian, was beautiful. I rarely drink coffee but I have dreams of theirs and their absolutely wonderful croissants. And best of all there was no TV which 'forced' us to go out and enjoy their beautiful surroundings. Everything was great, great, great!*" (B. Kudlo)

"*Our unique room was decorated beautifully and was both cozy and clean. We loved the big canopy bed and ocean view. We had dinner delivered both nights so that we could eat at our table by the fireplace. I recommend it to anyone wanting a quiet romantic retreat.*" (S. Nuttall)

"*We especially enjoyed the evening wine and cheese and room tour. Our room was just lovely and very comfortable.*" (L. Painter)

Berkeley

Elmwood House
2609 College Avenue
Berkeley, CA 94704
(510) 540-5123
Fax: (510) 540-5123
Innkeepers: Steve Hyske and John Ekdahl

♛♛ Rating: B+
Rates: Single/$55-85; Double/$65-95
Credit Cards: AE, MC, V

Redwood home built in 1902 is located near the fashionable Elmwood shopping district and Berkeley campus of the University of California. Choose from four guest rooms, each with private telephone and two with a private bath. Walk to an eclectic collection of ethnic restaurants, specialty shops, and evening entertainment. Public transit is available right nearby to San Francisco and all Bay Area attractions and off-street parking is available for your car if you drive to the area. Enjoy nearby golf, tennis, swimming, hiking, and bicycling. Continental breakfast. Facilities for small weddings and meetings. No smoking.

Bridgeport

The Cain House
11 Main Street
Bridgeport, CA 93517
(619) 932-7040 or (800) 433-2246.
Innkeeper: Marachal Gohlich

♛♛♛ Rating: A
Rates: Single or Double/$80-135
Credit Cards: AE, MC, V

Historic home built in the 1930's is located off highway 395 in the Eastern Sierra Mountains near the California/Nevada border. Each of the six guest rooms with private bath has been restored and features wicker, white washed pine, oak, and other antique furnishings. The newest room offers a private entrance and large canopy bed. Enjoy wine and cheese in front of the fireplace in the parlor, relax in the hot tub, and watch the beautiful sunsets over the

Eastern Sierra Mountains. Area attractions include fishing, hunting, and skiing. Yosemite, Bodie ghost town, and Mammoth Mountains are located nearby. A full country breakfast is offered. Families welcome. No smoking.

Calistoga

Foothill House
3037 Foothill Blvd.
Calistoga, CA 94515
(707) 942-6933 or (800) 942-6933
Fax: (707) 942-5692
Owners: Doris and Gus Beckert

♛♛♛   Rating: A
Rates: Single or Double/$115-170; Cottage/$220
Credit Cards: AE, MC, V

A variety of mature trees surround this turn-of-the-century farmhouse located in Napa Valley, less than two miles from the town of Calistoga. There are three guest suites in the main house, each with private bath, small refrigerator, wood burning stove or fireplace, private entrance, air conditioning, four-poster queen-size bed, and country antique furnishings. Some of the suites offer a Jacuzzi. A one-room cottage offers complete privacy and can sleep two comfortably. Calistoga is known for it's mud and mineral baths and bottled waters from geothermal wells. Area attractions: hot air balloon rides, glider rides, golf, hiking, bicycling, horseback riding, Monhoff Recreation Center, Sharpsteen Museum, Bothe State Park, and historic landmarks. Visit nearby world famous wineries and gourmet restaurants. A full gourmet breakfast served in the sunroom or guest suite features specialty dishes such as souffles along with fresh baked goods. Hors d'oeuvres and complimentary wine are served each evening. No smoking.

Guests write: *"The innkeepers hospitality really made us feel at home. There were numerous details — cookies at bedtime, sherry in the room. Breakfast was a feast with a lovely presentation. I make muffins myself. The ones served here were light and flavorful."* (C. Bray)

"Foothill House has gone beyond attention to detail to achieving perfection." (C. Turner)

Cambria

The Blue Whale Inn
6736 Moonstone Beach Drive
Cambria, CA 93428
(805) 927-4647
Innkeeper: Fred Ushijima

♛♛♛   Rating: A+
Rates: Single or Double/$135-170
Credit Cards: MC, V

Contemporary Cape Cod style inn built in 1990 is located 6 miles south of Hearst Castle, mid-way between San Francisco and Los Angeles on the central California coast. Each of the six guest rooms offer a private tiled bath with garden window, fireplace, canopied bed draped with French and English fabrics, as well as an armoire with hidden television, a writing desk, and an oversized dressing room. Visit with other guests in the dining, living, and library areas and enjoy the panoramic view of the ocean while having English tea. Explore the scenic Big Sur coast, nearby wineries and art galleries, and famous Hearst Castle. A full breakfast features such specialties as gingerbread pancakes with lemon sauce and whipped cream, Blueberry crepes, Mexican quiche, Eggs Benedict, or thick French toast with sautéed apples and sour cream. No smoking.

Guests write: *"The decor is Country French. It lends itself to the feeling of comfortable luxury. Very pleasing color schemes are interwoven with tastefully-selected wallpaper prints and borders, as well as materials used in bedspreads, canopies and furniture. One could literally throw a toothbrush and a change of clothes in a suitcase and head for the Blue Whale without needing to pack anything else. Amenities such as hairdryers, shampoos, lotions, refrigerators, fresh flowers, televisions, fireplaces, books, even cottonballs and Q tips are provided at this heavenly hide-away." (P&J Kirkwood)*

"Being able to look at the ocean—deep blue, populated by porpoises and whales. Sipping wine and using the telescope while the host and his lovely wife introduce you to other guests and invite you to explore the tide pools where we found starfish and hermit crabs. This is a very special inn." (K. Leugdon)

"My wife and I recently spent one of the most enjoyable weekends we have ever had at the Blue Whale Inn. The room was immaculate and the breakfast superb. We were made extremely welcome and comfortable by the owner and innkeepers. We have traveled the world and would highly recommend this inn to our friends." (J. Whitaker)

Davenport

New Davenport B&B Inn
31 Davenport Avenue
Davenport, CA 95017
(408) 425-1818 or 426-4122
Innkeepers: Bruce and Marcia McDougal

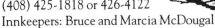

♛♛   Rating: B-
Rates: Single or Double/$60-115
Credit Cards: AE, MC, V

The New Davenport Cash Store and Restaurant is located halfway between San Francisco and Carmel on Coast Highway 1. Twelve guest rooms are available on the second floor of the main building or in the adjacent guest house. Each room offers a private bath and is furnished with antiques, ethnic treasures, collectibles, and local arts and crafts. Several rooms above the Cash Store have distant views of the ocean. The adjacent guest house offers smaller rooms as well as a common area for guests to enjoy breakfast and board games. The store on the main level offers a large variety of folk art, textiles, pottery, and jewelry. Area attractions include a secluded local beach, state redwood parks for hiking and picnics, seasonal whale watching, and elephant seal tours at Nuevo State Reserve. Full breakfast. No smoking.

Eureka

Old Town Bed & Breakfast Inn
1521 Third Street
Eureka, CA 95501
(707) 445-3951 or (800) 331-5098
Innkeepers: Leigh & Diane Benson

♛♛♛   Rating: A-
Rates: Single/$60-120; Double/$75-130
Credit Cards: AE, MC, V
Corporate discount

Greek Revival Italianate built in 1871 is on a quiet residential street in the heart of Eureka's Old Town, a city located on the Northern California coast, 280 miles north of San Francisco on Highway 101. Choose from seven guest rooms, five with private bath. Carlotta's Room is the inn's largest room and ideal for special occasions as it features a king-size brass bed, antiques, private bath, and a lavender and lace decor. The Maxfield Parrish room features Maxfield Parrish artwork and oak antiques. Gerri's room is quite spacious and features a collection of stuffed animals, king-size bed, and private bath with shower. The decor throughout each room combines whimsy with good fun which is evident by the Teddy Bears on each bed and rubber ducks by the bathtubs. An outdoor hot tub is surrounded by a privacy fence. Visit the nearby Redwood National Park, King Range Wilderness, and other Pacific Coast attractions. Full breakfast. No smoking.

Guests write: *"Dianne helps Jeff return to his childhood with his favorite breakfast of "Green Eggs and Ham" and Leigh serves it like a character right out of Dr. Seuss. It's one of the high points of our visits."* (P. Beardsley)

"If anyone has ever been unhappy in a B&B and said they would never try another, try this one and your mind will be changed." (R. Wayman)

"Leigh and Diane Benson have fine-tuned B&B innkeeping to an art form. All the requisite things are here, but the inn has a personality and a sense of humor all its own. The rest of the B&B industry should learn from these folks - they are the best." (H. Sharp)

"How to put it in a nutshell? We can't get over how the hominess feels like Grandma's. But there's something else - a touch of eccentricity that plays a big part in this B&B. We enjoyed everything from Vincent van Bear to the rose petals in the toilet. If Grandma ever could've cut loose, this is the way she would have lived." (N. Jackson)

"Every day the most delicious truffles would appear on the dresser. Made the whole room smell yummy! Lots of stuffed bears lounging on the bed and a huge stack of country magazines to read. The location is within walking distance to the beach and downtown restaurants. We go for the famous kinetic sculpture race and the contestants pedal by in front of the B&B." (A. Lehman)

Ferndale

The Gingerbread Mansion Inn
400 Berding Street
Ferndale, CA 95536
(707) 786-4000 or (800) 952-4136
Innkeeper: Ken Torbert

♛ ♛ ♛   Rating: A+
Rates: Single/$100-170; Double/$115-185
Credit Cards: AE, MC, V

1890's Victorian Queen Anne inn is located in the State Historical Landmark Village of Ferndale. The inn is famous for its classic gingerbread details such as carved, gabled turrets and an elaborately landscaped English garden. All of the nine guest rooms offer a private bath and individual decor theme. Special features of some rooms include beveled and stained-glass windows, fireplaces, claw-foot tubs, and French windows. One room has a private stairway leading to a second floor sitting room. Another room features "his" and "hers" claw-foot tubs. Guests are treated to many little extras such as bubble bath, bathrobes, and bedside chocolates. Enjoy the quiet privacy offered where no television or radio is present to interrupt conversation or board games being played in any of the four Victorian parlors. Borrow the inn's bikes to tour the historic town. Within driving distance is the ocean, redwood forest, and park recreation. A full breakfast is served each morning and includes baked egg entree, fresh fruits, homemade granola, locally-made cheeses and assorted baked items. No smoking.

Guests write: *"This Saturday evening will be our 85th visit to Gingerbread Mansion in the past seven years. My husband is a CPA and every tax season we get away to fantasy Ferndale where the quaint little shops and reasonable prices are delightful to seemingly step back in time. The mansion is always clean and pleasant, in a quiet neighborhood, there are beautiful antiques and delicious home-baked pastries with tea in the afternoon and a wonderful breakfast the next morning. It's a taste of heaven on earth."* (E. Staley)

"It is furnished with beautiful antiques. Tea and cookies are served every afternoon and a very nice, complete breakfast is served in the morning. Each room is unique, quiet and comfortable." (H. Green)

Ferndale

Shaw House
703 Main Street, P.O. Box 1125
Ferndale, CA 95536
(707) 786-9958
Innkeepers: Norma and Ken Bessingpas

♛ ♛ ♛   Rating: A-
Rates: Single or Double/$65-125
Credit Cards: AE, MC, V

Gothic inn with jutting gables, bay windows, and several balconies was built in 1854. The property is listed on the National Register of Historic Places and is situated on a one-acre landscaped lot in the village. Choose from six guest rooms, each with private bath. One large room is especially suitable for families. All feature floral wallpaper, quilted bedspreads, and fresh flowers. Relax on a secluded deck overlooking the creek or explore the gardens. Walk to village antique shops, galleries and restaurants. Area attractions include Avenue of the Giants, Pacific Ocean, Humboldt Bay, redwood forests, and wilderness hikes. Homemade continental breakfast. No smoking.

Fort Bragg

Grey Whale Inn
615 North Main Street
Fort Bragg, CA 95437
(707) 964-0640 or (800) 382-7244
Fax: (707) 964-4408
Innkeepers: Colette and John Bailey

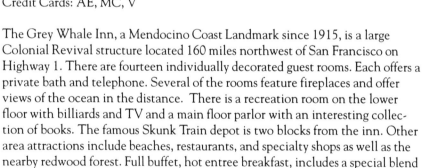

♛ ♛ ♛   Rating: A-
Rates: Single/$60-140; Double/$80-160
Credit Cards: AE, MC, V

The Grey Whale Inn, a Mendocino Coast Landmark since 1915, is a large Colonial Revival structure located 160 miles northwest of San Francisco on Highway 1. There are fourteen individually decorated guest rooms. Each offers a private bath and telephone. Several of the rooms feature fireplaces and offer views of the ocean in the distance. There is a recreation room on the lower floor with billiards and TV and a main floor parlor with an interesting collection of books. The famous Skunk Train depot is two blocks from the inn. Other area attractions include beaches, restaurants, and specialty shops as well as the nearby redwood forest. Full buffet, hot entree breakfast, includes a special blend of coffee and a sampling of the owner's many freshly baked breakfast breads or coffee cakes. Facilities available for meetings and social functions.

Guests write: *"I have been staying at the Gray Whale now going on five years, stopping by every five to six weeks. At first I stayed at John and Colette's B&B due to the wonderful rooms and the quiet relaxing evenings. Now I wouldn't think of staying anywhere else because Colette, Doddie, Linda and all the rest of the staff are just like family to me."* (J. Beck)

"There are two characteristics that set the Grey Whale above other B&B Inns. The first is the nature of the Inn itself. John and Colette Bailey have transformed the old local hospital into a "hospitality" inn. Having just celebrated its 15th anniversary, The Grey Whale is an original, not a come lately. Recently redecorated throughout, each room is an exceptional experience. We have stayed in over half of the rooms, but our

favorite is the Sunset room overlooking the water. The second characteristic concerns the innkeepers and the gang that go out of their way to make your stay friendly and comfortable without intruding on your privacy. All guests are immediately made to feel like long-time friends." (M&S Taylor)

"The breakfast was perfect, not too hearty - not too light for starting a full-day of business. The buffet style was relaxed and convenient since my day started very early. The staff took very clear and concise phone messages for me, even after 5:00 p.m." (R. Middleton)

"As career people we need to bring the romance back into our marriage. Our stay at the Grey Whale Inn met our expectations and more! We departed feeling the same way when we returned from our honeymoon." (M. Harmon)

Geyserville

Campbell Ranch Inn
1475 Canyon Road
Geyersville, CA 95441
(707)857-3476 or (800) 959-3878
Innkeepers: Jerry and Mary Jane Campbell

♛♛♛ Rating: A
Rates: Single/$90-155; Double/$100-165
Credit Cards: MC, V

California-style country home is situated on a hilltop estate of 35 acres. This area of Sonoma County is famous for its vineyards and is an easy 80 mile drive north of San Francisco. Five guest rooms each offer a private bath, king-size bed, fresh flowers and fruit. Most rooms feature a balcony with views of the surrounding countryside with its gently rolling hills. The newest guest suite is in a cottage and offers a private entrance, large balcony, sitting area, and fireplace. Guests enjoy gathering in the fireplaced living room as well as playing tennis on the professional court, swimming in the large swimming pool, and unwinding in the hot tub spa with a complimentary iced tea or lemonade. Hiking, horseshoes, Ping-Pong, and bicycling are available. Visit nearby wineries, Russian River, and Lake Sonoma. This is a good central location for taking day trips to the coast, Mendicino, or the Napa Valley. A full breakfast is served and homemade dessert and coffee or tea are offered each evening. Families welcome. No smoking.

Guests write: *"We first visited California in July 1981 and almost immediately had our greatest stroke of luck. We were in Healdsburg toward the end of a hot afternoon* and quite by chance heard of the Campbell Ranch B&B which had just opened. Off we drove to become Mary Jane and Jerry's first English guests, and what a right royal welcome we received. We had planned to stay one night but ended up by staying four, so comfortable and happy were we." (J. Moore)

"This B & B is on a hilltop overlooking a small scenic valley, truly a respite from a noisy city to a quiet relaxing getaway. Our private sunny cottage room with fresh flowers, fresh fruit basket, and a log for the fireplace, reflect the Campbell's attention to details that make their guest feel comfortable and special. There are endless choices of things to do: tennis on the court, swimming in a large outdoor pool, relaxing under the stars in the hot tub, horseshoes, hiking, biking, ping pong, or playing with a wonderful dog named Maggie. All the activities along with the warmth and charm of Jerry and Mary Jane changed any ideas that we had from straying from the ranch." (H&R Kirksey)

"Home away from home is how we would describe the Campbell Ranch Inn. Whether it's serve yourself ice tea or lemonade from the fridge or the truffles and fruit in your bedroom, you feel welcome the moment you arrive. Homemade breads and coffee cake make the full breakfast a real treat. Mary Jane always has a homemade cake or pie waiting each evening. To coin a current phrase, the deserts are to die for." (J. Giroux)

"We recommend this particular bed and breakfast very highly. They have lovely accommodations, beautiful pool and spa, gorgeous flowering gardens, and spectacular views of neighboring vineyards. The real plus about this B & B are the Campbell's— they have created a first class operation, and are the most personable and gracious hosts that you could imagine." (P. Williams)

Groveland

The Groveland Hotel
18767 Main Street
Groveland, CA 95321
(209) 962-4000 or (800) 273-3314
Fax: (209) 962-6674
Innkeeper: Peggy Mosley

♛♛♛ Rating: A
Rates: Single or Double/$85-165
Credit Cards: AE, MC, V

Historic 1849 Adobe-Monterey Colonial with 1914 Queen Anne wood-frame addition is found on Groveland's historic Main Street, less than one hour from Yosemite National Park and near Sonora. The hotel has been fully restored and offers seventeen guest rooms as well as a full-service restaurant. Each guest room offers a private bath, European antique furnishings, down comforter, and decor featuring Victorian-style fabric. There are three suites with fireplace and spa tub. Other common areas include the second floor parlor, restaurant, historic saloon, courtyard, and conference room. Recreation in the surrounding area includes tennis, golfing, white water rafting, fishing, and hiking. Local history is reflected in the area's antique stores as well as in the Historic Gold Country. Arrangements can be made for a day-long bus tour of Yosemite. Continental breakfast includes fresh croissants, breads, and seasonal fruit. A full service restaurant offers additional gourmet meals. Wedding and meeting facilities available with a private entrance, coffee service, and audio-visual materials. Families welcome. Wheelchair access. No smoking.

Hopland

Thatcher Inn
13401 South Highway 101
Hopland, CA 95449
(707) 744-1890 or (800) 266-1891
Fax: (707) 744-1219
Innkeeper: Carmen Gleason

♛♛♛   Rating: A
Rates: Single/$85.50; Double/$90-150
Credit Cards: AE, MC, V

Thatcher Inn is located 100 miles north of San Francisco and 50 miles north of Santa Rosa. This Victorian country inn built in 1890, sits in the heart of the Mendocino Wine country. Twenty guest rooms with private baths are available on the second and third floors. Each individually decorated room is furnished with antiques and fabrics. The grand dining room features authentic Italian cuisine with a fresh dinner menu three times a week as well as breakfast, lunch and Sunday champagne brunch. Patio dining is available weather permitting. Relax by the fire in the English style library, or visit the informal lobby bar. Within walking distance are winery tasting rooms, Mendocino Brewing company, The Cheesecake Lady, art gallery, antique shops and a country store. Area Attractions: University of California, wine country, Anderson Valley Winery, water sport facilities, Davis Hopland field station-experimental sheep ranching, and California Redwoods. Full breakfasts specialities may include the Thatcher Inn omelette, wild mushroom and herb omelette, eggs, French toast, griddlecakes, homemade granola and fresh fruit. Wedding and meeting facilities. Restricted smoking. Families welcome.

Long Beach

Lord Mayor's Inn B&B
435 Cedar Avenue
Long Beach, CA 90802
(310) 436-0324
Innkeepers: Laura and Reuben Brasser

♛♛♛ Rating: A
Rates: Single or Double/$85-105
Credit Cards: AE, MC, V

Historic restored Edwardian house located in the very heart of the city was home of the first mayor of Long Beach. Choose from five guest rooms with individual decor, private baths and access to a sundeck. The Eastlake Room is named for its Eastlake furnishings. The Hawaiian Room features a hand-carved oak bed and French doors that overlook the garden. Relax in the library or living room and enjoy tea and dessert in the evening. Area attractions: Long Beach Convention Center, Long Beach Grand Prix, marathon, Seafest, amphitheater events, sailboat regattas, ferry to Catalina Island, shops and restaurants at the Shoreline Village, and downtown's jazz clubs, coffee houses, and comedy club. Full breakfast specialties may include homemade cinnamon coffee cake, sourdough pancakes, popovers with lemon curd, or baked egg entrees. Families welcome. Restricted smoking

Guests write: *"It is said that home is where your heart is. And after spending two nights at Lord Mayor's Inn we can say that our host truly has his heart in this wonderfully restored B&B. From the moment we stepped in the door we felt like part of the family."* (S&L LeMere)

"This inn is like an oasis in the city. We loved the variety of flowers, trees, and shrubs. One time we were there for a succulent roast turkey Thanksgiving dinner event. Another time we went for the Mystery Weekend. The wine cellar crime scene gave the mystery additional ambiance. Laura's unique and delicious recipes made waking up worthwhile." (J. Wilkinson)

"This inn has a warm, welcoming atmosphere. The house was absolutely beautiful. Together, the innkeepers are an invaluable team with an award winning business for all ages to learn from and enjoy." (T. Caballero)

Mt. Shasta

Dream Inn
326 Chestnut St.
Mt. Shasta, CA 96067
(916) 926-1536
Innkeeper: David Ream

♛♛ Rating: B
Rates: Single or Double/$60-80
Credit Cards: AE, MC, V

Dream Inn is located 50 miles north of Redding off I-5. This 1904 Victorian inn, with its profusion of roses and perennials, is surrounded by a white picket fence. Choose from five guest rooms, one of which offers a private bath, TV, and VCR. Relax in the living room which offers antiques, a grand piano, wood pellet stove, and comfortable furniture. Walk to shopping, restaurants, tennis, baseball, city park, museum, fish hatchery, and nightclubs. Area attractions: excursion train, skiing at Mt. Shasta, fishing, Sisson Museum, white water rafting, hunting, camping, Pacific Crest Trail. A full breakfast, served on china with crystal glasses, includes coffee, teas, juice, cold cereal, and entrees such as waffles, pancakes, omelets, or egg dishes, homemade hash browns, and toast. Small weddings and meeting facilities. Restricted smoking. Families welcome.

Guests write: *"The brochure is beautiful and captures the lovely qualities of Dream Inn. The hosts have an unaffected welcoming air about them that is apparent as soon as you meet them. You'll see quality throughout the house and in the hospitality." (N. Skelly)*

Murphys

Dunbar House, 1880
P.O. Box 1375, 271 Jones Street
Murphys, CA 95247
(209) 728-2897 or (800) 225-3764 (ext. 321)
Fax: (209) 728-2897
Innkeepers: Barbara and Bob Costa

♛♛♛ Rating: A
Rates: Single or Double/$105-145
Credit Cards: MC, V

Italianate-style home built in 1880 is located southwest of Sacramento, 8 miles east of Angel's Camp on Highway 4. All four guest rooms offer a private bath and are decorated with antiques, lace, down comforters, and offer a TV/VCR with classic video collection, wood-burning stove, central air conditioning, and refrigerator stocked with a bottle of local wine. The Cedar Room is a two-room suite with a large two-person Jacuzzi. Relax on the wide porches or in front of the fire in the parlor. Calaveras Big Trees State Park nearby offers outdoor activities such as hiking, fishing, and skiing. Explore local wineries, historic towns, and caverns. Full breakfast may include house specialties such as crab cheese delight, lemon scone, muffins, and fresh fruit and is served in the fireplaced dining room, in the pleasant century-old garden or in the privacy of the guest room. Restricted smoking.

Guests write: *"The atmosphere is warm and comfortable, the breakfasts were superb. I especially enjoyed the view from our windows. My husband and I strolled the garden, sat on the swing under a tree and rocked, and read on the porch. Leisure time like we had here is very precious to us."* (L. Prinvale)

"Leaving the cold and fog of the valley behind, we came into sunshine and the warmth of Dunbar House hospitality. The is the perfect place to celebrate 30 years of marriage! If you think B&B stands for bed and breakfast, then you haven't stayed at Dunbar House long enough. We know that B&B stands for Bob and Barbara." (E. Moore)

"My favorite memories will be curling up in the chair by the fire with my book as the rain poured down, the wonderful music playing in the background, and all the yummy smells coming out of the kitchen." (C. Rucker)

"Eating the gourmet breakfasts in the garden is a wonderful start to each day. Also enjoyed reading for an hour in the garden at the end of a busy day of sightseeing - so relaxing!" (P. Schuck)

"Everything from the down comforter to the large claw-foot tub filled with bubbles was thoroughly enjoyed. The food was downright delicious." (D. Anderson)

"The porch outside our room is one of my favorite parts of this inn. Sitting out there in the late afternoon with a glass of the local wine and the wonderful appetizers, reading, playing checkers, or just visiting with your spouse is such a relaxing and wonderful treat! We've stayed in more elaborate places, but not many with such a warm comfortable feeling." (P. Schaller)

Napa -- See also Calistoga, Geyserville, Sonoma, and St. Helena.

Napa

Churchill Manor
485 Brown Street
Napa, California 94559
(707) 253-7733
Fax: (707) 253-8836
Innkeepers: Joanna Guidotti
and Brian Jensen

♕♕♕   Rating: A+
Rates: Single or Double/$75-145
Credit Cards: AE, MC, V

This 1889 three-story Second Empire mansion with mansard roof and extensive verandah, sits on an acre of manicured lawns and gardens with one-
hundred-year old cedars, redwoods, and formal landscaped fountain. Choose
from ten guest rooms with private baths. Each room boasts individual features
such as claw-foot tubs, carved antiques, mirrored armoires, writing desks,
secretaries, canopy beds, loveseats and sofas. Some rooms provide brass beds
and fireplaces accented by handpainted Dutch or Italian tiles. The grand foyer
of the mansion is enhanced with original redwood and beveled leaded-glass
doors, fluted columns of solid redwood, Oriental carpets, upholstered leather
and brocade chairs and sofas. Four parlors on the main level each feature an
ornate fireplace. The relaxing sunroom with all glass and leaded-glass windows
and original mosaic tile floor overlooks the gardens below. Walk to Napa
Valley Wine Train, historic tours through Old Town Napa, shopping and
dining. Tandem bicycles and croquet set-up are provided by the inn. Area
attractions: wineries, fine dining, galleries, golf, balloon rides, mud baths,
horseback riding, museums and hiking. Full breakfast buffet includes coffee,
teas, juice, fresh baked muffins, croissants, nut bread, and fresh fruit. Gourmet
omelets and French toast are made to order. Complimentary fresh-baked
cookies and refreshments are offered each afternoon as well as wine-and
cheese each evening. Wedding and meeting facilities. No smoking.

Napa

Hennessey House Bed & Breakfast Inn
1727 Main Street
Napa, CA 94559
(707) 226-3774; Fax: (707) 226-2975.
Innkeeper: Andrea Weinstein

♕♕♕ Rating: A
Rates: Single or Double/$80-155
Credit Cards: AE, MC, V
Senior discount

Queen Anne Victorian inn is listed on the National Register of Historic Places and located in California's famous wine country, 50 miles northeast of San Francisco. Choose from ten guest rooms which offer contemporary comfort blended with 1890's style. Nine of the rooms have a private bath and several feature working fireplaces, claw-foot tubs or whirlpool baths. Relax in the parlor with its cozy seating and varied selection of books and games. A guest sauna is available on the back porch. Walk to the famous Napa Valley Wine Train. Area attractions: balloon rides, mud baths, golf club, tennis, and winery touring. Full breakfast includes a hot entree and is served in the dining room which features a hand-painted tin ceiling. Small wedding and meeting facilities available. Restricted smoking.

Guests write: *"Breakfasts were superb in variety, quality, well-garnished, and presented and there was attention to personal preferences and dietary needs. Our room was large, well-maintained, and clean. We liked the period furnishings, skylight, fireplace, large Jacuzzi tub, tile floor, twin sinks, and fireplace. The gardens, well-lit staircases and parking areas, sauna, common room, and Heritage House added to the charm and pleasure of our stay and we appreciated the chance to use the bicycles."* (B. Dancik)

"Our room was tastefully decorated. The vanity in the bathroom was an old sideboard transformed into a vanity with two sinks. The location was perfect for visiting the wineries. The hostess was very willing to make a special breakfast dish for me which I had not informed her of until my arrival." (R. Faulkner)

Napa

La Belle Epoque
1386 Calistoga Avenue
Napa, CA 94559
(707) 257-2161 or (800) 238-8070
Innkeeper: Claudia Wedepohl

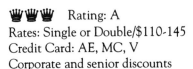   Rating: A
Rates: Single or Double/$110-145
Credit Card: AE, MC, V
Corporate and senior discounts

Queen Anne Victorian inn built in 1893 is located in the Historic District near the town center, just off Route 29. Choose from six guest rooms, each with private bath and period furnishings; two offer fireplaces. A fine example of Victorian architecture, the home features multi-gabled dormers, high-hipped roof, decorative carvings, and original stained-glass windows. Wine and appetizers are served in the evening in the Wine Tasting Room/Cellar. Relax in the living area which features a square grand piano and fireplace. TV/VCR are available in the upstairs parlor. Area attractions include wine tasting, hot air ballooning, mud and mineral baths, boutiques, gourmet restaurants, and Napa Valley Wine Train. Full breakfast. Facilities available for small meetings and social functions. Off-street parking available on the property. No smoking.

Guests write: *"Our five-day stay at the La Belle Epoque was delightful—rooms were decorated in the Victorian theme and were genuinely antique with florals, ruffles, lace, pillows and Tiffany-style lamps. Adjoining bathrooms were beautifully furnished, again in the Victorian theme. Both rooms were serviced every day with clean linens, fresh flowers and a mint on the pillow each night. Breakfasts were elegant—lovely china and both silver and gold flatware, fresh flowers each morning, fresh fruit, juice, elegant omelets and soufflés, baked French toast, baked asparagus and eggs and pastry."* (R&O Hargis)

"Merlin and Claudia are the two reasons we return to La Belle Epoque every year. The rooms at La Belle Epoque are all decorated differently with lovely antiques and appropriate wallcovering. Claudia puts a lot of effort into her gourmet breakfasts and always uses fresh herbs and ingredients—the results are first class." (R&G Morin)

"Comfort all around! Their artistic charm and abilities were profound; from the fresh flowers, right up to the marvelous ceiling fixtures. I've picked up more creative ideas during our stay than I could have from a year of magazines. Their attention to detail left no room for complaints." (M. Monthaven)

Newport Beach

Portofino Beach Hotel
2306 West Oceanfront
Newport Beach, CA 92663
(714) 673-7030
Innkeeper: Christine Luetto

♕♕♕ Rating: A+
Rates: Single or Double/$85-235
Credit Cards: AE, MC, V

Portofino Beach Hotel is on the oceanfront and boardwalk of this fashionable
beach town which is located just south of Los Angeles and fifteen minutes from
the Orange County Airport. Fifteen guest rooms or suites are available. Each
offers telephone, TV, private bath, and individual decor featuring lovely fabrics
and antiques. Several rooms include marble baths with Jacuzzis, private sun
decks, and fireplaces. Beach chairs and towels are available for a day on the
beach. Walk the boardwalk to visit nearby art galleries, bookstores, boutiques,
and historical sites. Disneyland is a short thirty minute drive and sailing, golf,
and tennis are available nearby. Continental breakfast buffet includes fresh
fruit, yogurt, and croissants. Facilities are available for meetings and weddings.

Palm Desert

Tres Palmas Bed & Breakfast
73135 Tumbleweed Lane
Palm Desert, CA 92261
(619) 773-9858
Innkeepers: Karen & Terry Bennett

♕♕♕ Rating: A+
Rates: Single or Double/$72-140

Tres Palmas Bed & Breakfast is approximately 130 miles east of Los Angeles and
San Diego and 15 miles east of Palm Springs. A circular drive leads to the
covered entrance of this Mediterranean/Spanish style inn with wonderful

views of the mountains. Three date palms dominate the garden and lawn in the front yard. Outlined by desert boulders, lawn, and citrus trees, is the pool and spa located in the back. Four guest rooms with private baths are uniquely decorated in Southwestern style. Room amenities include ceiling fans, individual climate controls, television, and welcome fruit or beverages. Relax in the living room with its Southwest decor and wet bar with fresh iced tea or lemonade. Walk to El Paseo, the "Rodeo Drive of the Desert," or Palm Desert Town Center with its many stores, movie theaters and indoor ice skating. Area attractions: biking, hiking, Living Desert Preserve, McCallum Theater/College of the Desert and Palm Springs Tram. Enjoy a continental buffet breakfast in the dining room. Seating up to 10, the large round dining table is set with placemats, linen napkins, and Southwest design tableware. Freshly baked muffins or breads, fresh fruits, juices, cereal, specialty coffees and teas are provided. A tray may be taken outside to the pool or to your room. Meeting facilities are available. No smoking

Guests write: *"We enjoyed the beautiful mountain view from the Jacuzzi, along with great shopping and dining a short walk away."* (G&P Smoak)

"This is a new facility, tastefully decorated to accommodate a select number of guests, each has their own private bath. Excellent hospitality and a family-run feeling. Their children even babysat for us. This is an excellent location within walking distance to galleries, shops, and restaurants." (W. Willard)

"Each morning our hostess prepared a different wonderful coffee, homemade muffins, granola-type cereal, and always fresh juice and fruit in a buffet setting. A no-host bar was available with lemonade and iced tea at any time of day, and a light after-hours snack each evening as a break from the day's activities." (R&G Ford)

"The authentic Southwestern decor including beautiful Navajo rugs was something we would have chosen ourselves. The fact that there are only four guest rooms created an intimacy we'd yet to find in a B&B." (K Carpenter)

"This new home, so close to the fine shopping at El Paseo you can carry your treasures home, has a private Jacuzzi and pool area. There is a beautiful common area with fireplace and bar as part of the dining space which is used for gathering and playing games. There were welcome snacks and a more than adequate breakfast." (T. Ruecker)

Palo Alto

Adella Villa
122 Atherton Ave.
Palo Alto, CA 94027
(415) 321-5195; Fax: (415) 325-5121
Innkeeper: Tricia Young

♕♕♕ Rating: A
Rates: Single or Double/$105
Credit Cards: AE, MC, V
Corporate and senior discounts

Large Tyrolean villa on an acre estate was built in 1920 and is located 25 miles south of San Francisco near US-101 and I-280. Three guest rooms provide private baths, (one with Jacuzzi tub), remote color TV, radio, and phone. The Champagne room with mini-kitchen has double French doors leading to the solar-heated swimming pool. Explore the estate with its surrounding trees, manicured gardens, and Japanese Koi pond or relax on the verandah while taking in the view. Area attractions include Silicon Valley, San Francisco, Stanford University, and Filoli Mansion. Full breakfast is served in the sunny breakfast room overlooking the fountain and gardens. Airport pickup available. Restricted smoking.

Guests write: *"All of the guests we met on our stay were return visitors and I can see why. The convenient location and lovely surroundings make this ideal for business or pleasure. No more hotels for me! What an opportunity to socialize with other guests or just spend time alone. The rooms are spacious and so well decorated. The layout of the house is such that you always have a private spot if you choose and never realize there's a full house."* (V. Smith)

"This was a very pleasant experience and my first stay at a B&B. It was a home away from home with breakfast served in a pleasant nook with a view of the grounds. My room was large with many personal touches — books, guides to the area, bric-a-brac, and a decanter of sherry. I had the run of the house and fresh fruit, coffee, and juice were always available." (J. Stevens)

"We love the Champagne room. Imagine a wonderful king bed with pillows like home and down cover so light and cozy it's like a cocoon. I cannot conjure up a detail overlooked. A bird aviary is in the back corner of the garden past the swimming pool and it's surrounded by all types of relaxing furniture." (M. Eaton)

Red Bluff

Faulkner House
1029 Jefferson Street
Red Bluff, CA 96080
(916) 529-0520
Innkeeper: Mary Klingler

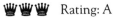 Rating: A
Rates: Single/$53-78; Double/$55-80

Red Bluff is in Northern California about thirty miles south of Redding.
Faulkner House is a Queen Anne Victorian home built in 1890 and is located
one mile off I-5 near downtown. Choose from four antique-filled guest rooms,
each with private bath. Special features of the individually decorated rooms
include carved bedroom sets, wicker accessories, and a brocade fainting couch.
The formal parlor or screened-in porch are great places to relax and meet other
guests while enjoying afternoon refreshments. Within walking distance are
restaurants, antique and specialty shops, and a historic house tour. Full breakfast
includes oranges from the trees in the yard, homemade muffins, and a baked egg
dish with meat. Facilities for meetings, weddings, and receptions. No smoking.

Redding

Palisades Paradise B&B
1200 Palisades Ave.
Redding, CA 96003
(800) 382-4649 or (916) 223-5305
Innkeeper: Gail Goetz

Rating: B
Rates: Single/$55-70; Double/$60-70
Credit Cards: AE, MC, V
Corporate and senior discounts

Contemporary home overlooks the Sacramento River, is surrounded by mountains, and located 160 miles north of Sacramento; 100 miles south of the
Oregon border. Two guest rooms share a one full and a half bath. The suite
offers a panoramic view of the city on the bluffs of the Sacramento River, has a
sitting area and a fifty-foot patio with spa. Both rooms offer contemporary
furnishings and a few antique pieces. The fireplaced living room has a wide
screen television. Guests also enjoy relaxing on the porch swing, or soaking in
the garden spa. Visit nearby Mt. Lassen Park, Shasta Lake and Caverns, or raft

or water ski on the Sacramento River. Expanded continental breakfast on weekdays and full breakfast on weekends may feature the house specialty, Palisades fruit puffs. Families welcome. Restricted smoking.

Guests write: *"I consider myself fortunate to have been referred to Palisades Paradise B&B. I have enjoyed warm hospitality in a comfortable, tastefully decorated contemporary home, close to all amenities. The breakfasts were nutritious and attractively presented. The bedroom is well-furnished, suitable for a single traveler like myself. The bathrooms are kept very clean — a must when I travel."* (M. McManus)

"We have never been anywhere with a more peaceful and beautiful view. The Sunset Suite is decorated with much charm and love." (J&J Schnittker)

"Palisades Paradise B&B is a real treat for those of us who enjoy the B&B setting. The view is incredible and the hostess is fantastic. When you combine this with a beautiful home you have a terrific combo." (L. McBride)

"Our room was large and comfortable, the breakfasts were delicious and our innkeeper very hospitable. The real high-point of our stay was relaxing under the stars in the hot tub after a long day of hiking. The inn overlooks the twinkling lights of Redding and a river — you could see all of that from our room." (A. Horvath)

Reedley

The Fairweather Inn
259 South Reed Avenue
Reedley, CA 93654
(209) 638-1918
Innkeeper: Vi Demyan

♛♛♛ Rating: A-
Rates: Single or Double/$75-85
Credit Cards: AE, MC, V

The Fairweather Inn is located 30 miles south of Fresno, 30 miles north of Visalia, and 12 miles off Highway 99. This two-story 1914 craftsman style inn, located on a row of historic homes, is surrounded by magnolias, oaks, and gardens filled with azaleas and rhododendrons. Choose from four bedrooms, two with private baths. The rooms vary in decor and may offer such amenities as clawfoot tubs, hand-carved furniture, a mirrored armoire, and polished hardwood floors with Oriental rugs. The antique-filled living room has hardwood floors, Oriental rugs, and fireplace. Visit the library filled with antique toys and a private radio collection. The dining room is a favored gathering place for many guests. Within walking distance is downtown Reedley which is full of shops and restaurants. Area attractions: Golf, Blossom Trail, Sequoia and Yosemite National Park, Kings Canyon National Park, Pine Flat Lake, and Kings River. Enjoy a full breakfast of coffee, tea, juice, fresh fruit, homemade muffins, coffee cake, and hot entree such as quiche, crepes, croissants, French toast, or homemade jam. Wedding and meeting facilities. No smoking.

Guests write: *"We loved the atmosphere and decor taking us back to another era through the marvelous yet functional antiques. The breakfast menu was a unique experience combining creative cooking with the use of fruit right off the backyard trees."* (K. Allgeyer)

"As someone who spends much of his life on the road, I can say the Fairweather Inn is like an oasis in the desert. The hospitality is unsurpassed and the breakfast dangerously good." (R. Rita)

"Spotlessly clean, comfortable bed, antiques in perfect condition, interesting antique collections of radios & period clocks, convenient location, entertaining hostess, quiet residential neighborhood." (T. Milbal)

"First time I ever stayed at a B&B. Usually when I travel I can't sleep. Slept like a baby! Plus great food in the morning. Like being at home on the road." (G.M. Hahman)

Sacramento

Amber House Bed & Breakfast Inn
1315 22nd Street
Sacramento, CA 95816
(916) 444-8085 or (800) 755-6526
Fax: (916) 447-1548
Innkeepers: Michael & Jane Richardson

♛♛♛ Rating: A+
Rates: Single/$80-135; Double/$90-195
Credit Cards: AE, MC, V

Amber House is located in an historic residential area of downtown Sacramento, 8 blocks from the state capitol and Convention Center. The inn is comprised of two adjacent historic homes; one a 1905 Craftsman and the other, a 1913 Mediterranean style building. Choose from nine guest rooms with private bath and individual decor. Special features may include French windows, canopy beds, and leaded-glass windows. Other rooms boast antiques and Jacuzzi tubs. Every room has its own full-service telephone, clock-radio/cassette player, and cable television. The main house, with stained glass windows, features a living area with fireplace, dining room, and cozy library. Columns and coved ceilings accent the living room of the Mediterranean style home. Within walking distance is the State Capitol, Sutters Fort, Governors Mansion, Convention Center, Downtown Plaza Mall, American River Parkway and bike trails. Area attractions: Railroad Museum, Old Sacramento State Historic Park, State Fair, Crocker Art Museum, Sacramento River Delta, University of California at Davis, California State University at Sacramento, historic Auburn and Folsom, and Folsom Prison Museum. Napa Valley is within a one hour drive. Full breakfast served on Royal Doulton china includes coffee, tea, hot chocolate, juice, fresh fruit plate, fresh croissants and special entrees such as quiche or potatoes with peppers. Meeting and wedding facilities. No smoking.

Guests write: "*A business trip brought me to the inn. From the beginning it was a joy! We were greeted by the sweetest staff, my room was comfortable and cozy with lovely antiques and books to relax with. After a very successful shopping jaunt, warm chocolate pecan cookies and hot chocolate were awaiting us.*" (B. Hart)

"*We arrived on Halloween night. After a relaxing soak in our ultra-large tub next to a bank of windows with moonlight streaming in, we asked if we could do the Halloween honors and played doorman the rest of the evening enjoying all the kids. We were thrilled to participate in a community spook night so far from home.*" (K. Brown)

"*Our room, the Longfellow, was well decorated with matching bedding and window treatments. The old furniture was in good condition and the room had lovely touches including cassette tapes and several volumes of Longfellow's writings. The service was exceptional.*" (L&V Beuder)

"*I have been in the hospitality business for six years now and consider myself a critic when I stay in other properties. The Degas Room has a canopy bed draped with rose and floral taffeta. The bathroom has rose marble floors, pedestal sinks, and Jacuzzi tub to drift away in. All of the sudden this critic is turned into just a happy and content guest.*" (C. Rachke)

"*We chose this particular inn because of its location near downtown Sacramento. Breakfast is scheduled by appointment. Some of the delicious and attractively served breakfasts we ate were Belgian waffles, quiche, crepes, and French toast.*" (E&A Budreika)

St. Helena

Bartels Ranch & Country Inn
1200 Conn Valley Road
St. Helena, CA 94574
(707) 963-4001; Fax: (707) 963-5100
Owner: Jami Bartels

♛♛♛   Rating: A
Rates: Single or Double/$125-$325
Credit Cards: AE, MC, V
Senior and government discount

Rambling stone and redwood ranch style inn was designed and built by the
innkeeper and is located in the heart of the Napa Valley Wine Country just
three miles east of downtown St. Helena. Bartels Ranch is a country estate set
atop a 60-acre valley and surrounded by award winning vineyards. Four guest
rooms each offer a private bath, air conditioning, Casa Blanca fans, and are
decorated in a distinctive decor. Two of the rooms provide Jacuzzis. All guest
rooms open onto a private deck surrounding a black bottom pool. Two
common areas are shared by guests: a massive game room and a sunken living
room with cathedral ceilings. In the game room, there is ping-pong and
billiards, and the living room has a baby grand piano, fireplace, and library.
TV/VCR for viewing movies is available and there are cassette recorders in
each guest room. Theaters, restaurants, wineries, and shopping are all conveniently close by. Other activities include winery tours, hot air balloon rides,
glider flights, bicycling, tennis, croquette, golf, fishing, petrified forests,
antique shops, and art galleries and therapeutic spa. Continental breakfast is
served in guest rooms or on private decks. Candlelit wine and cheese is served
every evening. Wedding and meeting facilities available. Fax, copier, computer, and secretarial services available. Restricted smoking.

Guests write: *"Little did we know when we picked Bartels Ranch out of a B&B
book, what a treat we had in store. Our welcome was warm and sincere and we
immediately felt at home. Our rooms were charming, the decks so inviting, the family
room loaded with so many things to do that it made it difficult for us to leave to visit
the wineries. I'm sure that all six of us could have stayed at the ranch. Jami's
preplanning of wineries, tours, and restaurants was such a great help and her choices
were superb."* (M. Davis)

*"I always feel like a bride when here. There's romance in your heart due to all of the
wonderful touches added to enhance the stay: bubble bath, candles, music,
breakfasts, and champagne."* (M. Woodard)

San Diego

The Cottage
3829 Albatross Street
San Diego, CA 92103
(619) 299-1564
Innkeeper: Carol Emerick

👑👑   Rating: B+
Rates: Single or Double/$49-75
Credit Cards: MC, V

Redwood cottage built in 1913 is located on a cul-de-sac in the Hillcrest section of the city. The private cottage in back of the main house can accommodate three and offers a bath, fully equipped kitchen, pump organ, wood-burning stove, and Victorian style furnishings. A guest room with private bath and separate entrance is also available in the main house. Area attractions include San Diego Zoo, Balboa Park, airport, beaches, and day trips into Mexico. Continental breakfast features freshly baked bread and seasonal fruit. Two night minimum stay. Families welcome. No smoking.

Guests write: *"The Cottage has proven to be the best attraction in San Diego not to mention the best bargain! No need to go anywhere else for a sumptuous breakfast."* (J. Varner)

"The cottage is decorated with lovely antiques including an antique organ in the sitting room. The bedroom has a magnificent, comfortable king-size bed decorated with tons of pillows. When we arrived there was a lovely bouquet of fresh flowers in each room. A bargain and a wonderful haven at only $65 a night." (J. McCarron)

"My husband and I were treated to breakfasts that demonstrated a caring, thoughtful touch — one that says, 'I have gone the extra mile to make you feel at home.' Mrs. Emerick must have arisen quite early to accommodate us at 7 a.m. with a different homemade from scratch coffee cake or bread each day." (S. Lynch)

"Absolutely delicious fresh fruits and homemade breads every morning. The zucchini bread—warm with the secret ingredient (chocolate) was to die for!" (G. Rengel)

"What a delightful cottage! The flower arrangement and garden added an elegance that was most appreciated. My favorite toy is the coffee machine. The breakfasts - they were special!" (M. Evans)

San Diego

Heritage Park B&B Inn
2470 Heritage Park Row
San Diego, CA 92110
(619) 299-6832 or (800) 995-2470
Fax: (619) 299-9465
Innkeepers: Nancy and Charles Helsper

♛♛♛   Rating: A
Rates: Single/$80-125; Double/$85-130; Suite/$200-250
Credit Cards: AE, MC, V
Corporate discount

Famous Old Town in San Diego is the setting for this Queen Anne Victorian
home built in 1889. It's situated in an unusual seven-acre park of historic
buildings and has some outstanding architectural features. Choose from ten
guest rooms, seven with private bath. Each is individually decorated with
Oriental rugs, handmade quilts, period antiques, and Victorian wallpaper. A
two-bedroom suite with private parlor, bath, shower and Jacuzzi is perfect for
honeymoons, business travelers and families. Attractions nearby include San
Diego Zoo, Mission Valley, and the San Diego Harbor cruise. Full breakfast is
served and there is an afternoon tea along with the showing of classic films.

San Francisco

Albion House Inn
135 Gough Street
San Francisco, CA 94102
(415) 621-0896; Fax: (415) 621-3811
Innkeepers: Aziz and Regina Bouagou

♛♛   Rating: B+
Rates: Single or Double/$75-150
Credit Cards: AE, MC, V

Edwardian brownstone built in 1906 is located in close proximity to the
Performing Arts Complex and the Civic Center. Nine guest rooms are
available. Seven rooms offer a private bath, phone, and TV. The high-
ceilinged living room with marble fireplace and grand piano is an inviting
place to relax with a complimentary beverage. Visit the nearby Moscone
Center, Performing Arts Complex, Civic Center, opera, symphony, and ballet

performances. Restaurants, shops, and art galleries are easily accessible. Homemade muffins, pancakes, and freshly squeezed orange juice are offered with the full breakfast. Small meeting facilities available.

Guests write: *"I thoroughly enjoyed my visit. The accommodations were wonderful as was the great breakfast of pancakes and cereal. It was my first stay ever in this city, and I just loved it. As the old song says, 'I Left My Heart in San Francisco,' and my appetite, too!" (P. Morton)*

San Francisco

The Chateau Tivoli
1057 Steiner Street
San Francisco, CA 94115
(415) 776-5462 or (800) 228-1647
Innkeeper: Rodney Karr

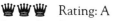 Rating: A
Rates: Single or Double/$80-200
Credit Cards: AE, MC, V

Victorian mansion, circa 1892, has undergone an authentic period restoration and is located in the Alamo Square Historic District. The inn's five guest rooms and two suites offer a step back into San Francisco's romantic golden age of opulence and are furnished with canopy beds, marble baths, balconies, fireplaces, stained glass, and antiques. Five rooms have a private bath. Walk to a variety of restaurants, shopping, theaters, Golden Gate Park, and Alamo Square Park. A continental breakfast is served weekdays and a full champagne breakfast is served on weekends. Meeting facilities available. No smoking.

San Francisco

Golden Gate Hotel
775 Bush Street
San Francisco, CA 94108
(415) 392-3702 or (800) 835-1118
Innkeepers: John and Renate Kenaston

Rating: B
Rates: Single or Double/$59-89
Credit Cards: AE, MC, V

Narrow four-story urban hotel of Edwardian architecture was built in 1913 and is now a small European-style hotel located two blocks north of Union Square and two blocks down from the top of Nob Hill. Choose from twenty-three guest rooms located throughout four floors with access by elevator. There is quite a variety in room size, prices, and amenities but each offers a bay window and fresh flowers; fourteen have a private bath. The small fireplaced parlor on the main floor is where guests enjoy a continental breakfast of fresh coffee and croissants as well as afternoon tea. Walk to many of the city's famous attractions, restaurants, and shops from this location. The main cable car line stops at the corner giving easy access to Fisherman's Wharf, North Beach, and Ghirardelli Square. Families welcome. No smoking.

Guests write: "As a French speaking visitor, I especially enjoyed speaking French with two employees of the staff. Foreign languages are welcome here. The owner speaks quite good German too. The owners are very nice innkeepers, always ready to help you discover a city which they love, looking for new information they could transmit to other customers." (P. Menard)

"Friendly atmosphere. It seems like coming home. Convenient location. Good coffee. Good value. Personal service." (A. Weber, M.D.)

"This has a charming, European feel and was put together with obvious loving care. Loved the tea and the cozy, top-quality breakfast. There was an interesting European-style openwork metal elevator. Best of all were knowledgeable hosts who clearly love what they do and interact graciously with a variety of guests with warmth, humor and grace." (B. Muc)

San Francisco

Washington Square Inn
1660 Stockton Street
San Francisco, CA 94133
(415) 981-4220 or (800) 388-0220
Fax: (415) 397-7242
Innkeeper: Karin Baird

♛♛♛   Rating: A-
Rates: Single or Double/$85-180
Credit Cards: AE, MC, V

Small European-style Victorian urban inn is located in the historic North Beach district, one block from Telegraph Hill. There are fifteen guest rooms throughout the building and there is quite a variety to the size, decor, and amenities offered in each room. All have a selection of English or French antiques, terry cloth robes, and down comforters. Four rooms which share baths offer an in-room sink and eleven rooms have private baths. The elegant parlor area features a fireplace and is an inviting setting for afternoon tea and evening hors d'oeuvres. Walk to many fine restaurants, coffee houses, and bakeries. Cannery shopping is ten minutes away. Take a cable car ride to Union Square, Financial District, or Fisherman's Wharf. Expanded continental breakfast served daily includes famous Graffeo coffee and fresh croissants. Families welcome. No smoking.

Guests write: *"I have been a guest here for five days. The staff couldn't have been more cooperative." (A. Law)*

"My mother and I thoroughly enjoyed the warm, efficient service you provided. The continental breakfast, tea hour, and the use of the terry cloth robes were quite nice." (J. Martin)

"The staff at the Washington Square Inn has consistently excellent service. During my recent visit to San Francisco, their patience and assistance helped to make my stay so much more enjoyable. Give them all big raises!" (M. Gould)

"They've restored our faith in customer service and are wonderful. The bottle of wine was perfect." (M. Patterson)

San Gregorio

Rancho San Gregorio
Route 1, Box 54
5086 La Honda Road
San Gregorio, CA 94074
(415) 747-0810
Innkeepers: Lee and Bud Raynor

♛♛   Rating: B+
Rates: Single or Double/$80-145
Credit Cards: AE, MC, V

Early California Spanish mission-style inn is a country retreat overlooking the San Gregorio Valley and is located 45 minutes south of San Francisco. There are four guest rooms, each with private bath. The San Gregorio room has a private deck overlooking the garden, king-size bed, two sofa-beds, woodburning stove, refrigerator, soaking tub, and Southwest decor. There is ample common space for guest conversation and relaxation and these areas feature interesting antiques, redwood beams, and terra cotta tile floors. The ranch is situated on fifteen acres and offers badminton, volleyball, horseshoes, lawn croquet, and quiet garden corners for contemplation. Area attractions: Ano Nuevo Seal Reserve, marshland bird byways, beaches (five miles away), and Redwood state parks. Full breakfast specialties vary day to day but may include apple-filled crepes, chocolate chip muffins, Rancho soufflé or Swedish egg cake with wild blackberry sauce. Families welcome. Restricted smoking.

Guests write: "*Breakfasts are a delightful melange of fresh fruits, savory dishes and homemade breads and cakes, different every morning! As in a true home, the kitchen is the heart of this house, and the door is never closed. Lee and Bud Raynor draw their visitors into their family. For us this was a real American welcome. It is an indication of how happy we were here, that we extended our visit from three to seven nights. The charming gardens which extend into surrounding woodlands and meadows create a peaceful and relaxing ambiance. In every direction are walks which are an education in the flora and fauna of this region. The house is full of books on the wildlife of the area, and there is even an excellent pair of binoculars for use of the guests.*" (D. Comerford)

"*We came to Rancho San Gregorio to get away and to cycle the scenic roads along the coast. Nothing can compare to bicycling along a quiet road, looking at the cows or catching glimpses of the ocean. Bud and Lee were very friendly and their breakfasts did a wonderful job of fueling these bicyclers!*" (T. Learmont)

"*When our lives become especially hectic, Rancho San Gregorio is the first place that comes to mind - it has become our retreat. Each room has a different flavor and they are all so comfortable. My favorite thing is a bubble bath in an old-fashioned tub with a fire in the wood burning stove followed by a glass of wine. Absolute perfection!*" (E. Swenson)

"*This was a delightful couple concerned about their guests and most helpful in planning tours. There were many little home touches such as a guest refrigerator on the second floor with soft drinks, beer, free wine coolers, VCR with large selection of movies, snacks, coffee, tea, and fruit were available in the kitchen at all times.*" (D. Grant)

"*We have stayed in three of the four rooms and each is absolutely charming. I would have a difficult time choosing my favorite but maybe the claw-foot tub in Corte Madera would be my choice. The food is excellent. Something fresh from the garden is always part of the breakfast meal.*" (M. Johnson)

San Luis Obispo

Garden Street Inn
1212 Garden Street
San Luis Obispo, CA 93401
(805) 545-9802
Innkeepers: Dan and Kathy Smith

 Rating: A
Rates: Single or Double/$90-120; Suites/$140-160
Credit Cards: AE, MC, V

Built in 1887, this Victorian Italianate/Queen Anne inn has been recently restored and is located four hours south of San Francisco off Highway 101. Choose from nine guest rooms and four suites. Each offers a private bath, king or queen-size bed, armoire, attractive wall coverings, rich fabrics, and antiques. Enjoy the Victorian decor in the McCaffrey Morning room with its original stained glass windows or sit on one of the outside decks with a good book from the Goldtree Library. Walk to the 1772 mission and historic downtown or drive to nearby Hearst Castle, Pismo Beach, Morro Bay, and Cambria. Outdoor activities nearby include tennis, golf, horseback riding, and hiking. A homemade full breakfast includes specialty breads and can be served in the suites by request. Facilities for small weddings and meetings available. Wheelchair access. No smoking.

Guests write: *"The reception was warm. They had wine, cider, cheese very well set up for two guests. The room was tastefully decorated. The bathroom was spacious. Breakfast was succulent and bountiful with fresh strawberry fruit salad and the best muffins I had in California."* (P. Meunier)

"Charming inn—probably the nicest of all the B & B's I've ever stayed in (approximately 50). The decor is beautiful and peaceful and the amenities very modern and up-to-date." (S. Murphy)

"Concourse suite has a delightful visiting area with fireplace for entertaining a few friends. An antique auto theme makes this room very interesting to anyone with even the faintest interest in autos. The host and hostess are most cordial and accommodating. The breakfasts were unique combinations of eggs and muffins with fresh fruit, orange juice and plenty of hot coffee." (J. Hogue)

Santa Barbara/Summerland

Inn on Summer Hill
2520 Lillie Avenue
Summerland, CA 93067
(805) 969-9998 or (800) 845-5566
Fax: (805) 969-9998
Innkeeper: Lin Richardson

♛♛♛♛   Rating: AA+
Rates: Single or Double/$160-275
Credit Cards: AE, MC, V

New England-style inn in a quiet seaside village is surrounded by rolling
foothills and located 2 miles south of Santa Barbara, 90 miles north of Los
Angeles. Choose from sixteen exceptionally well-furnished guest rooms. Each
features a private bath, canopy bed, gas fireplace, down comforter, antiques,
original art, and distant ocean view. The decor in each room is outstanding
with rich fabrics, lovely wall coverings, and unique accessories. The large
armoire in each room hides a TV/VCR and guest refrigerator stocked with
beverages. The whimsical garden features English country benches, bird
houses, and observation deck with spa. Full breakfast and evening refreshments served daily. No smoking. Facilities available for small meetings and
social functions.

Guests write: *"It is amazing how many conveniences were in our room—love seat,
lounge, desk, fireplace, Jacuzzi, refrigerator, boiling water, as well as the wonderful
abundant lighting everywhere! Nothing to add, and terrace overlooking the ocean!"*
(W. Brochman)

*"Every room has a wonderful balcony overlooking the ocean across the road. As soon
as we saw the fireplace, Jacuzzi tub, down quilt on canopy bed, pine ceiling,
beautiful wallpaper and window coverings, fresh flowers (even in the bathroom) —
we knew that we were in an exceptional place! The room also has complimentary
tea, coffee, cocoa, and mineral water. The quiche and bread pudding with banana
sauce were fantastic and the chocolate chip cookies were out of this world! I looked in
several rooms and each was just beautiful."* (J. Harold)

*"I will never be able to stay anywhere else without being disappointed. I have never
had such a wonderful stay. I was made to feel like their most important guest."* (G.
Altshuler)

Santa Barbara

Simpson House Inn
121 East Arrellaga
Santa Barbara, CA 93101
(805) 963-7067 or (800) 676-1280.
Innkeeper: Gillean Wilson

♛♛♛♛ Rating: AA-
Rates: Single or Double/$76-185
Credit Cards: AE, D, MC, V

Victorian inn built in 1874 is secluded on an acre of gardens within the city.
Choose from ten guest rooms with private bath each featuring antiques, lace,
Oriental rugs, goose-down comforters, fresh flowers, claw-foot tub and private
deck. A newly renovated carriage house on the property offers well-designed
guest suites with private entrances and spacious quarters. Enjoy a relaxing stroll
through the extensive gardens with curving paths, mature oaks, magnolias, and
pittosporums. Walk to restaurants, theaters, downtown shops, and museums.
Among area attractions are swimming, boating, and bicycling. Full breakfast
featuring homemade breads and house specialties is served overlooking the
gardens. Afternoon tea, wine and hors d'oeuvres served daily. No smoking.

Guests write: *"We especially enjoyed our breakfast on the sun room deck. The scones
were light and airy and homemade lemon curd! It was then a joy to lie out on our teak
sun lounges to digest and read, to look out over the mountains and beautiful gardens
below. There was no need to go anywhere."* (P. Young-Wolff)

*"We felt so rested and pampered by the elegant furnishings, romantic gardens and
sumptuous food - especially by Gillean's hospitality. The artful hors d'ouevres brought
to our room on a silver tray were a wonderful treat."* (B. Kendall)

*"Staying here is like coming home to the English country house which haunts my
dreams. Nestled behind tall Eugenia hedges, surrounded by lawns and gardens, the
house itself soothes and comforts world-weary travelers. Sumptuous breakfasts on the
balcony with a view of the mountains, wine and cheese in the late afternoon, pleasant
chats with the staff - these are memories to savor."* (P. Dickson)

Santa Cruz

Babbling Brook Inn
1025 Laurel Street
Santa Cruz CA 95060
(408) 427-2437 or (800) 866-1131
Fax: (408) 427-2457
Innkeeper: Helen King

♛♛♛   Rating: A+
Rates: Single or Double/$85-165
Credit Cards: AE, MC, V

The Babbling Brook Inn is located 90 miles south of San Francisco and was built on the foundation of a former 1795 tannery and grist mill. Its name comes from the extensive gardens, brook, waterwheel, and waterfalls which surround the inn. Twelve guest rooms with private bath are available. Each is unique in size, amenities, and decor but some special features include French Country decor, antiques, fireplaces, skylights, color cable TV, private phone, whirlpool baths, private outside entrances and decks. The Degas Room features a unique bed used by a local repertory group in their production of Shakespeare's "Romeo and Juliet". The inn is within walking distance of the beach, wharf, boardwalk, shopping, and tour of historic homes. Full country breakfast includes fresh-baked croissants. Wine and cheese are offered in the evening along with Mrs. King's special cookies. No smoking.

Guests write: *"We loved the gardens and the Honeymoon suite. The bath tub is great and big enough for two." (J. Sczepanski)*

"We stayed in the Renoir room until the last minute enjoying the view and music of the waterfall." (I. Lusebrink)

"The Countess room was spacious, charming, and lovely. The Talouse Lautrec room on the 2nd night was beautiful. Breakfast here was delicious and staff are so generous and attentive, yet unobtrusive." (S. Nachenberg)

"Our room was the Farmer's Garden room - very quaint and so nice we didn't want to be away from it too much." (G. Metzler)

"We're real homebodies because nothing is usually as comfortable but Babbling Brook is every bit as comfortable plus being enchanting." (C. Unruh)

Santa Monica

Channel Road Inn
219 West Channel Road
Santa Monica, CA 90402
(310) 459-1920
Fax: (310) 454-9920
Innkeeper: Susan Zolla

♛♛♛ Rating: A+
Rates: Single or Double/$95-200
Credit Cards: MC, V
10% corporate discount

Channel Road Inn is a large Colonial Revival home built in 1910 and located 2 miles north of I-10 in the Los Angeles metropolitan area. This building is the oldest residence in the surrounding vicinity and is convenient to cultural attractions as well as the beach. Fourteen guest rooms with large private baths are available. Each has distinctive period decor and furnishings but all offer an ocean or garden view, fresh cut flowers, and home-baked cookies. Bicycles are available for the oceanside bike paths and horseback riding as well as tennis are nearby. Area attractions include Getty Museum, pier, beaches, and Will Rogers Park. Full breakfast served in the mint-green and pink breakfast room features fresh California fruits and baked egg dishes. Complimentary refreshments are offered each evening. No smoking. Families welcome.

Guests write: *"The comfort and warmth provided by the staff are wonderful for someone who's homesick. They patiently answer all my questions, serve a fabulous breakfast, give great directions for driving, and stop to chat when I'm feeling lonely. I'll be coming back here as long as my business keeps bringing me to Los Angeles."* (S. Rosenberg)

"The inn is beautifully decorated in a Victorian manner - lots of wicker furniture and chintz covers. It is all new furniture - not old and musty. Our bedroom was very special and the bed had a wonderful pink and white hand-made quilt and there was an adjoining bathroom." (J. Kennedy)

"It's the little touches that make the Channel Road Inn a special hideaway. The Battenburg lace, the ocean view, the blooming hillside, waking to the smell of fresh coffee, and blueberry coffeecake, and your own key to the front door. I enjoyed reading the thoughts of past guests in the diaries in each room - especially Room #6 - the Honeymoon suite!" (D. Riley)

Seal Beach

Seal Beach Inn and Gardens
212 5th Street
Seal Beach, CA 90740
(310) 493-2416 or (800) 443-3292
Fax: (310) 799-0483
Innkeeper: Harty Schmahl

♛♛♛   Rating: A
Rates: Single or Double/$118-18; Penthouse/$255
Credit Cards: AE, MC, V

Seal Beach Inn and Gardens is located in a seaside village south of Los
Angeles and is a complex of French/Mediterranean architecture with a lush
garden setting. There are twenty-three distinctive guest rooms or suites. Each
offers a private bath and several have full kitchens. A Victorian library and tea
room offer quiet relaxation. Stroll through the gardens with European
fountains. Walk one block to the beach or pier. Interesting sites and activities
in the area include gondola rides, candlelight dining, seaside strolls, harbor
cruises, specialty shops, Disneyland, and Knott's Berry Farm. Full breakfast.
Facilities available for small meetings.

Guests write: *"I would say that visiting the inn is like coming home—only home is
never this pleasant. As a book lover, the first thing I do on each visit is search
thoroughly the volumes in my room and in the library. On each visit I end up
spending an evening in fron of the fireplace with a mug of cider and a wonderful old
book. Coming from Minnesota, having fresh berries for breakfast in February is a
great treat—but the highlight of breakfast is always the cheerful conversation with the
staff."* (J. Jalkie)

*"The location makes walks to the beach town and marina easy and pleasant.
Restaurants are in close proximity to the inn, and the very romantic Gondola Cruise
in Napals topped off a most romantic stay."* (D&P Durling)

*"Although I had lived in Seal Beach for three years prior to moving to New Jersey, I
always wanted to stay at the Seal Beach Inn. I got my wish and was more than
pleased. The staff was so accommodating with my off hours of arrival and departure.
The breakfast was beautiful each morning—arranged so invitingly with a lot of
variety. Fresh flowers abound everywhere. Truly refreshing for a travel weary soul.
This place is a labor of love with antiques lovingly arranged."* (D. Salamore)

Sonoma

The Hidden Oak
214 East Napa St.
Sonoma, CA 95476
(707) 996-9863
Innkeeper: Catherine Cotchett

♛♛♛ Rating: A
Rates: Single or Double/$105-170; Suite/$225
Credit Cards: AE

The Hidden Oak is located 45 minutes north of San Francisco and is a restored 1913 California Craftsman Bungalow with a brown shingled exterior and high gabled roof. Three guest rooms offer a private bath and antique or wicker furniture. The luxury suite, with its three rooms, has a private patio, bath, and many amenities. Browse through the library, sit by the fire in the reading room, borrow the inn's bicycles to explore the nearby wineries, or tour the Mission or the historic Plaza, just a block and a half away. Restaurants, art galleries, concerts, and plays are all a part of the surrounding area. Full breakfast is offered and dietary restrictions are taken into consideration. No smoking.

Sonoma

Sonoma Hotel
110 West Spain Street
Sonoma, CA 95476
(707) 996-2996 or (800) 468-6016
Fax: (707) 996-7014
Innkeeper: Dorene Musilli

♛♛ Rating: B
Rates: Single or Double/$75-120
Credit Cards: AE, MC, V

Historic hotel situated on the city's tree-lined plaza has been completely restored by the present owners who have worked hard at retaining the historic atmosphere of the building. There are seventeen individually decorated guest rooms with pleasant decor, antiques, and brass and iron appointments. Several rooms offer private baths with deep claw-foot tubs and herbal bubble bath. Most rooms on the third floor share two large "his" and "hers" baths at the end of the hall. Nearby attractions include wineries, hot air balloon rides, art galleries, shops, and historic landmarks. Continental buffet breakfast is served in the lobby and often includes fresh-baked pastries. Dining available on the premises. Families welcome.

Tahoe City

Chaney House
PO Box 7852 4725 West Lake Blvd.
Tahoe City, CA 96145
(916) 525-7333
Innkeepers: Gary and Lori Chaney

♛♛   Rating: B+
Rates: Single or Double/$95-110

Old European-style stone home with gothic arches was built in the 1920s and is nestled among native pine trees along the shore of Lake Tahoe, 5 miles south of Tahoe City and 60 miles west of Reno. Four guest rooms are available, three in the main house with the main level guest room having a private bath. The large master bedroom on the second floor has a private half bath and shares a shower with another room on this floor. A private entrance, alcove with futon couch, separate bedroom, and full kitchen is offered in the apartment over the garage. Guests enjoy gathering in front of the massive stone fireplace that reaches to the top of a cathedral ceiling. Just across the road is a private beach and pier. Rent a paddle boat or bicycle to explore the area. There's an abundance of recreation in the area including golfing, hiking, rafting, boating, and skiing. A full breakfast is served in the dining room or on the patio overlooking the lake and often features quiche, blackberry French toast, or egg stratas. Afternoon refreshments are offered in front of the fireplace. Restricted smoking.

Guests write: *"For complete relaxation in pleasant surroundings with the use of a private pier deck on the beautiful Lake Tahoe, Chaney House was ideal for providing a break in our travels. If you want to be kept busy however, you can spend your evenings guessing what imaginative, culinary treat Lori will present you with for breakfast! As English tourists in the States, we felt completely at home with the hospitality we were offered and the comfort of our stay."* (S. Moser)

"Besides Chaney House being warm and comfortable, we found our host to be extremely hospitable. We enjoyed wine and cheese with them after skiing, and there was always a really superb breakfast waiting for us each morning." (D. Thompson)

"We enjoyed our stay at the Chaney House. Our hosts, Gary and Lori were warm and friendly. We spent a romantic weekend in front of their big stone fireplace, watching the snow fall." (C. Penney)

Walnut Creek

The Mansion at Lakewood
1056 Hacienda Drive
Walnut Creek, CA 94598
(510) 945-3600; Fax: (510) 945-3608
Innkeepers: Angie and John Senser
Owners: Sharyn and Michael McCoy

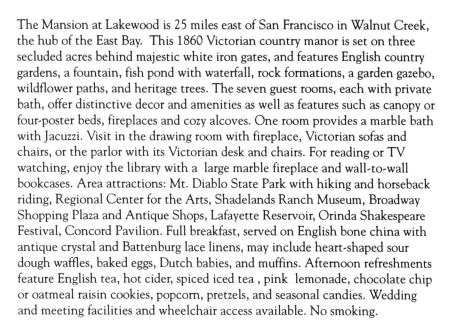

♛ ♛ ♛   Rating: A+
Rates: Single/$95-105; Double/$105-300
Credit Cards: AE, MC, V

The Mansion at Lakewood is 25 miles east of San Francisco in Walnut Creek, the hub of the East Bay. This 1860 Victorian country manor is set on three secluded acres behind majestic white iron gates, and features English country gardens, a fountain, fish pond with waterfall, rock formations, a garden gazebo, wildflower paths, and heritage trees. The seven guest rooms, each with private bath, offer distinctive decor and amenities as well as features such as canopy or four-poster beds, fireplaces and cozy alcoves. One room provides a marble bath with Jacuzzi. Visit in the drawing room with fireplace, Victorian sofas and chairs, or the parlor with its Victorian desk and chairs. For reading or TV watching, enjoy the library with a large marble fireplace and wall-to-wall bookcases. Area attractions: Mt. Diablo State Park with hiking and horseback riding, Regional Center for the Arts, Shadelands Ranch Museum, Broadway Shopping Plaza and Antique Shops, Lafayette Reservoir, Orinda Shakespeare Festival, Concord Pavilion. Full breakfast, served on English bone china with antique crystal and Battenburg lace linens, may include heart-shaped sour dough waffles, baked eggs, Dutch babies, and muffins. Afternoon refreshments feature English tea, hot cider, spiced iced tea , pink lemonade, chocolate chip or oatmeal raisin cookies, popcorn, pretzels, and seasonal candies. Wedding and meeting facilities and wheelchair access available. No smoking.

Guests write: *"This beautiful country inn evokes the quiet nostalgic heritage of turn-of-the-century California. Every detail has been seen to from decor to delicious gourmet breakfast specialties with fresh fruit and baked goods. My wife and I were truly pampered."* (J. Boyer)

Aspen

Crestahaus Lodge
1301 East Cooper Avenue
Aspen, CO 81611
(303) 925-7081 or (800) 344-3853
Fax: (303) 925-1610
Innkeeper: Melinda Goldrich

♛   Rating: C+
Rates: Single or Double/$50-185
Credit Cards: MC, V.

This two-story contemporary country B&B inn is just one-quarter mile from downtown Aspen and offers a view of Aspen Mountain. Choose from any of the thirty-one rooms, each with private bath, and decor ranging from Victorian to European country to contemporary. Relax in front of the fireplace in the large lounge or library, where in addition to reading, there are games, a television, and VCR. The dining room has a large screen TV. Main attractions include downhill skiing, cross-country skiing, hiking, bicycling, river rafting, and horseback riding, fine dining, and historic tours. An expanded continental breakfast is served. In winter, warm up with some complimentary apres-ski hot appetizers, desserts, and hot drinks. Wedding and meeting facilities available. Fax and copier available. Wheelchair accessible. Families welcome. Restricted smoking.

Guests write: *"Charming decor in a very homey, friendly atmosphere. It's a good value, especially for Aspen." (S. Sterling)*

Breckenridge

Allaire Timbers Inn
9511 Hwy., #9 South Main Street
Breckenridge, CO 80424
(303) 453-7530 or (800) 624-4904
Fax: (303) 453-8699
Innkeepers: Jack and Kathy Gumph

♛♛♛ Rating: A+
Rates: Single or Double/$115-250
Credit Cards: AE, MC, V

Allaire Timbers Inn is 87 miles west of Denver off I-70. This newly constructed log cabin bed and breakfast sits at the south end of historic Main Street. Nestled among the trees and sitting on a knoll overlooking the valley, the Inn offers views of Breckenridge Ski Area and the Ten Mile Range. Ten guest rooms, each with private bath, in-room phone, and private deck, are uniquely decorated with locally hand-crafted furniture. Two spacious suites each contain a hot tub and gas-operated, river-rock fireplace. Relax in the log and beam Great Room with large stone fireplace or sit in the sun room with love seat, garden furniture, sign-in desk, and telephone. The loft provides a love seat, recliner, or rocker where you can rest and watch television or play board games. Within walking distance is Alpine skiing, hiking, ice skating, museums, historic tours, and the Breckenridge Summer Music Festival Series. Area attractions: Alpine skiing, cross-country skiing, ice skating, mountain biking, sailing, hiking, golf, historic mining towns and sites, museums, shopping, National Repertory Institute, Breckenridge Classical & Jazz series. Full or extended continental breakfast may include homemade granola, cereal, fresh fruit, yogurts, quiche, croissants, homemade breads, cakes, rolls, muffins, and strawberry jams. During winter months hot entrees, such as French toast, Belgian waffles, and Mexican scrambled eggs are added to the menu. An afternoon happy hour includes complimentary beer and wine, appetizers, desserts, iced tea, and homemade hot citrus cider. Wedding and meeting facilities and wheelchair access available. No smoking.

Guests write: "*Visiting the inn is like visiting family. Jack and Kathy do everything to make guests feel welcome and at home, even supplying ski clothes when my luggage was lost. The atmosphere is very quiet and decor is rustic, yet beautiful.*" (D. Adams)

"*The inn is a new log home. Each room has a theme from a local mountain pass. One room is Bear Pass complete with a trophy bear! The fluffy quilts make it hard to leave bed in the morning for one of Kathy's spectacular breakfasts!*" (K. Weller)

Colorado Springs

Cheyenne Cañon Inn
2030 W. Cheyenne Blvd.
Colorado Springs, CO 80906
(719) 633-0625; (719) 633-1348
(719) 633-8825; Fax: (719) 633-8826
Innkeepers: Barbara and John Starr

  Rating: A+
Rates: Single/$65-105; Double/$75-115
Credit Cards: AE, MC, V

Secluded 2 1/2-story Mission style mansion, with over 100 windows, is located at the entrance to north and south Cheyenne Canons, with spectacular views to the south and west and Cheyenne Mountain to the south. Over 1,000 feet of terraced rock gardens surround the property. Each room with private bath reflects a unique region of the world. Sample a Swiss chalet, an Oriental tea house, a Mexican hacienda, or a Colorado lodge. These rooms offer television and telephone and complimentary beverage. Relax in the 1,000 square foot Great Room with 60 feet of 7-foot tall windows overlooking Cheyenne Mountain. Other common rooms include the library with stone fireplace, dining room, formal entry, gift shop, upstairs sitting area and hot tub room. Within walking distance is Seven Falls, Starsmore Discovery Center, Broadmoor Hotel, numerous hiking trails, and Starr-Kempf Sculptures. Area attractions: hiking and mountain biking, restaurants, Pikes Peak, Air Force Academy, Seven Falls, Broadmoor Hotel, Pioneer's Museum, and Old Colorado City. Full breakfast with china and crystal includes fruit muffins, bacon and egg muffins, coffee cake, oven-baked apple pancakes, crab quiche, juices, hot and cold cereals, coffee and tea. Retreat and meeting facilities available. No Smoking.

Guests write: *"Our corner room had a beautiful view of the mountains. After hiking and dinner, we relaxed in the hot tub which was next to our room and had another breathtaking view of the mountain. The location is convenient to many attractions."* (L. Gibson)

"I have never had baked fruit for breakfast 'til I went to the Cheyenne Canon Inn. Peaches one morning, pineapple the next - delightful! The rooms are each uniquly decorated for a specific area of the world. We stayed in the Italian villa which has by far the best view in the house. Watching the sunrise turn the Cheyenne Mountains red was worth the early wake-up call. If there weren't so many trails to hike or so many sights to see, I would have been content to sit and read for hours on end in the Great Room." (T. Edgington)

Crested Butte

Alpine Lace Bed & Breakfast
726 Maroon
Crested Butte, CO 81224
(303) 349-9857
Innkeepers: Ward and Loree Weisman

♛♛♛ Rating: A
Rates: Single or Double/$75-150
Credit Cards: MC, V

Swiss chalet-style inn is surrounded by mountain and valley views and is situated in the National Historic District near Highway 135. Three guest rooms are available, each with balcony, garden, or valley views. A two-room suite offers a TV, refrigerator, private balcony, and can accommodate up to four guests. A sunroom on the main floor has a Jacuzzi tub, guest refrigerator, wine glasses, and towels. The main living room features a large stone fireplace and interesting collection of books on Colorado. The mud room offers secure and accessible storage for skis, bicycles, hiking equipment, and a boot dryer. The large redwood deck is a great place to relax and unwind in the summer. This is a year-round recreation area which offers skiing, snowmobiling, snow shoeing, sleigh rides, biking, hiking, and horseback riding. Walk to unique shops and restaurants in the village area. Full gourmet breakfast served. Beverages and snacks are available throughout the day. Facilities available for small social functions. No smoking.

Guests write: *"Spending Christmas alone is a bummer unless you're at the Alpine Lace in which case it becomes a memorable high. The genuine warmth here quickly took off the chill for this flatlander. The food was excellent and will be missed immediately when I wake up in Florida upon my return. Also, if Ward can teach me to ski, he can teach anybody anything."* (R. Booth)

"Alpine Lace is our home away from home. The luxurious towels, the flowers on the table, Loree's warmth and friendship, Ward's efficiency and attention to detail, the hot tub soothing our tired muscles, the wonderful atmosphere of town - these are the things that made our trip a wonderful memory." (S. Sabo)

"We loved our week here and lost all track of time. A really great spot! The shuttle bus to the slopes made life effortless. Every breakfast was better than the one the day before." (D. Killen)

Denver

Capitol Hill Mansion
1207 Pennsylvania
Denver, CO 80203
(303) 839-5221 (800) 839-9329
Fax: (303) 839-9046
Innkeeper: Kathy Robbins

♛♛♛♛   Rating: AA
Rates: Single/$79-139; Double/$89-149
Credit Cards: AE, MC, V

Capitol Hill Mansion is located in the heart of Denver approximately four blocks from the state capitol and six blocks from the central business district. The three-story Richardsonian Romanesque architecture is from the Victorian period and features turrets, balconies, curved porches, bays with curved windows, elaborate oak and stained glass. Choose from eight guest rooms with private baths. Each room, uniquely decorated, offers various amenities. Some rooms feature fireplaces and whirlpool tubs, while other rooms may boast private balconies and curved glass windows. One of the three suites available includes a modern kitchen. Refrigerators, cable TV, a hot water maker, and hair dryers are provided in all rooms. The living room has a number of easy chairs for relaxation, and the dining room has two tables with chairs which can be used in non-breakfast hours for board games. Within walking distance is the state capitol, numerous museums and galleries, 16th Street Mall, mountain views, shopping, dining, and entertainment. Area attractions: government and business offices, historic architecture, Western history, parks, museums, theaters, clubs, shopping, dining, entertainment, and carriages (for the urban romantic), national forests, historic towns and districts, fishing. A continental breakfast includes fresh fruit, juice, cereals, breads, jams, jellies, yogurts, teas and coffee. Meeting facilities available. No smoking.

Guests write: *"My room, the Elk Thistle Suite was spacious, the bed was comfortable, the suite was equipped with a desk, telephone, easy chairs, and TV. The inn itself is within an easy walk to several interesting restaurants - I had buffalo for the first time! I found the other guests interesting and the proprietor and staff kind. I had been on the road for some time and felt thoroughly at home and well pampered!" (J. Crabb)*

"We have many incoming phone calls and the innkeepers were very gracious in keeping our calls in order, writing down messages, and bringing them to our room. The rooms are sunny, cheerful, spacious, and decorated with loving attention to detail." (C. Drake)

Denver

Castle Marne B&B
1572 Race Street
Denver, CO 80237
(303) 331-0621 or (800) 92-MARNE
Innkeeper: Melissa, Jim, and Diane Peiker

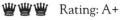 Rating: A+
Rates: Single/$70-180; Double/$85-180
Credit Cards: AE, MC, V
Auto club, corporate, and senior discounts

Historic Victorian mansion built in 1889 is now a luxury urban inn located near the intersection of Routes 40 and 287, 20 blocks east of downtown. Nine guest rooms or suites are available, each with period antiques, family heirlooms, and private bath. The spacious guest suites feature Jacuzzi bath tubs. The original character of the mansion is still evident in its hand-rubbed woods, circular stained-glass peacock window, and ornate fireplaces. Business travelers will appreciate the quiet office setup in the lower level with desk and office equipment ready for use. Full breakfast and afternoon tea served daily. Candle-light dinners are available on Friday and Saturday evenings by advance reservation. Facilities available for small meetings. No smoking.

Guests write: *"Wonderful turn-of-the-century decor featuring an unparalleled attention to details. Every horizontal surface is graced with wonderful period photos, toys or other period objects of art. Soaps and toiletries are tied with ribbons. What detail! The Castle itself is a large Victorian architectural beauty that has been painstakingly restored to its original grandeur from the peacock stain-glass window to the wall sconces. It has clearly been a project from the heart."* (C. Perry)

"Breakfast was tastefully served and delicious. The menu on one day included juice, coffee, muffins, green chili quiche and fresh fruit. Another day, breakfast included fruit cup, whole wheat strawberry pancakes, juice and coffee. All sauces and jams are homemade. Afternoon tea was a highlight also with herbal or regular tea, scones, gingerbread and lemon squares. Convenient location for business travelers like me. I will return." (S. McManigal, Ph.D.)

Denver

Queen Anne Bed & Breakfast Inn
2147 Tremont Place
Denver, CO 80205
(303) 296-6666 or (800) 432-INNS
Fax: (303) 296-2151
Innkeeper: Tom King

♛♛♛   Rating: A
Rates: Single or Double/$75-125; Suite/$135-155
Auto club and business travel discount
Credit Cards: AE, MC, V

Two large Queen Anne Victorian homes facing a quiet city park offer the atmosphere and ambiance of Denver's Historic District, yet are located only four blocks from the center of downtown. There are fourteen guest rooms with private bath. Each has a unique decor, fresh flowers, classical music intercom system, period lighting, air conditioning, and telephone. The Aspen Room's unusual architectural features are enhanced by an original mural of aspen trees and this central theme is carried out with unique wood lighting fixtures. Four new suites have been recently added which feature spacious rooms, upscale furnishings, and special deep tubs. The Capitol, 16th Street Pedestrian Mall, specialty shops, galleries, and restaurants within walking distance. Horse-drawn carriages are available for special occasions. Full breakfast and evening refreshments served daily. Off-street parking is available on-site. No smoking.

Guests write: *"Forget the elevators, front desk and all of the inconveniences of the typical hotel. In fact, forget hotels. I have. From here on out we'll search out the bed and breakfast inns."* (S&L Davies)

"The Queen Anne Inn is a charming B&B which is filled with antiques, fine books, and piped chamber music. We stayed in the Garden Room with antique furnishings, huge wardrobe, desk, rocking chair, comfortable double bed, and private bath. We would wholeheartedly recommend the inn to readers." (L. Edwards)

"The Queen Anne is my port of choice in Denver. What I count on is a peaceful place in a busy city, rooms that are nicely furnished—mostly antiques, some modern— always delightful and complete, a nourishing, hot and complete breakfast, and a wise and warm innkeeper. With many to choose from, my favorite room has been the Aspen which is filled with a delightful hand-painted mural and octagonal walls. Gazing into the trees and sky as I drift away into slumber is the best medicine I could take." (L. Be)

Denver/Arvada

The Tree House
6650 Simms Street
Arvada, CO 80004
(303) 431-6352
Innkeeper: Sue Thomas

♛♛♛ Rating: A-
Rates: Single or Double/$49-$89
Corporate discount
Credit Cards: MC, V

Chalet style inn is set far back from the road on ten wooded acres and is located only 20 minutes west of downtown Denver near the Ward exit off I-70. Each of the five guest rooms offers a private bath and is furnished with brass bed, handmade quilts, and interesting antiques. Four rooms feature a wood-burning fireplace. Several balconies provide a quiet spot for taking in the wooded views. Enjoy a leisurely walk through the forest that surrounds the inn. A large parlor offers a fireplace and comfortable oak and leather furniture. Area attractions: Rocky Mountains, Denver Mint, Denver Zoo, and Coors Brewery. Full breakfast includes special homemade cinnamon rolls, omelets, and fresh fruit. Families welcome. No smoking.

Guests write: "*Beautifully decorated and comfortable interior and wooded surroundings. The crowning touch was the gourmet breakfast. As a host of breakfast eaters who feel the day should begin with a good meal, we were all delighted with Amanda's wonderful cooking.*" (N. Arnold)

Leadville

Delaware Hotel
700 Harrison Ave
Leadville, CO 80461
(719)486-1418 or (800) 748-2004
Innkeeper: Susan Brackett

 ♛♛ Rating: B-
Rates: Single/$50-85; Double/$55-90
Credit Cards: AE, MC, V

Historic cornerstone inn built in 1886 is in the heart of downtown, 70 miles west of Denver. Period antiques, brass fixtures, oak paneling, and crystal chandeliers are all a part of the recent renovation restoring the original Victorian atmosphere. Thirty-seven guest rooms with private baths feature antique furnishings, brass or iron bedsteads, wooden dressers and quilt wall hangings. Many of the rooms offer views of the Continental Divide and the Arkansas Valley; all have color cable television. Relax in the Jacuzzi or listen to the baby grand piano in the lobby. Visit nearby National Mining Hall of Fame, Matchless Mine Heritage, Healy House, Tabor Opera House, or Tabor Home. A full breakfast in the restaurant features Eggs Callaway, crepes, or Huevos Rancheros. Wedding and meeting facilities available. Families welcome. Restricted smoking.

Guests write: *"We loved the renovation, the Victorian floor, and the decor was very well done. The breakfasts were also wonderful with very generous portions!" (T. Young)*

"The Historic Delaware Hotel has and excellent atmosphere for capturing the spirit of Colorado. It has a traditional western motif. In the city of Leadville, it stands as a renovation example for renewing the entire city." (H. Cleary)

"Comfortable, restored with the look an feel of the past, with a few modern additions for comfort. Bathrooms were added to the rooms. A hot tub was added to the lobby for the benefit of the many skiers that flock to the hotel." (K. Cope)

Ouray

The Manor B&B
317 Second Street
Ouray, CO 81427
(303) 325-4574
Innkeepers: Joel and Diane Kramer

♕♕♕ Rating: A-
Rates: Single or Double/$55-80
Credit Cards: MC, V

Built in 1890 during Ouray's mining boom, this Victorian home offers views of the mountains, is on the Natiomnal Historic Register, and can be found one block west of Main Street in Ouray. Each of the seven guest rooms features a private bath, period decor, queen size beds fitted with feather beds and down comforters during the winter months, and views of the surrounding mountains. Relax in the parlor or on the sunny, second story balcony. The patio has a Jacuzzi for soaking while taking in the mountain views. Arrange for an in-house therapeutic body massage or tour the town with its historic turn-of-the-

century homes. Area attractions: jeep tours and rentals, hiking and mountaineering, hot air ballooning, rock or ice climbing, horseback riding, mine tours,
fishing, hunting, museums, galleries and autumn foliage. Full breakfast
includes fresh brewed coffee, homemade breads and muffins and a specialty
entree such as upside-down peach or apple French toast, whole wheat buttermilk pancakes, or souffle blintzes. No smoking.

Guests write: *"The historic Victorian house was tastefully decorated, quiet, and in a
convenient location. The hosts were extremely helpful in discovering and enjoying
Ouray with its hiking, fishing holes, restaurants, and galleries. The food was fresh,
interesting and of the highest quality in taste and presentation." (S. Chase)*

*"The hospitality that was extended to us at this B&B far exceeded our expectations.
The rooms were cheerful and comfortable with real down comforters and a view of
the ampitheater in the San Juan mountains. The breakfasts were both tasty and
healthy with the blintz souffle being my favorite. There was usually a fire in the living
room in the evening where we could sit and read while enjoying tea and cookies." (R.
Harrison)*

Redstone

Cleveholm Manor
0058 Redstone Boulevard
Redstone, CO 81623
(303) 963-3463 or
(800) 643-4837(Outside Colorado)
Innkeeper: Cyd Lange

♕♕♕   Rating: A
Rates: Single or Double/$95-180
Senior discounts
Credit Cards: AE, MC, V

English Manor-style mansion built originally for a wealthy mining baron at the
turn-of-the-century sits overlooking the Crystal River and red mountain cliffs
and is located south of Glenwood Springs, 200 miles west of Denver, and 45
miles southwest of Aspen. Sixteen guest rooms are available which offer a
variety in price, decor and amenities. Eight rooms have private baths. Several
small rooms which share baths offer fresh, updated decor. Other choices
include the suites with period furnishings and decor, private baths, and
fireplaces. The main floor has an impressive entry, parlor, and dining rooms
whose features include elegant woodwork, stone and marble fireplaces, inlaid
floors, gold leaf ceilings, and Persian rugs. The lower level offers a small

television room, and billiards room. Outdoor recreation available nearby includes high country skiing, hiking, bicycling, horseback riding, and fishing. Continental buffet breakfast. Large common areas are available for private parties, dinners, lunch tours, or special events. Families welcome. No smoking.

Steamboat Springs

The Inn at Steamboat, Bed & Breakfast
3070 Columbine Drive
Steamboat Springs, CO
(303) 879-2600 or (800) 872-2601
Fax: (303) 879-9270
Innkeepers: Tom & Roxane Miller-Freutel

♛   Rating: C+
Rates: Single or Double$62-159
Children age12 and under are free.
Credit Cards: AE, MC, V

The Inn at Steamboat, Bed & Breakfast is nestled in the Colorado Rockies and located 3 miles from the heart of downtown Steamboat Springs; three hours northwest of Denver off of Hwy. 40. The three-story inn, reminiscent of a Swiss chalet, sits on a hillside overlooking the Yampa Valley and Mt. Werner. Western accents and an A-frame entrance add a touch of Colorado's past. Choose from 32 guest rooms with private baths. Each is decorated with wood wainscoting, brass lighting, and a small sitting area. Other amenities include television with VCR, telephone, and clock radio. Relax by the huge rock fireplace in the parlor that features hurricane lamps, wine cabinet, and oversized sofas. A game room offers a pool table and video games. Relax in the outdoor heated pool or sauna. Walk to skiing (cross-country & downhill), tennis, golf, hiking, biking, hot air ballooning, swimming, fishing, river rafting, kayaking, and classical music performances. Area attractions: snowmobiling, horse drawn sleigh, hot air ballooning, bobsledding, ice skating, dog sledding, mountain biking, sailing, fishing and horseback riding. Full breakfast offered during winter months varies each day with specialties such as pancakes, eggs and bacon, sourdough French toast, Buckwheat pancakes, and omelettes. Continental breakfast is provided during spring, summer and fall. Meeting facilities available. No smoking. Families welcome.

Telluride

Alpine Inn Bed & Breakfast
440 West Colorado Ave.
Telluride, CO 81435
(303) 728-6282 or (800) 707-3344
Fax: (303) 728-3424
Innkeepers: Denise and John Weaver

Rating: B+
Rates: Single or Double/$50-200
Credit Cards: AE, MC, V

Retored Victorian built in 1903 is located on main street of this historic town which is secluded in the San Juan Mountains, 330 miles southwest of Denver; 67 miles south of Montrose. Each of the eight guest rooms has been individually decorated with antiques and Victorian accents. Six rooms offer a private bath. Breakfast is served in the sun room which offers panoramic views of the mountains. Relax on the outside deck or in the hot tub room after a day of hiking, skiing, or cycling. Main Street offers interesting shopping and a good variety of restaurants. Area attractions include the Telluride Ski Resort, Bridal Veil Falls, Hot Air Balloon Rally, and several choices of music and film festivals. Fresh fruit accompanies a full breakfast. No smoking.

Guests write: *"I found the Alpine Inn a thoroughly delightful place to stay. The hospitality is in the tradition of the Southwest. The accommodations are very immaculate and comfortable. The added extras of a hearty breakfast and beverages after skiing made it a truly desirable place to stay."* (L. Longo)

"Cozy, different rooms are very inviting — like going to Grandma's house. The sunroom that looks out on the mountain is very nice." (J. Knopinski)

"The inn was clean, neat, and beautifully decorated. The hosts' stories of the town were interesting and amusing." (L. Gouthro)

Telluride

Bear Creek Bed & Breakfast
221 E. Colorado Avenue
Tulluride, CO 81435
(303) 728-6681 or (800) 338-7064
Innkeeper: Colleen Whiteman

👑👑   Rating: B
Rates: 1 or 2 persons/$65-180
Credit Cards: AE, MC, V

Bear Creek Bed & Breakfast is located on Highway 145, seven hours southwest of Denver. This three-story brick European-style structure in the heart of Telluride offers a bed & breakfast on the second and third floors. Choose from eight guest rooms with private baths. Rooms on the third floor offer a stunning wall of windows and skylights. Available in these rooms are telephones, clock radios, and televisions. Relax in the common area which offers a fireplace and opens to second story skylights. A steam room and sauna is provided for the comfort of guests. For summer enjoyment, there is a roof deck which offers a 360 degree view of the surrounding mountains and Telluride. Area attractions: fly fishing, tennis, swimming, hiking, jeep trails, horseback riding, mountain biking, hang gliding, museum, opera house (plays & special events), sleigh/wagon rides, golf, Nordic skiing, ice skating, ski lifts, gold panning, rafting, Herb Walker tours, volleyball, snow mobile tours, and waterfalls. Full breakfast includes coffee, assorted teas, juice, locally baked breads, assorted cereals, stewed fruit, yogurt, and granola. Examples of hot entrees, which vary daily, include pancakes, Southwestern eggs, corn quiche, Mexican quiche, stuffed German toast, and breakfast casserole. Meeting facilities. No smoking.

Guests write:*"This was my first stay at a B&B. I thoroughly enjoyed my vacation and was most pleased with the accommodations. The banana and pecan pancakes made quite a hit and I am still trying to duplicate them."* (B. Smith)

"Breakfasts were made from typical ingredients cooked up in unique fashion with Southwestern flair. The most enjoyable feature is the sun roof overlooking downtown. The lawn chairs allowed me to sit back in the sun and gaze above at Colorado's blue sky. The Jacuzzi was welcomed after the daily jazz concerts and/or hiking. Rooms were quiet and well decorated to reflect the area culture. I looked at some of the other B&Bs while in Telluride and came to the conclusion that I chose the right one for location, food, friendliness, and ambience." (D. Ansel)

Telluride

San Sophia
330 West Pacific Avenue
Telluride, CO 81435
(800) 537-4781
Innkeepers: Diane and Gary Eschman

👑👑👑 Rating: A+
Rates: Single or Double/$90-250
Credit Cards: AE, MC, V

Newly built contemporary inn is well-situated in town and is within walking distance to either the historic downtown shopping area or the base of the ski area and lifts. The atmosphere of the inn combines Victorian architecture with modern conveniences. Choose from sixteen guest rooms with private bath. Each offers a brass bed, comfortable furnishings, and handmade quilts. There is a fireplaced library, English garden, and gazebo with sunken Jacuzzi for relaxing after hiking, shopping, or skiing. A small observatory tower on the third floor offers waterfall and mountain views. Secure ski lockers and boot dryers along with a computerized map routing service are some of the special services provided guests. Full gourmet buffet breakfast and afternoon refreshments offered daily. Facilities available for meetings and social functions. No smoking.

Connecticut

Essex

The Griswold Inn
36 Main Street
Essex, CT 06426
(203) 767-1776 or (203) 767-0481
Innkeeper: William G. Wintuer

👑👑👑 Rating: A
Rates: Single or Double/$90-175
Credit Cards: AE, MC, V

The Griswold Inn is located on the river at the foot of Main Street in Essex Village, a location convenient to either I-95 or I-91. The inn, built in 1776, is one of the oldest structures in Connecticut and is set on the banks of Connecticut River. Choose from 26 guest rooms including standard rooms, petite suites,

suites, and luxury suites. All have air conditioning, private baths, telephones, and piped-in classical music. Some offer fireplaces. Visitors can warm up by the potbelly stove or relax by one of the many fireplaces. A handsome taproom is available and a library of firearms boasts weapons dating from the 15th century. Enjoy a meal from one of the four dining rooms: the Covered Bridge, the Steamboat, the Library and the Gun Room. Walk to shops, and the nearby Connecticut River Museum. Area Attractions: Connecticut River Museum, Valley Railroad, Mystic Aquarium, Mystic Seaport, beaches, steamboat rides, Gillette Castle, and boating. Continental breakfast is provided. Lunch and dinner are available as well as wedding and meeting facilities. Families welcome.

New London

Queen Anne Inn
265 Williams Street
New London, CT 06320
(800) 347-8818 or (203) 447-2600
Innkeepers: Tracey and James Cook

♛♛♛   Rating: A-
Rates: Single/$73-150; Double/$78-155
Credit Cards: AE, MC, V

Victorian inn built in 1903 is located off I-95 in a shoreline resort area. Choose from ten guest rooms, eight with private bath. Each room offers antique furnishings, air conditioning, and unique decor. Several rooms feature working fireplaces. A private cable TV and telephone are available in certain rooms upon request. The home's original beauty has been retained and is showcased in its carved alcove, fireplaced foyer, stained-glass windows, and main staircase circular landing. Transportation by bus, train, and ferry is within walking distance. Area attractions include Mystic Seaport and Aquarium, US Coast Guard Academy, Nautilus Submarine Memorial, and Block Island. Full breakfast and afternoon tea served daily.

New Preston

Boulders Inn
East Shore Road (Route 45)
New Preston, CT 06777
(203) 868-0541; Fax: (203) 868-1925
Innkeeper: Kees & Ulla Adema

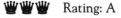 Rating: A
Rates: Single/$100-190; Double$125-235
Credit Cards: AE, MC, V

Boulders Inn is located two hours northeast of New York City. Built in the late 1800's, this Victorian home, named for the enormous boulders used to build parts of the house, sits at the foot of Pinnacle Mountain overlooking Lake Waramang. Twenty-eight acres offers expansive lawns with wildflower and herb gardens, as well as a wooded area on the mountain for hiking. Fifteen guest rooms and two suites with private baths are available. Guest rooms in the inn are furnished with a combination of country classics and antiques. Behind the inn four guest houses provide country decor, lake views, private decks, and fireplaces. The carriage house shelters three traditionally furnished guest rooms, each with its own stone fireplace. The large living room with fireplace, overlooks the lake. The library offers television, and a game room provides billiards and a piano. Within walking distance is hiking, swimming, bicycling, boating, fishing, tennis, ice-skating, and antiques. Area attractions: 18th century villages of Litchfield and Washington, Connecticut, antique and craft shops, summer theater and music festivals, hiking, bicycling, cross-country and downhill skiing, golf, horseback riding. Hot breakfast specials are created fresh each morning along with yogurt, fresh fruit, cereals, fresh baked coffee cake and Danish, fresh juice, coffee and tea. The acclaimed restaurant serves dinner and Sunday brunch in addition to breakfast. Wedding and meeting facilities available. Wheelchair access. Restricted smoking.

Ridgefield

West Lane Inn
22 West Lane
Ridgefield, CT 06877
(203) 438-7323
Innkeeper: N. M. Mayer

 Rating: A+

Rates: Single/$90-115; Double/$120-165
Credit Cards: AE, MC, V

Victorian inn built in 1848 is set at the end of a broad lawn and surrounded by
majestic maples, and located one hour north of New York City and three hours
southwest of Boston. Choose from twenty individually decorated rooms, each
with private bath, temperature control, and color television. Several rooms
feature working fireplaces. There are ample common areas for guest relaxation
in front of a fireplace or with a good book. Take long walks on the wooded trails
or visit nearby historic sites, museums, art galleries, and antique stores. Area
recreation includes swimming, sailing, bowling, skating, and skiing. Continental breakfast is included in the rates but a full breakfast is available. Families
welcome. Wheelchair access.

Washington, DC
(See Silver Spring, Burtonsville, and Olney, Maryland)

Additional information on B&Bs throughout Florida is available through the following reservation agency: B&B Scenic Florida (904) 386-8196.

Amelia Island

Elizabeth Point Lodge
98 South Fletcher Street
Amelia Island, FL 32034
(904) 277-4851 or Fax: (904) 277-6500
Innkeepers: David and Susan Caples

♛♛♛   Rating: A
Rates: Single/$80-115; Double/$95-125
Senior and auto club discounts
Credit Cards: AE, MC, V

New oceanfront Nantucket-style inn built in a turn-of-the-century manner is found just off Route A1A, 25 miles north of Jacksonville, and fifteen miles off I-95. Twenty guest rooms, each with private bath, have been carefully decorated to emphasize a maritime theme and include oversized tubs and fresh flowers. Enjoy a glass of lemonade and a homemade snack on the main floor's wrap-around porch or step out the back door for beachcombing. Special children's activities are regularly scheduled and assistance is given in arranging special tours and outings with sailing, fishing charters, golfing, biking, and horseback riding nearby. A full breakfast is served in the oceanfront sunroom and includes special egg dishes and fresh baked goods. Meeting and reception facilities available. Families welcome. Wheelchair access.

Guests write: *"Absolutely exquisite. The little extras were great! Whirlpool tubs, afternoon wine, the veranda overlooking the beach, and all the other extras made it a perfect romantic weekend getaway. The breakfasts—unbelievable!"* (R. Mock)

Amelia Island

The Fairbanks House
227 South Seventh Street
Amelia Island, FL 32034
(904) 277-0500 or (800) 261-4838
Fax: (904) 277-3103
Innkeepers: Nelson & Mary Smelker

♕♕♕ Rating: A+
Rates: Single or Double/$85-150
Credit Cards: AE, MC, V

Set on an acre of landscaped oaks, magnolias, and palms, this three story Italianate Villa listed on the National Register of Historic Places has four piazzas, ten fireplaces, arches all around, and two historic cottages. It is located in the historic district of Fernandina Beach on Amelia Island just 30 miles north of Jacksonville. Choose from ten guest rooms with private baths, four-poster or canopied beds, Jacuzzis, claw foot tubs or showers, television, and telephones. Four rooms are suites. The inn's hardwood floors, carved moldings, carved fireplaces, antiques, Oriental rugs, and period pieces reflect the mid-19th century architecture and style. Explore the surrounding grounds with swimming pool and gardens. It's only a short walk to historic Fernandina's Centre Street shops, art galleries, and restaurants. Area attractions: Amelia Island's beaches, Fort Clinch, Cumberland Island National Seashore, zoo, fishing, tennis, and golf. A sample continental breakfast includes specialties such as homemade raw apple or cranberry-raspberry muffins, layered breakfast bake, fresh fruit, and baked banana with fresh blueberries. Weddings and meeting facilities available with the gardens and piazzas serving as garden party or reception backdrops. Families welcome. Wheelchair access. Restricted smoking.

Daytona Beach

Live Oak Inn and Restaurant
448 South Beach Street
Daytona Beach, FL 32114
(904) 252-4667 or (800) 881-4667
Fax: (904) 255-1871
Innkeeper: Vinton Fisher

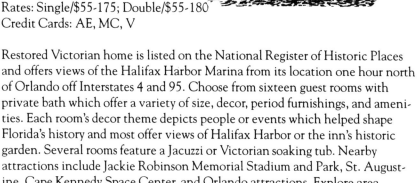

♛♛♛ Rating: A-
Rates: Single/$55-175; Double/$55-180
Credit Cards: AE, MC, V

Restored Victorian home is listed on the National Register of Historic Places
and offers views of the Halifax Harbor Marina from its location one hour north
of Orlando off Interstates 4 and 95. Choose from sixteen guest rooms with
private bath which offer a variety of size, decor, period furnishings, and amenities. Each room's decor theme depicts people or events which helped shape
Florida's history and most offer views of Halifax Harbor or the inn's historic
garden. Several rooms feature a Jacuzzi or Victorian soaking tub. Nearby
attractions include Jackie Robinson Memorial Stadium and Park, St. Augustine, Cape Kennedy Space Center, and Orlando attractions. Explore area
beaches, art galleries, museums, and historic sites. Continental plus breakfast is
served in the restaurant and includes fresh fruit and orange juice, muffins,
cheese, and breakfast beverage. Facilities available for meetings and weddings.
Wheelchair access. Restricted smoking.

Gainesville

Sweetwater Branch Inn
625 E. University Avenue
Gainesville, FL 32601
(904) 373-6760
Innkeeper: Cornelia Holbrook

♛♛♛ Rating: A
Rates: Single/$55-60; Double $60-90

Victorian two-story home surrounded by over an acre of gardens is located two
hours north of Orlando on I-75; 1 1/2 hours east of Jacksonville on I-10.
Choose from six guest rooms, four with private sitting rooms. Each offers
antique furnishings and hardwood floors. The entry parlor offers a place to relax
with fireplace, Victorian sofa, and comfortable chairs. A sitting area is also

provided in the main formal parlor with Persian rug, chandelier, and fireplace. Within walking distance is Matheson Historical Center. Area attractions: fresh water springs and rivers, historic town of Micanopy, Paynes Prairie State Park, University of Florida, Matheson Historical Center, antique shops in Micanopy and High Springs, Gulf Coast 50 miles west and Atlantic Coast 80 miles east. Full breakfast includes homemade muffins, fresh fruit salad, Camelia's French toast, pancakes with sautéed apples, orange juice and the inn's own blend of coffee. Herbal tea and vegetarian breakfast is also provided. In the afternoon, enjoy homemade snacks. Wedding and meeting facilities available. Wheelchair access. Restricted smoking.

Holmes Beach

Harrington House B&B
5626 Gulf Drive
Holmes Beach, FL 34217
(813) 778-5444
Innkeepers: Frank and Jo Davis

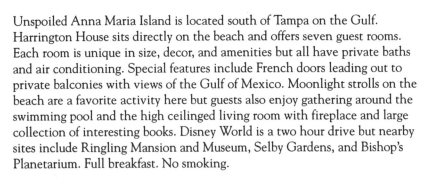

♛♛♛   Rating: A
Rates: Single or Double/$79-159
Credit Cards: MC, V

Unspoiled Anna Maria Island is located south of Tampa on the Gulf. Harrington House sits directly on the beach and offers seven guest rooms. Each room is unique in size, decor, and amenities but all have private baths and air conditioning. Special features include French doors leading out to private balconies with views of the Gulf of Mexico. Moonlight strolls on the beach are a favorite activity here but guests also enjoy gathering around the swimming pool and the high ceilinged living room with fireplace and large collection of interesting books. Disney World is a two hour drive but nearby sites include Ringling Mansion and Museum, Selby Gardens, and Bishop's Planetarium. Full breakfast. No smoking.

Guests write: *"What can we say to describe our trip here? The welcome was warm and inviting. We loved the room - so cozy and super clean. Breakfast was delicious. We just had a great time. And our only sorrow was it wasn't long enough."* (D. Yeager)

"Our room was lovely and I most appreciated the attention to detail - iced tea on the porch, mints on the dresser, refrigerator in the room, and the little basket with shampoo, etc. in the bath. Those are the things that make it special. Breakfasts were delightful." (K. Goss)   (Continued)

"The setting was wonderful. We want the Sunset Room when we return. Friendliness of staff and guests was like home. Food was wonderful. I appreciated the little touches - decor, accessories, colors, warmth." (C. Cavanagh)

"These folks treat their guests like kings and queens. The service is second to none. The atmosphere is very unique and enjoyable. They create a warm and friendly environment for all." (D. Traudt)

"The room, the ambiance, the staff, breakfasts, the view, the beach - all too nice for words." (T. Ennis)

Key West

Heron House
512 Simonton Street
Key West, FL 33040
(305) 294-9227 or (800) 294-1644
Fax: (305) 294-5692
Innkeeper: Fred Geibelt

♛♛♛ Rating: A-
Rates: Single/$75-145; Double/$105-195
Credit Cards: AE, MC, V

Heron House is a historic property built in 1856. It is centrally located near all major tourism attractions in Key West yet located on a quiet residential street off Route 1. There are twenty-one guest rooms with private bath available. Each is unique in size, decor, and amenities. Several luxury rooms feature large mirrored walls and unusual wood decorative artwork as well as marble baths. The rooms are located in four buildings that surround a swimming pool and patio with lush foliage, large pots of tropical plants, and orchids. Nearby attractions include Hemingway House, Mel Fischer's Treasure Museum, snorkeling cruises, tennis, golf, fishing, and hiking. Continental breakfast includes waffles or French toast, bagels and muffins. Wheelchair access.

Guests write: *"The Heron House was everything we were looking for during our stay in Key West…atmosphere, relaxation, and charm. Lush tropical gardens surround a beautiful pool and sundecks. The large guest rooms are all furnished in their own tropical flair. Our favorite, room #10 was very luxurious, spacious and beautifully appointed with mirrored walls, wet bar, marble bath and a king bed with a beautiful inlaid teak wood headboard. French doors open into a private tropical garden." (J&J DiBello)*   (Continued)

"This is my sixth visit to the Heron House. It certainly won't be the last. The grounds here make you feel as though you are a guest at a wonderful botanical garden. The staff always sees to your every need. I love the new sundeck." (R. Abplanalp)

Key West

La Mer Hotel
506 South Street
Key West, FL 33040
(800) 354-4455 or (305) 296-5611
Innkeeper: Matthew and Carrie Babich

♛ ♛ ♛   Rating: A
Rates: Single or Double/$110-245
Credit Cards: AE, MC, V

Located directly on the Atlantic Ocean, this Victorian Conch house is surrounded by tropical foliage and palm trees in the heart of Old Town Key West. Each of the newly renovated guest rooms, eleven in all, feature private bath, cable television, air conditioning, in-room safe, and private phone. Most rooms, decorated with a contemporary theme, offer private patios or balconies overlooking the ocean or tropical surroundings. Relax at one of the three pools, a Jacuzzi, or the sunning pier. Bike and moped rentals are available for exploring the area. Visit the only coral reef in the country, take a sunset cruise, scuba dive or snorkel, or take advantage of the ample shopping, historic attractions, and nightlife found in the resort area. Extensive continental breakfast is served and daily newspaper delivery is complimentary.

Guests write: *"The thoughtfulness of the managers, Matt & Carrie Babich and all the their supporting staff is exceptional and greatly appreciated. The sun brightly shining, the blue sky and water, with the waves washing against the shore, and a sand beach are at your door. The decor is eclectic soft pastels and wicker furniture with just the right feeling of casual living and relaxing." (B. Isabel)*

"My wife and I find La Mer to be perfectly located. It's at the quiet end of Duval Street with a pool and beach on the Atlantic, a sunning pier from which we can enjoy a drink watching Key West's legendary sunsets. Elegant verandah for watching the parade of character's pass on South Street. The rooms are well-appointed and quiet (recently renovated) and breakfasts are generous and varied." (A. Wimett)

Key West

The Watson House
525 Simonton Street
Key West, FL 33040
(305) 294-6712 or (800) 621-9405
Innkeeper: Ed Czaplicki

♕♕♕   Rating: A+
Rates: Single or Double/$95-360
Credit Cards: AE, MC, V

Bahamian-style guest house built in 1860 has been fully restored and expanded and is located in the heart of the Historic District. Choose from two guest accommodations in the main house or the Cabana which is a four-room private apartment. Each is individually furnished and features hardwood floors, paddle fans, wicker and rattan furnishings, floral patterns and textures, private bath, telephone, color cable TV, fully equipped kitchen, and air-conditioning. Private decks overlook a tropical garden setting enhanced by a waterfall, large spa, and heated swimming pool. Walk to many fine restaurants, live theater, Hemingway House, boating, deep sea fishing, Conch train tours, and the nightlife of Duval Street. Continental breakfast basket is brought to each suite.

Key West

Westwinds
914 Eaton Street
Key West, FL 33040
(305) 296-4440 or (800) 788-4150
Innkeeper: Ingrid Ford

♕♕   Rating: B
Rates: Single or Double/$50-145
Credit Cards: AE, MC, V

Victorian inn located in Old Town consists of four guest buildings, a tropical garden and waterfall that spills into a pool. Choose from nineteen guest rooms and three suites. Seventeen of these rooms and three suites offer private baths.

(Continued)

Common space provides a combination registration office and boutique. Within walking distance are San Carlos Institute of Cuban Culture, The Mel Fisher Maritime Museum, Old City Hall, city docks at Key West Bight, The Little White House and Duval Street, and Fort Zachary Taylor. Area attractions: historic sites, nautical museums, snorkeling and diving on the coral reef, back country and deep sea fishing, Naval Air Station at Boca Chica, beach, state park at Bahia Honda. Continental breakfast consists of fruit juices, hot beverages, seasonal fruit, and fresh breads and pastries from local bakeries. Guests serve themselves and enjoy eating on the rear deck in the garden or around the pool.

Guests write: "*Westwinds is my French connection and European haven in Key West. Having been disappointed by the big American cities and hotel chains, I chose this as an experiment. They had no TVs and little advertising. But what they had was what I needed: a tranquil green, fresh breakfast around the pool, crisp rooms, and affordability.*" (O. DeTarragon)

"*We felt quite at home because of the familiar European touch of Westwinds. It meant fundamental relaxation and recreation far from our worldly, usual activities, and allowed us to explore the Keys in quite an interesting way.*" (F. Schmied)

"*They have one of the cleanest establishments in the Keys, their hospitality is genuine and remarkable, their breakfast is as fresh and attractive as I have eaten, and their rates are reasonable.*" (C. Verbeck)

"*Having lived in Key West for 11 years and now an avid and frequent visitor, I would like to recommend Westwinds as a fabulous and inexpensive retreat. The inn offers the guest a collection of five or so Conch houses clustered around a free-form pool with waterfall, lusciously landscaped gardens and a sunning platform. The rooms are gracious with island-style furnishings. If Westwinds sounds enchanting, it truly is.*" (E.A. McGee)

"*Westinds certainly remains for us the quintessential tropical place to enjoy a short or a long stay among the flowers and birds under the sun and ocean breeze in a peaceful atmosphere, enhanced by courteous and competent personnel and other civilized, educated and cosmopolitan guests.*" (B. Bochatay)

Lake Wales

Chalet Suzanne Country Inn & Restaurant
3800 Chalet Suzanne Drive
Lake Wales, FL 33853
(813) 676-6011 or (800) 433-6011
Fax: (813) 676-1814
Innkeepers: Carl and Vita Hinshaw

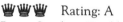 Rating: A
Rates: Single or Double/$125-185
Credit Cards: AE, MC, V
Corporate discount

Chalet Suzanne is an unusual private estate that is a family-owned and operated European-style inn with restaurant. The inn is listed on the National Register of Historic Places and located in central Florida off US-27. Choose from thirty individually decorated guest rooms with private bath. There is a variety in the size, decor, and amenities of the rooms but each features air conditioning, telephone, and TV. The complex includes a ceramic studio, antique shop, and historic chapel. There are extensive grounds which include a swimming pool and secret garden area where special guests have been invited to sign tiles which are fired in the ceramic studio and used to create a garden wall. Area attractions include Bok Tower Gardens, Cypress Gardens, Disney World, Epcot Center, Sea World, and Busch Gardens. Full breakfast and gratuity are included in the room rate. Lunch and candlelight dinner available at additional charge. Families welcome. Facilities for meetings and social functions. Guests can fly in as there is a private landing strip on the property.

Guests write: *"Our stay at Chalet Suzanne was exceptional (as usual). It's amazing how we can make Lake Wales on our way to everywhere we go in Florida. From the warm welcome greeting on arrival to the excellent service at dinner, to the morning smiles from staffers and the come again waves as we left, we were made to feel this is our Southern home. Although we brought our children, we purposely fed them early so we could enjoy our candlelight romantic dinner alone. The presentation of each course was superb. The melody of flavors and textures and color makes our memories of dinner here linger long after we've left."* (D. Thorsen)

"We think the Chalet Suzanne is fabulous. Since we have flown in 475 times for breakfast, it must be great! The food is superb and the hospitality of the Hinshaws and their staff is simply marvelous." (E. Bowman)

Ocala

Seven Sisters Inn, Bed & Breakfast
820 SE Fort King Street
Ocala, FL 34471
(904) 867-1170;
Fax: (904) 732-7764
Innkeepers: Bonnie Morehardt
and Ken Oden

♛♛♛   Rating: A
Rates: Single or Double/$85-135
Credit Cards: AE, MC, V

A sweeping baluster porch hugs this Queen Anne style Victorian with its angular cupola, gables, bays and red brick chimneys and flowering border gardens. The inn is located in the historic district 90 miles north of Orlando, 120 miles north of Tampa. Four guest rooms and four suites feature private baths, telephone, television, and "welcome" fruit or beverages. A common room offers television, phone, games and a good collection of books and is decorated in plaid and hunter green with an equestrian theme. Seven Sisters offers a game of "Whodunit" in its Suspect Theatre where guests are invited to join the cast of characters and staff in a search for clues. Walk to antique shops, gift shops, and an art gallery. Area attractions: Silver Springs, Appleton Museum, and thoroughbred farms. Full breakfast served on china, silver, and crystal includes such specialties as 3-cheese French toast, tomato zucchini quiche, macadamia nut pancakes, blueberry cobbler, chicken-pecan puffed pastry, baked apple-walnut oatmeal, fresh fruit, yogurt, homemade muffins, fresh juices, and coffee or herbal tea. Candlelight dinners are offered several times a month on Friday or Saturday night by advance reservation. Wedding and meeting facilities and wheelchair access. Restricted smoking on porch.

Guests write: *"They have convenient, secluded parking, the inn is well organized with great attention paid to detail, decor, and lay-out, amenities are home-like with comfort a top priority, and breakfast is attractively presented and delicious."* (C. Lazier)

"The inn is gracious, very clean, decorated tastefully. There is a bounty of white towels and ample light for reading. The manager and owner are most hospitable. Quite a change from the chain motels." (R. Stone)

"Beautiful as are the physical surroundings, the staff makes the different as they are terrific!" (H. Thompson)

Orange Park

Club Continental Suites
2143 Astor Street
Orange Park, FL 32073
(904) 264-6070 or (800) 877-6070
Innkeeper: Caleb Massee

♛♛♛   Rating: A
Rates: Single or Double/$60-120
Credit Cards: AE, MC, V

Italian Renaissance inn with classic Mediterranean red tile roof, multiple arches, and wrought iron, is 12 miles south of downtown Jacksonville. Built in 1923 as the Palmolive family estate, it is surrounded by giant live oaks and native palms. All of the twenty-two guest rooms, including several two-rooms suites, are individually decorated and have oversized private baths. Several rooms offer special features such as a fireplace, Jacuzzi, and view of the St. Johns River. A third floor tower apartment has a full kitchen and large balcony. Stroll the manicured courtyard or relax by one of the two full-sized pools. Play tennis on one of the inn's seven courts or take the path to the river where a Pre-Civil War cottage is now a local gathering place featuring entertainment Thursday through Saturday. St. Augustine and First Coast Beaches are thirty-five minutes away and Orlando attractions are two hours south. Continental breakfast is served daily. The riverfront view and spacious grounds are an ideal setting for weddings and meetings and can accommodate up to 250 people. Families welcome. Wheelchair access.

Orlando

The Courtyard at Lake Lucerne
211 North Lucerne Circle East
Orlando, FL 32801
(407) 648-5188 or (800) 444-5289
Fax: (407) 246-1368
Innkeeper: David Gardner

♛♛♛   Rating: A-
Rates: Single or Double/$65-150
Senior, corporate, and auto club discounts
Credit Cards: AE, MC, V

Comprised of three historic buildings built in 1883, 1916, and 1947 successively, this B&B inn is located in the heart of Downtown Orlando. Choose from twenty-two guest rooms with private bath. Six rooms with Victorian decor are located in the Norment-Parry Inn. Thirteen one-bedroom suites with kitchenette are in the Wellborn building which feature Art Deco decor. Three suites in the Victorian/Edwardian style are found in the I.W. Phillips House. Two honeymoon suites provide Jacuzzis. Explore the private garden, turn-of-the-century English fountain, and wide verandah porches. A burled oak grand piano graces the large reception hall. Just a few blocks away is downtown Orlando with its many attractions including Church Street and the Arena. Disney World and Sea World are only minutes away. Expanded continental breakfast plus complimentary bottle of wine are included in the rate. Wedding and meeting facilities available. Families welcome. Restricted smoking.

Guests write: *"For the last two years I have been staying at The Courtyard at Lake Lucerne at least one night per week for virtually every week of the year. I sincerely consider the inn my home away from home. The overall facility, location, food, and most importantly, the quality of the service, are all consistenly exceptional. I would enthusiastically recommend the inn to anyone who wants to experience a truly class operation."* (L. Richey)

Orlando

Perri House Bed & Breakfast Inn
10417 State Road 535
Orlando, FL 32836
(407) 876-4830 or (800) 780-4830
Fax: (407) 876-0241
Innkeepers: Nick and Angi Perretti

♛♛♛   Rating: A-
Rates: Single/$60-70; Double/$65-85
Senior discounts
Credit Cards: AE, MC, V

Nestled in Disney's back yard, this 5,400 square foot home is located 3.6 miles North of exit 27 off I-4 on State Road 535 North. Six guest rooms are available, each individually furnished with contemporary decor theme, air conditioning, private bath, private entrance, and brass queen-size bed or four-poster king-size bed. There is a Jacuzzi as well as swimming pool on the property for guest use. Historic downtown Orlando is twenty minutes away and DisneyWorld, Sea World, Universal Studios, and Pleasure Island are only minutes away. Visit fine area restaurants, golf courses, shopping areas, and water parks. Continental breakfast features fresh fruit, giant muffins, danish, and cereals. Families welcome. Restricted smoking.

Guests write: *"The Perrettis run a wonderful B&B. In addition to charmingly furnished rooms and lovely surroundings, they are extremely warm, friendly, and helpful. They repeatedly asked us if we had any special needs and met each and every one. Breakfast was a potpourri feast of fresh fruit, cereals, juices, and always a special muffin or cake. The house was immaculate. The breakfast area overlooked the yard and pool. There are many birds and the Perrettis are encouraging guests to donate bird feeders as they intend to start a bird sanctuary."* (F. Leoussis)

"The house is modern and each individually decorated room has its own entrance and private bath. At night, you can sit in the Jacuzzi by the pool and sip a glass of wine. I particularly liked the fact that Perri House combines the best elements of a first-class hotel (it's completely private and you can come and go as you please) with the hominess and hospitality you expect in a B&B." (K. Monaghan)

Orlando/Maitland

Thurston House
851 Lake Avenue
Maitland, FL 32751
(407)539-1911
Innkeeper: Carole Ballard

♛♛♛   Rating: A
Rates: Single or Double/$80-90
Corporate discount
Credit Cards: AE, MC, V

Boasting a cross gable roof and three screened-in porches, this circa 1885 Queen Anne Victorian is situated in a rural lakefront setting just 5 miles from downtown Orlando. All four newly restored guest rooms have a private bath and feature period decor. Each room is named after one of the four families that have occupied the house over the last one-hundred years. Common rooms include a front and back parlor as well as wrap-around porch. The grounds offer gardens, acres of fruit trees, and lakefront view. Visit nearby museums, restaurants, state parks, beaches, and Disney attractions. An expanded continental breakfast and afternoon snack are offered daily. No smoking.

Guests write: *"Our room at Thurston House was comfortable, attractive, clean with a lovely view of the lake. We had never before been offered a 'nightcap' of peach liqueur. What a nice touch! Fresh flowers in our room—camellias from the yard, were lovely. Candlelight at breakfast was something new to us." (R&S Corcoran)*

"Thurston House is an oasis and a jewel within the Central Florida/Orlando area. No where can a more beautiful and pastoral setting be found right in the middle of a big city. You have all the amenities of the city of Orlando coupled with the peacefulness of five acres and a lake." (B. Felkel)

"I have considerable experience in custom quality renovation. The attention to detail would warrant a stop by anyone interested in quality work whether or not they had time to stay. We were not disappointed. Details of decor kept us interested for our full two days." (P. McGonigle)

Palm Beach

Palm Beach Historic Inn
365 South County Road
Palm Beach, FL 33480
(407) 832-4009
Fax: (407) 832-6255
Innkeepers: Harry and Barbara Kehr

♛♛♛   Rating: A
Rates: Single or Double/$75-250
Credit Cards: AE, MC, V

Restored Mediterranean-style inn built in 1923 is situated in the heart of Palm Beach, one block from the beach. Each of the guest rooms and suites feature individual decor, private bath, air conditioning, telephone, cable TV, and deluxe amenities. Walk to the beach or to Worth Avenue; enjoy water sports as well as cruises, golfing, tennis, world class dining, galleries, theater, and shopping. Cultural events and performing arts as well as museums and concerts are nearby. Continental breakfast features fresh Florida fruits and baked goods served in your room. Restricted smoking.

Sanibel

Sanibel's Song of the Sea
863 East Gulf Drive
Sanibel Island, FL 33957
(813) 472-2220 or (800)231-1045
Innkeeper: Patricia Slater

♛♛♛ Rating: A
Rates: Single or Double/$124-263
Credit Cards: AE, MC, V

Surrounded by tropical foliage and flowering plants, this recently renovated, European-style seaside inn is located on the Gulf of Mexico, 10 miles west of Fort Myers. Thirty guest rooms offer private baths as well as Mediterranean tile floors, Country French furnishings, fresh flowers, ceiling fans, fully equipped kitchens, and screened terraces. Relax in the whirlpool, borrow a book to read from the lending library, or borrow a bicycle to explore the island bike paths. Recreation here includes golf, fishing, sailing, tennis, and shelling on the miles of private beaches that Sanibel Island is famous for. Expanded continental breakfast is offered with a complimentary newspaper each morning and guests are encouraged to take their breakfast out onto the terrace. Weddings on the beach can be planned. Families welcome.

St. Petersburg

Mansion House
105 5th Avenue Northeast
St. Petersburg, FL 33701
(813) 821-9391
Fax: (813) 821-9391
Innkeepers: Suzanne and Alan Lucas

♛♛ Rating: B+
Rates: Single/$55-60; Double/$60-65
Credit Cards: MC, V

English-style inn built at the turn-of-the-century is within the St. Petersburg city limits, just 2 minutes off of Highway 375. Each of the six guest rooms with private bath has been decorated with a English Country theme. The Carriage room boasts a beamed ceiling and four poster bed. Relax on the indoor porch with its peach and green cane furniture and white and teal tiled floor or on the outdoor screened porch which sits under a large oak tree. The formal lounge has a variety of reading material, big chairs for relaxing, and a piano. The second floor has a guest library and TV room. Take a short walk to Straub Park where open air concerts and festivals are held or to the Pier, where live music, fishing, and boating are available. Take a thirty minute drive to Busch Gardens or visit nearby Sunken Gardens, Museum of fine Arts, Dali museum, and the Pat Buckley Moss Gallery. A full English breakfast offered in two dining rooms serves specialties such as Welsh cakes, sausage, bacon, eggs, and fried tomatoes. No smoking.

Guests write: *"The Welsh breakfast of eggs as you like them, sausage, bacon, crisp fresh country fried potatoes, sliced tomatoes along with wheat or white toast was memorable; but the Welsh cakes were fantastic. There was also a banana orange fruit juice, dry cereals, and coffee. The cook, Alan, often sang in the kitchen."* (G. Boyd)

"This B&B has a special charm not often found in the United States. Alan and Suzanne welcomed us into their newly restored home and made us feel like a part of the family." (T. Kurzweg)

"Better than home for two retired guests. Cheery-light living and reading rooms- clean, comfortable- nicely decorated bedroom- very well located for a walking visit of St. Petersburg Bay Front. Excellent breakfasts." (B. Harmon)

"Meticulously clean, friendly, personal attention; Privacy was respected." (T. McEachern)

"What a wonderfully pleasant surprise to find such a fresh and clean, large older home remodeled to perfection and operated by a young, friendly Welsh couple. Allan's a great English breakfast cook- even to the Welsh cake he prepares along with a full breakfast to your order." (D. Lapworth)

Additional information on B&Bs throughout Georgia is available through the following reservation agencies: B&B Atlanta at (800) 96-PEACH.

Atlanta

Oakwood House
951 Edgewood Avenue, NE
Atlanta, GA 30307
(404) 521-9320 or (404) 688-6034
Innkeepers: Judy and Robert Hotchkiss

♛♛   Rating: B+
Rates: Single/$60-80; Double/$65-85
Credit Cards: MC, V

Turn-of-the-century Craftsman-style inn still shows off its original woodwork and is located in the historic neighborhood of Inman Park, near downtown and midtown Atlanta. The four guest rooms, each with a newly built private bath, have been furnished to compliment the style of the early part of this century and include modern fixtures and telephones. Relax on the front porch, the backyard decks, or under the shady oak tree, for which the inn was named. Take a short walk to Little 5 Points, Atlanta's Off Broadway, or Soho. Visit nearby Underground Atlanta as well as Downtown, World Congress Center, zoo, Cyclorama, World of Coke, Martin Luther King Jr. Grave and National Park, as well as many wholesale marts, universities, and stadiums. Health oriented continental breakfast includes home baked goods and fresh fruit. Wedding and meeting facilities available in the historic Trolley Barn found immediately next door to the inn. Families welcome. No smoking indoors.

Guests write: *"It was a delightful overnight as guests in the Oakwood Bed and Breakfast, with breakfast the highlight of our stay. The poppyseed cake was such a special treat, and we will make an effort to produce the same in our kitchen, hoping to give some of our friends such a happy surprise."* (M&B Mitchell)

"We stayed in the master suite and it was nicely appointed and very spacious. The high ceilings and large rooms give the whole house an airy feel." (A. Bowden)

"I recently had the enjoyment of staying at the Oakwood House. A very convincing recommendation from a friend led me to plan the stay. The immaculate upkeep, warm atmosphere, and even more so, the genuine hospitality of both Judy and Robert, made my several days in Atlanta a pleasurable experience." (C. Smith)

Blairsville

Souther Country Inn
2592 Collins Lane
Blairsville, GA 30512
(706) 379-1603 or (800) 297-1603
Innkeeper: Linda Sudnik

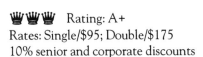 Rating: A
Rates: Single or Double/$75-125
Credit Cards: AE, MC, V

Set in a rural area and built in the style of an English country manor, this 1992 inn is located 112 miles north of Atlanta. Choose from eight guest rooms, each with private bath; one is a suite. Enjoy the area's many outdoor activities such as white-water rafting, hiking on the Appalachian Trail, fishing, swimming, boating, and golf. Antique shopping as well as seasonal fairs and festivals round out vacation plans here. Full breakfast. Facilities available for corporate or religious retreats and weddings. Wheelchair access. No smoking.

Savannah

Ballastone Inn and Townhouse
14 East Oglethorpe Avenue
Savannah, GA 31401
(912) 236-1484 or (800) 822-4553
Innkeeper: R. F. Carlson

Rating: A+
Rates: Single/$95; Double/$175
10% senior and corporate discounts

Built in 1838, this restored four-story Federal and Victorian mansion is situated in the center of Savannah's historic district. All of the twenty-four guest rooms feature a private bath, color TV, air conditioning, period antiques, and decor that reflects Savannah's rich past. Some rooms have fireplaces and whirlpools. Visit the area's two historic districts, museum houses, riverfront attractions, historic forts, and the nearby beach. A continental plus breakfast offers specialties such as Southern-style muffins and fruit compote, and is served in guest rooms, the courtyard, or the downstairs parlor. Wheelchair access.

Savannah

Eliza Thompson House
5 West Jones Street
Savannah, GA 31401
(912) 236-3620 or (800) 348-9378
Innkeeper: Arthur Smith

 Rating: B+
Rates: Single or Double/$88-108
Senior and auto club discounts

The Eliza Thompson House is a Federal home built in 1847 and located in the heart of Savannah's Historic District. Choose from twenty-five guest rooms, each with private bath, heart pine floors, period furnishings, telephones, and color television. A relaxing parlor is offered as well as an inviting landscaped courtyard with fountains. Area attractions within walking distance include museums, Forsyth Park, and River Street shopping. Deluxe continental breakfast includes croissants, muffins, danish, homemade quiche, cereal, fresh fruit, and orange juice. Afternoon wine and cheese and evening sherry offered. Families welcome.

Senoia

The Veranda
252 Seavy Street
Senoia, GA 30276-0177
(404) 599-3905 or Fax: (404) 599-0806
Innkeepers: Jan and Bobby Boal

Rating: A-
Rates: Single/$70-90; Double/$90-110
Credit Cards: AE, MC, V

Victorian, neo-classic two-story frame building, with verandah on front and side, is located in the historic district of Senoia, a small town with a population of approximately one thousand. Choose from nine bedrooms with private baths. Each room, furnished with turn-of-the-century antiques, offers a different theme and contains a collection of family memorabilia. Visit the five common rooms with their collection of kaleidoscopes. A 1923 Estey pump organ can be played in the front parlor; television may be watched in the den, and board games may be found in the upstairs hall. The downstairs hall boasts a collection antique hats, and the formal dining room displays handpainted china and crystal. The gift shop houses the rare old Wurlitzer player-piano/organ with chimes and is a good place for guests to browse at gift items such as kaleidoscopes, puzzles, games, toys and handcrafted items. Walk to the old historic district of Senoia, antique stores, old hardware store, and city park with tennis courts. Area attractions: pond fishing, horseback riding, F.D.R.'s Little White House at Warm Springs, Callaway Gardens, metro Atlanta art, music, sports, shopping. A full breakfast includes fresh fruit, various juices, homemade granola, meats, and entree choice such as poached eggs Florentine, potato-cheese omelet, Veranda French toast, Belgium waffles, fruit crepes, fruit pastries, and coffee or tea. Five-course formal gourmet candlelight dinners are available by advance reservation. Wedding and meeting facilities. Wheelchair access. Restricted smoking on the verandah.

Guests write: *"Jan and Bobby Boal are the quintessential B&B hosts. Never has the fabled 'Southern Hospitality' been more warmly demonstrated. We stayed in the Walking Stick room where we found more than 100 walking sticks collected by Bobby's father. The most fascinating was one made from Coca-Cola bottle glass which was said to protect a home from germs. The breakfast was served with special attention to little details such as fresh flowers on the table, soft music in the background, and with the morning paper nearby. Breakfast was a compote of fresh fruits and yogurt, lingonberry juice, homemade granola with blueberries, poached eggs with spinach and bacon, beef hash on hot biscuits, fresh sliced tomatoes, hot muffins and a loaf of hot whole wheat bread. All of this topped off with an apple crepe with whipped cream!" (E. W. Woolf)*

"The first sight of the rocking chairs on the porch, the organ, piano, old and new books, and a house filled with kaleidascopes makes you feel you must stay days to see it all." (L. Hughes)

"The hospitality was supreme! The rooms are clean and comfortable. They offer a breakfast for champions and the gourmet dinners are a real experience in good food. This is a wonderful town unchanged by time." (H.G. Hutchinson)

Additional information on B&Bs in Hawaii is available from the following B&B reservation agencies: B&B Honolulu (Statewide) (800) 288-4666 or Hawaii's Best B&B (800) 262-9912.

Hilo, Island of Hawaii

Hale Kai-Bjornen
111 Honolii Pali
Hilo, HI 96720
(808) 935-6330
Innkeeper: Evonne Bjornen

♛♛♛ Rating: A+
Rates: Single or Double/$75-98

Modern home of Scandinavian and Japanese design sits on a bluff facing the ocean and is located 2 miles from downtown Hilo. Choose from four guest rooms (2 kings and 2 queens) with private bath, cable TV, ocean view, and easy access to the bar room, pool, Jacuzzi, patio, and lanais. The guest cottage offers a living room, kitchenette, bedroom with king-size bed, private bath, cable TV, and faces the ocean. Explore the entire island from this location including nearby Rainbow Falls, Botanical Gardens, Akaka Falls, the volcano, Waipio Valley, and cities of Hilo and Kona. Full breakfast features dishes such as macadamia nut waffles, Portugese sausage, fruit platters, and Kona coffee. Restricted smoking. Three day minimum for the main house and five day minimum reservation for the guest cottage.

Guests write: *"We found our Blue Hawaii as we sipped champagne in Evonne's Jacuzzi and watched the tangerine sunrise on the Pacific Ocean through her swaying coconut and papaya trees. A real second Honeymoon!" (P. Butler)*

"We enjoyed a view of Hilo Harbor that is beautiful and can be seen from the room, pool, or Jacuzzi. The breakfast was as good as I've eaten with island fruits and breads, and macadamia nut waffles, Portugese sausage and Norwegian eggs. The best thing was the friendliness of the hosts who can tell you all the do's and don'ts of the island." (D. McHugh)

"We didn't want to leave! The hosts shared their collections and personal travel experiences with us. Such an interesting and warm couple! They directed us to delicious restaurants for dinner and served delicious full course breakfasts. They treated us as family and kings." (J. Glass)

Kamuela, Island of Hawaii

Waimea Gardens Cottage
PO Box 563
Kamuela, HI 96743
(800) 262-9912 or (808) 885-4550
Innkeeper: Barbara and Charles Campbell

♛♛♛   Rating: A
Rates: Single or Double/$100-105

Country cottage with rambling stream running through the back yard, is situated on 1.5 acres and located two miles west of the ranch town of Waimea, 8 miles from the beach, and 45 miles from Kailua-Kona. Each cottage offers two guest rooms that feature a private bath, hardwood floors, wainscoting, antique furnishings, and French doors opening to brick patios. Sit by the fireplace in the Waimea Wing, explore the Parker Ranch and the island's white sand beaches. Guests gather their own eggs and prepare their own breakfast with provisions provided, including homemade bread. Hosts live on the premises in the main house. Families welcome. Wheelchair access. No smoking.

Guests write: *"Waimea Gardens was special and unique from the moment of our arrival. The lights on in our little cottage and soft music playing. Fresh cut flowers greeted us with beauty and scent. Warm robes hung in the closet. Clear and simple instructions on 'how to do things here' awaited our perusal. We awoke to birds chirping and fresh Hawaiian coffee."* (J. Bell)

"A charming, architect-designed cottage, with living area, kitchen, bedroom and large bath. A formal, brick and stone-tiled sitting garden made this a great private retreat. It's ideally located for day-trips to the beach, upland areas and north coast. Very professional hosts. This was like staying in our own first-class hotel." (L. Livingston)

"The peaceful and attractive patio and garden created an ideal place for reading, relaxing, and enjoying the birds' songs. We were especially impressed with the cleanliness of the entire cottage. All was in perfect order." (B. Kraig)

Kailua-Kona, Island of Hawaii

Hale Maluhia Bed & Breakfast
76-770 Hualalai Road
Kailua-Kona, HI 96740
(808) 329-5773 or (800) 559-6627
Fax: (808) 326-5487
Innkeepers: Ken and Ann Smith

  Rating: B
Rates: Single/$45-75; Double/$50-80;
Cottages/$100-200
Charge Cards: AE, MC, V

Hale Maluhia is located ten minutes from Kailua-Kona village and resort area. Rambling Hawaiian style home with shingled exterior walls sits on one acre of old Kona coffee land and is found at the 900-foot elevation of Hualalai Mountain in the Holualoa fruit belt. Within three separate buildings are five guest rooms, all with private baths. Each room offers a clock radio, and telephone. The Banyan Cottage offers a kitchen and Jacuzzi. The interior of Hale Maluhia boasts open beam ceilings and lots of natural woods. The furnishings are a blend of Victorian and Hawaiian with family antiques, wicker, koa, lauhala, and oriental rugs. Two living rooms are available for relaxation, each with television, and one with kitchenette. The family room offers a pool table, television, and VCR library. Within walking distance are excellent views and the Holualoa town and art center. Area Attractions: horseback riding, Hapuna Beach, skiing on Mauna Kea. Breakfast includes cereal, fresh fruit, juice, assorted muffins, coffeecake, and coffee, tea, and juice. Wedding and meeting facilities. Wheelchair access. No smoking. Families welcome.

Guests write: *"Our large guest room was beautifully decorated with a floral cushions, bedspread, antique desk, rocking chair, and Polynesian dresser with exquisite arrangement of fresh Hawaiian flowers. The room was bright and had its own private bath and door out to a garden area. Breakfast was a fruit plate (decorated with a fresh orchid), assortment of cereals, muffins, fresh bread, jams, jellies, three types of juices, and fresh eggs from the family's chickens."* (M. Todd)

"We had a wide assortment of breads and muffins for breakfast along with an abundant supply of fruit. We really like the fresh eggs and the fact we could prepare them ourselves. We felt very comfortable as we were free to move about the house and use the amenities such as the spa and snorkeling equipment." (L. Stevermer)

Volcano, Island of Hawaii

Chalet Kilauea at Volcano
P.O. Box 998
Volcano, HI 96785
(808) 967-7786 or (800) 937-7786
Fax: (808) 967-8660
Innkeepers: Lisha and Brian Crawford

♛♛   Rating: B+
Rates: Single or Double/$75-225
Credit Cards: MC, V

Hawaiian chalet has a lush tropical setting outside the village of Volcano.
Choose from three guest rooms in the main house which are decorated with
Oriental, African, or Victorian themes. The two-level Treehouse suite is
adjacent to the main building and offers complete privacy with a bedroom
upstairs, a sitting area on the lower level, and private bath. A large parlor with
fireplace offers ample comfortable seating among an interesting collection of
art from around the world. The grounds are spacious and include a hot tub.
Volcano National Park is nearby where visitors enjoy hiking, golfing, biking,
swimming, birdwatching, and lava viewing. A candlelit full two-course
gourmet breakfast boasts international and local dishes as well as Kona coffee.
Complimentary afternoon tea is served every day between 4 and 5 PM in the
guests living room. Families welcome. Restricted smoking.

Guests write: *"Chalet Kilauea is a most unique B&B that is beautifully decorated
and serves delicious breakfasts. The hosts are a gracious, well-traveled couple who
have considered all needs. I especially liked the Tree House Suite." (H. Haan)*

Volcano, Island of Hawaii

Kilauea Lodge
P.O. Box 116
Volcano, HI 96785
(808) 967-7366
Innkeepers: Lorna and Albert Jeyte

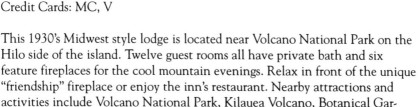

♛♛♛ Rating: A
Rates: Single or Double/$85-105
Credit Cards: MC, V

This 1930's Midwest style lodge is located near Volcano National Park on the Hilo side of the island. Twelve guest rooms all have private bath and six feature fireplaces for the cool mountain evenings. Relax in front of the unique "friendship" fireplace or enjoy the inn's restaurant. Nearby attractions and activities include Volcano National Park, Kilauea Volcano, Botanical Gardens, hiking, golfing, and bird watching. Full breakfast frequently features specials such as pancakes and French toast. Families welcome. Wheelchair access.

Guests write: *"Excellent food, hospitality, accommodations in a beautiful surrounding. Would recommend this lodge to anyone and everyone. Can't think of any way in which improvement could be made. Lodge staff has an excellent first-aid kit available for minor injuries, falls, and scrapes on the lava flows."* (E. Murray)

"Life doesn't get any better than this. We have been home for three months and still feel the same way about the Kilauea Lodge." (F. Harman)

"I almost didn't want to say anything nice about this place because I would like to keep this charming B&B to ourselves. Philip kept wanting to hike around the Volcano while I wanted to return to our cozy room and sip a cocktail by our own fireplace. The staff couldn't have been more courteous, the food was consistently excellent." (A. Rauenhorst)

"Our cottage was beautifully maintained and wonderfully cozy. The staff was exceptionally polite and helpful, and our meals at the lodge were delicious and reasonably priced. Our stay at the lodge will certainly be one of our favorite Honeymoon memories." (J. Lowe)

Kapaa, Island of Kauai

Kay Barker's B&B
P.O. Box 740
Kapaa, Kauai, HI 96746
(808) 822-3073 or (800) 835-2845
Innkeeper: Gordon Barker

♛♛   Rating: B
Rates: Single/$30-60; Double/$40-70
Credit Cards: MC, V

Kay Barker's B&B is a ranch home set on the slopes of Sleeping Giant Mountain in a quiet residential area. There are four guest rooms in the main house, each with a private bath. A separate cottage offers complete privacy along with a king-size bed, living room, private lanai, and kitchenette. Guests relax and gather together on the lanai or in the living room of the main house which has a comfortable TV viewing area and extensive library. Beach supplies such as boogie boards, ice chests, towels, and beach mats are available as well as a washer and dryer. Popular attractions in the area include Wailua River and the Fern Grotto. Area recreation includes snorkeling, tennis, and hiking. Full breakfast often includes fresh fruit, banana nut muffins, macadamia nut hotcakes, or quiche. Families welcome.

Poipu, Island of Kauai

Gloria's Spouting Horn B&B
4464 Lawai Beach Road
Poipu, Kauai, HI 96756
(808) 742-6995
Innkeeper: Gloria Merkle

♛♛♛   Rating: A
Rates: Single or Double/$125
Credit Cards: MC, V

Gloria's Spouting Horn B&B is located on the ocean at Spouting Horn which offers a marvelous secluded beach and famous ocean vistas. Guest accommodations have been completely rebuilt in 1993 and offer a private bath and entrance. A hammock is strategically located near the water for those who've dreamed of sleeping under a coconut palm tree on the beach. Whales have been spotted from the private decks off the guest rooms. Popular attractions in the area include Spouting Horn, Waimea Canyon, Hanalei Bay, and Poipu Beach as well as golfing, tennis, and horseback riding. The area offers a good selection of galleries, shops, and restaurants. Tropical continental breakfast features Gloria's own fresh homemade pastries and fresh island fruits and juices. No smoking.

Guests write: "*As we laid on our bed and looked to our left, the only thing that separated the ocean from us was the lanai. It was almost like as if we were on the deck of a cruise ship. After spending a week at a fancy high-rise with an ocean view, we learned that ocean view is definitely a relative term. At Gloria's you are literally on top of the Pacific Ocean. The rooms were spacious and carefully appointed, the bathroom was bigger than most four star hotels and our lanai was fifteen-twenty feet long.*" (D&S Rosenfeld)

"*Gloria and Bob Merkel's aloha spirit of hospitality and their true love for this beautiful island was evident at our return visit to their newly rebuilt B & B. We really relaxed, lying in the hammock secured between coconut palms. Other amenities we were impressed with: sunken tub and shower in private bathroom, microwave oven and wet bar, VCR with TV, panoramic views of mountains and ocean from our room.*" (M.& J. Haynes)

"*It is not just beautiful, but homey and very unique. We slept in a willow bed, had coffee each morning and evening on our own lanai. Snorkeling and swimming beaches are nearby (beach towels and mats are provided). Whales frequently spout just offshore.*" (J. Miniken)

Poipu Beach

Poipu Bed & Breakfast Inn
2720 Hoonani Road
Poipu Beach, Kauai, HI 96756
(808) 742-1146 or (800) 22-POIPU
Fax: (808) 742-6843
Innkeeper: Dottie Cichon

♕♕♕   Rating: A
Rates: Single/$105-170; Double/$110-175
Auto club, senior, and government discount

1933 plantation house located 12 miles south of Lihue Airport is in the heart of Poipu Beach. Situated on one-third acre of lushly landscaped gardens where mangos, bananas, and papayas grow, it is on an inlet only half a block from the Pacific Ocean. The inn offers four guest rooms each with private bath, several having whirlpool tubs. All guest rooms are furnished in antique pine with white wicker and an authentic carousel horse. A large great room contains several areas for different activities, such as reading, a video library, and wicker loveseats for relaxing. The carousel horse that is the inn's logo is also in this room. Relax on the beautiful beaches, or choose from a variety of water sports such as swimming, boating, surfing, scuba diving, body surfing, and kayaking. Other activities include golf, tennis, and horseback riding. Restaurants, shopping, and the Spouting Horn are all within walking distance. Just a short drive away is the Waimea Canyon (the Grand Canyon of the Pacific), the beautiful Na Pali Coast, the National Tropical Botanical Gardens, Grove Farm Homestead Museum, the Wailua River Valley, and the Waimea Falls. Helicopter tours offer excellent sightseeing opportunities. A tropical continental breakfast is served on the lanai. Fax and copier available for guest use. Families welcome. Restricted smoking.

Idaho

Information on additional B&Bs in Idaho is available from the following: B&B Western Adventure (406) 259-7993.

Ketchum

The River Street Inn
100 Rivers Street West
Ketchum, ID 83340
Mail: PO Box 182, Sun Valley, ID 83353
(208) 726-3611
Assistant Manager: Gundl Taylor

♕ ♕ ♕   Rating: A
Rates: Single/$95-165; Double/$105-175
Credit Cards: AE, MC, V

Built in 1985 and just a few blocks from the center of Ketchum , this country inn boasts Palladian windows, whitewashed oak, and polished brass. Nine guest rooms with private baths feature mountain or Trail Creek views and offer queen-sized beds, small refrigerators, color television, radio, and telephone. Most have Japanese-style soaking tubs and vanities with large mirrored walls behind the sinks. Sit in front of the natural brick fireplace in the living room or enjoy late night star gazing and early morning bird watching on the large redwood deck where iced tea is served during the summer. Four season area attractions include world class skiing on Mt. Baldy in nearby Sun Valley, trout stream fishing, hiking in the Sawtooth Mountains, golf, tennis, ice-skating, and horseback riding. Within walking distance are restaurants, boutiques, and art galleries. Inn guests have special privileges at a nearby health club. A gourmet breakfast promises to keep guests full until lunch with such specialties as Hootenanny topped with home made applesauce, lemon ricotta pancakes with raspberry butter, breakfast meats, and freshly baked coffee cake or scones. Afternoon tea offered. Restricted smoking. Weddings and meeting facilities available. Wheelchair access. Families welcome.

Guests write: *"Great to be on Ketchum time watching the moon rise through the trees and listening to the creek outside our bedroom window. This is the place to stay." (W. & S. Lock)*

"We returned from skiing each afternoon and were greeted by a warm and welcoming fire, afternoon tea, and refreshments. The inn is on a quiet street, yet it is an easy walk to town, the bus, restaurants, shops, and galleries. Ginny and her staff are most cordial and hospitable." (L. & C. Goodyear)

Sun Valley

Idaho Country Inn
134 Latigo Lane
Sun Valley, ID 83340
(208) 726-1019
Innkeeper: Julie and Terry Heneghan

♛♛♛♛ Rating: AA
Rates: Single or Double/$95-145
Credit Cards: AE, MC, V

Contemporary mountain-style inn built of logs and river rock is located high on a hill with panoramic mountain views. Choose from ten guest rooms which offer a private bath, remote control, color TV, refrigerator, and special themes ranging from the "Wagon Days" room to the "Wildflower" room. Many of the pieces of furniture and artwork are created by the host who is also an accomplished fishing guide. Six rooms have air conditioning. There are two parlors with fireplaces, a well-stocked library including books on Idaho, 24 hour beverage service, and well-organized information center. A specially-designed Jacuzzi in the back yard offers views of surrounding mountain peaks. This is a major year-round recreation center offering skiing, ice skating, sleigh rides, trout fishing, and golfing. Generous "Idaho-style" full breakfast. Meeting facilities available. Families welcome. No smoking.

Guests write: *"Beautiful Inn, spotlessly clean and very well decorated. Every morning an unusual breakfast: Sun Valley eggs (homemade potato scone, smoked trout, and poached egg) or fresh blueberry pancakes."* (J&M Frankel)

Illinois

Evanston

The Margarita European Inn
1566 Oak Avenue
Evanston, IL 60201
(708) 869-2273 or (708) 869-2283
Fax: (708) 869-2353
Innkeepers: Barbara and Tim Gorham

♛♛   Rating: B-
Rates: Single/$45-80; Double/$55-90

Originally a woman's private club, this Georgian mansion north of Chicago has been reopened as an inn with an Italian restaurant on the main level. Choose from thirty-four guest rooms, half with newly decorated private baths. Several rooms share a dormatory-style bathroom in the hall. Relax in the spacious parlor which features a molded fireplace and floor-to-ceiling arched windows. A paneled library and party rooms are also available. Explore Evanston's fine restaurants, art galleries, theater companies, cultural arts center, specialty shops an five universities. Nearby Lake Michigan offers sand beaches, historic walking paths, and biking trails that begin at Northwestern University and lead to downtown Chicago. Continental breakfast includes muffins, pastries, and fresh fruit. Lunch and dinner are available in the restaurant. Facilities for weddings and meetings available.

Galena

Hellman Guest House
318 Hill Street
Galena, IL 61036
(815) 777-3638
Innkeeper: Merilyn Tommaro

♛♛♛ Rating: A-
Rates: Single/$75-110; Double/$80-115

A fully restored Queen Anne Victorian built in 1895 of Galena brick with
corner tower and wrap around porch is on a hill overlooking the downtown
area and surrounding country side; 150 miles west of Chicago and 250 miles
southeast of Minneapolis. Four guest rooms have private baths. The Hellman
master bedroom feautres a spectatuclar view of the town from its tower alcove
along with queen-size bed. Relax in the front parlor with period furnishings,
and a telescope for special views of the countryside. The library features
wicker furniture, antique bookcases, and stereo for guest's use. Walk to the
Main street shops of Galena, the Galena/Davis Historical Society, Grant's
Home, historic homes (85% are listed on the National Register of Historic
Places), and state historic sites. Area attractions: Mississippi Palisades State
Park, Apple River Canyon, Eagle Point Park, Chestnut Mountain Ski Resort,
and local golfing. Full breakfast specialties may include triple cheese strata or
sour cream pancakes with sausage links. Small meeting and wedding facilities.

Galena

The Goldmoor
9001 Sand Hill Road
Galena, IL 61036
(815) 777-3925 or (800) 255-3925
Innkeeper: Jim Goldthorpe

♛♛♛ Rating: A+
Rates: Single or Double/$95-225
Credit Cards: AE, D, MC, V

Grand estate in the country offers quiet seclusion and views of the mighty
Mississippi River. Six guest rooms with private bath are available. Two special
honeymoon suites each feature an extra large room with sitting area, Jacuzzi,

fireplace, and entertainment system with stereo. An atrium spa and sauna are located on the main level of the inn and there are several private decks and patios along with extensive landscaped grounds. Romantic getaway, honeymoon and anniversary packages available. Area attractions include twenty-five antique shops, General Grant's home, and Chestnut Mountain Resort Ski Lodge. Full breakfast includes homemade jams and jellies and fresh baked rolls, muffins, and breads as well as house specialties.

Geneva

Oscar Swan Country Inn
1800 West State Street
Geneva, IL 60134
(708) 232-0173
Innkeepers: Nina and Hans Heymann

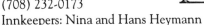

♕♕♕   Rating: A-
Rates: Single/$65-85; Double/$88-139
Charge Cards: AE, MC, V

Oscar Swan Country Inn is located 35 miles west of Chicago off Interstate 88. This Colonial Revival, built in 1902, sits on a large front lawn which boasts beautiful gardens, a pool, and a rustic refurbished 1850's barn. Choose from eight guest rooms, six with private baths. Each of these rooms offers a different decor. One may have a canopy bed while another provides a king-sized waterbed. The Swan Loft includes a kitchen and dining area. The Twin Rooms feature a complete suite for 4 persons. Other amenities include television and VCR. The living room, with its large Colonial Williamsburg fireplace, is furnished in antiques. Within walking distance is Fox River, bike paths, and cross country skiing. Area attractions: museums, riverboat gambling, and Chicago. A full breakfast served on fine china includes fresh fruit, juice, homemade cinnamon raisin French toast, country thick sliced bacon, scrambled eggs with chives, hazelnut coffee and herbal tea. Hot oatmeal, muffins, scones, and corn bread may be ordered by request. Wedding facilities available. Restricted smoking. Families welcome.

Morrison

Hillendale Bed & Breakfast
600 Lincolnway West
Morrison, IL 61270
(815) 772-3454
Fax: (815) 772-7023
Innkeepers: Mike and Barb Winandy

♛♛♛   Rating: A-
Rates: Single or Double/$50-135
Charge Cards: AE, MC, V

Hillendale B&B is twelve miles east of the Mississippi River on Route 30, 2.5 hours west of Chicago. Victorian English Tudor built in 1891 is an asymmetrically designed house with twenty-nine rooms, gabled roof, portico over the driveway, and three tiered water garden in front of a replica of a Japanese teahouse. Each of the nine guest rooms with private baths are decorated in an international theme such as French Country, Oriental, Italian, African, Hawaiian, Mayan, Dutch, Irish, or Australian. Some of the rooms have fireplaces and/or whirlpool spas. Breakfast is served in the conservatory and a game of pool may be played in the Billiard Room. Walk to antique shops, a quilt shop, and the Carlton House, a Morrison historical museum. Area Attractions: Rockwood Morrison State Park for cross country skiing, hiking, and fishing, restaurants, quilt shops, antiquing, Lock and Dam Number 13, Mississippi River, Dillion House Museum, Heritage Canyon, and the Mississippi Belle Casino. A sample full breakfast includes orange juice, coffee/tea, cheddar cheese and bacon omelet, oatmeal raisin muffins, and cantaloupe. Meeting facilities. No Smoking

Guests write: *"My room was cozy and comfortable. Breakfast included German applecake like my mother used to bake for me while growing up. It was a very pleasant experience."* (B. Wagoner)

"Our family stayed at Hillendale while visiting family. Our hosts were very hospitable and obviously enjoyed having people around. They took time to talk about climbing mountains, building greenhouses, and to show our grandson's their exotic fish. We enjoyed the breakfasts, the decor, and the cleanliness of everything." (H. Rempe)

"The house is elegant. The decor in each room was very interesting because it was from different parts of the world." (J. Williams)

Rockford

Victoria's B&B Inn
201 North 6th Street
Rockford, IL 61107
(815) 963-3232
Innkeeper: Martin Lewis

♛♛♛ Rating: A
Rates: Single or Double/$69-169
Credit Cards: MC, V
Corporate discounts

Victoria's B&B Inn was built at the turn-of-the-century and is centrally
located in the city which is 90 miles west of Chicago off I-90. There are five
guest suites with private baths. Each has been decorated with antiques, rich
wallpaper and fabrics, and offers a TV and Jacuzzi. The Victorian parlor on the
main floor has been the setting for weddings, and it features unusually detailed
wallpaper which in itself is a work of art. Popular attractions in the area
include Burpee Museum, Tinker Cottage, riverboat rides, and Victorian
Village's seventy shops and restaurants. Continental breakfast. Facilities for
meetings, receptions and weddings.

Wheaton

The Wheaton Inn
301 West Roosevelt Road
Wheaton, IL 60187
(708) 690-2600 or (708) 690-2623
Innkeeper: Judith Ottoson

Rating: A
Rates: Single or Double/$99-195
Credit Cards: AE, MC, V
Senior, business and auto club discounts

Built in 1987 in a design to reflect Colonial Williamsburg, this urban inn is
located 25 miles west of Chicago. Several of the sixteen rooms feature a
Jacuzzi tub or gas fireplace. All offer a private bath with European towel
warmers and amenities. There are several common rooms including a living
room with fireplace, breakfast atrium room with French doors leading onto the

patio, and lower-level conference rooms. Explore the historic town of
Wheaton or nearby Geneva for shopping and unique restaurants. Nearby
attractions include Morton Arboretum, Cantigny War Museum, McCormick
Mansion, Wheaton Water Park, or the Billy Graham Center found on the
Wheaton College campus. A full breakfast and afternoon refreshments are
offered daily. Two meeting rooms available for family reunions, weddings, and
business functions. Families welcome. Wheelchair access.

Indiana

Columbus

Columbus Inn
445 5th Street
Columbus, IN 47201
(812) 378-4289
Fax: (812) 378-4289
Innkeeper: Paul Staublin

♛♛♛   Rating: A-
Rates: Single/$80-90; Double/$95-275
Credit Cards: AE, MC, V
Corporate discounts

Columbus Inn, noted for its Romanesque architecture, is listed on the National Register of Historic Places. Originally built as City Hall, the inn has
been completely restored and rivals other examples of fine architecture
throughout this city. Thirty-four individually decorated guest rooms are
available, each with private bath. The Sparrell Suite is reached by a grand
staircase and its main floor serves as an impressive parlor or meeting area with
a two-story ceiling, antique furnishings and fine fabrics and upholstered pieces.
Columbus is known as the "architectural showplace of America," with more
than fifty buildings providing a concentrated and outstanding collection of
contemporary architecture. Full breakfast. Facilities for meetings and social
gatherings.

Hagerstown

Teetor House
300 West Main Street
Hagerstown, IN 47346
(317) 489-4422 or (800) 824-4319
Innkeepers: Jack and JoAnne Warmoth

♛♛♛   Rating: A
Rates: Single/$70-85; Double/$75-90

Imposing private mansion built in 1936 is situated on a ten acre wooded estate in a small town just 5 miles north of Route 70 in the east/central part of the state. There are four large air-conditioned guest rooms with twin or king sized beds and private bath. Explore this historic home which features carved cherry paneling in the foyer and living room, Steinway concert piano, and in-house museum; or just sit and relax on the pleasant screened-in porch. Popular attractions in the area include fine restaurants, unusual shops, the world's largest antique mall, tennis, golf, and historic tours. Full breakfast. Families welcome. Facilities available for meetings and social functions. Restricted smoking.

Guests write: *"Jack did a fine job both describing the house and telling about one of the great minds of the 20th Century. Hosts were very cordial with prompt attention. Good breakfast was well served. The screened-in porch was especially nice in the evenings." (C. Tucker-Ladd)*

"Exceeded our expectations. The Warmoth's add warmth and a unique perspective." (P. Healey)

"The tour was a highlight that impelled us to bring guests for the weekend on our second visit. The house is an expression of the genius and character of Ralph Teetor. The hosts, through their devotion to the house and to the guests, properly memorialize that genius." (H. Hensold)

"We appreciated all the extra touches. The omelet was superb! The tour was fascinating and inspiring. I'd rather stay at a bed and breakfast than any hotel if others are as nice as the Teetor House." (K. Hudson)

Middlebury

Patchwork Quilt Country Inn
11748 County Road #2
Middlebury, IN 46540
(219) 825-2417
Innkeeper: Maxine Zook

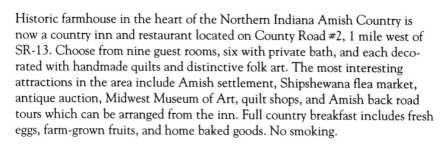

♛♛   Rating: B+
Rates: Single/$43; Double/$53-95
Credit Cards: MC, V

Historic farmhouse in the heart of the Northern Indiana Amish Country is now a country inn and restaurant located on County Road #2, 1 mile west of SR-13. Choose from nine guest rooms, six with private bath, and each decorated with handmade quilts and distinctive folk art. The most interesting attractions in the area include Amish settlement, Shipshewana flea market, antique auction, Midwest Museum of Art, quilt shops, and Amish back road tours which can be arranged from the inn. Full country breakfast includes fresh eggs, farm-grown fruits, and home baked goods. No smoking.

Middlebury

Varns Guest House, Inc.
205 South Main Street
Middlebury, IN 46540
(219) 825-9666 or (800) 398-5424
Innkeepers: Carl and Diane Eash

♛♛♛   Rating: A-
Rates: Single/$65; Double/$69
Credit Cards: MC, V

Varn's Guest House is a modest turn-of-the-century home built in 1898 and located on a tree-lined street in the heart of town. This area is known as Amish country and it is located 5 miles south of the Indiana Toll Road's Middlebury exit. Choose from five guest rooms. They offer a variety of size, decor, and amenities, but each has a private bath, air conditioning, comfortable furnishings, and has been named after relatives and childhood memories. A wrap-around porch is a popular place to watch the activities in this small town but in cold weather guests enjoy gathering around the parlor's brick fireplace. Popular attractions nearby include the giant Shipshewana flea market, Amish communities, and a selection of interesting shops and restaurants with good home-cooked food. Continental plus breakfast includes homemade pastries. No smoking.

Guests write: *"Varn's Guest House is a jewel. After more than 200 B&Bs and inns it takes a lot to impress us! Ask for the China Rose Room. It is exquisite."* (K. Wellage)

Richmond

Philip W. Smith Bed & Breakfast
2039 East Main Street
Richmond, IN 47374
(800) 966-8972 or (317) 966-8972
Innkeepers: Chip and Chartley Bondurant

♛♛♛   Rating: A-
Rates: Single/$60-70; Double/$65-75
Charge Cards: MC, V

Queen Anne Victorian home built in 1890 and located in the historic district of town is convenient to I-70 near the Indiana and Ohio border. The two and a half story brick structure has Romanesque details and features stained glass windows and ornate carved wood. Choose from four second floor guest rooms with full or queen-size beds and private baths. A large living room offering comfortable seating is where homemade snacks are served in the evening. Full breakfast is served on fine china and linens in the dining room. Area attractions: four historic districts, arboretum, hiking Whitewater River Gorge, and hunting for prehistoric fossils along the shore, outdoor concerts in the park, and an abundance of antique shops. Wedding and meeting facilities available. Restricted smoking. Families welcome.

Warsaw

White Hill Manor
2513 East Center Street
Warsaw, IN 46580
(219) 269-6933
Innkeeper: Gladys Delow

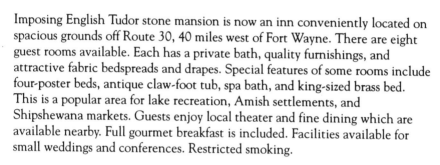

♛♛♛   Rating: A
Rates: Single/$68-105; Double/$75-112
Charge Cards: AE, MC, V

Imposing English Tudor stone mansion is now an inn conveniently located on spacious grounds off Route 30, 40 miles west of Fort Wayne. There are eight guest rooms available. Each has a private bath, quality furnishings, and attractive fabric bedspreads and drapes. Special features of some rooms include four-poster beds, antique claw-foot tub, spa bath, and king-sized brass bed. This is a popular area for lake recreation, Amish settlements, and Shipshewana markets. Guests enjoy local theater and fine dining which are available nearby. Full gourmet breakfast is included. Facilities available for small weddings and conferences. Restricted smoking.

Guests write: *"Top notch service from friendly and diligent innkeepers make the Whitehill Manor outstanding. Living accommodations are deluxe with cozy rooms, furnished in a luxury decor, each with its own special atmosphere. I prefer the "library" with loft bathroom, brass iron bed and walls of classical novels. No request is unreasonable, such as special service, catering, special dietary requirements, or office support. The best place to stay while visiting Warsaw, Indiana."* (J. Spar)

Amana Colonies/Homestead

Die Heimat Country Inn
Amana Colonies
Homestead, IA 52236
(319) 622-3937
Innkeepers: Warren and Jacklyn Lock

♛♛   Rating: B
Rates: Single or Double/$41-63
Charge Cards: MC, V

Historic inn is conveniently situated on Main Street at the junction of US-151 and SR-6. This century-old restored building features a wide variety in the size of the rooms. Each has a private bath, television, quilt, and traditional Amana furniture. Relax on the shaded lawn in the Amana wooden glider or visit nearby "family-style" restaurants, Colony wineries, antique stores and unique craft shops. Take a tour of the colonies and discover the seven historic villages that make up the Amana Colonies which were founded by settlers in 1844. Full breakfast is served buffet style in the lobby. Facilities for small groups.

Dubuque

The Hancock House
1105 Grove Terrace
Dubuque, IA 52001
(319) 557-8989
Innkeeper: Eric Fish

♛♛♛   Rating: A
Rates: Single or Double/$75-150
Charge Cards: AE, MC, V

Imposing Queen Anne Victorian mansion is set on the bluffs of this historic town and is located at the intersections of Routes 151, 61, 52, and 20 in the Northeast corner of the state. Nine individually decorated guest rooms (some with operable fireplaces) are available, each with private bath (four with whirlpool tub). Enjoy a spectacular view of the Mississippi River from this location. Nearby downtown offers restored Victorian mansions serving as museums, art galleries, and antique and specialty shops. Don't miss taking a riverboat ride on the Mississippi River. The area's mountains offer hiking, biking, and skiing. Full breakfast. A beverage/snack center is available to all guests and is included in room rate. Families welcome. No smoking.

Guests write: *"There are small touches there that distinguished it from other B&B's. Our room was comfortable and complete with every amenity we could have wanted, including comfy bathrobes for after relaxing in the hot tub."* (M&R Knutsa)

"This great B & B is a beautifully restored Victorian home. Our bedroom suite had a large living area, separate bedroom with all antique furnishings from the period and a full bath with a separate whirlpool tub. The breakfasts were complete with eggs, fruit, French toast (caramelized) and a variety of sweet rolls and breads. Also, there was an open kitchen that could be used with wine, pop, beer, cheeses and other snacks at all times. We loved the player piano!" (B. Miller)

Fort Madison

Kingsley Inn
707 Avenue H
Fort Madison, IA 52627
(319) 372-7074 or (800) 441-2327
Innkeepers: Myrna Reinhard

♛♛♛   Rating: A
Rates: Single or Double/$65-105
10% senior, corporate, or auto club discounts
Charge Cards: AE, MC, V

Century-old Victorian hotel is located in a Mississippi River town one-hundred miles south of Davenport. Fourteen guest rooms with private bath offer individual decor and Victorian antiques. Several rooms have a whirlpool tub or a view of the river. Within walking distance are antique and specialty shops, galleries, and the historic Victorian residential area where the Sheaffer Pen Company is headquartered. Take a historic tour on the "Little Red Train". Visit nearby Old Fort Madison, Mississippi River, Lee County Historical Museum, Mormon Settlement, or the villages of Van Buren, Lock, and Dam at Keokuk. A continental plus breakfast includes granola, home made pastries, and Kingsley Inn coffee. Wedding and meeting facilities available. Wheelchair access. No smoking.

Guests write: "We have enjoyed the hospitality, service, and the beauty of this luxury inn. This is the type of quality that hopefully one day will become the standard in

America. 'The Dream Facility' ! We look forward to returning. " (T. Evans)

"We love this place! The elegant surroundings and pampering by the staff are very much appreciated. In our hectic lives we have little time for such pleasures." (D. Johnson)

"This was the perfect get-away. The room was very romantic. The staff was very hospitable." (B. Gerst)

Maquoketa

Squiers Manor Bed & Breakfast
418 West Pleasant
Maquoketa, IA 52060
(319) 652-6961
Innkeepers: Kathy and Virl Banowetz

♕♕♕   Rating: A
Rates: Single or Double/$65-125
Charge Cards: AE, MC, V

Queen Anne brick mansion built in 1882 is located 30 miles south of Dubuque and 40 miles north of Davenport. The inn retains its original features including the butternut and walnut staircase, three fireplaces, and American Victorian antiques. Six guest rooms are named for Squiers family members and former residents of the mansion. Each has a private bath with single or double whirlpool tub, telephone, color TV, and queen-size antique bed. The down-stairs guest room is often used for special occasions such as honeymoons and anniversaries and is available as a suite with adjoining private parlor. Walk to the library, churches, restaurants, and movie theater. Take a short drive to the Quad Cities, Cedar Rapids, Iowa City, Clinton, and Galena, Illinois. Explore the Maquoketa Caves State Park. A full breakfast might include seafood quiche or Eggs Katrina and is accompanied with fresh fruit and home made breads. A candlelight evening dessert is served nightly in the parlor or in Victorian dining room. Families welcome. Restricted smoking.

Guests write: "The home was wonderfully decorated with pieces that fit the era of the house. It was a well-planned mixture of the old and the new. Nice extras included a box of chocolates, dessert at night, and coffee delivered in the morning. The breakfast served was a banquet of huge portions and gourmet flavors. We didn't eat for the rest of the day. " (P. Ochrlein)

"Virl and Kathy make my business trip seem like a mini-vacation. Their hospitality, scrumptious breakfasts and beautifully decorated manor always makes me feel like someone special. I'm sure that other guests would agree." (S. Henderson)

"Squiers Manor is the best of the best in uniqueness and elegance. Service is delivered to perfection from the rooms that look like you're the first to ever stay in them with the little 'Thank you for staying with us' on the nightstand or pillow, to the evening desserts and morning feeding extravaganzas accompanied by the charming host. The conversation and warmth shared at the breakfast table not only encourages you to kick your shoes off and relax but also reminds you to do this again soon!" (D. Day)

Wichita

Inn at the Park
3751 East Douglas
Wichita, KS 67218
(316) 652-0500 or (800) 258-1951
Innkeeper: Kevin Daves

♛♛♛♛   Rating: AA-
Rates: Single/$75-125; Double/$85-135
Senior, auto club, and corporate discounts
Charge Cards: AE, MC, V

The Inn at the Park is a mansion built in 1910 that has been completely renovated. In 1989 the entire inn was professionally decorated by a number of well known area designers for use as a Designer's Showcase. There are ten guest rooms with private bath in the mansion and their decor ranges from French Country to Oriental, from Neoclassical to Art Nouveau. A carriage house on the grounds offers two private suites. Amenities include fireplaces, private courtyard, hot tub, cable TV, VCR, and phone. Continental breakfast features fruits, pastries, and often includes quiche or chili rellenos. Special services for business travelers include a conference room, secretarial services, and fax machine. Families welcome.

Guests write: *"They are doing a fine job of providing people with a quality place to spend a night or a Honeymoon. I think that next year we will spend our anniversary at the Inn at the Park."* (T. Chamberlain)

Wichita

Max Paul, An Inn
3910 East Kellogg
Wichita, KS 67218
(316) 689-8101
Innkeepers: Jill and Roberta Eaton

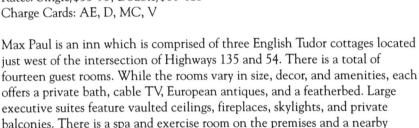

   Rating: B+
Rates: Single/$55-95; Double/$80-125
Charge Cards: AE, D, MC, V

Max Paul is an inn which is comprised of three English Tudor cottages located just west of the intersection of Highways 135 and 54. There is a total of fourteen guest rooms. While the rooms vary in size, decor, and amenities, each offers a private bath, cable TV, European antiques, and a featherbed. Large executive suites feature vaulted ceilings, fireplaces, skylights, and private balconies. There is a spa and exercise room on the premises and a nearby public park for tennis, jogging paths, and children's pool. Airport, downtown shopping centers, and major corporate headquarters are nearby. Continental breakfast. Facilities for business meetings or social functions.

Bardstown

Jailer's Inn
111 West Stephen Foster Ave
Bardstown, KY 40004
(502) 348-5551; (800) 948-5551
Innkeeper: Fran McCoy

Rating: A-
Rates: 1 or 2/$ 55-90
Charge Cards: AE, MC, V

1819 Federal-style building with 30 inch limestone walls was originally a jail and has been completely renovated and decorated with antiques and heirlooms. 35 miles South of Louisville, 17 miles from I-65, and 60 miles south west of Lexington, 1 mile from the Bluegrass Parkway. Choose from of the six guest rooms with private baths decorated with themes such as the Victorian, Colonial, Garden, and Jail Cell Bedroom complete with black and white decor and jail cell bunks, and waterbed. Two large hallways, one upstairs and one on the main floor serve as guest areas with television, a grand piano, and easy chairs. Area attractions: St. Joseph Cathedral, My Old Kentucky Home State Park, Stephen Foster outdoor Drama, Lincoln's Birthplace, Oscar Getz Museum, local distillery tours, and unique shops. Continental breakfast is served out in the gazebo in summer and may include Peach French toast, Strawberry & Cream French toast or Blueberry coffee cake. No smoking. Weddings facilities available. Families welcome. Wheelchair access.

Guests write: *"We found Jailer's Inn B&B to be charming and comfortable. The owners made us feel welcome and took care of our every need." (D. Homel)*

This was my first time to stay at a B&B and I just loved it. It was neat knowing you were staying in an old jail." (L. Green)

Louisiana

Additional information on B&Bs in this state is available from the following B&B reservation agency: Lincoln Ltd. B&B (601) 482-5483.

Lafayette

T'Frere's House
1905 Verot School Road
Lafayette, LA 70508
(318) 984-9347 or (800) 984-9347
Innkeepers: Pat & Maugie Pastor

♛♛♛ Rating: A-
Rates: Single or Double/$75-85
Charge Cards: MC, V

T'Frere's House is 50 miles west of Baton Rouge and 150 miles west of New Orleans off I-10. Restored Cajun home with T-shaped architecture is built of Louisiana Red Cypress. This home boasts three fireplaces and original pine flooring. Choose from four unique guest rooms with private bath and television. Antique furnishings adorn each room. The parlor, dining room, and glassed porch, filled with antiques, are used upon arrival for complimentary "T" Juleps and Cajun canapés. Area attractions: Cajun music, dancing, dining, shopping, sightseeing, swamp tours, and historic homes. Full breakfast served on elegant china may include specialties such as potatoes with onions, cheese, and bacon, or cheese grits, fresh fruit salad or grapefruit baskets, sausage Ettouffe, T' pancakes, hot French bread, and French toast. Restricted smoking.

New Orleans

Bed and Breakfast As You Like It
3500 Upperline Street
New Orleans, LA 70125
(504)821-7716
Innkeeper: Ann Hallock

 Rating: B
Rates: Single/$60; Double/$80; Suite/$90
Credit Cards: MC, V; Special event rates

Turn-of-the-century, Mediterranean-style home is in the University area near Tulane and Loyola, just 3 miles from the heart of New Orleans, the French Quarter, and Convention Center. Two guest rooms feature American antiques. Each has a phone and color TV. Enjoy welcome drinks and hors d'oeuvres in the living room and relax on the porch or garden deck. Tipitina's jazz and several of the city's finest restaurants are within one mile, as are the Garden District, St. Charles Avenue Trolley, Audubon Park and Zoo, and the Mississippi River Cruise. Awaken to Cafe Du Monde coffee or tea waiting outside your door. Continental breakfast includes New Orleans' croissants, breads, or muffins with fresh fruit and juice. Public transportation three blocks away. No smoking. Special events rates.

Guests write: "A most enjoyable stay in a lovely home. The hospitality was the highlight of our short visit." (J. Wheeler)

"Now we know the meaning of Southern hospitality. " (E. Ulrich)

New Orleans

La Maison Marigny
Bourbon Street near Esplanade
Mail to: Box 52257
New Orleans, LA 70152-2257
(800) 729-4640 or (504) 488-4640
Fax: (504) 488-4639
Innkeeper: Jeremy Bazata

Rating: A
Rates: Single or Double/$81-126

Restored Colonial Revival is located at the edge of the French Quarter in the heart of New Orleans. Three guest rooms with private bath are decorated with a blend of antiques and rich fabrics that soothe the senses after a long day of seeing sights in the city. A small sitting room with TV on the lower floor overlooks the traditional New Orleans walled garden and courtyard. Stroll to Jackson Square with its street performers and artists, famous restaurants and Bourbon Street. Sit at an open air cafe by the river. Visit the many galleries, jazz clubs, and antique shops, or take a Mississippi Riverboat ride. A riverfront streetcar or minibus is available for trips to convention centers and the Riverwalk Mall. Continental plus breakfast. Families welcome. Restricted smoking.

Guests write: *"I fell in love with New Orleans and with this wonderful and warm home. Why leave the house when you've got those wonderful scones in the morning and Frank's PB&J sandwiches in the evening!"* (*D. Blakney*)

"We suggest that guests use Jeremy and her knowledge of the area to the hilt. Her observations are rational, reasonable and down to earth. Fortunate are those of us whose paths cross hers!" (*E. Schubert*)

"For our first stay in a B&B, she certainly has shown us how it should be done. Such a warm, generous accommodating person! We're glad she gave up the law stuff to open up this very quaint, very comfortable, very homey Maison Marigny. We'll be back." (*K. Parker*)

"Her expert knowledge of New Orleans helped me to fully enjoy this most sensuous of cities - its sights, its sounds, its smells, and most importantly of all, its people. Her hospitality, attention to detail, and patience knew no bounds." (*N. Kent*)

New Orleans

Lafitte Guest House
1003 Bourbon Street
New Orleans, LA 70116
(504) 581-2678 or (800) 331-7971
Innkeeper: John Maher

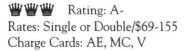 Rating: A-
Rates: Single or Double/$69-155
Charge Cards: AE, MC, V

Lafitte Guest house is an historic mansion with French architectural influence which is conveniently located in the heart of the French Quarter of the city. Choose from fourteen guest rooms which offer a variety in size, decor, and amenities but each has a selection of period furnishings, rich fabrics and appointments, and a private bath. Several rooms have private balconies with views of the city skyline and French Quarter and these rooms are especially popular during Mardis Gras. Walk to an abundance of world famous restaurants, renowned nightclubs, specialty shops, museums, and colorful Creole and Spanish cottages. Complimentary Continental breakfast features fresh pastries. Wine andhors d'oeuvres are served each evening in main parlor.

New Orleans

Lamothe House
621 Esplanade Avenue
New Orleans, LA 70116
(504) 947-1161
Fax: (504) 943-6536
Innkeeper: Carol Chauppette

♕♕♕   Rating: A
Rates: Single/$59-87; Double/$72-99
Charge Cards: AE, MC, V

Lamothe House is located at the edge of the French quarter on Esplanade, between Royal and Charters Streets. 150-year-old Victorian Inn displays pink stucco walls, white trimmed balconies, and green shuttered windows. Choose from eleven guest rooms and nine suites, all with private baths. Many rooms offer canopy beds, and all have color television and telephone. The Inn's most elegant suites, Mallard and Lafayette, are located on the first floor and offer such amenities as antiques, oriental rugs, and adjoining sitting rooms with
museums, historic sites, shopping, restaurants, Bourbon Street and Dixieland Jazz, Jackson Square, river and lakes. Continental breakfast, served in the dining room or taken to the courtyard, includes juice, croissants, and New Orleans dark roast coffee. Wheelchair access. Families welcome.

Guests write: "*I found the Lamothe House charming and the staff very efficient and friendly. The rooms are delightful and comfortable. The morning coffee fantastic!*" (P. Goodyear

Shreveport

2439 Fairfield "A Bed & Breakfast"
2439 Fairfield Avenue
Shreveport, LA 71104
(318) 424-2424 or Fax: (318) 424-3658
Innkeepers: Jimmy & Vicki Harris

♕♕♕   Rating: A+
Rates: Single or Double/$95-150
Credit Cards: AE, D, DC, MC, V
Corporate discounts available

The 2439 Fairfield "A Bed & Breakfast" is located 150 miles east of Dallas, TX. Three-story, red brick Victorian Inn, located in the historical district, is surrounded by turn-of-the-century mansions. English rose and herb gardens, A Victorian swing, gazebo, and water fountain are nestled among oak trees. Four guest rooms with private baths are available. The Jana Roberta Suite boasts a full-size brass and iron bed with a white hand-cut linen canopy. The Honeymoon Suite, with its hand-carved, king sized canopy and goose-down duvet, offers a wet bar and whirlpool. A wet bar is also provided in the Vicki Gail Suite. Each room has its own private balcony. An 1893 concert grand piano, a 1900 pump organ, and a victrola can be found in the drawing room. Phones are available in every room. Area attractions: LA Downs, riverboats, Strand Theatre, and American Rose Center. Full breakfast includes cereals, selected cheeses, fresh fruit, eggs, Canadian bacon, sausages, homemade breads, jellies, jams, English muffins, imported teas and coffees. Afternoon tea is also provided. Meeting Facilities. Restricted smoking

Guests write: *"They have all the conveniences of a successful hotel plus a lot more to offer. During our stays this B&B has always been immaculately clean and well furnished. The English antiques throughout the entire house are plentiful and beautifully maintained. When we arrive our room is always well lit and inviting. If we go out in the evening, our bed is turned down when we return. They serve a full English breakfast including fresh fruit, cheeses of all kinds, homemade muffins, choice of cereal, scrambled eggs, sausage, Canadian bacon, sauteed mushrooms, and a wide selection of juices, hot teas, and coffees."* (C&V. Walker)

"We have often noted the genuine hospitality given to each guest by Mr. and Mrs. Harris. Their home is filled with many beautiful pieces of art and antiques and many a story can be told of where and how each piece managed to find its way there. Each room is quite grand though our favorite is the Jamie Alice suite, a romantic hideaway." (M. Crawford)

Bar Harbor

Breakwater-1904
45 Hancock Street
Bar Harbor, ME 04609
(207) 288-2313 or (800) 238-6309
Innkeeper: Bonnie Sawyer

♛ ♛ ♛ ♛   Rating: AA
Rates: Single or Double: $155-295
Credit Cards: AE, MC, V

Turn-of-the-century English Tudor estate is located on Bar Harbor's historic shore path which over looks Frenchman Bay and the Porcupine Islands. Recently restored and listed on the National Register of Historic Places, the inn offers six guest rooms. Each is spacious and elegantly furnished with private bath, fireplace, queen or king-size bed, and four offer ocean-front views. There are ample common areas for guest relaxation including the front verandah, formal parlor, and billiard room. Explore nearby Acadia National Park and surrounding areas by hiking, biking, kayaking, canoeing, and beach combing. A full breakfast is served in the formal dining room overlooking the ocean. Specialties of the house include raspberry almond French toast, eggs Benedict, or apple crepes with homemade sausage. No smoking.

Guests write: *"Whether it is the morning homemade donuts, egg soufflés and freshly prepared granola or the late afternoon snacks of lemon bars and brownie bites, your tummy is in for a treat! Relax and retire in spacious rooms filled with history. Each room tells a story of the past from the impeccable footed tub, the four-postered bed, to the original flooring and crown molding. The Breakwater 1904 is truly a treat for the mind and a comfort for the body."* (R&W Lively)

"The Breakwater is an extremely luxurious, pampering experience. Because there are only seven guest rooms, you feel that you're staying in a private home. The inn's management is very friendly and helpful without being overly intrusive. We are seasoned travelers, and this is the most spectacular inn we've ever seen!" (D. Dauman)

Bar Harbor

Clefstone Manor
92 Eden Street
Bar Harbor, ME 04609
(207) 288-4951
Innkeepers: Pattie & Don Reynolds

♛♛♛ Rating: A
Rates: Single or Double: $65-185
Credit Cards: AE, MC, V

Clefstone Manor is located 30 miles east of Bangor on 1-A East. Three-story Victorian summer cottage sits on one acre of terraced gardens with long distance views of the bay from the third level. Each of the sixteen rooms with private bath, is reminiscent of an English country house with imported lace curtains and goose-down comforters. Guests can relax and share experiences in the spacious fireplaced public rooms. Within walking distance is Acadia National Park, hiking, biking, climbing, kayaking, canoeing, swimming, shopping, tennis, sailing, whale watching, and nature cruises. Enjoy a full breakfast in the dining room with such specialties as French vanilla toast, ham and egg strata, pattie puffs, and blueberry delight. Served on a daily basis is cereal, hot cereal, coffee cake, muffins or sticky buns, tea bread, English muffins, bagels, three types of juice, various teas and coffee. Smoking is restricted to outside porches.

Bar Harbor

Manor House Inn
106 West Street
Bar Harbor, ME 04609
(800) 437-0088 or (207) 288-3759
Innkeeper: Mac Noyes

♛♛♛ Rating: A
Rates: Single or Double/$50-165
Credit Cards: AE, MC, V

Three story Victorian mansion set on a landscaped acre is situated on an historic, tree-lined street in the West Street National Historic District. The Manor House complex consists of the summer mansion, original chauffeur's cottage, and two guests cottages. There are fourteen guest accommodations throughout the complex. Each has individual Victorian wall coverings, original maple floor, period antiques and accessories, and a private bath. Some rooms offer working fireplaces and a garden view. Walk to Bar Harbor's shops, restaurants, whale watching events, schooner rides, and Bar Island. Explore Acadia National Park. A full breakfast is served and specialty of the house includes baked stuffed blueberry French toast. Restricted smoking.

Bar Harbor

The Tides
119 West Street
Bar Harbor, ME 04609
(207) 288-4968
Innkeeper: Kim Swan-Bennett

♛♛♛   Rating: A
Rates: Single or Double/$145-195
Credit Cards: MC, V

Classic Greek Revival oceanfront inn is located on historic West Street, just off of Route 3 in the village. Three guest rooms with private bath feature period furnishings and a full ocean view. The impressive foyer leads into gracious living and dining rooms. Take an easy walk downtown to the shops, restaurants, and wharf, or drive to nearby Acadia National Park. A full breakfast and afternoon tea are served daily on a wrap-around verandah with fireplace and ocean views. No smoking.

Belfast

Frost House
6 Northport Avenue
Belfast, ME 04915
(207) 338-4159
Innkeeper: Joanie Lightfood

♛♛♛   Rating: A-
Rates: Single/$50-70; Double/$60-80

Victorian turn-of-the-century home is less than a mile off Route 1 on a 1.2 acre lot with gardens. Choose from three guest rooms which are decorated with period antiques and offer views of the water. Two rooms have connecting baths and the third offers a private bath next to the guest room. Special features include a sleigh and step-up four poster bed. The Beatrix Potter room has a water view framed by trees. Relax in the second floor sitting room or in the first floor oak parlor with stained glass windows. The harbor is just blocks away with bay cruises, live theater, concerts, shopping, and dining. Bar Harbor is an hour drive and Camden can be reached in 20 minutes by car. Blueberry pancakes, Amaretto French toast, Belgian waffles, and fresh muffins are some of the full breakfast specialties. Tea and flavored coffee are offered with a light snack at check-in time. No smoking. Closed October 31 - May 20.

Blue Hill

Mountain Road House
Mountain Road
Blue Hill, ME 04614
(207) 374-2794
Innkeepers: Carol and John McCulloch

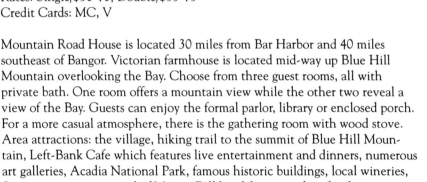

 Rating: A-
Rates: Single/$50-70; Double/$55-75
Credit Cards: MC, V

Mountain Road House is located 30 miles from Bar Harbor and 40 miles southeast of Bangor. Victorian farmhouse is located mid-way up Blue Hill Mountain overlooking the Bay. Choose from three guest rooms, all with private bath. One room offers a mountain view while the other two reveal a view of the Bay. Guests can enjoy the formal parlor, library or enclosed porch. For a more casual atmosphere, there is the gathering room with wood stove. Area attractions: the village, hiking trail to the summit of Blue Hill Mountain, Left-Bank Cafe which features live entertainment and dinners, numerous art galleries, Acadia National Park, famous historic buildings, local wineries, Searsport, antique capital of Maine. Full breakfast, served in the dining room, includes stuffed French toast with blueberry or Maple Syrup, fresh fruit, and a variety of homemade muffins. Enjoy afternoon refreshments of lemonade, coffee, tea or wine. No smoking.

Boothbay Harbor

Atlantic Ark Inn
64 Atlantic Avenue
Boothbay Harbor, ME 04538
(207) 633-5690
Innkeeper: Donna Piggott

♛♛   Rating: B+
Rates: Single or Double/$65-215
Credit Cards: AE, MC, V

Small, intimate Victorian inn built in 1875 is found across the harbor on the east side of the village, 11 miles from Route 1. Six guest rooms with private bath are available. Each has been decorated with period antiques, fresh flowers, mahogany poster beds with firm mattresses, and Oriental rugs. A new suite addition features sixteen windows, vaulted ceiling, two sets of French doors, and panoramic views. Several rooms offer private balconies with harbor views, double Jacuzzi, or Greek tub. A separate guest cottage on the property is also available. The front porch is a good spot to view the sunset each evening. Crossing the small foot bridge at the edge of the property leads to the Inner Harbor shops, galleries, and fine restaurants. Full breakfast is served on fine linen and china and features specialties such as English scones, old-fashioned biscuits, cinnamon popovers, and sweet baked goods such as apricot nut bread or strawberry muffins. Complimentary wine and beverages are offered each afternoon. No smoking.

Guests write: *"Waking up in a four-poster bed with the sun shining in through lace curtains is one of our most lasting memories. We truly enjoyed the beautiful front porch where we could watch the fishing boats in the harbor with our morning coffee, or evening cordials. We happened upon the Atlantic Ark the first weekend they opened, and have been back every summer since."* (M. Sternberg)

"It is especially clean, well-managed, and comfortable. The hosts are able to get your day started on the right course by serving a unique and delicious breakfast. Its charm is evident throughout." (H. Craig)

"As we arrived we were greeted and escorted past beautiful petunias to a private chalet overlooking views of a pond to the side and the harbor in front. Tall glasses of iced-tea adorned with fresh mint from the garden were over-shadowed only by the specially prepared muffins, fresh fruit, and full breakfast served at a private table overlooking the veranda." (M. Caporaso)

Camden

Hartstone Inn
41 Elm Street
Camden, ME 04843
(207) 236-4259
Innkeepers: Peter and Elaine Simmons

👑👑👑 Rating: A-
Rates: Single/$60-85; Double/$75-90

Intimate Victorian inn is located in the heart of the village, a stones throw from the harbor. There are eight guest rooms with comfortable antiques and private baths. Two have fireplaces. There is also a parlor with fireplace and a library with a variety of good books and cable TV. Two efficiency apartments are in the carriage house and available at weekly rates. Shops, galleries, and restaurants are only steps away from the front door. Skiing, golf, swimming, sailing, or kayaking are all nearby. Full breakfast. Candlelight dinners and picnic lunches available by advance reservation.

Camden

Maine Stay Inn
22 High Street
Camden, ME 04843
(207) 236-9636
Innkeepers: Peter and Donny Smith
and Diana Robson

👑👑👑 Rating: A+
Rates: Single or Double/$65-110
Credit Cards: AE, MC, V

Built in 1802 and listed on the National Register of Historic Places, this Colonial inn is located in the center of Camden's historic district, 3 blocks north of the village center and harbor. Eight guest rooms, four with private bath, have brass or oak beds. A new room on the lower level offers a contemporary feel with traditional comfort, private bath, separate entrance, view of the woods, and a pellet stove. Two fireplaced parlors and a TV lounge are decorated with oriental rugs and period furnishings. Stroll through the two-acre wooded glen, walk to the harbor, or hike along miles of well maintained trails in the Camden Hills State Park. Alpine and cross-country skiing, golf, tennis, fishing, sailing, bicycling and ferry service to picturesque islands are available close by. Information is provided for suggested tours and day trips. Tasty egg dishes, French toast, or whole wheat pancakes are frequently part of the full breakfast offered.

Guests write: *"The innkeepers at the Main Stay have spoiled me! Breakfast is a special treat—from the homemade granola to Grandma's Pancakes and stuffed French toast. I've never stayed in lodgings anywhere that we felt as much at home as the Maine Stay." (S. Stonestreet)*

"Warm welcomes, afternoon tea, blazing fires perfectly laid (even this detail isn't missed), stories of Down East (the accent and humor perfected by Peter), breakfast to die for (blueberry compote followed by their favorite recipe for good eggs and cranberry-orange muffins), and always fresh ironed sheets and thirsty towels. A pampering even the queen would love!" (J&A Boardman)

"We have two favorite bedrooms. If you don't mind sharing a bath, #3 at the top of the stairs is my all time favorite. The side window overlooks the woods, and the rocker by the back window is perfect for catching the afternoon breeze. The bath out the door has a shower and the one across the hall has an old claw-foot bathtub to soak away your worries. The custom bath salts the trio have blended is so nice; even my husband uses them! For a private bath the downstairs is definitely the one. The walls are lined with bookcases and window seat to prop yourself up on while you toast your toes on the wood stove. The sitting area opens on a fieldstone terrace which overlooks the grounds." (C. Brimson)

"Upon arrival each summer we are served lemonade on the wooden patio overlooking a wonderful garden." (M&K Armijo)

"Each guest room is tastefully appointed to provide the guest with comfort, privacy, a feeling as if you are staying in your 'own' room while at their house. You don't feel crammed in, nor is road noise apparent in the front rooms. The lighting is ample and adjustable. The bath facilities are modern, sparkling clean, and have great fluffy towels. The morning room service is impeccable." (J. Newton)

"The Maine Stay has superior quality in hospitality, accommodations and location. During our visits, we were given specific details and maps for activities in the area and could also preview menus from local venues." (J. Frower)

"The innkeepers couldn't be more gracious. Even after the first visit, you feel like family. I've stayed with them on several occasions. Breakfasts are delicious! I especially appreciate their knowledge of the area offering ideas for daily trips and local eateries if you are undecided on what to do or where to go. Definitely a high quality inn! I've referred many to the Camden Maine Stay Inn." (D. West)

Freeport

Porter's Landing Bed & Breakfast
70 South Street
Freeport, ME 04032
(207) 865-4488
Innkeepers: Peter and Barbara Guffin

♛♛♛   Rating: A-
Rates: Single/$70-85; Double/$80-95
Credit Cards: MC, V

Carriage house built in 1870 is located in Freeport's quiet Maritime district, one mile from town and L.L. Bean's retail store. Three guest rooms on the second floor offer private baths and feature handmade quilts and fresh cut flowers. Also upstairs is a quiet loft for reading. On the main floor is a parlor with Count Rumford fireplace and comfortable window seats with views of the flower gardens. Walk along Main Street and explore more than 100 factory outlet stores. Visit nearby Wolf Neck or Winslow Parks and enjoy biking, sailing, fishing, cross-country skiing, or hiking along the edge of the ocean. A hearty breakfast features fresh fruits, homemade breads and muffins, and specialties such as Belgian waffles with spiced apples and wild Maine blueberry pancakes. No smoking.

Guests write: *"We enjoyed a small but very lovely room with private bath. The common area was warm and attractive with lots of information available on the Freeport area."* (T. Lane)

"I had intended to come up for the cross-country skiing but my husband is deployed in the Persian Gulf. You can be sure upon his return we'll be up for a weekend. After all, he's an L.L. Bean addict and I can't think of a more peaceful and romantic haven to spend time with a long-lost spouse. I can't say enough about Porter's Landing. Upon our arrival, Peter, who had been washing windows, greeted me by name and welcomed me. He ushered us in and Barbara took over and cooled our parched throats with fresh iced tea in the sitting room. The decor was beautiful but comfortable. Our hosts offered us their knowledge about the area and acted on our behalf when making reservations for us locally." (M. Smith)

"The most memorable part of my trip to Maine was my stay at Porter's Landing. Barbara and Peter made us feel welcome the moment we arrived and went out of their way to accommodate us. Their hospitality is second to none." (J. Dodgson)

Fryeburg

Admiral Peary House
9 Elm Street
Fryeburg, ME 04037
(800) 237-8080 or (207) 935-3365
Innkeepers: Ed and Nancy Greenberg

♛♛♛   Rating: A+
Rates: Single/$65-100; Double/$70-108
Credit Cards: MC, V

Once the home of the famous American explorer, this historic Victorian home
is now an inn and is located 50 miles west of Portland. Choose from four guest
rooms with private bath, sitting area, dressing table, air conditioning, and
individually controlled heat. Some rooms feature mountain views, king-sized
brass beds, or slanted roof lines that create interesting nooks and crannies.
Soak in the outdoor spa, play tennis on the inn's clay court, read a book from
the library in the guest living room, play pool in the Billiard room, or relax on
the large screened-in porch where afternoon tea is offered daily. Area attractions: White Mountains National Forest, hiking and touring, Saco River
Canoeing, Fryeburg Fair, alpine and Nordic skiing, golfing, antiquing, and
outlet shopping. A full breakfast offers such specialties as Maine blueberry
pancakes, Belgium waffles, or Admiral Peary breakfast pie, served with home
made-muffins and breads. Wedding and meeting facilities available. No
smoking.

Guests write: *"Their breakfasts are well planned, imaginative and bountiful. Their
personalities and the clientele they attract promises diverse and interesting
conversations continuing most of each morning. They are well suited to the B & B
industry. The Admiral Perry House—aside from its' historical connections, is located
in a 'post card' New England village—well suited for a family or group in safe
setting. An hour drive from everything of meaning and interest."* (W. Poulin)

*"We are very pleased with the personal attention of Nancy and Ed. They always
remember personal requests, including requests for friends to stay that occurred over
a year before."* (W. Neiman)

*"Although each guest room possesses its own attractiveness, the one room located on
the third level — not surprisingly named the North Pole, has an uninterrupted view
of the lush green lawn behind the inn, the tennis courts, and a small vegetable
garden. The furniture in this room is most pleasing to the eye."* (V&F Francesconi)

Kennebunk Beach

Sundial Inn
P.O. Box 1147
48 Beach Avenue
Kennebunk, ME 04043
(207) 967-3850
Fax: (207) 967-4919
Innkeeper: Lawrence Kennedy

♛♛♛ Rating: A+
Rates: Single or Double/$65-150
Credit Cards: AE, MC, V

Large oceanfront inn offers a quiet setting with beach access. There are thirty-four guest rooms with private bath, cable TV, air conditioning, and turn-of-the-century antique furnishings. Several luxury rooms offer ocean views and whirlpool baths. An living room furnished with Oriental rugs and chintz-covered chairs and sofa offers a pleasant area for conversing or just enjoying the ocean breezes. Popular attractions in the area include shopping at the local art galleries, gift and outlet shops, whale-watching, deep-sea fishing, and hiking at the nearby wildlife refuge and estuary. Continental breakfast features homemade muffins. Wheelchair access.

Kennebunkport

1802 House Bed & Breakfast Inn
15 Locke Street, PO Box 646-A
Kennebunkport, ME 04046-1646
(207) 967-5632 or (800) 932-5632
Innkeepers: Ron and Carol Perry

♛♛ Rating: B-
Rates: Single/$55-135; Double/$65-145
Credit Cards: AE, MC, V

1802 House Bed & Breakfast Inn is approximately 25 miles south of Portland, Maine and is located a half mile from Dock Square, the town center, and near the Kennebunk River. Surrounded by lawns, gardens and trees, this 1802 two-story Colonial offers an extensive view of the Cape Arundel Golf Club. Each of the six guest rooms provides a private bath; one of which has a two-person whirlpool bathtub. Some rooms have sitting areas with working fireplaces; others have romantic four-poster beds. Two guest parlors are available, one with wood stove and piano. Within walking distance are ocean beaches, historic sights, antique shops, fine restaurants, and golfing. Other area attractions: President Bush's summer home, Electric Trolley Museum, art museums, Narrow Gauge (two foot) Railroad Museum, working waterfront, shopping, professional sports teams. Full breakfast includes fresh fruit, Eggs Benedict, banana pancakes served with Maine maple syrup, soufflés, and a variety of muffins. Served with this is ham, sausage, or bacon. Facilities available for meetings and small weddings. No Smoking

Guests write: *"We were extremely pleased by the hospitality of the owners. The decor and cleanliness of our rooms was impeccable. The location was beautiful." (V. Baker)*

"We celebrated our 39th wedding anniversary at this inn. The hospitality was warm and always gracious. A fan was provided immediately upon request. The food at breakfast was most attractive and delicious particularly the Eggs Florentine." (E. Feeney)

"They were the best hosts of all our B&Bs due to the tips provided (best beaches, restaurants, etc.). What suits us very well was the quiet location near the golf club." (M. Petri)

Kennebunkport/Cape Porpoise

Inn at Harbor Head
41 Pier Road
Kennebunkport, ME 04046-6916
(207) 967-5564
Fax (207) 967-8776
Innkeepers: Joan and Dave Sutter

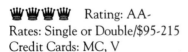

♕♕♕♕ Rating: AA-
Rates: Single or Double/$95-215
Credit Cards: MC, V

Inn at Harbor Head is a century-old saltwater farmhouse located at the harbor's edge on the rocky shore of Cape Porpoise Harbor, 2 miles east of Kennebunkport. Five guest rooms are available. Each is individually furnished and offers queen or king-size bed, a private bath, and view of the lobster boats, islands, and ocean. Two rooms feature whirlpool tubs and one boasts a fireplace. Other amenities include bed turndowns and robes in rooms. Explore nearby beaches, tranquil walking paths, and bike routes. Use the inn as a central base for day trips to the New Hampshire mountains, Boston, Salem, or further along the coast to Boothbay Harbor or Camden. Full breakfast is served in a dining room full of crystal, pewter, and original stenciling, and offers varying specialties such as stuffed French toast, eggs Florentine, or homemade sherry-creamed chicken. Individual dietary needs are happily considered. No smoking.

Guests write: *"Our bed had an excess of six pillows and the comforter was just as thick. The faucets on the sink were birds, and the mirrors reflected the art work. There were chocolates on our beds after we returned from a delicious dinner at a restaurant recommended by our hosts, and candied bananas and personal quiches for breakfast the next morning."* (L. Taber)

"The 'Summer Suite' is so comfortable, it would do very well as a Spring or Fall suite too. Melissa, Sarah, and Alyse took very good care of us. We hope to return to the beautiful view and these very comfortable and relaxing accommodations." (J&J Rogers)

"What a pleasant retreat from the Chicago hustle and bustle…An extension of family in Maine?…it felt like it. This is the first B & B where the hosts have encouraged interaction among the guests—just an overflow of your warm personalities. It was grand!" (B. Blick)

"The Greenery room is wonderfully tranquil and comforting with its walls wrapped in windows and the bed sinking under all those pillows. Joan and David's gourmet breakfasts have turned us into morning people." (M. Costa)

"Joan is the epitome of a bed and breakfast hostess reaching that rare balance of attention to every detail while maintaining a warm, cozy, friendly, inviting haven for her guests. My soul is restored from the classical guitar, the crystal, silver, starched linens, hammock, and my own bird singing to me from outside the window." (D. Beto)

"The Harbor Suite with its beautiful murals and view is by far the best room in which we've ever stayed and we've been all over the world." (E. Volk)

"The Summer Suite was romantic, done in exquisite taste, the view divine. The breakfasts were more than delicious and they were presented as a work of art." (A. Ferraro)

"The chocolate covered French toast made my daughter Barbra's day." (F. Johnson)

Kennebunkport

Inn on South Street
PO Box 478A
Kennebunkport, ME 04046
(207) 967-5151
Innkeepers: Eva and Jack Downs

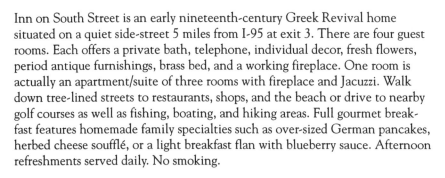

♛♛♛ Rating: A+
Rates: Single/$85-165; Double/$95-185
Credit Cards: MC, V

Inn on South Street is an early nineteenth-century Greek Revival home
situated on a quiet side-street 5 miles from I-95 at exit 3. There are four guest
rooms. Each offers a private bath, telephone, individual decor, fresh flowers,
period antique furnishings, brass bed, and a working fireplace. One room is
actually an apartment/suite of three rooms with fireplace and Jacuzzi. Walk
down tree-lined streets to restaurants, shops, and the beach or drive to nearby
golf courses as well as fishing, boating, and hiking areas. Full gourmet breakfast features homemade family specialties such as over-sized German pancakes,
herbed cheese soufflé, or a light breakfast flan with blueberry sauce. Afternoon
refreshments served daily. No smoking.

Guests write: *"Upon our first arrival (we were guests at the Inn on 3 different
occasions) Eva let us take our pick of the available rooms. 'Our room' was easily
identified. Even when the sun wasn't shining, the room was bright, warm and cozy.
Eva's ability to create an overall effect with eclectic furnishings cannot be duplicated.
The brass bed, dhurrie rugs, Chinese vase lamps and stenciled borders all represent
different decorating styles and eras, but Eva has a knack for pulling it all together."*
(J. Henry)

*"This inn should be used as an example of how to run an inn properly. All the
comforts such as clean, well-appointed rooms were provided but somehow the whole
was greater than the sum of its parts. Jack and Eva were delightful hosts not just
innkeepers. You felt extremely comfortable yet there was still a degree of elegance that
comes only with knowledge and experience. This gives you the feeling of living in
Maine, not just being a tourist."* (E. DuBose)

*"Breakfast is in the tree tops in the 2nd floor kitchen with a view of the Kennebunk
River. Featured on the menu were homemade breads and jams, colorful and tasty
combinations of fresh fruits and egg dishes served on blue and white china. Elegant,
yet unpretentious."* (J. Chalmers)

Kennebunkport

Kennebunkport Inn
P.O. Box 111, Dock Square
Kennebunkport, ME 04046
(207) 967-2621
Innkeeper: Rick Griffin

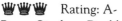   Rating: A-
Rates: Single or Double/$60-179
Senior and business travel discounts
Credit Cards: AE, MC, V

Large sea captain's home situated along the Kennebunk River was built in 1899 and is now an inn with restaurant. There are thirty-four guest rooms available. Each offers a private bath, color TV, and period furnishings. The restaurant lounge with fireplace and swimming pool with patio are popular spots for relaxation in the evening. Antique shops, boutiques, and restaurants are within walking distance from the inn. Local theaters, horseback riding, golf, and fine beaches are within a short drive. A full breakfast and candlelight dinner are served daily, but not included in the nightly rate. However, special packages and a Modified American Plan are available that do include meals. Families welcome. Meeting facilities available.

Kennebunkport

Kilburn House
P.O. Box 1309, Chestnut Street
Kennebunkport, ME 04046
(207) 967-4762
Innkeeper: Samuel Minier

Rating: B+
Rates: Single or Double/$45-125
Credit Cards: AE, MC, V

Small Victorian home built in 1890 is situated on a quiet side street one block from the village center. The four guest rooms offer twin or double beds; three have a private bath. A third floor suite offers complete privacy, two bedrooms, separate living room, and private bath. Specialty shops and restaurants are within easy walking distance from the inn. Beaches, nightly entertainment, and the L.L. Bean retail store are a short drive away. Continental breakfast. No smoking.

Kennebunkport

Kylemere House 1818
P.O. Box 1333
Kennebunkport, ME 04046-1333
(207) 967-2780
Innkeepers: Ruth and Helen Toohey

♛♛♛   Rating: A
Rates: Single/$80-125; Double/$95-135
Credit Cards: MC, V

Historic Federal inn is located on a quiet street a few minutes walk to shops, beaches, and restaurants. Choose from four guest rooms with private bath. All are furnished with period antiques and soft colors that enhance the ambiance and true New England decor of this seaport inn. Guests enjoy afternoon refreshments in the sitting room or on the porch overlooking the gardens. The inn is a short walk from the ocean and Dock Square. Nearby sights include beaches, Trolley Museum, Monastery, Maritime Museum, and Portland Museum of Art. A variety of outdoor sporting activities available. Full gourmet breakfast. No smoking.

Guests write: *"Our room, like all the other rooms, was individually furnished with beautiful antiques. Simply a beautiful place to spend several peaceful and relaxing days." (D&G Kimmerly)*

Kennebunkport

Maine Stay Inn and Cottages
P.O. Box 500-A, 34 Maine Street
Kennebunkport, ME 04046
(207) 967-2117 or (800) 950-2117
Fax: (207) 967-8757
Innkeepers: Lindsay and Carol Copeland

♛♛♛   Rating: A
Rates: Single or Double/$75-195
Credit Cards: AE, MC, V

Victorian inn and ten garden cottages built in 1860 are located in the National Historic District just 5 minutes from the village center. The main house offers four guest rooms and two suites, each with private bath. Cottages on the property each offer a small kitchen. Five accommodations have working fireplaces. The inn boasts a suspended stairway, sunburst-crystal glass windows, and a cupola with panoramic view of the town. Relax on the spacious porch or explore the beautiful sandy beaches, picturesque harbor, galleries, antique, and gift shops. Full breakfast features homemade scones, muffins, granola, and specialties such as baked omelets, Maine Stay French toast, apple blintz soufflé, or apple bread pudding. Afternoon tea is served daily. Small wedding facilities available. Families welcome.

Guests write: *"The bungalow efficiencies at the back of the main building are excellent for a family, particularly if one needs to be able to provide food to children at 3 a.m. because of the time change (from Europe) without annoying other guests. As a vegetarian, I also found the healthy breakfasts a far cry from the usual animal-fats-with-everything level of American cuisine."* (S. Yarnold)

"They know how to make their guests feel comfortable. The accommodations and the pleasant atmosphere provided made us feel right at home." (D. Goegelman)

"The bottle of wine was such a nice gesture. The food, fireplace, and advice on activities in the area were all excellent. We enjoyed the backyard area for reading." (N. Johnson)

"On our 2nd Anniversary we were introduced to another couple at the inn. The four of us have become fast friends and see each other often. Carol and Lindsay have always been helpful in making reservations for evenings out, picnics, and other places of interest." (J. Ellison-Taylor)

Portland

Andrews Lodging Bed & Breakfast
417 Auburn Street
Portland, ME 04103
(207)797-9157
Fax: (207)797-9040
Innkeeper: Elizabeth Andrews

♕♕ Rating: B+
Rates: Single/$45-65;
Double/$50-75; Suite/$85-155
Senior discount
Credit Cards: AE, MC, V

Circa 1740s Colonial house situated on 1.5 acres is surrounded by country gardens and located five miles from the center of Portland on the outskirts of the city. There are a total of six guest rooms and one offers a private bath. Each room has been decorated with antiques and traditional furnishings and features a unique decor theme. The Golf room has antique golf pictures while the Victorian Room offers 1860 furniture including a signed Miller lamp. The Wicker room has wicker furniture and Oriental bird prints while the Shaker suite offers the timeless simplicity of Shaker furniture and also has a whirlpool tub. The Amish room has pencil post beds and folk quilts. A guest kitchen provides a sitting area with cable television and laundry facilities and there's a comfortable living room with fireplace. Explore the gardens, sit on the deck, relax on the brick patio or in the comfortable library and solarium. Downtown Portland, a short drive away, offers the Historic Old Port, museums, restaurants, and the waterfront. Within a day trip by car are the L.L. Bean and the Freeport Factory outlets and nearby ocean activities. Continental breakfast is served in the formal dining room on silver and crystal and often features hot oatmeal with Maine syrup, fresh muffins and sweet breads, as well as fresh fruits grown in the summer garden. Wedding facilities available. Families welcome. No smoking.

Guests write: *"The 200-year-old house had been re-constructed throughout and an additional remodeling for guest rooms was superbly finished and decorated. The room we stayed in was very private and quiet. If we wanted to stroll or take a walk, the neighborhood complimented the Andrew's and their dwelling. Safe and very pleasant. We were asked when we wanted breakfast the night before. In the morning a note on the upstairs dining table stated that breakfast was being served. Fresh fruit with whipped cream and a hot round oven-baked (twelve inch) scone greeted us as we sat down at the formal dining table downstairs. Cereal with fruit was also available at the sideboard. Upstairs they have a small library/reading room and a complete suite with private bath (w/skylights) and whirlpool."* (C&D Rose)

Searsport

Thurston House B&B
P.O. Box 686, 8 Elm Street
Searsport, ME 04974
(207) 548-2213 or (800) 240-2213
Innkeepers: Carl and Beverly Eppig

♛/♛   Rating: B
Rates: Single/$40; Double2/$45-60
Senior, military, and veteran discounts

Colonial home built in 1831 is located on a quiet side street of the village opposite Penobscot Marine Museum and just off US-1. Four guest rooms are available with pleasant decor and selected antique furnishings. Two rooms offer a private bath. Walk to local restaurants, galleries, specialty shops, and beach park. Popular local attractions include state parks and forts, ocean cruises, and day trips to Blue Hill, Castine, Bar Harbor, and Camden. Indulge in a "forget-about-lunch" full breakfast. No smoking.

Guests write: *"We could literally go on ad infinitum about Thurston House, its warmth and charm, the lovely inviting way Beverly and Carl open their arms and make you feel a part of their lives, a Valentine Celebration, provide a personalized tour of the bay, concern themselves with the needs and comfort of their guests even to the extent of making sure that recipes are altered to allow an allergic person to enjoy all the food pleasures others enjoy."* (M. Glorioso)

"The rooms were clean and kept that way. Every time we traveled in the area, we followed Carl's advice as to where we ate. Each time his recommendation was 'on the money' and added to our enjoyment. His specialty was breakfast (spelled with a capital B). This man literally knocked himself out coming up with the most unusually, totally filling, and healthy approach to food." (S. Browner)

"We stayed in the attached carriage house. This was ideal. The surprise for us was that we had such wonderful hosts. The Eppigs were a terrific resource of things to do and places to visit. Thurston House lives up to its billing as the one where you 'forget about lunch.' Each morning Carl dons his special chef's toque and prepares a distinctly different potpourri of delights. Hearty is an understatement for this morning meal...it's a feast fit for kings." (F. Cavalier)

Southwest Harbor

Harbour Cottage Inn
9 Dirigo Roads
Southwest Harbor, ME 04679—0258
(207) 244-5738
Innkeepers: Ann & Mike Pedreschi

♛♛♛   Rating: A-
Rates: Single/$55-130; Double/$60-140
Credit Cards: AE, MC, V

Sitting opposite the harbor on a long, sweeping lawn, this 1870s three story mansard inn boasts clapboard on the first two floors and cedar shakes on the mansard. All eight guest rooms have private bath and room amenities that include hair dryers, ceiling fans, individual heating controls, and alarm clocks. Several rooms offer a telephone and TV. The sitting room features a piano, TV with VCR, books, and games. Relax on the deck which faces the harbor or walk to museums, fishing, boating, shopping, lobster wharves, a live oceanarium, and the Wendell Gilley Bird Carving Museum. Area attractions: snow mobiling, skiing, sailing, sea kayaking, as well as Acadia National Park, museums, shopping, and the Blue Nose ferry to Nova Scotia. Continental breakfast includes a daily chef's special such as Banana Delight, eggs Benedict, fruit roll ups, and various quiches. An afternoon snack is offered on the porch when weather permits. No smoking.

Guests write: "*We found the inn one year ago and have been back six times. The rooms are attractive, cheerful, and immaculate. Baths are all new with either Jacuzzi or steam baths — all have hairdryers, heat lamps, and good exhaust fans. Individual thermostats and excellent mattresses contribute to a comfortable night. We enjoy the harbor views and quiet location. And always we look forward to sumptious breakfasts which still manage to respect our needs for low-fat foods.*" (R&P Trub)

"*The rooms are lovely with water views. Mike and Ann are fascinating conversationalists making it easy to quickly get to know each other on a first name basis. Breakfasts are creative, delicious, and delightful. Snacks, tea, coffee, and ice are available.*" (R Nostrand)

Spruce Head

Craignair Inn
Clark Island Road
Spruce Head, ME 04859
(207) 594-7644
Innkeepers: Norman and Tery Smith

 Rating: B+
Rates: Single or Double with shared bath: $42-67;
Single or Double with private bath: $76-91
Credit Cards: AE, MC, V

Waterfront country inn is surrounded by natural beauty and located 8 miles from Route 1 in Thomaston. There are twenty-two guest rooms in the main house or annex. Each is furnished with homemade quilts, hooked rugs, and colorful wallpaper; eight offer a private bath. A comfortable porch overlooks the water and there are attractive gardens whose paths lead to the coastline's tidal pools, clam flats, meadows, and offshore islands. Within a short drive are Rockland, Camden, antique shops, art galleries, museums, tennis, golf, sailing, and festivals. Full breakfast. There's a restaurant on the premises as well as facilities for meetings and social functions. Families welcome. Open March through November.

Guests write: *"The hospitality shown led to a lasting friendship. Terry, upon my 1st visit, invited me to go antiqueing with her and gave me the use of her car for my independent excursions. If I missed meals, I was made to feel welcome to take my meals with her family." (B. Sajdak)*

"The setting is beautiful and not crowded - right on the ocean. The food and service was excellent and moderately priced. The innkeepers have always made our stays fun." (J. Dacey)

Sullivan Harbor

Island View Inn
HCR 32, Box 24
Sullivan Harbor, ME 04664
(207) 422-3031
Innkeepers: Evelyn and Sarah Joost

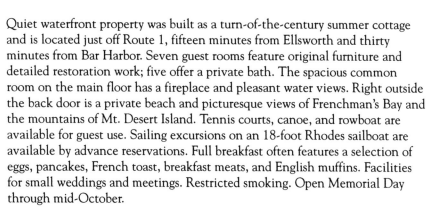

♛♛♛ Rating: A-
Rates: Single or Double/$40-70
Credit Cards: MC, V

Quiet waterfront property was built as a turn-of-the-century summer cottage and is located just off Route 1, fifteen minutes from Ellsworth and thirty minutes from Bar Harbor. Seven guest rooms feature original furniture and detailed restoration work; five offer a private bath. The spacious common room on the main floor has a fireplace and pleasant water views. Right outside the back door is a private beach and picturesque views of Frenchman's Bay and the mountains of Mt. Desert Island. Tennis courts, canoe, and rowboat are available for guest use. Sailing excursions on an 18-foot Rhodes sailboat are available by advance reservations. Full breakfast often features a selection of eggs, pancakes, French toast, breakfast meats, and English muffins. Facilities for small weddings and meetings. Restricted smoking. Open Memorial Day through mid-October.

Tennants Harbor

The East Wind Inn
PO Box 149
Tenants Harbor, ME 04860
(800) 241-VIEW or (207) 372-6366
Innkeeper: Tim Watts

Millikan

 Rating: B
Rates: Single/$48; Double/$74-130
Credit Cards: AE, MC, V

East Wind Inn built in 1920 was fully restored in 1974 and sits at harbor's edge offering views of the ocean. It is located nine miles from Thomaston and thirteen miles outside of Rockland in the heart of mid-coast Maine. A total of twenty-six guest rooms are available. The Meeting House offers one full apartment, two suites, and seven rooms with private baths. The inn has fourteen guest rooms with shared baths as well as one suite and a room with private bath. The inn's lobby is a place to relax, watch television, read, or play the baby grand piano. Additional common areas in the Meeting House include a living room with television, books, and magazines. Take a bike ride to explore the peninsula. Walk to the beach and explore the tidal pools or board a ferry to Monhegan, Vinalhaven, or North Haven Island. Visit nearby museums, antique shops, lighthouses, or just relax watching the harbor activity from the large porch. Continental breakfast features blueberry muffins. A full breakfast and dinner are available at extra charge in the dining room. Meeting facilities include a conference room with up-to-date audio visual equipment. Families welcome.

Wiscasset

The Squire Tarbox Inn
RR-2 Box 620
Wiscasset, ME 04578
(207)882-7693
Innkeepers: Karen and Bill Mitman

Rating: A
Rates: Single/$65-85; Double/$75-160
Credit Cards: AE, MC, V

The original board floors, timbers, and wainscoting of this 1763 farmhouse are still visible today in what is known as the Squire Tarbox Inn. The inn is found on Westport Island 8.5 miles off Route 1 between Wiscasset and Bath. Choose from eleven guest rooms, each with private bath. There are four rooms in the main house which feature fireplaces. The connected carriage barn houses seven more rooms with exposed beams and country decor. Relax in front of the fireplace with a book from the inn's bookshelves, play a game in the barn after dinner, take a walk down to the saltwater marsh, or sun on the open deck overlooking the woods. Bicycles are also provided for island touring. The innkeepers raise floppy-eared, friendly Nubian dairy goats and process natural cheeses from their own dairy and cheese samples are offered by the fire before dinner. The inn is in the country, away from tourist centers but near many Maine coast attractions such as beaches, harbors, antique and craft shops, museums, and lobster shacks. A full breakfast for B&B guests offers granola, fresh fruit, quiche, and a choice of five cakes and breads. Dinner is available at an additional charge. Smoking restricted to weather protected deck.

Guests write: *"Our stay at the Squire Tarbox was the highlight of our entire trip. This place was the very best in every way—overall appearance, rooms, furnishings, food, ambiance, history, goats and all. The walk to the water was just great as was the milking routine."* (M&I Sell)

"Being a tour operator, I have stayed at many B&Bs. The Squire Tarbox Inn is a very special place. We had a lovely, although short, visit. The animals are delightful, the marsh is peaceful, the food is healthy and delicious. I have already highly recommended the inn to some of our Maine guests for the 1993 season." (D. Mann)

"Never stayed at a nicer place. The best food I've ever tasted! And the best atmosphere!" (L. Smith)

"We thoroughly enjoyed the stay, the room, the goats, and especially the food! Eveyone was friendly and gracious. We continue to relate our wonderful experience at the Squire Tarbox to our friends." (J. Miller)

"We along with another couple, were on a two-week vacation in New England where we stayed exclusively in B&Bs. Squire Tarbox was our very favorite — the food, cordiality, atmosphere, and our spotless room were super." (R. Graydon)

York Harbor

York Harbor Inn
Route 1 A
York Harbor, ME 03911
(207) 363-5119 or (800) 343-3869
Fax: (207) 363-3545 X295
Innkeeper: Garry Dominguez

♕♕   Rating: B
Rates: Single/$ 65-105; Double/$79-139

Surrounded by large Victorian homes and gardens, this white, two and a half story, clapboard Colonial with dormers sits in the heart of town, a short walk from a protected beach; 50 miles north of Boston on I-95. Thirty-two guest rooms, twenty-eight with private baths, vary in decor with special rooms such as the Honeymoon Suite with king-size bed, antique dresser and dressing table, and a large tiled bath with a two person tub/spa. Gather in the fieldstone, fire-placed Common Room or explore the surrounding grounds with shade trees and flower beds. Walk to the beach for boating and swimming, art galleries, scenic cliff walk overlooking ocean, boutiques, deep sea fishing, Lobster tours, and Old York Historic Society Museum Houses. Area attractions: scenic coast, lighthouses, outlet shopping district, cross country skiing, sailing, lobster fishing, Portsmouth, NH, Seaport Town, Strawberry Bank Historic District, and York's wild Kingdom Zoo and Amusement Park. Continental breakfast includes freshly baked pastries, bagels, muffins, breads, cereal, fresh fruit and yogurt. Meeting and wedding facilities. Families welcome.

Baltimore

The Paulus Gasthaus
2406 Kentucky Avenue
Baltimore, MD 21213
(410) 467-1688
Innkeeper: Lucie Paulus

♛♛ Rating: B
Rates: Singe/$70; Double/$75
Credit Cards: AE, MC, V

Three-story European Tudor with secluded garden and patio is location in a quiet tree-lined residential neighborhood easily accessible to all major highways. Two guest rooms are available, one with private bath. Each room is comfortably furnished with down comforters, television, and clock radios. Relax in the living room with fireplace, large bay window, entertainment center, radio, and cassette recorder. Tennis courts, public golf course, biking and fitness track are within walking distance. Area attractions: Inner Harbor, Balitmore Aquarium, museums, cultural centers, Memorial Stadium, theaters, restaurants, horse farms, Annapolis Naval Academy, Chesapeake Bay, and Washington, DC. Choose from a German or American style full breakfast with specialties such as Apfelpfannkuchen, Creole bread pudding, Moselle toast with berries. Other amenities include chocolates, fresh flowers, fresh fruits and sherry. Fluent German spoken and some French. No smoking.

Berlin

Merry Sherwood Plantation
8909 Worcester Highway
Berlin, MD 21811
(410) 641-2112 or (800) 660-0358
Innkeeper: Kirk Burbage

♛♛♛ Rating: A+
Rates: Single or Double/$95-150
Credit Cards: MC, V

Victorian mansion with over 8,500 square feet was completed in 1859 and built for lavish parties — the perfect home for accommodating discerning guests. It sits on over eighteen acres and is located on Maryland's Eastern Shore, 130 miles east of Baltimore and 140 miles East of Washington, D.C. Choose from eight guest rooms, six with private marble bath. Each room has authentic period antiques and interesting architectural details such as large scaled baseboard, loblolly pine flooring, nine fireplaces, window moldings, and floor to ceiling "peer" mirrors. The first floor has a formal ballroom, grand entrance hall with four-story mahogany stair railing, a sitting parlor, rosewood dining room, library, sun parlor, and wrap-around verandah. Explore the surrounding grounds that are still landscaped in a typical 19th-century style, sit in the outdoor Victorian patio setting, or stroll the walking path. Visit nearby beaches and the National Wildlife Reserve. Activities in the area include swimming, fishing, boating, tennis, hunting, and antiquing. A full breakfast offers puffed apple pancakes, tomato rarebit, "Bubble and Squeak", as well as home-made muffins, jams, and jellies. Wedding, retreat, and meeting facilities available. No smoking.

Burtonsville

Upstream at Water's Gift
3604 Dustin Road
P.O. Box 240
Burtonsville, MD 20866
(301) 421-9562 or 421-9163
Innkeeper: Marceline Murphy

♛♛♛   Rating: A+
Rates: Single or Double/$85-105

Country home situated on a fifty-three acre Colonial horse farm is surrounded by several thousand acres of secluded woods and located halfway between Baltimore and Washington, D.C. The guesthouse offers two rooms, each with air conditioning and a private bath. The great room features a large fireplace, cathedral ceilings and unusual antique pine paneling. An expansive glass wall provides a spectacular view of the rolling landscape and horse pastures. Enjoy the many outdoor activities available such as hiking and mountain biking. Full gourmet breakfast. Restricted smoking.

Hagerstown

Beaver Creek House B&B
20432 Beaver Creek Road
Hagerstown, MD 21740
(301) 797-4764
Innkeeper: Don and Shirley Day

♛♛♛ Rating: A-
Rates: Single/$55-75; Double/$65-85

Beaver Creek House is a restored farmhouse built at the turn-of-the-century and located 4 miles east of Hagerstown in historic Beaver Creek. Five guest rooms are available with air conditioning, antique furnishings, and family memorabilia. Hosts have an extensive collection of Civil War books and tapes on the Antietam battlefield. A common room on the main floor offers an area for watching TV or reading. Explore the country garden and courtyard with fountain. Popular local attractions include antique shops, Civil War battlefields, Appalachian Trail hiking, skiing, golf, and trout fishing. Full breakfast features homemade muffins, biscuits, and rolls, as well as a hearty serving of eggs, sausage, and pancakes. Afternoon tea is served in the parlor. No smoking.

Guests write: *"Don and Shirley Day are so warm and welcoming that we instantly relaxed upon entering their cozy and inviting home. Their large white country home perches on a hill overlooking the rolling Maryland countryside, and we woke up to the smells of Don preparing his outstanding breakfast of pecan pancakes and country sausage. I've also had their raspberry cream cheese strudel and baked apples not to mention the most scrumptious coconut banana in English custard (I was able to persuade Don to share some of these recipes with me). All of this is served in their dining room of lace and crystal on antique china." (N&E Leisher)*

"The wonderful antique beds, the original French doors and abundance of family memorabilia added the perfect ambiance to the aged but well-preserved home. Every facet of the Beaver creek House seems to tell a story of past history. Our visit at Beaver Creek House was one of the most relaxing and comfortable vacations we've had." (C. McFall)

"The hosts were friendly and extremely helpful without ever being overbearing. They had a thorough library of books on local interests available. Sherry and snacks in every room. Innumerable knickknacks, clocks and antiques throughout the house." (A. Moseley)

(Continued)

"I like the fresh outdoors in the springtime, the birds singing and the horses to pet and talk to. The room is very attractive and complete with television and radio plus a bed rarely found outside of home. A great variety of books, a fire in the fireplace, a cup of tea , and a rocking chair provide a relaxing evening after a busy day touring the area. I enjoyed the peaceful setting. The house was so much like home especially with the fireplace. The hospitality was so gracious." (J. Weingartner)

"Don and Shirley are perfect hosts. And Don makes the best breakfasts! I wanted to move in. Very helpful with points of interest and history. There were wonderful snacks. This is a lovely home with very comfortable beds. I can't say enough!" (H. McCrae)

Oxford

1876 House
110 North Morris Street
Oxford, MD 21654-0658
(410) 226-5496
Innkeepers: Eleanor and Jerry Clark

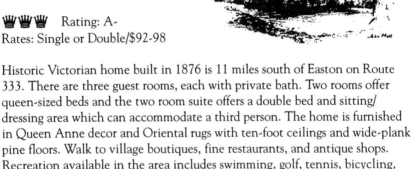

♕♕♕   Rating: A-
Rates: Single or Double/$92-98

Historic Victorian home built in 1876 is 11 miles south of Easton on Route 333. There are three guest rooms, each with private bath. Two rooms offer queen-sized beds and the two room suite offers a double bed and sitting/ dressing area which can accommodate a third person. The home is furnished in Queen Anne decor and Oriental rugs with ten-foot ceilings and wide-plank pine floors. Walk to village boutiques, fine restaurants, and antique shops. Recreation available in the area includes swimming, golf, tennis, bicycling, fishing, boating, and hunting. Continental breakfast served in formal dining room usually includes English muffins, croissants, fruit-filled turnovers, and fresh-brewed coffee and tea.

St. Michaels

Parsonage Inn
210 North Talbot Street
St. Michaels, MD 21663
(800) 394-5519
Innkeeper: Will Workman

👑👑👑 Rating: A
Rates: Single/$70-120; Double/$80-130
Credit Cards: MC, V

Brick Victorian home built in 1883 is situated in the heart of this small coastal village on Maryland's Eastern Shore. Choose from eight guest rooms with king or queen-size bed, private bath, ceiling fans, Queen Anne-style furnishings, and Laura Ashley linens. Three rooms have working fireplaces. Popular gathering spots include the library with collection of good books, upstairs deck for sunbathing, and quiet parlor with fireplace. Bicycles are available for exploring the village. Walk to great seafood restaurants, antique and gift shops, the historic harbor, and Maritime Museum. Full breakfast. Families welcome. Restricted smoking.

Snow Hill

River House Inn
201 East Market Street
Snow Hill, MD 21863
(410) 632-2722
Innkeeper: Larry and Susanne Knudsen

👑👑👑 Rating: A
Rates: Single or Double/$65-125
Family, senior, and auto club discount
Credit Cards: MC, V

Historic river-front Victorian country home built in 1860 is situated on two acres of rolling lawn on Maryland's Eastern Shore about fifteen miles south-west of Ocean City on Route 394. Nine guest rooms are available. Each of five rooms in the main has a private bath and air conditioning, and several feature a marble fireplace and wrap-around porch. The Little House, built in 1835, provides three additional rooms. A carriage barn has become the River Cottage, which is ADA handicapped accessible. There are several common areas throughout the inn including two spacious parlors, breakfast room, and dining room, each with fireplace. Porches with ceiling fans overlook the back lawn, gardens and the river front. Popular activities in the area include walking the village's picturesque streets and exploring the Pocomoke River which offers canoeing and fishing. Assateague and Chincoteague are nearby as are Ocean City beaches. Guests have their choice of full breakfast from a variety of entrees and afternoon refreshments are served daily. Box lunches and dinners can be prepared by advance arrangement. Small wedding and meeting facilities available. Restricted smoking.

Guests write: *"We had a lovely time here. Everything was perfect including their attention to our two-year-old."* (D. Pankratz)

"Our host family was very hospitable. The breakfasts were delicious. The house and grounds are lovely and well-kept. We were within walking distance of canoe rentals and enjoyed canoeing on the Pocomoke River. They provided us with a pass to enjoy Assateague Island and the ocean beaches there. We look forward to a return visit." (J. Nieberding)

"We gathered our closest friends together for a wedding on their property and it was beautiful! They took care of so many details and made each of our guests feel at home. I cannot think of another inn at which such an event could be carried out with such ease." (J. Christodoulon)

"What makes the River House Inn so special, besides its lovely decor, large comfortable rooms, and quiet location, is the Knudsen's. They love people and running their inn. Their rare enthusiasm for life makes their inn a pearl indeed." (S. Jones)

Solomons Island

Davis House
PO Box 759
Solomons, MD 20688
(410-326-4811)
Innkeepers: Runa and Jack Howley

 Rating: B+
Rates: Single or Double/$65-125
Credit Cards: MC, V

Turn-of-the-century Victorian inn commands a frontal view of the harbor and is located 60 miles southeast of Washington, DC on Maryland's Western Shore. Seven guest rooms, five with private bath, have been restored and feature air conditioning and queen-size beds. Four offer a harbor view as does a loft suite occupying the third floor. Relax in the living room or library, both of which open to the verandah. Explore the surrounding grounds, enjoy the view, and go boating, fishing, hiking, golfing, or antiquing nearby. Calvert Cliffs and St. Mary's City are a short drive. Full breakfast offers such specialties as eggs Benedict, crab deviled eggs, or country hash. Restricted smoking.

Guests write: *"Breakfast was accompanied with classical music on lovely antique dishes and was delicious. Runa was willing to supply us with anything we particularly wanted. For example, we asked her if there was a convenient store nearby so that we could purchase club soda. While we were unpacking, she left in her car and arrived back with two bottles of club soda brought to our room on a tray."* (W. Hoag)

"We have been a guest at the Davis House for the past 8 years. During this time accommodations have been enhanced, including the "loft" and private bath without compromise to the historical factors of this home." (H&J Patchak)

"The Davis House is our favorite escape place in that it is comfortable but still creates a special atmosphere. Breakfast is spectacular! Runa and her personal touch make Davis House unique!" (L. Smith)

"I would recommend Davis House to anyone. It's everything a B&B should be." (E. Fitzsimmons)

Additional information on bed and breakfasts in Massachusetts can be obtained from the following B&B Reservation Agencies:
B&B Associates Bay Colony (800) 347-5088
Be Our Guest B&B (617) 837-9867
B&B Cape Cod (508) 775-2772
Golden Slumber Accommodations (800) 892-3231 (Outside MA)

Amherst

Allen House Victorian Inn
599 Main Street
Amherst, Ma 01002
(413) 253-5000
Innkeepers: Alan and Ann Zieminski

♛♛♛   Rating: A
Rates: Single/$45-85; Double/$55-95

Constructed in 1886 in the Victorian Queen Anne "stick style", this historic inn sits on three acres and is found in a small college town, 20 miles north of Springfield. Eastlake-style furnishings, "Aesthetic Movement" decor, period art, and art-wall coverings fill the five guest rooms, each of which has a private bath. Visit the five-college area, Historic Deerfield, and Old Sturbridge Village. Walk to nearby Emily Dickinson House, Amherst College, and the University of Massachusetts as well as fine galleries, museums, theaters, concerts, shops, and restaurants. Stuffed French toast, eggs Benedict, Swedish pancakes, and eggs Southwest are some of the special dishes offered at the full breakfast. Also offered are refreshments with afternoon and evening tea . Restricted smoking.

Guests write: "The Allen House is an oasis in the New England area. The hosts are warm, convivial people. I never knew that authentic Victorian furniture could be so comfortable. The hearty breakfasts and personal attention to my wife and I have made us come back frequently." (G. Garrow)

"It was a wintry day when I arrived for a weekend. My bones were stiff from the cold until I walked into the Allen House. My room was cozy with a down mattress and comforter. The bath was immaculate. The decorating of the room was in true "livable" Victorian style. My breakfast of oatmeal was laced with sweet maple syrup. It's just great!" (E.L. Roif)

"This was our first experience with B&B and it was just great. We were there for four days and found the owners very friendly and knowledgeable about their Victorian house and furniture. The breakfasts were excellent, particularly the Swedish pancakes. We had a very comfortable queen-size bed." (R. Schloerb)

"I have traveled around the world and have never encountered an inn, hotel, or motel equal to the Allen House in Amherst where we stayed during my recent visit to Amherst College for my 50th reunion. There is plenty of parking and the area is quiet. As the brochure indicates, it is extremely close to the cultural life of Amherst and the beauty of the surrounding countryside. These are overnight accommodations at their best." (S. Hess)

Attleboro

The Colonel Blackinton Inn
203 North Main Street
Attleboro, MA 02703
(508) 222-6022
Innkeepers: Allana Schaefer
and Ann Jenkins

♛♛ Rating: B
Rates: Single/$42-68; Double/$52-72
Business travel discount
Credit Cards: AE, MC, V

Colonial Blackinton Inn is a Greek Revival structure built in 1850 and located just south of I-95, exit 5. Sixteen guest rooms are available and eleven have a private bath. The rooms have a simple yet comfortable furnishings and pleasant decor. Two guest parlors are on the main floor with a fireplace, TV viewing area, and sunny porch. The turret offers a view of the river nearby. Recreation in the area includes golf, tennis, and fishing. Full breakfast is served in the two dining rooms on the main floor. This is also the setting for a formal tea in the afternoon that is open to the public. A remodeled carriage house on the grounds is available for social functions. Wheelchair access.

Guests write: *"In the past 3 or 4 years my job has me staying in hotels and inns four nights a week and I must say that this fine B&B is the best. The warmth and friendliness made me feel quite at home except more pampered. From the peach pancakes to the Victorian sitting room, this B&B rates a top shelf rating. The large common room with comfy couches and fireplace is right out of a magazine." (J. Walsh)*

Barre

The Jenkins House Bed & Breakfast Inn
RT. 122/ Barre Common
Barre, MA 01005
(508) 355-6444 or (800) 378-7373
Fax: (508) 355-6449
Innkeeper: David Ward and Joe Perrin

♛♛ Rating: B+
Rates: Single/$50-90;Double/$60-100
Senior and corporate discount
Credit Cards: MC, V

1834 Victorian is due north of Barre Common on scenic Route 122. Five guest
rooms offer a mix of antiques from several different periods and three of the
rooms have a private bath. Special features in the guest rooms include a
fireplace, semi-private balcony overlooking North Park on the Common, and
a queen-sized canopy bed surrounded by three walls of cafe windows. Relax in
front of one of the four fireplaces, sit on the wrap-around porch, rent a bicycle
to explore the area, or take a walk on the common. It's just a short drive to
Sturbridge Village and State Parks, Wachusett Mountain, Quabbin Reservoir,
and Cooks Canyon Audubon Society. Take in the view from the breakfast
room while enjoying a full breakfast which features oat scones, various
muffins, pancakes, or French toast. Enjoy the Tea Room and Coffeehouse
which provide an assortment of coffees and espresso drinks, sodas, juices, light
lunches, breads, pastries, and desserts. No smoking.

Guests write: *"David and Joe are considerate and caring hosts. Their facility is
always tidy and clean with a solid touch of Americana in its decor. They have a
variety of rooms including one with a four-poster and eleven windows! Our favorite
is the Winter Room, a large room well adorned and with a full bathroom attached. It
is truly our 'home away from home.' Caring and efficient innkeepers, attractive
surroundings, quietness and great food!"* (J.&D. Seeley)

*"We like to stay in the Terrace Room, with the small balcony looking out toward the
town common. The room is always cozy with big fluffy pillows and a warm
comforter on the bed. In the morning, the breakfast room is bright with the light from
its many windows. The room is set with small tables, and we usually chose one
where we could watch the goldfinches at the birdfeeder outside. After breakfast, I*

usually stop in the common room to work on a jigsaw puzzle (they seem to remember my affection for them and always have one set up for my arrival). In the early evening, we sit by the living room fireplace, and Dave seems to sense our mood to talk or to be left to ourselves. We've visited many B&B's, but this is our favorite, and we always look forward to our annual visit here." (G. Webb)

"I've stayed at Jenkins on three separate occasions and have found the accommodations very pleasant. Breakfasts are delightful, especially the baked items. Hosts are friendly but not obtrusive." (W. Hosley)

Boston — (Also see listings in Cambridge, Concord, Essex, Lynn, and Rockport)

Boston

Newbury Guest House
261 Newbury Street
Boston, MA 02116
(617) 437-7666
Innkeepers: Nubar and Mark Hagopian

♕♕♕ Rating: A-
Rates: Double/$85-125
Credit Cards: AE, MC, V

Nineteenth-century brick brownstone was completely renovated in 1991 and is located in the heart of the Back Bay area of Boston. Thirty-two guest rooms are located on three different floors of adjoining brownstone buildings with an elevator. Each offers a private bath, period furniture, accent rugs on hardwood floors, telephone, and individual heat and air conditioning. A new lobby on the main floor offers a comfortable area for watching TV. The inn is located in one of Boston's best known areas for specialty shops, restaurants, and art galleries. Walk to the Charles River nearby which offers jogging or biking trails. Many of Boston's famous landmarks are nearby including the Museum of Fine Arts, Museum of Science, Freedom Trail, Fenway Park, and Harvard University. Continental breakfast. Families welcome. Wheelchair access. Limited off-street parking available in the back of the building.

Cambridge

Cambridge House B&B
2218 Massachusetts Avenue
Cambridge, MA 02140
(617) 491-6300 or (800) 232-9989
Innkeeper: Ellen Femmino

♕♕♕   Rating: A
Rates: Single/$59-119; Double/$79-149
Credit Cards: AE, MC, V

Historic Colonial Revival home built in 1892 is located near Harvard Square
and only three minutes from the subway to downtown Boston. Choose from
seventeen guest rooms, nine with private bath. The inn has undergone
extensive renovation during 1993 and several new private baths have been
installed. One spacious room on the second floor offers a full private bath,
working fireplace, telephone, color TV, and elegant furnishings. There are two
parlors on the main floor. Both feature fireplaces, comfortable upholstered
furnishings, and rich drapery fabric. This location is near all major colleges
and hospitals and is easily accessible to Routes 2 and 93 or Mass-Turnpike. Full
breakfast and evening refreshments are served in the parlors. No smoking.

Chatham, Cape Cod

The Old Harbor Inn
22 Old Harbor Road
Chatham, MA 02633
(508) 945-4434 or (800) 942-4434
Innkeepers: Sharon and Tom Ferguson

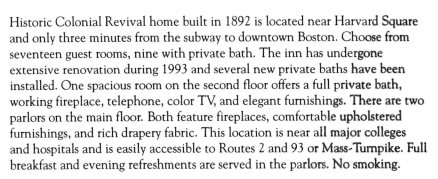

♕♕♕   Rating: A
Rates: Single/$85-145; Double/$95-155
Credit Cards: AE, MC, V

Classic Colonial Cape Cod-style inn built in the early 1930's is situated in a
residential area one block from the village center of Chatham which is located
on the elbow of Cape Cod. The inn was carefully restored in 1986 and offers
six guest rooms. Each has individual English country decor accented with
designer linens and antique and wicker furnishings. Choose from king, queen

or twin beds. A fireplaced living room offers a quiet spot to read, relax, play the baby grand piano, or converse. Walk to the nearby beaches, gift and antiques shops, art galleries, outdoor concerts, museums, wildlife sanctuary, restaurants, golf, tennis, and boating. Continental buffet breakfast includes home-baked muffins and scones, fresh fruit, yogurt and granola, juices, gourmet coffee and tea and is served in the sun room or on the outside deck overlooking flower gardens.

Guests write: *"Charming and flawless, as always!" (L. Palmer)*

Concord

Hawthorne Inn
462 Lexington Road
Concord, MA 01742
(508) 369-5610
Innkeepers: Marilyn Munro
and Gregory Burch

♛♛   Rating: B+
Rates: Single/$75-110; Double/$110-150.

Ralph Waldo Emerson, the Alcotts, and Nathaniel Hawthorne once owned the land on which this 1870 Colonial is situated. Choose from seven guest rooms, each with private bath and individual decor. Each room features a selection of antique furnishings, handmade quilts, and wood floors graced with Oriental and rag rugs. Popular attractions in this area steeped in history include Wayside, Walden Pond, Great Meadows Wildlife Sanctuary. Many guests have enjoyed canoeing and quiet picnics in the area. Continental breakfast. Families welcome. No smoking.

Guests write: *"We particularly appreciated the attention to guest "TLC" by daily change of all towels and linens, and room tidiness, assisting us with our daily outings and travel plans and general good 'make us feel at home' hospitality. The breakfast breads, juices, cereal and fruits were delightful! It made our first trip to Boston a wonderful one." (M&J Hakanson)*

"I'm happy to report that the law of diminishing returns has spared Marilyn and Gregory Burch's charming Hawthorne Inn. I returned recently and the place (and therefore I) was undiminished. The nurturing and enriching ambiance of the inn with its books, art, distinctive beds, masterful quilts, location, location, location, and appetizing aromas nudges me into planning yet another stay." (D. Dasch)

Dennis, Cape Cod

Isaiah Hall B&B Inn
152 Whig Street
Dennis, MA 02638
(508) 385-9928 or (800) 736-0160
Fax: (508) 385-5879
Innkeeper: Marie Brophy

♛♛♛ Rating: A
Rates: Single/$52-92; Double/$57-102
Credit Cards: AE, MC, V

Greek Revival farmhouse built in 1857 and located on a quiet side street 10 miles north of Hyannis on a quiet historic side street. There are eleven guest rooms in the main inn or the adjacent restored barn. Ten offer a private bath. Each room features fine antiques, Oriental rugs, and handmade quilts. There are several common rooms offering private areas for reading, playing board games, or conversing with other guests although the gardens that surround the inn are perfectly suited for these activities as well. Within walking distance can be found the beach, Museum of Fine Arts, Playhouse, and cinema. Bicycle trails and golf courses are nearby. Continental plus breakfast. Limited wheelchair access. Restricted smoking. Open April 2 through October 17.

Guests write: *"Marie Brophy is the most delightful and personable innkeeper we have encountered in our travels. She makes Isaiah Hall the friendly, unpretentious, and comfortable home to travelers that it is." (J. Meuse)*

"Our first visit to Cape Cod was much enhanced by our stay at the Isaiah Hall B&B Inn. The hospitality was excellent, the comfort and decor in our rooms and the house in general reflected the true New England style we had hoped to find." (M. Kunle)

Breakfasts are always fun at the Isaiah Hall Inn - good food, especially the cranberry muffins, and good conversation with Marie and the other guests. Marie's good spirits and enthusiasm are very much what makes the inn a special place to stay. The inn is lovely with common rooms that are warm and inviting. The guest rooms are spacious and always immaculate. Our favorite room is #10, overlooking the flower gardens in the back of the house." (L. Garavalia)

"We have never experienced anything but clean rooms with everything in working order. Every room we have stayed in has had good lighting for reading at night and windows to open to savor the Cape breezes. We have stayed in both the main house and the attached renovated barn. We've had a hard time deciding which we enjoy the most, but have over time found we like the barn. Furnishings are country casual with

a mix of antiques. The innkeepers are there when you need them but don't force themselves upon you." (T. Stapleton)

"The historic house is homey, beautiful and furnished with authentic antiques. However, the one thing that makes Isaiah Hall Inn different from any other inn we have visited and brings us back year after year is the warm hospitality of the host and hostess. They make their guests feel at home. The comforts, cleanliness, and amenities we pay for but this sincere interest and caring is priceless." (A. Coveney)

Dennisport, Cape Cod

Rose Petal B&B
152 Sea Street
P.O. Box 974
Dennisport, MA 02639
(508) 398-8470
Innkeepers: Dan and Gayle Kelly

 Rating: A-
Rates: Double/$45-84

Quaint New England-style farmhouse built in 1872 is located 7 miles east of Hyannis on Cape Cod. There are four second-floor guest rooms with shared baths. A parlor on the main floor offers a piano, selection of reading material, and comfortable area for watching TV. Warm-water beaches of Nantucket Sound are nearby as are several antique shops, theaters, museums, and restaurants. Recreation available in the area includes golf, fishing, boating, and bicycle trails. The ferries to Nantucket and Martha's Vineyard are a short drive away. Full breakfast includes home-baked goods. Families welcome. Restricted smoking.

Guests write: *"This home is lovely. We found the accommodations tastefully decorated, meticulously clean, and very comfortable. Breakfast was always a treat. A hearty breakfast that gave us a great start to the day." (D. Ewing)*

"Genuine friendliness but non-intrusive - a tough balance to strike and done with graciousness and topped with some of the most delicate buttery pastry we've ever had." (K. McLeod)

"Perfect. Every detail was appreciated. Breakfast was tasty and the right way to start our day. The map and guides Gayle gave us were extremely useful. We also like having the bathrobes and fan. Everything was very comfortable and homey." (B. Polk)

(Continued)

"We were made to feel at home almost immediately. Nothing was missing: comfortable bed, nice bath, conveniences. Breakfast was a welcome day's beginning; — ample and tastefully done." (J. Bulkley)

"They were extremely helpful in pointing us in the right direction and making suggestions. Always a smile and friendly conversations each morning. The accommodations were very charming and like Old New England. The rooms and bathrooms were immaculate. Breakfast was delicious. They really won my husband over with the Eggs Benedict. He is sure to return just for that." (L. Grimm)

East Orleans, Cape Cod

Ship's Knees Inn
186 Beach Road, P.O. Box 756
East Orleans, MA 02643
(508) 255-1312
Innkeeper: Donna Anderson

♛♛ Rating: B+
Rates: Double/$45-100

160-year-old sea captain's home has been restored and is located a short walk from Cape Cod's Nauset Beach. Twenty-two guest rooms are available, eight with private bath. All rooms offer a selection of antique furnishings and several have ocean views, beamed ceilings, quilts, and old four-poster beds. Two housekeeping cottages on the water are available for weekly rentals and off-season on a daily basis. The landscaped grounds feature a tennis court and swimming pool with golf and horseback riding available nearby. Continental breakfast offers muffins, baked breads, and jams. Open year round.

East Sandwich, Cape Cod

Wingscorton Farm Inn
11 Wing Boulevard
East Sandwich, MA 02537
(508) 888-0534
Innkeeper: Dick Loring

♛♛ Rating: B-
Rates: Single/$95; Double/$115-150
Credit Cards: AE, MC, V

Colonial landmark built in 1758 is situated on seven landscaped acres off Route 6A on Cape Cod. Seven guest rooms each offer a private bath, working fireplace, and restored antique furnishings. An historic carriage house on the property features completely modern decor and amenities with fireplace, full kitchen, private sun deck, and brick patio. There is a private ocean beach within a short walk and other area attractions include golf, whale watching, antique shops, and outdoor recreation. Full breakfast includes eggs, breakfast meats, and vegetables from the inn's own livestock and gardens. Families welcome.

Eastham, Cape Cod

Over Look Inn
3085 County Road
P.O. Box 771
Eastham, MA 02642
1-800-356-1121 or (508) 255-1886
Fax: (508) 240-0345
Innkeepers: Ian and Nan Aitchison

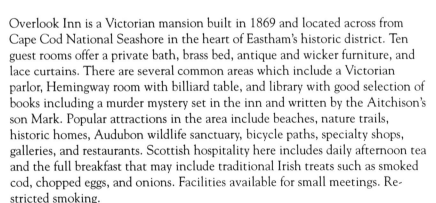

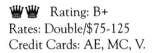 Rating: B+
Rates: Double/$75-125
Credit Cards: AE, MC, V.

Overlook Inn is a Victorian mansion built in 1869 and located across from Cape Cod National Seashore in the heart of Eastham's historic district. Ten guest rooms offer a private bath, brass bed, antique and wicker furniture, and lace curtains. There are several common areas which include a Victorian parlor, Hemingway room with billiard table, and library with good selection of books including a murder mystery set in the inn and written by the Aitchison's son Mark. Popular attractions in the area include beaches, nature trails, historic homes, Audubon wildlife sanctuary, bicycle paths, specialty shops, galleries, and restaurants. Scottish hospitality here includes daily afternoon tea and the full breakfast that may include traditional Irish treats such as smoked cod, chopped eggs, and onions. Facilities available for small meetings. Restricted smoking.

Eastham, Cape Cod

The Whalewalk Inn
220 Bridge Road
Eastham, MA 02642-3374
(508) 255-0617; Fax:(508) 240-0017
Innkeepers: Carolyn and Dick Smith

♛♛♛ Rating: A
Rates: Double/$75-165.

Originally an 1830s whale master's home, this restored, "outer cape" area inn is 90 miles from either Boston or Providence. Choose from twelve guest rooms with private bath that are housed in the main inn, or suites found in the restored barn, the Salt Box, and the guest house. Each room has been decorated in pastel colors with a mix of antiques, painted furniture, and brass and wooden beds. Accessories include comforters, extra pillows, decorator bed skirts, and fresh flowers. Visit with other guests in the living room with fireplace and antiques, relax on the patio surrounded by the garden, or explore the nearby forty miles of sandy beaches and nature trails. Attractions nearby include Cape Cod National Seashore, Audubon Wildlife Sanctuary, fishing, sailing, antiquing, whale watching, and golfing. Grand Marnier French toast, cranberry/blueberry pancakes, or apple raisin crepes are some of the specialties offered for a full breakfast. Hors d'oeuvres are served each evening. No smoking.

Edgartown (see Martha's Vineyard)

Essex

George Fuller House
148 Main Street
Essex, MA 01929
(508) 768-7766
Innkeepers: Cindy and Bob Cameron

♛♛♛ Rating: A
Rates: Double/$75-115
Credit Cards: AE, MC, V

George Fuller House was built in 1830 and is located 30 miles north of Boston on Cape Ann. There are seven guest rooms and each offers a private bath, television, telephone, country decor, antique furnishings, braided rugs, comfortable rockers, and a brass or canopy bed. Three rooms have working fireplaces. The inn's original architectural features have been retained and include folding Indian shutters, fireplaces, Colonial paneling and woodwork. There are over fifty antique shops to visit in Essex as well as the Shipbuilding Museum. The inn offers a mid-week sailing package on board a thirty-foot cruising sailboat. Full breakfast may include Grand Marnier French toast or Belgian waffles.

Guests write: *"My husband and I have stayed at many B&Bs all over New England and in the Midwest. The George Fuller House is our favorite! It's a wonderful location overlooking the salt marshes and within walking distance of great restaurants and antique shops. The decor is warm, relaxing, and very tasteful"* (N. McRay)

"The owners have lovingly restored an old New England house with Oriental rugs, beautiful art work, colonial antiques, rooms with four-poster beds, fireplaces, and their warmth pervades the whole thing. Cindy is a par-excellence cook and our breakfast was served on Lenox china." (L. McKinley)

"The hospitality was extraordinary and the accommodations superb! The availability of the telephone, TV, and individual control of heating and air conditioning in our room was very much to our liking." (M. Cominsky)

"Cindy and Bob were friendly and helpful hosts. The room had everything - private bath, a phone, a fireplace, TV. We had the best breakfast ever. The food was 4-star. We had pears in cream, Belgian waffles with yogurt and orange sauce, apple strudel, coffee, juice, and seconds on anything we wanted. After this I'm afraid other B&Bs might be a let down!" (J. Saggerer)

"The Andrew Suite we relished is The Best. From the canopy bed to the blazing fireplace, we couldn't have dreamt of a nicer inn. The breakfast is without equal in our experience. If George Fuller was awarded only three crowns, what does a four or five crown inn have that they don't? I would like to visit one of them because I think it would be hard to beat our favorite."
(J. Donaher)

"I travel 50% of the time throughout the Eastern U.S. As a business traveler I try to stay in B&Bs whenever I can. The George Fuller House has provided the best stay I have had anywhere. What really makes a noticeable difference at places to stay are the innkeepers. All three mornings I had to leave by 6:30 a.m. for meetings. Each morning I woke to a full gourmet breakfast at 6:00 a.m.!" (Rosenwinkel)

Falmouth, Cape Cod

Hewins House Bed & Breakfast
Care of: B&B Cape Cod
P.O. Box 341
West Hyannisport, MA 02672-0341
(508) 775-2772; Fax: (508) 775-2884
Innkeeper: Virginia Price

♛ Rating: C
Rates: Double/$90
Credit Cards: AE, MC, V

Suggesting southern architecture, this Inn, built in 1822, faces Falmouth's
Village Green with a lovely view of the Congregational church. It is on Cape
Cod about 15 miles South of the Bourne Bridge on Route 28 in the historic
district of Falmouth. A garden containing an antique cast iron bird bath and a
small water garden with gold fish surrounds the house. Choose from three
guest rooms, two with private baths. These rooms are decorated in a country
style and two offer four-poster canopy beds. All rooms have telephone and
clock radio. A Steinway grand piano may be played in the living room and
guests will enjoy breakfast in the dining room. An upstairs kitchen with sink,
stove, dishwasher, and refrigerator can be used by guests. This room furnishes a
table and chairs. Within walking distance is Bonanza Bus Depot, shuttle bus to
Ferry dock, Highfield Theater, walking trails, Falmouth Sports Center (with
full gym, racquetball, and tennis), downtown shopping, restaurants, Falmouth
Historical Society Museum, Shining Sea Bike Path, and beach. Area attractions: Cape Cod, fishing, beaches, boating, golf, wind surfing, bicycling,
Martha's Vineyard, Nantucket ferries, Falmouth Historical Society Museum,
shopping, restaurants, Plymouth, Massachusetts, Plymouth Plantation,
Mayflower II, Sandwich, Heritage Plantation, Sandwich Glass Museum, JFK
Museum, Woods Hole-ferries to islands. A full breakfast includes coffee, tea,
juice, muffins, toast, or breads, a hot entree; such as, bacon and eggs, pancakes
and sausage, or waffles, and fresh fruit. A specialty in August is waffles with
fresh blackberries and homemade blackberry syrup topped with whipped
cream. No Smoking. Families welcome.

Guests write: *"Everything about our stay was wonderful. The hostess, the
hospitality, and the room were a joy. I would highly recommend this B&B to anyone
who planned on visiting this area. (D. & D. Deily)*

Falmouth, Cape Cod

Peacock's "Inn on the Sound"
313 Grand Ave., PO Box 201
Falmouth, MA 02541
Innkeepers: Bud and Phyllis Peacock
(508) 457-9666

♛♛ Rating: B
Rates: Single/$50-85; Double/$65-125
Credit Cards: AE, MC, V

1880s Victorian with multiple additions is situated across the street from the ocean in a quiet residential area of Falmouth which is located 75 miles south of Boston and 85 miles east of Providence. Ten newly renovated guest rooms each offer a private bath and are decorated in a country style. Most offer ocean views. Relax on the front porch or beside the large stone fireplace in the common room with its view of the ocean. Read a book in the library or sip hot cider during the cooler months. Attractions in the area include miles of beaches, whale watching, local historic sites, museums, and live band concerts and theater. Full breakfast specialties include banana-stuffed French toast with blueberry compote, raspberry poached pears, or Belgium waffles with fruit. No smoking.

Guests write: *"The bed was very comfortable, view outstanding, and warm hospitality. Also, heavenly gourmet breakfasts." (H. Cook)*

"The Peacocks know their community extremely well and know instantly what to recommend for activities, entertaining, or dining." (K. Coll)

"They made our honeymoon extra special! The hospitality was out of this world! The rooms are homey and beautiful. I can't forget to mention the breakfasts were outstanding!" (C. Underwood)

"Bud gave us a computerized map of what roads to take, the amount of time on each stretch of highway, and our time of arrival. This was a very kind gesture. We're planning on going to the Peacock Inn for our 3rd straight year." (K. Cashatt)

Falmouth, Cape Cod

Village Green Inn
40 West Main Street
Falmouth, MA 02540
(508) 548-5621
Innkeepers: Linda and Don Long

♛♛♛ Rating: A
Rates: Single/$70-110; Double/$80-120

The Village Green Inn is a combination Victorian/Colonial structure built in
1804 and located on the village green, 15 miles south of Cape Cod Canal.
Four guest rooms and one suite each offer a private bath and working fireplace.
The parlor offers a setting where guests relax and converse during tea-time.
Popular area attractions include beaches, museums, plantations, and Woods
Hole Oceanographic Institute and Aquarium. Walk to village specialty shops
and a variety of restaurants. Borrow the inn's bicycles for exploring the
Shining Sea bike path. Full breakfast includes homemade specialties such as
blueberry-almond bread or nutmeg muffins. Seasonal beverages and home-
made treats are offered. No smoking.

Guests write: *"We've been guests in each room and are always charmed by the*
Victorian style decor, the immaculate conditions and thoughtful amenities there for
our enjoyment. Our comfort and the comfort of all guests is their primary concern
with strict attention paid to all detail in the rooms and bathrooms as well. Fresh,
flowers, books to read, iced tea and cookies in summer, hot mulled cider in fall and
winter and sherry available in the living room for afternoon. The delicious aroma of
Linda's baking fills the house. The front porch is an ideal comfortable place to sit with
that second cup of coffee and the newspaper." (I. Gould)

"The Longs are outstanding hosts (they even remember what we've had for breakfast
in past visits, so they never duplicate the menu). The location is the best in
Falmouth; the suite is great, and the breakfasts are incredible! We're back several
times a year—not often enough." (J&R Kilianski)

"Each room has a theme which is tied together in the entire home. There is no
question that breakfast is always prepared with fresh foods, fresh coffee beans, and

homemade breakfast pastries. Breakfast often lasts for over an hour and thirty minutes, as we enjoy the food, the ambiance, including soft music, and the gracious company of everyone." (P. Langton)

"The Pineapple Room we stay in is like a Victorian dream right out of 'Better Homes & Gardens,' beautiful, yet completely comfortable with all the little touches that Don and Linda do for their guests (such as foil wrapped candies, flowers, candles, etc.). It has a beautiful fireplace that invites a romantic interlude for people of all ages." (D&M Mageau)

"We have stayed at others where the owners were very cold and not very polite. You can tell from the very first moment Don and Linda love and enjoy what they are doing." (M&D Munson)

Harwichport, Cape Cod

Dunscroft By-The-Sea Inn & Cottage
24 Pilgrim Road
Harwichport, MA 02646
(800) 432-4345 or (508) 432-0810
Innkeepers: Alyce and Wally Cunningham

♛/♛ Rating: B
Rates: Single/$75-165; Double/$85-165
Credit Cards: AE, MC, V

Gambrel roofed Colonial inn was built in 1920 and is located on Cape Cod's South Shore. Nine guest rooms with private bath are available. Each has a romantic decor with unusual quality linens. A fireplaced living room is a popular gathering spot for guests and there is an extensive library with an interesting selection of books. Walk to the nearby mile-long private beach. Popular attractions in the area include Plymouth Rock, Plymouth Plantation, National Seashore, Kennedy Memorial, sand dunes, nature trails, fishing, and sailing. Full breakfast includes fresh-ground coffee and homemade breads. Facilities for small meetings available. Restricted smoking.

Hyannis, Cape Cod

Sea Breeze Inn by the Beach
397 Sea Street
Hyannis, MA 02601
(508) 771-7213, or 771-2549
Innkeeper: Patricia G. Battle

W W Rating: B
Rates: Double/$45-95
Credit Cards: AE, MC, V

Historic Victorian inn is in a secluded setting a short walk from the Sea Street
Beach. Fourteen guest rooms each offer a private bath, TV, radio, canopy beds,
and air conditioning. Several feature ocean views. Popular area attractions
include the Kennedy family Compound, summer theater, nightclubs, whale
watching, boating, golfing, and shopping at local galleries and specialty shops.
The dock for ferry boats to Nantucket and Martha's Vineyard is nearby.
Expanded continental breakfast includes fresh fruits, cereals, muffins and
bagels.

Hyannisport/Centerville

Copper Beech Inn
Care of: B&B Cape Cod
P.O. Box 341
West Hyannisport, MA 02672-0341
(508) 775-2772; Fax: (508) 775-2884
Innkeepers: Joyce and Clark Diehl

W W W Rating: A
Rates: Double/$80-$90
Credit Cards: AE, MC, & V

Cape-Cod style home built before 1830 by an intercostal sea captain, is
located in the heart of the historic district amid private estates and antique
homes. It is located 80 miles south of Boston in the Mid-Cape section, 3 miles
from Hyannis where the ferry to Nantucket or Martha's Vineyard is
located.Manicured grounds, lawns and gardens create a picturesque setting for
this bed and breakfast. Three air-conditioned guest rooms with private baths
are available. Each room is decorated in traditional decor. Visit the parlor for
relaxation, reading, and conversation. Sunning areas outside offer another
pleasant change after a day at the beach. Area attractions: Craigville

Beach, 3/4 mile from Inn, warm water swimming, deep sea fishing, whale watch boats and discount shopping within a few miles, museums, golf, tennis, fishing, sailing, ferry to Nantucket or Martha's Vineyard, Cape Cod Melody Tent in Hyannis, restored homes that date from the seventeenth century. Full breakfast, served with china and silver, includes special egg dishes, griddle cakes, French toast, eggs benedict, bacon, fresh fruit, coffee and tea. Restricted smoking.

Lenox

Blantyre
16 Blantyre Road, P.O. Box 995
Lenox, MA 01240
(413) 637-3556 (May 1- Nov. 1st)
(413) 298-3806 (Nov. 1 - Apr. 30)
Fax: (413) 637-4282
Innkeeper: Roderick Anderson

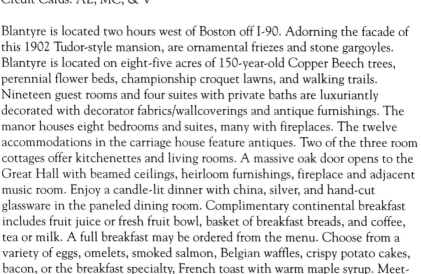

♛♛♛♛   Rating: AA-
Rates: Double/$160-575
Credit Cards: AE, MC, & V

Blantyre is located two hours west of Boston off I-90. Adorning the facade of this 1902 Tudor-style mansion, are ornamental friezes and stone gargoyles. Blantyre is located on eight-five acres of 150-year-old Copper Beech trees, perennial flower beds, championship croquet lawns, and walking trails. Nineteen guest rooms and four suites with private baths are luxuriantly decorated with decorator fabrics/wallcoverings and antique furnishings. The manor houses eight bedrooms and suites, many with fireplaces. The twelve accommodations in the carriage house feature antiques. Two of the three room cottages offer kitchenettes and living rooms. A massive oak door opens to the Great Hall with beamed ceilings, heirloom furnishings, fireplace and adjacent music room. Enjoy a candle-lit dinner with china, silver, and hand-cut glassware in the paneled dining room. Complimentary continental breakfast includes fruit juice or fresh fruit bowl, basket of breakfast breads, and coffee, tea or milk. A full breakfast may be ordered from the menu. Choose from a variety of eggs, omelets, smoked salmon, Belgian waffles, crispy potato cakes, bacon, or the breakfast specialty, French toast with warm maple syrup. Meeting and wedding facilities.

Guests write: *"The first image of Blantyre as one enters the driveway and follows the beautifully manicured tree-lined grounds up to the mansion is breathtaking. The guest rooms in the main house are the best ones and it's definitely worth paying the extra to experience these rooms. The dinner presentation did not disappoint us. Our soup was roast chicken consume with leeks and truffles. This was followed by smoked trout in a horseradish sauce and potato pancake with marinated greens. Entrees were grilled snapper or beef tenderloin. It was a dining experience to please the most discriminating guest." (S&D Sidney)*

"The inn has beautiful period decor and is always maintained in a very clean and professional manner. All personnel are warm, friendly, and very helpful. You feel like you're staying at your own weekend retreat!" (C&F Gervais)

Lynn/Boston's North Shore

Diamond District Bed & Breakfast
142 Ocean Street
Lynn, MA 09102
(617) 599-4470 or (800) 666-3076
Fax: (617) 599-4470
Innkeepers: Sandra & Jerry Caron

♛♛♛ Rating: A-
Rates: Single or Double/$70-95
Credit Cards: AE, MC, & V

Diamond District Bed and Breakfast is 7.5 miles north of Boston's Logan International Airport (22 minutes), 8 miles north of Boston. This turn-of-the-century Georgian-style clapboard mansion with mansard roof sits on a half acre of yard and gardens just 300 feet from the Atlantic Ocean. Choose from eight guest rooms, (four with private bath), and each featuring antique furnishings, down comforter, quilt, color television, and telephone. Relax in the large living room with mahogany woodwork, marble fireplace, French doors, and view of verandah, grounds, and ocean. Within walking distance is the beach, Lynn Historical Society and Museum, Lynn Heritage State Park and Museum, Mary Baker Eddy home, Elihu Thompson house, Grand Army of the Republic meeting hall and museum. Area attractions: Witch Museum, House of Seven Gables, historic districts and attractions in Boston, Newburyport, Rockport, Salem, Marblehead, Gloucester and Cambridge. A full breakfast on antique English china and crystal is served in the spacious dining room with fireplace. Entrees may include French toast, lobster quiche, or sour dough pancakes accompanied by fruit, home baked breads, muffins, or pastries and fresh brewed coffee or tea. Guests can help themselves to tea, hot chocolate and cookies from the butler's pantry. Meeting facilities. Restricted smoking. (Continued)

Guests write: *"The house is grand in every respect and very tastefully decorated. Our innkeepers were warm, gracious, friendly, and understanding what the word 'hospitality' really means. She serves a full gourmet breakfast which is ample, varied, and interesting."* (M. Powell)

"They have the perfect sea-viewing porch in warm weather, a crackling fire in the dining room fireplace for cold weather, antique furnishings, Oriental rugs, privacy, and most pleasant, hospitable hosts. It's living with a grace of Victorians, but with 20th century understanding." (S&R Gunn)

"This home is furnished invitingly and from the porch is a lovely view of the ocean. We were encouraged to make ourselves at home which was easily done. Breakfast was served at a large dining table and a friendly fire was crackling in the fireplace. When we unexpectedly returned to stay another night because of weather delays, we were again welcomed and treated to their warm hospitality." (M&J Rodrick)

"We had a queen-size canopy bed with goose down warm comforters which made us feel like we were sleeping on a fluffy cloud." (A. Barry)

Martha's Vineyard, Edgartown

Daggett House
PO Box 1333, 59 North Water Street
Edgartown, MA 02539
(508) 627-4600 or (800) 946-3400
Fax: (508) 627-4611
Innkeepers: John & James Chirqwin/ Celeste Jones

♛♛ Rating: B+
Rates: Single or Double/$75-175

Located on historic Edgartown Harbor on Martha's Vineyard with gardens that extend to the water's edge, this Shingled Colonial inn constructed in 1660 has been in operation for over 240 years. It is one and one half hours south of Boston off the coast of Cape Cod. Choose from twenty-six guest rooms, all with private baths, and Early American decor. Discover the secret walkway, walk along the harbor front lawn, or relax in front of the antique paneled fireplace found in the old breakfast room. Walk to the Vineyard Museum, Fishing Charters, historic whaling seaport, and many shops. Area attractions: Gay Head Cliffs, Chicama Winery, Flying Horses Carousel, beaches, "gingerbread" houses, wildlife sanctuaries, and water activities. Full breakfast features daily specials. Dinner available. Meeting and wedding facilities. Families welcome.

Martha's Vineyard/Edgartown

The Governor Bradford Inn of Edgartown
128 Main Street
Edgartown, MA 02539-0239
(508) 627-9510
Innkeepers: Brenda and Ray Raffurty

♛♛♛ Rating: A
Rates: Single or Double/$60-210
Credit Cards: AE, MC, V

Restored Gothic Revival inn is located on the main road into Edgartown near
the village center. The sixteen guest rooms all have a private bath, ceiling fan,
and king sized brass or four-poster beds. Relax with other guests in the comfortable wicker room with bar, curl up with a book in the library in front of the
fireplace, or share a complimentary sherry at the day's end with other guests in
the parlor. There's a large meeting room on the lower level with TV and
movies. Enjoy historic Edgartown's attractions including sunning, swimming,
fishing, and sight seeing. Shops, galleries, restaurants, and beaches are all
nearby. Full breakfast specialties include Belgium waffles, omelets, pancakes,
or frittatas. Wedding and meeting facilities available. Wheelchair access.
Restricted smoking.

Martha's Vineyard, Oak Bluffs

Dockside Inn
Box 1206, Circuit Ave. Extension
Oak Bluffs, MA 02557
(508) 693-2966 or (800) 245-5979
Fax: (508) 696-7293
Innkeeper: Susan Convery

♛♛♛ Rating: A-
Rates: Double/$75-220
Credit Cards: AE, MC V

Two-story inn with colorful paint and flower baskets on the porch is across
from the ferry dock in Oak Bluffs and an easy walk to the village center.
Choose from twenty guest rooms. Each offers a private bath, queen-size bed,
color cable TV, and air conditioning. Several rooms offer water views. There is
a small yard with a grill for guest's use. Walk to village specialty shops,
restaurants and the beach. The inn's lobby is where a continental breakfast

buffet is served each morning. Families welcome. Restricted smoking.

Martha's Vineyard, Oak Bluffs

Oak House
Seaview Avenue, P.O. Box 299-BB
Oak Bluffs, MA 02557
(508) 693-4187 or Fax: (508) 696-7385
Innkeeper: Betsi Convery-Luce

♕♕♕ Rating: A-
Rates: Double/$125-220
Credit Cards: AE, MC, V

Quintessential Victorian Cape Cod inn across the street from the beach offers
ten guest rooms or suites, each featuring private bath and Victorian furnishings. Most rooms also have private balconies and water views. This Victorian
seaside resort includes miles of bicycle paths and beaches. Walk to Oak Bluffs
landing and the village from the inn. Continental breakfast includes fresh
baked breads. Afternoon tea is also provided. Facilities available for small
meetings and social functions. Open mid-May through mid-October.

Martha's Vineyard, Vineyard Haven

The Hanover House
P.O. Box 2107
10 Edgartown Road
Vineyard Haven, MA 02568
(508) 693-1066
Innkeepers: Ronald and Kay Nelson

♕♕♕ Rating: A-
Rates: Double/$50-158
Credit Cards: AE, MC, V

Walk to the ferry from this renovated inn built in 1930. Twelve guest rooms
each offer a private bath, cable TV, and individually controlled air conditioning and heating. Many rooms open onto large sun decks. Three housekeeping
units with full kitchens are available in a separate carriage house. The village
of Vineyard Haven offers quaint shops and restaurants. Shuttle buses are
convenient to take guests to Oak Bluffs and Edgartown. Nearby beaches
provide swimming, sailing, fishing, and windsurfing. Fresh baked muffins
round out a hearty continental breakfast served on an enclosed sun porch.
Families welcome.

Nantucket Island

Corner House
49 Centre Street
Nantucket, MA 02554
(508) 228-1530
Innkeepers: Sandy and John Knox-Johnson

👑👑   Rating: B
Rates: Double/$ 55-160

1790s Historic Nautical Colonial home is lined by a brick paved terrace and flower borders. Each guest rooms offers a private bath, down comforter, and canopy bed. Some rooms have a refrigerator and television. Relax on the screened-in porch overlooking the garden terrace or sit in front of the fire by hearth. Walk to Nantucket's Historic district, ferries, shops, restaurants, theaters, museums, beaches, and tennis. Continental breakfast includes home baked specialties. An afternoon tea is served daily. Small wedding facilities. Families welcome.

Nantucket Island

Eighteen Gardner Street Inn
18 Gardner Street
Nantucket, MA 02554
(508) 228-1155 or (800) 435-1450

👑👑   Rating: B+
Rates: Single or Double/$95-185
Credit Cards: AE, MC, V

Restored Colonial Nantucket inn built in 1835 is in the historic residential district; 90 miles south of Boston on the island of Nantucket. The seventeen guest rooms, fifteen with private baths, have been decorated with antiques and period reproductions, including canopied or four-poster beds. Some have working fireplaces; all are air conditioned and offer cable television. All are air conditioned. Relax by the fireplace in the main parlor or sip champagne outside in the garden. The guest pantry is stocked with beach towels, coolers, and picnic baskets. Borrow one of the inn's bikes for an easy ride to one of the many beaches. Go golfing, sailing, or fishing, play tennis, or explore the nearby shops and museums. A full "Nantucket" breakfast is offered in the dining room. Wedding and meeting facilities available. Families welcome. No smoking.

Nantucket Island

The Four Chimneys
38 Orange Street
Nantucket, MA 02554
(508) 228-1912
Innkeeper: Bernadette Mannix

👑👑👑 Rating: A
Rate: Double/$150-250

Greek Revival sea captain's home built in 1835 is a short walk from
cobblestoned Main Street. Choose from ten guest rooms with private baths
that have been authentically restored and furnished with period antiques,
Oriental rugs, and canopy beds. A suite on the third floor features pine and
country furnishings and a harbor view. Many of the area attractions are a short
walk away including shops, art galleries, golf, windsurfing, fishing, tennis, fine
restaurants, and beaches. Continental breakfast can be served in guest rooms
or on the porch furnished in white wicker. A large double parlor with twin
fireplaces easily accommodates weddings.

Nantucket Island

Ten Lyon Street Inn
10 Lyon Street
Nantucket, MA 02554
(508) 228-5040
Innkeeper: Anne Marie Foster

👑👑👑 Rating: A
Rates: Double/$65-150
Credit Cards: MC, V

Colonial inn built in 1849 has been completely renovated and is located in
the center of town on a quiet side street near the harbor. Choose from seven
guest rooms with double or queen-size beds and private bath. Each room offers
antique furnishings, linens, down comforters and pillows, and interesting
prints. Walk to historic sites, beaches, water sports such as sailing and
windsurfing, fine restaurants, or rent bicycles to tour the island. Continental
breakfast.

Oak Bluffs (See Martha's Vineyard)

Rockport

Ralph Waldo Emerson Inn
1 Cathedral Ave P.O. Box 2369
Rockport, MA 01966
(508) 546-6321 or Fax: (508) 546-7043
Innkeeper: Gary Wemyss

 Rating: B
Rates: Single/$57-124; Double/$86-137
Credit Cards: MC, V

Imposing Greek Revival inn overlooking the rocky coastline was built in 1840 and is located 40 miles northeast of Boston. The inn has been renovated several times and now blends modern amenities with the atmosphere of an earlier era. Choose from thirty-six guest rooms with telephone, private bath, and a choice of single, twin, or double bed. Relax on the old-fashioned verandah with ocean view or several common areas inside the inn. Nearby attractions include Hammond Castle, Rocky Neck, and Halibut State Park. Stroll along the shady streets, visit art galleries and shops, go boating, fishing, sightseeing, or whale watching. A full breakfast features such specialties as strawberry pancakes and a variety of omelets. Wedding and small meeting facilities available. Families welcome. Wheelchair access. Tour and business meeting discount.

Rockport

Yankee Clipper Inn
96 Granite Street
Rockport, MA 01966
(508) 546-3407 or 546-3408
Innkeepers: Bob and Barbara Ellis

👑👑👑 Rating: A
Rates: Single/$60-175; Double/$98-208
Credit Cards: AE, MC, V

Impressive oceanfront Victorian mansion is located 45 minutes north of

Boston near the northeast end of Route 128. There are twenty-six guest rooms in the mansion or two smaller inns on adjacent properties. Each room differs in size, decor, and amenities but special features found in some rooms include ocean views, canopy beds, glass-enclosed porches, and 19th-Century furnishings. The landscaped grounds invite exploration and feature a heated salt-water swimming pool and paths that end at the rocky water's edge. Two of the three buildings offers a parlor with television lounge. The mansion's living room features floor to ceiling bookcases, fireplace, and original wall murals. Full breakfast. Candlelight dinner available at the restaurant. The lower level offers an attractive function room with large windows. Families welcome. Restricted smoking.

Guests write: *"We had one of the most romantic vacations ever! The grounds and food of the inn were excellent."* (L. Burke)

Sandwich, Cape Cod

Bay Beach B&B
1-3 Bay Beach Lane
Sandwich, MA 02563
(508) 888-8813
Innkeepers: Emily and Reale Lemieux

🐾🐾🐾🐾 Rating: AA
Rates: Double/$125-195

New oceanfront contemporary inn overlooks a private beach and Cape Cod Bay. Choose from five spacious guest suites, each with ocean view, private balcony, contemporary wicker furnishings, and ceiling fans. Two Honeymoon suites feature a whirlpool bath, and each room offers a private bath, cable color TV, phone, refrigerator, and air-conditioning. There are several common rooms for guest relaxation and an exercise room for work-outs. Visit nearby museums, historic sites, and fine restaurants within walking distance. Full breakfast. No smoking.

Sandwich, Cape Cod

Captain Ezra Nye House
152 Main Street
Sandwich, MA 02563
(508) 888-6142 or (800) 388-2278
Innkeepers: Harry and Elaine Dickson

Captain Ezra Nye House
Sandwich, MA

♛♛   Rating: B+
Rates: Double/$55-90
Credit Cards: AE, MC, V

Historic clapboard Federal-style home is located in the heart of Sandwich near
Route 6, exit 2. Nine guest rooms have hand-stenciled walls, original artwork,
and furnishings collected from around the world including Oriental rugs,
spindle beds, sleigh beds, and claw-foot tubs. Five of the rooms offer a private
bath. A small den houses a fine library of books and comfortable seating for
watching TV. Area attractions include Sandwich Glass Museum, beaches,
Heritage Plantation, Thornton Burgess Museum, Doll Museum, Shawme Lake,
and Hoxie House, the oldest house on Cape Cod. Full breakfast. No smoking.

Guests write: *"Wonderfully clean and welcoming room. Temperature was perfect—
warm and cozy. Breakfast was plentiful and delicious. Atmosphere was friendly.
Very helpful in area restaurants and shops to visit and local attractions."* (K&P
Rodrigues)

*"Genial host, friendly, comfortable, fresh clean facility. Very helpful. We had an
enjoyable stay and will return if we are in the area. Excellent breakfast."* (E.
Monohan)

South Dennis

The Captain Nickerson Inn
333 Main Street
South Dennis, MA 02660
(508) 398-5966 or (800) 282-1619
Innkeepers: Dave and Pat York

♛♛   Rating: B-
Rates: Single/$45-80; Double/$50-85
Credit Cards: V, MC

Three-story Queen Anne inn is lined by privet hedges and boasts gingerbread trim and leaded glass windows. The Captain Nickerson Inn is 15 miles East of Hyannis off Rt. 6. Choose from five guest rooms, three with private bath. The rooms feature four-poster, white iron, or a pineapple mahogany bed as well as Oriental or hand-hooded wool rugs. The large living room is separated into two areas, one offering television and VCR, while the other has a bookcase and easy chairs for quiet contemplation. A faux marble fireplace is located in the large dining room featuring parquet floors and a ceiling rosette. Within walking distance can be found fishing, historic sites, and antique shops. Area attractions: beaches, ferry to Nantucket, JFK Memorial, museums of natural history, and lighthouses. A full breakfast includes pancakes, French toast, or eggs, muffins or homemade breads, cereal, fruit, bacon or sausage. Weekend dinners are available to guests for an additional $12.50 when purchased in advance. Meeting facilities. Restricted Smoking. Families welcome

Stockbridge

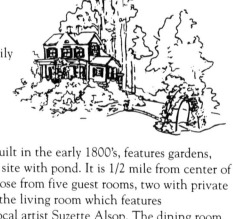

Arbor Rose Bed & Breakfast
8 Yale Hill
Stockbridge, MA 01262
(413) 298-4744
Innkeepers: Christina Alsop & family

♛♛ Rating: B-
Rates: Single or Double/$55-135
Credit Cards: AE, MC & V

New England clapboard colonial, built in the early 1800's, features gardens, mountain view and an old saw mill site with pond. It is 1/2 mile from center of Stockbridge, 4 miles from I-90.Choose from five guest rooms, two with private baths. Sit by the Franklin Stove in the living room which features television,VCR, and paintings by local artist Suzette Alsop. The dining room, boasting shaker furniture and silver tea service, sits ten. Tennis, restaurants, hiking and shopping are all within walking distance. Area attractions: Tangelwood Music Center (summer home of Boston Symphony), art, theatres, skiing, lakes, winter sports, hiking, shopping at outlet stores, Norman Rockwell Museum.Continental breakfast served weekdays includes muffins, rolls, or coffeecake, fresh fruit, homemade granola, English muffins, bagels, toast, coffee and juice. A full breakfast served on weekends includes an entree as well such as omelettes, waffles, French toast, or beer pancakes with maple syrup. Meeting and small wedding facilities. Restricted Smoking, Families welcome.

Guests write: *"With fruit and herbs from the garden we had a delicious breakfast of omelettes and muffins. The inn is charming and comfortable with a large cozy bed, airy room, and big modern bathroom." (J. Charrette)*

"This is a very charming home. Good taste is shown in furnishings as well as a good breakfast with home made bread. The most important is that the owner, Christina, is a very nice and sensative person." (F. Alvarez)

Stockbridge/South Lee

Historic Merrell Inn
1565 Pleasant Street
South Lee, MA 01260
(413) 243-1794
Innkeepers: Charles and Faith Reynolds

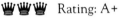 Rating: A+
Rates: Single/$75-135; Double/$85-145
Credit Cards: MC, V

This historic Federal home built in 1794 is celebrating its bicentennial year in 1994. Originally built as a stagecoach inn, Merrell Tavern Inn is now listed on the National Register of Historic Places and is situated in a small village 3 miles from exit 2 on I-90. The front entrance hall is graced by a hand painted mural and 18th-Century furnishings. There are nine guest rooms available and each has a private bath, direct dial telephone, antique furnishings, and period decor. Some feature fireplaces and most have canopy beds. Relax in the parlor, sit by the fire in the tavern room, or stroll on the grounds, which extend to the banks of the Housatonic River. A screened riverside gazebo is a favorite spot to imbibe in a complientary glass of ice tea or lemonade. The gardens feature the original stone walls of the inn's barns and livery stables. Area attractions include Norman Rockwell Museum, Tanglewood Music Festival, golf, tennis, fishing, hiking, and skiing. A choice of full breakfast is offered from a menu. Families welcome. No smoking.

Guests write: *"The peace of a riverbank at the bottom of the garden where you can recline for hours in a gazebo is guaranteed to dispel every care. Inside the house, the antiques are tastefully used as furnishings which makes the inn a home and not a museum. They are thoughtful innkeepers, ready to give any advise or assistance requested but never imposing themselves. It is a pleasure to chat with such cultured* hosts and have the benefit of their gentle but richly informed enthusiasm for history and the arts." (L. McRedmond)

"Over a span of ten years my wife and I have enjoyed the warm hospitality and gracious accommodations afforded by the Merrell Tavern Inn. The rooms are meticulously attended to. Their bright, warm period atmosphere is made all the more pleasant by the unobtrusive and thoughtful attentiveness of our hosts." (D. Scheufele)

"The rooms were wonderful — cozy and comfortable, and the entire inn had the exact feeling that you need on a brisk New England Fall day. There was a crackling fire in the sitting room where the sound of the grandfather clock chiming made you feel all's well with the world. Breakfast was fabulous! Each day you have choices and you can sit at your own private table where you can choose to talk to your neighbors or have a quiet time for yourself. The price was excellent!" (B. Huff)

"We chose room #10 which had a bath tub and was beautifully decorated with antiques and checked fabrics. The breakfast was substantial with a good choice. We chose pancakes with maple syrup and sausages and scrambled eggs and sausage. Delicious!" (C. Harvey)

"The Merrell Tavern Inn is a rare find. Not only is it a very comfortable late 18th-Century timepiece but it is also the source of very generous and gracious hospitality. The innkeepers serve tea and freshly-baked cake at 5 p.m. We felt very much at home." (W. Nicholls)

Sturbridge

Colonel Ebenezer Crafts Inn
Fiske Hill
Sturbridge, MA 01566
(508) 347-3313 or (800)-PUBLICK
Fax: (508) 347-5073
Innkeeper: David Cashill Lane

♛♛♛ Rating: A
Rates: Double/$69-150
Auto club, business, family, and senior discounts
Credit Cards: AE, MC, V

Historic Colonial home built in 1786 stands at the summit of Fiske Hill in Sturbridge off I-84, exit 2. A total of eight guest rooms are available, each with private bath and air conditioning. They reflect Colonial living with decor that includes antiques and period reproductions. The Cottage Suite with living room, TV, and telephone, adjoins the main house and offers perfect accommodations for families of four. Relax by one of the inn's two fireplaces, or in the summer sit by the outdoor pool. Explore nearby Old Sturbridge Village with its restored homes, farms, shops, a general store, and working grist mill. Other area attractions include tennis, golf, fitness center, and skiing. Fresh-baked muffins are part of the daily continental breakfast and afternoon tea features sweet baked goods. Meeting and wedding facilities available. Call for a calendar of special events including Yule Log and Thanksgiving weekends.

Vineyard Haven (See Martha's Vineyard)

Williamstown

River Bend Farm
643 Simonds Road, Route 7N
Williamstown, MA 01267
(413) 458-3121 or (800) 418-2057
Fax: (413) 458-5504
Innkeepers: Jeffrey Miller & Bob Horan

♛♛　Rating: B+
Rates: Single or Double/$87-99
Credit Cards: AE, MC, V

224 year old Georgian Colonial Tavern Farmhouse listed on the National Register of Historic Places, is a post and beam constructed two story house with original gray exterior. The stone chimney in the center of the house contains five separate fireplaces and two ovens. Five guest rooms with shared baths have been furnished with period pieces, hand braided rugs, and woven antique bedspreads to create an authentic Colonial restoration. Gather with other guests in the Keeping Room with its stone fireplace, beehive oven and collection of wrought iron cookware or in the Tap Room, a historic tavern room. Enjoy views of the Berkshires, wander through the vegetable, herb, and flower gardens, or experience the fall foliage and pastoral winter views. Walk to Williams College with its Museum of Art, The Sterling and Francine Clark Institute and town shops and restaurants. Area attractions: Historic Deerfield, the Shaker Village, and Bennington with historic battle sites. Full breakfasts

vary with specialties like spinach, ham and egg timbales accompanied with freshly baked blueberry lemon muffins and oatmeal bread spread with home-made jams and local honey. Small weddings and meeting facilities available. Families welcome. No smoking.

Guests write: *"All the rooms we saw had been painstaking and authentically restored giving the inn just the right air of 18th-Century charm including the period furnishings, fixtures, and fireplaces. Jeff went out of his way to make us feel at home, served us a delightful breakfast and provided helpful advice on the local sights."* (S. Dewhurst)

"We felt welcome every minute we were here. The rooms were decorated authentically and were very comfortable. Th breakfasts were super. Jeff is nominated for the society of Great Guys. Can't say enough good things." (B. Piff)

Yarmouthport, Cape Cod

The Colonial House Inn
Route 6A, 277 Main Street
Yarmouthport, MA 02675
(508) 362-4348 or (800) 999-3416
Innkeeper: Malcolm Perna

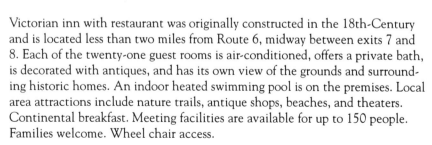

♛♛   Rating: B+
Rate: Single/$45-80; Double/$60-95
Rates include breakfast and dinner
Auto club, business travel, family, and senior discounts
Credit Cards: AE, MC, V

Victorian inn with restaurant was originally constructed in the 18th-Century and is located less than two miles from Route 6, midway between exits 7 and 8. Each of the twenty-one guest rooms is air-conditioned, offers a private bath, is decorated with antiques, and has its own view of the grounds and surrounding historic homes. An indoor heated swimming pool is on the premises. Local area attractions include nature trails, antique shops, beaches, and theaters. Continental breakfast. Meeting facilities are available for up to 150 people. Families welcome. Wheel chair access.

Guests write: *"We had the two most beautiful rooms one could ask for. Ours had a canopy bed and complete bathroom with claw-foot tub. My parent's had a fireplace ready to use. We will never forget the warm reception."* (M. de Prada)

Yarmouthport

Wedgewood Inn
83 Main Street
Yarmouthport, MA 02675
(508) 362-5157 or 362-9178
Innkeepers: Milt and Gerrie Graham

♛♛♛   Rating: A-
Rates: Single or Double/$90-150
Credit Cards: AE, MC, V

Greek Revival home on the north side of Cape Cod is surrounded by majestic elms and original stone walls. Originally built in 1812, the inn was completely refurbished in 1983. Each of the six guest rooms offers a private bath (some with tub only), vintage quilt, period wallpaper, and fresh flowers. Most have a working fireplace, wide board floors, and a canopy or pencil post bed. Two of the rooms are suites with a private sitting room and porch. A gazebo graces the two acres of lawns and gardens. Popular attractions in the area include beaches, nature and bike trails, whale watching, and antique shops, art galleries, and museums. Belgian waffles and home-baked goods are a part of the full breakfast offered in an elegant dining room. Small function rooms available for meetings and weddings. Restricted smoking.

Michigan

Battle Creek/Augusta

The Lodge at Yarrow
10499 North 48th Street
Augusta, MI 49012-9500
(616) 731-2090; Fax: (616) 731-2091
Innkeeper: Christa Quandt

Millikan

♛♛♛   Rating: A+
Rates: Single/$89-109; Double/$99-129
Credit Cards: AE, V, MC

The Lodge at Yarrow is a unique retreat and conference center situated on 350 acres between Battle Creek and Kalamazoo. Three secluded cottages house nine guest accommodations. Each room offers two queen-size beds, private entrance, screened-in porch, TV/VCR, phone, and private bath. The American Gothic style farmhouse lodge, a short walk from each cottage, overlooks the Potawatomi Valley. Here is where guests gather to converse and dine. The grounds off over eight miles of trails for hiking, biking, bird watching, and cross-country skiing; a 57 acre pristine lake for canoeing, fishing, and swimming, and a 50-foot Alpine Tower used by groups to help teach self-confidence and group problem solving. Nearby attractions: golf and horseback riding. A continental breakfast is included in the overnight rate although a full breakfast, lunch, and dinner are available for an additional charge. No smoking. Wheelchair access.

Fennville

Hidden Pond Bed & Breakfast
5975 128th Avenue
Fennville, MI 49408
(616) 561-2491
Innkeepers: Larry and Priscilla Fuerst

♔♔♔   Rating: A
Rates: Single or Double/$64-110

Hidden Pond combines modern amenities with a secluded rural atmosphere on twenty-eight acres of private, wooded grounds, 40 miles southwest of Grand Rapids. Two guest rooms are available, each with private bath. There is a large common room with comfortable seating for conversing with other guests, playing board games, or reading. Bird watching and hiking on the property have proven popular with guests and golf, tennis, skiing, hiking, bicycling, and water sports are nearby. Area attractions: Lake Michigan beaches, Saugatuck boutiques, and Fennville's winery and cider mill. Full breakfast is served at the time guest's request it on the enclosed porch overlooking a wildlife pond and includes fresh fruit, breads, muffins, and a hot entree. Turndown service, complimentary soft drinks, tea or an evening sherry are offered daily.

Guests write: *"The entire second floor is shared by two guest rooms which are beautifully decorated. The two guests have their own rooms and bathroom and share a wonderfully stocked kitchen with a refrigerator full of soda. Also shared are a beautifully decorated living room with fireplace and a reading room fully stocked with books, magazines and puzzles." (A&D Shachter)*

"Hidden Pond Bed and Breakfast was a secluded hideaway where we recharged our

hectic life. We felt pampered with fresh flowers all over the house, chocolates on our pillows, fluffy white robes in the closet, and our king-size bed made up for us each night." (C&B Riesadecki)

"Hospitality was first rate. The grounds (woods, pond) really aded a nice opportunity to walk, relax and enjoy nature." (C. Copper)

Ludington

Synder's Shoreline Inn
903 West Ludington Avenue
Ludington, MI 49431
(616) 845-1261; Fax: (616) 843-4441
Innkeeper: Tom & Sharon Snyder

♛♛♛   Rating: A-
Rates: Single/$55-199; Double/$ 65-189

Two-story gable roof inn is located at the west end of Ludington Avenue at Lake Michigan with 1/2 mile of beach and is 100 miles northwest of Grand Rapids. Twenty-one guest rooms have private balconies and nine have individual patios — all with a panoramic sunset view of Lake Michigan. All rooms private baths, telephones, cable TV with remotes, guest controlled heat and air, hand-stenciled walls, and handmade quilts. The upper level suites offer hand built furniture—some with lace canopy beds— wet bars, microwaves, and VCR. The lower level rooms have themes such as the log cabin room, the tulip room, and the Victorian bedchamber. The guest lending library is in the lobby where guests gather for conversation or reading. Walk to the beach, the harbor walk, museums, theater, restaurants, shops, city marina, and outdoor band shell where concerts are performed in season. Area attractions: beaches, state parks for swimming, fishing, and canoeing, historic village, historic lighthouses, and miles of biking trails. Continental breakfast includes fresh juice, gourmet coffees and teas, muffins, pastries, toast, bagels, and assortment of condiments. 98% of the rooms are designated smoke-free and three rooms are handicap accessible.

Guests write: *"As 30-year nomads of the beautiful State of Michigan, we were captivated by the quaintness of Snyder's Shoreline Inn. From the miles of stenciling to the crosstitch on the wall, each appointment was carefully selected. The sense of a country inn and the warmth of gracious hosts promises a return visit. In addition, the sunsets are spectacular and the local restaurants are among the best. We have rediscovered Ludington!" (D&C Juras)*

Saugatuck

Sherwood Forest Bed & Breakfast
PO Box 315 938 Center St.
Saugatuck, MI 49453
(616) 857-1246 or (800) 838-1246
Fax: (616) 857-1996
Innkeepers: Keith and Susan Charak

♛♛ Rating: B+
Rates: Double/$70-130
Credit Cards: MC, V

Victorian-style home built in the 1890s boasts a wrap-around porch and is located near the village center, 40 minutes south of Grand Rapids. Five newly renovated guest rooms are named for their color scheme and each has a private bath, queen size bed, and traditional furnishings. The Black and White room on the second floor is spacious and offers an oversized Jacuzzi tub. Gas fireplaces can be found in the Apricot room and cottage. Original features of the home have been preserved and are visible in the hardwood floors, oak trim, and leaded glass windows. Relax on the patio or take a dip in the heated swimming pool. The surrounding forests are perfect for hiking or cross country skiing in winter. The Douglas Public Beach is within walking distance and Saugatuck Oval Beach is just minutes away. The area's white sandy beaches are the perfect place for strolling, swimming, or watching sunsets. Visit art galleries, restaurants, public golf courses, state parks, summer theater, and boat charter tours. Continental plus breakfast may feature such specialties as lemon-yogurt bread, blueberry muffins, and fresh fruit salad. Wedding and small meeting facilities available. No smoking. A separate cottage adjacent to the inn is also available.

Guests write: *"Hosts are a fun young couple. Theirs is a lovely Victorian home in a nice, quiet residential neighborhood a bit out of town. They are a short walk to a lovely stretch of beach and provide bicycles for those who want to explore this quaint, historic area. " (E. Davis.)*

"The room we stayed in was a delight. It was warmly decorated and had a fireplace. The bed was comfy and large. The bathroom adjoined the room and was perfect with a nice hard shower and plenty of hot water. We were happy campers." (S. Cowen)

"Our family of four (including two children) really love Sherwood Forest. We found the meticulously decorated and remodeled guest rooms very pretty, quiet, and restful. Our children particularly liked the swimming pool in its wooded setting and the one-block walk to a great Lake Michigan beach." (N. McGarrity)

Additional information about B&Bs in Mississippi is available through the following B&B reservation agency: Lincoln Ltd Mississippi Reservation Service (601) 482-5483.

Missouri

Kansas City

Southmoreland on the Plaza
116 East 46th Street
Kansas City, MO 64112
(816) 531-7979
Fax: (816)531-2407
Innkeepers: Susan Moehl
and Penni Johnson

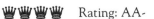

♛♛♛♛   Rating: AA-
Rates: Single/$90-135; Double/$100-145
Credit Cards: MC,V, AE

The Southmoreland on the Plaza is located within the heart of Kansas City's historic, cultural, shopping, and entertainment district in the Southmoreland and Country Club neighborhoods. Nestled on an urban "green" space in between carefully designed condominiums, this restored, 4,200 square-foot, 1913 Colonial Revival inn once served as a city residence. A new carriage house, courtyard, and 6,200 suare foot sympatehic addition has been added with period tile baths and vintage mill work used throughout the structure. Twelve guest rooms offer private baths and all have antiques and special touches such as Civil War-era furnishings, Chippendale pieces, oak and copper four-poster beds, hand-made shaker furnishings, and a "gentleman's library" decor. All rooms have either private decks, wood-burning fireplaces, or double Jacuzzi baths. Relax in the living room with television and VCR, classic film collection, and wet bar, or in two all-weather solariums with books and magazines, antique wicker furniture, and porch swing. Walk to the Nelson-Atkins Museum of Art, University of Missouri, Missouri Repertory Theatre and Country Club Plaza with 350 upscale shops, restaurants, and horse-drawn carriage rides. Area attractions include museums, art galleries, Kansas City Zoo, Truman Library/Museum, Pony Express, Historic River Market and Steamship. A full breakfast may offer apricot-bananna frappe, stuffed French toast with Swiss cheese, brown sugar ham, maple syrup, and almonds, and homemade chocolate-zucchini bread. Small meeting facilities. Wheelchair access. No smoking.

Kimberling City

Lakehouse Bed & Breakfast
Rt. 3, Box 704
Kimberling City, MO 65686
(417)739-1440 or (800) 739-1440
Fax: (417) 739-1450
Innkeepers: Dotty Peck

♛♛　Rating: B+
Rates: Single or Double/$75-95
Credit Cards: AE, MC & V

Contemporary house with long covered decks overlooking Table Rock Lake is located in wooded area which gently slopes to the lake and dock. It is10 miles from the "Branson Entertainment Strip" (Rt. 76). Each of the three guest rooms, all with private bath, has its own entrance and deck overlooking the lake. Lounging in comfortable furniture can be done in the airy family room also with the lake view. This room provides a wet bar, refrigerator, coffee maker, cable television, and videos. Swimming, boating, and fishing are all within walking distance at Table Rock Lake and a boat dock is available. Area attractions: country music shows in Branson, winery, Silver Dollar City, Civil War Museum, Craft Stores.A continental breakfast served on china in the spacious family dining room consists of juice, asparagus and ham fritatta, home-fried potatoes, stuffed tomatoes, toast or muffins, coffee and tea. Picnic lunches may be provided for hikers and conoeists. Elegant dinners are available upon request with advance notice. Meeting facilities. Restricted smoking

Springfield

Walnut Street Inn
900 East Walnut
Springfield, MO 65806
(800) 593-6346 or (417) 864-6346
Fax: (417) 864-6184
Innkeeper: Karol Brown

♛♛♛　Rating: A
Rates: Double/$75-150
Senior and corporate discounts
Credit Cards: AE, MC, V

Turn-of-the-century Victorian urban inn with hand-painted Corinthian columns, wide verandah with porch swing, and beveled-glass front door is listed as a National Historic Site and is located in the heart of the city. Each of the fourteen guest rooms has individual decor, a private bath, in-room telephone, writing desk, chairs for reading, and Turkish bathrobes. Some suites offer a Jacuzzi, fireplace, or claw foot tub. Relax in one of the soft chairs by the fireplace, play games, watch television, or read books in the sitting room with its leaded, lace covered windows. The back deck is shaded by large sycamores and the front porch offers wicker rockers and a porch swing. Regional specialties are featured at the full breakfast which can be eaten in the dining room, on the deck, or as a romantic breakfast-in-bed. Visit nearby Southwest Missouri State, Bass Pro Shops, performing art centers, theater, restaurants, antique shops, boutiques, art museums, and Wilson Creek National Battlefield. Wedding and meeting facilities available. Families welcome. Wheelchair access. No smoking.

Guests write: *"I stayed at this B & B for three days, and each day I was greeted with a fabulous breakfast, ranging from gingerbread pancakes to apple crepes, all served on fine china. The staff was always friendly and accommodating. Every detail, from coffee and popcorn in the sitting room of an evening, to luxurious bathrobes hanging in my room, were attended to. What hospitality!"* (C. Donica)

"This is an excellent place to stay for the money. There was plenty of room, we were very comfortable and enjoyed the good breakfast, cheerful hosts, and excellent parking. What a reasonable rate for everything you get!" (D. Dryer)

Montana

Additional information on B&Bs throughout this state is available through the following: B&B Western Adventure (406) 259-7993.

Columbia Falls

Bad Rock Country Bed & Breakfast
480 Bad Rock Drive
Columbia Falls, MT 59912
(800) 422-3666
Innkeepers: Jon and Susie Alper

♛♛♛   Rating: A+
Rates: Single or Double/$90-125
Credit Cards: AE, MC, V

Experience the Montana country lifestyle in this farmhouse filled with Old

West antiques and located in a farming valley 11 miles east of Kalispell and 125 miles north of Missoula. All of the guest rooms feature a private bath, antique furniture, and queen sized beds. Four new rooms have been built from hand-hewn square logs peeled down to the bare wood. Each is furnished with lodge pole pine furniture and feature gas log fireplaces. Two living rooms offer guests a place to relax, read, sit by the fireplace, or watch satellite television. Look out on the nearby Swan Mountain range or soak in the secluded hot tub while gazing out at the Big Mountain ski resort. Winter recreation nearby includes downhill or cross county skiing, snow mobiling, dog sledding, and ice skating. Glacier National Park is fifteen miles south and offers breathtaking views. Flathead Valley and Flathead Lake offer fishing, hiking, rafting, horseback riding, and swimming. Museums, art galleries, antique shops, casinos, and antique stores are all found in the nearby towns of Kalispell, Whitefish, Bigfork, and Columbia Falls. "Sundance" eggs, Montana potato pie, and huckleberry muffins are some of the unusual, Montana-style specialties offered at a full breakfast. Non smoking guests only.

Helena

Upcountry Inn
2245 Head Lane
Helena, MT 59601
(406) 442-1909
Innkeeper: Lynne Albright

♛♛ Rating: B+
Rates: Single/$50;Double/$60
Credit Cards: MC

Upcountry Inn is nestled in the Helena Valley on the east slope of the Rocky Mountains, 2 miles west of Helena off US-12. Quilts, stencils, iron beds, and wicker chairs fill the eight guest rooms and add to the inn's home-style hospitality. All have been named after the quilt patterns that adorn them. One room offers a private bath. The dining hall and great room are decorated country-estate style with wood, wool, and leather. Area attractions include Spring Meadow Lake State Recreation Area, historic Helena, Green Meadow Golf Course, and the Archie Bray Pottery Studio. Visit the inn's country store which offers hand crafted pottery, quilts, books, and paintings by Montana artists. Enjoy a full breakfast by the fire which includes homemade muffins and specialty entrees. Afternoon tea and dining in the Red Fox Restaurant are available by advance reservation. Facilities for weddings and meetings available. Families welcome. Wheelchair access. No smoking.

Three Forks

Sacajawea Inn
5 North Main Street
Three Forks, MT 59752
(406) 285-6515 or (800) 821-7326
Fax: (406) 285-4210
Innkeepers: Smith and Jane Roedel

♛♛♛ Rating: A-
Rates: Single/$49-59; Double/$59-99
Senior, business, and auto club member discount
Credit Cards: AE, MC, V

Guests have enjoyed the Sacajawea Inn since William Howard Taft was
president! This mid-19th-Century Western lodge has been in operation as an
inn since 1910 when it was built to serve the travelers on the Milwaukee
Railroad and it's located 50 miles east of Butte and 28 miles west of Bozeman
off I-90. The inn was totally renovated in 1992 and offers thirty-three guest
rooms with private bath. The large lobby with polished wood beams, high
ceilings, and original light fixtures serves as a gathering place for summer
guests and outdoorsmen visiting Yellowstone National Park. A large front
verandah offers comfortable rocking chairs. Popular attractions in the area
include Yellowstone Park, Gallatin Valley, Lewis and Clark Caverns, Madison
Buffalo Jump State Monument, Three Forks Museum, and Museum of the
Rockies. Area recreation includes hunting, fishing, skiing, horseback riding,
biking, and hiking. Continental breakfast includes home-baked pastries.
Restaurant open year-round. Meeting and conference facilities available.
Families welcome. No smoking.

Nevada

Additional information on B&Bs in this state is available from Mi Casa Su Casa (800) 456-0682.

New Hampshire

Cornish

The Chase House
Chase Street, Route 12A
RR #2, Box 909
Cornish, NH 03745
(603) 675-5391 or (800) 401-9455
Fax: (603) 675-5010

♛♛♛ Rating: A
Rates: Single/$75-85; Double/$85-115
Credit Cards: MC, V

This completely restored inn is the birthplace of Salmon Portland Chase and is one of New Hampshire's few historic designated landmarks. The inn is located on the banks of the Connecticut River, less than two miles south of the Cornish/Windsor covered bridge — the longest such bridge in the United States. The inn is a classic example of the early New England tradition of combining two houses: a 1766 Settlement Colonial with a 1795 Federal style home. Choose from seven guest rooms with private baths, individual heat thermostats, freshly ironed sheets, and antique furnishings. A large 30x40 foot air conditioned gathering room features exposed post and beam architecture, fieldstone fireplace, dance floor, and piano and is used for casual gatherings, business meetings, and wedding receptions. Additional common areas offer television or quiet conversation areas. Recreation within thirty miles includes hiking, fishing, bicycling, skiing, snowshoing, sleigh rides, canoeing, antique shops, flea markets, auctions, country fairs, and fine restaurants. Area attractions: Mt. Ascutney, American Precision Museum in Windsor, Saint-Gaudens Museum in Cornish, and Dartmouth College with its Hood museum, Shaker Village and Museum, and restaurants. Full breakfast includes homemade breads as well as pancakes or waffles served with warmed Cornish syrup and is served in two fireplaced dining rooms. Afternoon tea or evening dessert are available on request. Computer, fax, and copier services available. No smoking. Kennel for boarding pets is nearby; advance reservations are required.

Guests write: *"We have been going to B&Bs for about 40 years. This is among our favorites and I wouldn't change a thing. It has outstanding features, cleanliness, cozy atmosphere, attention to details, and breakfasts that defy descriptions." (R&L Spalthoff)*

"Our room was beautifully decorated with simple yet elegant furniture and pale blue wallpaper. The bed is four-posted with a delicate, crocheted canopy. For Valentine's Day, Bill and Barbara served a heart-shaped pastry filled with glazed cherries. Among my favorite breakfasts here is the quiche filled with mushrooms, blueberry pancakes with real maple syrup, and apple crisp. We are fed enough that we do not eat again until dinner time." (J. Mannick)

"History types will enjoy the parlor books on Salmon Chase, the would-be-president who Honest Abe cleverly made a Cabinet member, and who started the U.S. Treasury system." (M&R Barker)

Concord/Hopkinton

Windyledge Bed & Breakfast
1264 Hatfield Road
Hopkinton, NH 03229
(603) 746-4054
Innkeepers: Dick and Susan Vogt

♛♛♛   Rating: A
Rates: Single/45-65; Double/$55-75
Senior, family, business, and auto club discounts
Credit Cards: MC, V

Colonial home overlooks the White Mountains and is located eleven miles west of Concord. Three guest rooms are available, one with private bath. Special features of the rooms include pencil-post bed, hand-stenciled walls, hand-made antique furnishings, and Oriental rugs. The sitting room has a fireplace, piano, and comfortable seating for viewing TV. Popular spots for relaxation include the deck and swimming pool. Area attractions include antique shops, New England College, St. Paul's School, country fairs, concerts, boating, fishing, golfing, skiing, canoeing, and biking. Rooms for small functions available. Full gourmet breakfast features house specialties such as apricot glazed French toast, sour cream soufflé, and honey and spice blueberry pancakes. No smoking. Families welcome.

Guests write: *"When my husband announced that he had found a place for us to stay outside of Concord for only fifty-five dollars per night for the two of us, plus breakfast, I was understandably leery. How nice could this place be? Happily my fears were groundless. The Windyledge B&B would have been a bargain and a treat at twice the price. We were served breakfasts that were simply wonderful ranging from fruit-filled pancakes to vegetable frittatas. The Vogts have set up a wonderful, cozy family room which not only has a video library of immense proportions but also comes with a nice fire in the winter and glass of wine. A truly memorable stay."* (K. Berky)

"Windyledge was a cinch to find and what a haven on a blustery, frigid night! The warmth of their welcome was only equal to the warmth and charm of the home. Also, those blueberry-spice pancakes are destined for fame." (R. Willcox)

"After a five-hour drive and our arrival at Windyledge, Dick and Susan greeted us with warmth and friendliness and most importantly a much needed cold beer to unwind and relax. Our stay was like a visit with friends." (E. Botz)

"Susan thought of every detail to make our room beautiful and cozy from the white eyelet bedding on the four-poster bed to the fresh flowers on the antique dressing table." (B. Whyte)

Franconia

The Franconia Inn
Easton Valley Road
Franconia, NH 03580
(603) 823-5542 or (800) 473-5299
Fax: (603) 823-8078
Innkeepers: Alec and Richard Morris

♛♛♛ Rating: A-
Rates: Single/$60-80; Double/$78-113
Credit Cards: AE, MC, V

Traditional New England white clapboard structure, situated on 107 acres, is located in the northwestern side of the state off I-93 near Littleton. There are thirty-four guest rooms, most with private baths. Ten rooms have an extra bed for a third guest. Two suites are especially suited for families. The Honeymoon suite includes a Jacuzzi tub and queen-size bed. An oak-paneled library and large living room offer beautiful views of the mountains. Two porches offer seating and views of the surrounding countryside. The Rathskeller Lounge on the lower level has a hot tub and game room with movies available. Year-round recreation includes riding, tennis, swimming, trout fishing, hiking, skiing, and sledding. Area attractions include the Robert Frost home, Franconia State Park, and Maple Sugar Museum. Full breakfast served. Dinner is available at the restaurant at an additional cost. Facilities for weddings and functions available. Families welcome.

Guests write: *"We can suggest nothing to improve. Everything and everyone was very nice and pleasant."* (R. Stavnitsky)

"This year we are going to stay in the same room on the 1st floor next to the library. This place has fantastic food, plenty to do and the people are just great." (A. Greenberg)

"Our return stay (the 3rd or 4th time), was just as enjoyable as the previous visits. It is heartwarming to return and recognize members of the staff and have them recognize you - acknowledging your previous visits! It is like a homecoming of sorts and certainly increased our desire to continue our treks to Franconia Inn." (J. Wright)

Gorham

Gorham House Inn
55 Main Street
P.O. Box 267
Gorham, NH 03581
(603) 466-2271 or (800) 453-0023
Innkeepers: Ron and Maggie Cook

 Rating: B-
Rates: Single/$38; Double/$60

Victorian inn built in 1891 is located on the town common at the junction of Routes 2 and 16, the northern gateway to the White Mountains. Choose from three guest rooms with shared baths. An fireplaced parlor offers a relaxing area in which to unwind, socialize, or enjoy the entertainment center. Area attractions include Mount Washington auto road and train, ski areas, golf, hiking, and fishing. Ski packages available. Full breakfast. Families welcome.

Guests write: *"During my family's stay in New England, we encountered many people and enjoyed many fine bed and breakfasts, but the Gorham House topped the* list. *We found 'down' home Texas style hospitality as well as the best nights sleep we had had in eight nights of traveling." (D&B Shrum)*

Hampton

The Victoria Inn
430 High Street
Hampton, NH 03842
(603) 929-1437
Innkeeper: William Beynon

♛♛♛   Rating: A-
Rates: Single/$55-75; Double/$75-95
Credit Cards: MC, V

Victorian home recently renovated was originally built as a carriage house and is located on the coast, 20 minutes south of Portsmouth near I-95, exit 2. Six guest rooms are available, three with private bath. Area attractions include Hampton Beach, Seabrook Race Track, and the White Mountains. Boston is a forty-five minute drive. Full breakfast is included in the rates with dinner for 10 or more available by advance reservation. Facilities available for weddings, reunions, and functions. No smoking.

Guests write: *"We keep returning to the Victoria Inn because we are treated like royalty. The food is served with all the extra attention food can be given. It looks beautiful and delicious. There are a choice of places to eat breakfast, formal dining room or porch that is surrounded by glass doors overlooking a beautiful little park with a gazebo. The rooms each have their own theme, with a hundred and one special little touches, such as a Burgundy room trimmed in burgundy with a Victorian doll in burgundy." (L.&M. Gelinas)*

"Rooms are beautifully decorated in an elegant Victorian style. They are big, spacious and well ventilated with an overhead fan in each room." (J.&E. Mahoney)

"We were married at the inn on June 26, 1993. It will be the most memorable day of our whole wedding experience." (S. & M. Dube)

Jackson

Inn at Jackson
P.O. Box H
Jackson, NH 03846
(603) 383-4321 or (800) 289-8600
Innkeeper: Lori Tradewell

♛♛   Rating: B+
Rate: Single/$41-90; Double/$56-105
Credit Cards: AE, MC, V

Victorian inn built in 1902 is located near the village's covered bridge on
Route 16A in the White Mountain National Forest. Choose from nine guest
rooms, each with private bath. Enjoy panoramic views of the village or
Presidential Mountain Range. Among area attractions are cross-country skiing
from the inn's front door, outlet shops, and hiking. Full breakfast is served in
the fireside dining room or on the glassed-in porch. Families welcome. 10%
service charge is added on to the bill.

Jackson

Nestlenook Farm on the River
P.O. Box Q
Jackson, NH 03846
(603) 383-9443
Innkeepers: Robert and Nancy Cyr

♛♛♛♛   Rating: AA
Rates: Single or Double/$125-295

Riverfront estate on 65 acres was built in 1780 and is reached through a
covered bridge which sets the scene for escaping into a Victorian past. The inn
is located 3 hours north of Boston off Route 16. Choose from seven guest
rooms or suites, each with private bath and oversized Jacuzzi, fine antique
furnishings, and original paintings. Special features of the inn include horse-
drawn Austrian sleigh rides, ice skating, cross-country skiing on groomed
trails, heated pool, gazebo, and a gingerbread chapel. Full family-style breakfast. No smoking.

Guests write: *"When walking into the inn, you feel as if you are walking into the
'Walton's home'. It has large rooms with high ceilings and cozy fireplaces. After a
day of skiing, their outdoor hot tub made it the end of a perfect day. Breakfast*

consisted of homemade strawberry muffins, French toast, juice, coffee or tea. All was made to perfection. For my husband and I, this was our first getaway from our children in 3 years. We couldn't have chosen a better romantic spot." (J. Whitaker)

"There was a nice variety of specialty pancakes served on the porch or dining room with pleasant alpine views. We have used them twice as base camp for spring skiing. The Jacuzzi after skiing is always ready, and being outdoors and seeing the moon and stars while healing aching muscles is extremely pleasant." (M. Stein)

"The atmosphere and decor are something out of a magazine. The rooms and outside grounds were great. This place will be highly recommended." (P. Fritz)

"It was our 36th Wedding Anniversary and what a wonderful place to celebrate here at Nestlenook. This place takes you into Fantasyland. My husband and I have only one regret. The fact that we have to leave this beautiful setting." (F. Rattigan)

"A step into the past with eyes to the future. What a wonderful place to reflect on the blessings of the past and the expectations for the future." (B. Kokko)

Keene/Jaffrey

Benjamin Prescott Inn
Route 124 East
Jaffrey, NH 03452
(603) 532-6637
Innkeepers: Barry and Janice Miller

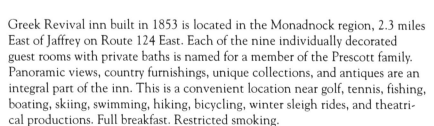

♛♛♛ Rating: A-
Rates: Single/$60-80; Double/$65-130
Credit Cards: AE, MC, V

Greek Revival inn built in 1853 is located in the Monadnock region, 2.3 miles East of Jaffrey on Route 124 East. Each of the nine individually decorated guest rooms with private baths is named for a member of the Prescott family. Panoramic views, country furnishings, unique collections, and antiques are an integral part of the inn. This is a convenient location near golf, tennis, fishing, boating, skiing, swimming, hiking, bicycling, winter sleigh rides, and theatrical productions. Full breakfast. Restricted smoking.

Guests write: "The decor reflects the region as well as the personality of the innkeepers. The use of floral patterns in a choice of pleasing colors lends itself to a relaxing atmosphere. Each room is unique and the variety can serve everyone's taste. The breakfasts they served were beyond our expectations; they run a hot breakfast *rotation so you never receive the same meal unless you spend 17 days at the inn. In addition to the usual muffins and pastries, the hot breakfast item was outstanding. This particular morning they were serving apple crepes with bacon." (D. Jankura)*

"I've now stayed at the inn twice, and each time I've found the rooms both inviting and interesting. By using antiques, country crafts, and reproduction quilts and coverlets, Jan and Barry Miller have created an atmosphere that makes visitors feel they are staying as house guests, not lodgers. My favorite breakfast was a blackberry pancake soufflé, a delicious, light, puffy creation served in a ramekin with a few pieces of fresh fruit on the side." (M. Wood)

"The innkeepers, Janice Miller and her husband, were very accommodating giving the guest the feeling of visiting a relative or a close friend. The inn and rooms reflects the charm of this New England area with its tastefully appointed decor. Immaculate and spacious are descriptions used to describe the rooms." (A. Stewart)

"I found the room very comfortable. The food was delicious and the folks at the inn were very congenial." (W. Petty)

"It turned out to be the perfect place for a family get-together. The rooms were charming and unique, and we loved the handmade chocolates left each night in our rooms." (H. DeAngelis)

Manchester/Wilton Center

Stepping Stones Bed & Breakfast
Bennington Battle Trail
Wilton Center, NH 03086
(603) 654-9048
Innkeeper: Ann Carlsmith

♛♛   Rating: B
Rates: Single/$35; Double/$45-50

Built as an addition to a pre-Revolutionary period structure, this 19th century Greek Revival home is found 60 miles north of Boston and 20 miles west of Nashua. Guests are accommodated in three guest rooms that have been decorated in the country style with natural fibers and soft colors. Each room has hand-woven throws, down pillows and puffs, fresh flowers and feature windows overlooking the countryside. One room offers a private bath. Guests gather in the solar breakfast room with plants, pottery, and views of the garden. The parlor offers a fireplace, books, games, television, and stereo. There is a sheltered porch and secluded lawn area within the extensive garden for quiet contemplation. Take a country walk to a waterfall, antique mill, or around the reservoir. Visit local antique markets, summer theaters, and chamber music. The back roads in the area offer excellent bicycling and hikers regularly explore the nearby Wapack Trail. Home baking and local fresh fruit are a part of the full breakfast served. Small, private garden wedding facilities available. Families and well-behaved pets welcome. Restricted smoking.

Guests write: *"The house itself is a treasure. Furnished with simple, elegant Shaker furniture and throws, rugs and pillows hand-woven by Ann, it is full of special touches, like fresh flowers and candies in the bedrooms. A woodstove in the kitchen and fireplace in the living room make it very cozy in winter. The kitchen, with its sunny, airy atrium-style windows and plants galore is a natural gathering place for guests. We've spent many a leisurely morning basking in the sunlight of the kitchen after a gourmet breakfast of fluffy waffles or a soufflé with asparagus and hollandaise sauce, watching birds at the bird feeders."* (J. Rottenberg)

"From the afternoon herbal tea to the scrumptious Belgian waffles served with fresh fruit, everything done for you has the stamp of Ann's earthy touch and kind hospitality. Breakfast in the bright and homey greenhouse-like room is a bird watcher's delight. Any season of the year, we're treated to an array of birds in the various shrubs and bird feeders viewed right from the breakfast table!" (M. Stone)

"Steppingstones is a charming, white farm house, comfortably furnished with Shaker furniture, softened by pillows, rugs and throws hand-loomed by Ann. Reading materials abound—quiet corners are stocked with a variety of books, magazines and maps." (G. Stormes)

Manchester/Hampstead

Stillmeadow Bed & Breakfast at Hampstead
P.O. Box 565
545 Main Street
Hampstead, NH 03841
(603) 329-8381
Innkeepers: Lori and Randy Offord

🏅🏅🏅   Rating: A
Rates: Single/$50; Double/$60-90
Credit Cards: AE

1850 Greek Renaissance Colonial home located on Main Street (Route 121) near the junction of Route 111, is accessible to both the mountains and the sea coast. Four guest rooms or suites are available, each with private bath. A large suite offers queen-size bed and sitting room with trundle bed. Another suite is ideal for families with crib, changing table, and stairs leading to a playroom - all child-proof. Children will also enjoy the fenced-in play yard. The home is adjacent to the Hampstead Croquet Association's twin grass courts. There is also golf and swimming nearby. Other area attractions include the Robert Frost Farm, America's Stonehenge, Rockingham Park Race Track, and Kingston State Park. This location is convenient to Manchester, NH and is less than an hour from Boston. Expanded continental breakfast. Small meeting facilities available. Families welcome. No smoking.

Guests write: *"We have stayed at Stillmeadow on several weekends. This has given us a chance to be in four different rooms, each of them immaculate and decorated (each very different from the others in color scheme) with taste and charm down to the last little pin cushion on a dresser. The rooms are bright and room temperature both in winter and summer was comfortable. The hosts are delightful, interesting people and paid attention to our every need and desire. Breakfasts are filled with surprises—there's a different home baked bread or muffin or cake each time. A staple, however, is the wonderful granola/yogurt fresh fruit cup that Lori presents in a beautiful dessert dish. It's a place where you feel relaxed and pampered."* (P&H Hersh)

"Our stay at the Stillmeadow was the only peaceful and pleasant time in our lengthy moving-in process. We can wholeheartedly recommend their hospitality to future visitors." (P. Broadwater)

"You can't go too many places where someone would even loan you their own makeup. They sure helped me get off to a good start. They've done such a lovely job here that we felt right at home." (R. Snyder)

"They played a part in our big reunion weekend and smaller clan gathering. It had been four years since we had all been together. All week long one or another of us would say how we have to get together at a place like Stillmeadow more often. It was perfect." (D. Rozeboom)

North Conway

Buttonwood Inn
P.O. Box 1817, Mt. Surprise Road
North Conway, NH 03860
(603) 356-2625 or
(800) 258-2625 (U. S. and Canada)
Fax: (603) 356-3140
Innkeepers: Claudia and Peter Needham

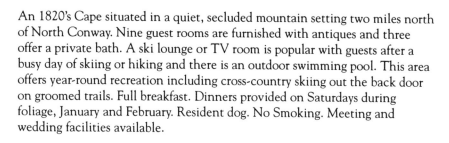

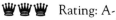 Rating: A-
Rates: Single/$45-70; Double50-100
Credit Cards: AE, MC, V

An 1820's Cape situated in a quiet, secluded mountain setting two miles north of North Conway. Nine guest rooms are furnished with antiques and three offer a private bath. A ski lounge or TV room is popular with guests after a busy day of skiing or hiking and there is an outdoor swimming pool. This area offers year-round recreation including cross-country skiing out the back door on groomed trails. Full breakfast. Dinners provided on Saturdays during foliage, January and February. Resident dog. No Smoking. Meeting and wedding facilities available.

North Conway

Cranmore Mountain Lodge
859 Kearsarge Road
P. O. Box 1194
North Conway, NH 03860
(603) 356-2044 or (800) 356-3596
Innkeeper: Dennis E. Helfand

Rating: A
Rates:Single or Double/$59-99
Auto club discount
Credit Cards: AE, MC, V

New England farmhouse inn built in 1865 is located in Mt. Washington Valley, less than 2 miles northeast of town off Route 16. The lodge has sixteen guest rooms, each with private bath. Stay in either the main house or the renovated barn which has spacious rooms ideal for families and groups with private bath, cable TV, and fireplaced recreation room. Abundant area recreation includes hiking, bicycling, rock climbing, kayaking, cross-country and downhill skiing, golf, and fishing. Enjoy the on-site swimming pool, Jacuzzi, tennis, volleyball, tobogganing, ice skating, and the farm animals on the property. Full breakfast. Families welcome.

North Conway/Intervale

Old Field House
P. O. Box 1, Route 16A
Intervale, NH 03845
(603) 356-5478 or (800) 444-9245
Innkeeper: Tim Merritt

♛♛♛ Rating: A-
Rates: Double/$59-109
Auto club and corporate discounts
Credit Cards: AE, MC, V

Colonial-style motor inn with a stone facade is located 3 miles north of North Conway on Route 16A. Choose from eighteen guest rooms, each with private bath, air conditioning, phone, TV, and queen or king-size beds. Two suites offer a Jacuzzi and fireplace. Sit in front of the fireplace in the living room, relax with a book, or listen to soothing music. On the premises are clay tennis courts, an outdoor heated swimming pool, Jacuzzi, shuffleboard, and cross-country skiing. Area attractions include alpine ski resorts, hiking, mountaineering, fishing, canoeing, and factory outlets. Continental breakfast. Families welcome. No smoking.

North Conway

Victorian Harvest Inn
28 Locust Lane
North Conway, NH 03860
(603) 356-3548 or (800) 649-0749
Fax: (603) 356-8430
Innkeepers: Linda and Robert Dahlberg

♛♛♛ Rating: A
Rates: Single/$55-65; Double/$55-100
Credit Cards: AE, MC, V

Restored 1850s multi-gabled Victorian inn is found one-half mile south of

North Conway off Route 16 tucked away on a quiet side street. Each of the six guest rooms, four with private bath, have ample sitting room, air-conditioning, and antique furnishings. Two rooms with queen-size beds can serve as a suite for families or couples traveling together. Swim in the Victorian decorated pool, relax on the enclosed porch or large deck, play the new piano in the library-sitting room. Four-season recreation nearby includes downhill and cross-country skiing, ice skating, kayaking, canoeing, hiking, swimming, and viewing the magnificent autumn leaves. Full country breakfast. Facilities available for social functions. No smoking.

Guests write: *"We have stayed at this inn enough times to try all the rooms and each one has been so wonderfully comfortable. The innkeepers are exceptional. We feel so at home and wake up to the wonderful aromas of a great breakfast."* (E. LaVena)

"I am a fairly private person and avoided B&Bs for that reason. A friend finally talked me into joining her at the Victorian Harvest for some cross-country skiing. I had a wonderful time and was extremely comfortable. I experienced a true interest in my well-being and comfort with a deep respect for my privacy. This takes real sensitivity on the part of the innkeepers." (L. Howard)

"We enjoyed our previous stay here so much that we returned for a week with our family. We've had a wonderful week — great food, beautiful and comfortable accommodations with warm, thoughtful and caring hosts. If all B&Bs were like this the hotel/motel business would be in trouble." (D. Wills)

"As always, we thoroughly enjoyed ourselves when visiting the inn. Their warmth and hospitality are wonderful as are the delicious meals and the acceptance as family. The music was great - like everything else."
(I. McDonald)

"Since I discovered the Victorian Harvest Inn in the Autumn of 1988, I have had the pleasure of staying there nine times. It's elegant yet comfortable, and the atmosphere is always warm and welcoming. The innkeepers, Bob and Linda, have a flair for making people feel special. The breakfasts were exceptional. They are quite talented in the kitchen" (V. Hagstrom)

North Woodstock

Wilderness Inn Bed & Breakfast
Rtes. 3 & 112
North Woodstock, NH 03262
(603) 745-3890 or (800) 200-WILD-200
Innkeepers: Michael and Rosanna Yarnell

♛♛   Rating: B+
Rates: Single/$30-80; Double/$40-90
Credit Cards: AE, MC, V

1912 Craftsman cottage in the White Mountains overlooks Lost River and the south ridge of Loon Mountain and is 120 miles north of Boston. Choose from seven guest rooms or a cottage that offer a view of the river, mountains, or garden. Five of the rooms have a private bath. Enjoy a winter's evening sitting in front of a fire with a cup of hot mulled cider, swim in the swimming hole in the summer, or leaf watch in the fall. Visit the nearby White Mountain National Forest, Franconia Notch State Park, Loon Mountain, or Cannon Mountain. Full breakfast specialties include crepes with home-made applesauce or cranberry- walnut pancakes. Breakfast is served on the front porch or is available on a tray for breakfast in bed. Wedding and meeting facilities available. Families welcome. Restricted smoking.

Guests write: *"There aren't enough superlatives to do justice to the Wilderness Inn. This large, well-kept house is comfortably and functionally furnished, the common rooms inviting, the bedrooms cozy, and the grounds peaceful. They make every guest feel as if you're being pampered in your own home."* (K. Reagon)

North Woodstock

Woodstock Inn
80 Main Street
North Woodstock, NH 03262
(603) 745-3951 or (800) 321-3985
Innkeepers: Scott and Eileen Rice

♛♛♛   Rating: A
Rates: Double/$45-135
Credit Cards: AE, MC, V

Century old Victorian inn is nestled in the middle of the White Mountains.

Seventeen guest rooms are available in the main house or the inn; eleven offer a private bath. All rooms feature air conditioning, color TV, and telephone, with some offering Jacuzzis, a separate sitting area, or porch overlooking the Pemigewasset River. The Cascade swimming area is a short walk from the inn and additional recreation nearby includes hiking and skiing. Popular attractions in the area include Old Man of the Mountain, Kancamagus Highway, Lost River, Fantasy Farm, Mount Washington Cog Railway, the Whales Tale Water Slide. Full breakfast is served in the glass-enclosed porch. Lunch and dinner are available in the area's original train station that is attached to the back of the inn. Facilities available for large functions. Families welcome.

Wentworth

Hilltop Acres
East Side and Buffalo Road
Wentworth, NH 03282
(603) 764-5896
Innkeeper: Marie Kauk

♛♛ Rating: B-
Rates: Double/$65-80
Credit Cards: MC, V

Colonial inn and cottages built in 1806 are located at the foot of the White Mountains, approximately 20 minutes from I-93, exit 26. There are five guest rooms with private bath and double brass or twin beds in the main inn. Each has scenic views, plants, a selection of books, and a ceiling fan. Two housekeeping cottages especially suited for families are available May through mid-November and include full kitchen unit, separate bedroom, fireplace, and screened-in porch. A pine-paneled recreation room offers games, a large collection of books, and cable TV. Wentworth has three swimming holes, several hiking trails, and fishing streams. Area attractions include Polar Caves, Ruggles Mine, Lost River, and Franconia Notch. Continental breakfast includes an assortment of muffins, pastries, and breads. Families welcome.

Guests write: ""*For those of us enmeshed in the 9-5 syndrome, my recent stay at Hilltop has become a memorable experience. It was a reminder that the simple things in life often times are the most wonderful.*" (R. Doukas)

"*They've done a splendid job of decorating with a modest Victorian touch that allows a visitor to enjoy the uniqueness of the accommodations while feeling completely at home. After a long country walk, the jazz concert on the lawn made our stay even more memorable.*" (R. Jorgensen)

Bay Head

Conover's Bay Head Inn
646 Main Avenue
Bay Head, NJ 08742
(908) 892-4664 or (800) 956-9099
Innkeeper: Beverly Conover

♕♕♕ Rating: A
Rates: Single/$80-185; Double/$90-195
Business travel discount
Credit Cards: AE, MC, V

Shingle-style inn built in 1905 as a summer cottage is located in a small town at the seashore. Choose from twelve guest rooms, each offering private bath, air conditioning, and featuring dramatic color-coordinated decor including matching spreads and ruffled pillows. Enjoy the views of the ocean, bay, and marina from one of the expansive porches or large windows. Area attractions: ocean and bay recreation, quaint shops, golf, tennis, fishing, and hiking. Full breakfast includes fresh-baked goods and is served in the dining room, front porch, or on the manicured front lawn. No smoking.

Cape May

Inn at 22 Jackson
22 Jackson Street
Cape May, NJ 08204
(609) 884-2226 or (800) 452-8177
Fax: (609) 884-2226
Innkeeper: Barbara Carmichael

♕♕♕ Rating: A-
Rates: Single/$95-155; Double/$180-240; 4/$250
Credit Cards: AE, MC, V

Located 90 miles from Philadelphia in the heart of the primary historic district, this historic beach resort is a three-story Queen Anne Victorian. Constructed in 1898, it lies just half a block from the Atlantic Ocean and is on the National Register of Historic Buildings. Choose from five suites, each with private bath, furnished with antiques, lace, and fresh flowers. Delight yourself with a ride in a horse-drawn carriage down streets lined with gas lights, or take in a sunset boat trip around the island. Fishing, miniature golf, and, of course, the beach are some other activities waiting for you. There are also over 600 historical Victorian homes still in Cape May. Full breakfast is served inside or take a tray to the front porch. Wedding and meeting facilities available. Fax and copier available. Restricted smoking.

Guests write: *"We was our first time at a B&B and we loved it. The house itself was wonderfully decorated in the Victorian tradition with antiques true to the period. We had the Turret Room with a sitting room, kitchen, porch, two bedrooms, and a private bath. What made this place so special were the innkeepers who go out of their way to make guests feel comfortable, at home, and part of the family. Not to be missed are the wonderful breakfasts — one day sweet, the next, savory." (I&K Weinstein)*

Cape May

The Mason Cottage
625 Columbia Avenue
Cape May, NJ 08204
(609) 884-3358 or (800) 716-2766
Innkeepers: Dave and Joan Mason

♛♛♛ Rating: A-
Rates: Double/$85-255
Senior discount
Credit Cards: MC, V

Victorian seaside home with lofty ceilings, sweeping verandah, and full length windows was built in 1871 and is located two hours from Philadelphia at the end of the Garden State Parkway. Choose from five guest rooms with antique furnishings and private baths; several with air conditioning. Four new suites scheduled for completion soon will offer whirlpool baths, air conditioning and sitting areas. This construction project will also add a large new dining room. The verandah offers a distant ocean view. Popular attractions in the area include Lewes Ferry, village shopping, golf, tennis, fishing, boating, swimming, hiking, and bicycling. Continental breakfast is served on trays in the parlor until the new dining room is finished.

Guests write: *"This was our first stay in a B & B, and it was great fun. They made us feel very special and more like house guests than customers. Breakfast in comfortable rockers on the front porch, beautifully served and carefully prepared will be a happy memory." (M. Klauder)*

"Our thoughtful hostess created a warm and welcoming atmosphere. Special treats made for a special stay." (E.&G. Dingle) (Continued)

"The hospitality and attentiveness to our needs were outstanding; and her breakfasts, with dishes such as apple-crusted French toast, were all that one could wish for. The cottage has a true Victorian charm without being overdone. The location is extremely convenient to points of interest in the historic neighborhood." (D&N Reiner)

"When our daughter was married in Cape May the summer of 1991, we reserved the Mason Cottage for ourselves, family, and friends. The Mason's gracious hospitality is unsurpassed! In the midst of all the wedding preparations, the Mason Cottage was a haven to which we could return, rock on the porch, feel the ocean breezes, enjoy the aroma of flowers and be pampered. Being from the Midwest, we especially enjoyed the location near the ocean and in the center of the Victorian district. One of our favorite activities was strolling the lanes of the Victorian homes in the neighborhood during the day and night." (J. Colson)

Cape May

Queen Victoria ®
102 Ocean Street
Cape May, NJ 08204
(609) 884-8702
Innkeepers: Dane and Joan Wells

♛♛♛   Rating: A+
Rate: Single or Double/$75/245
Credit Cards: MC, V

Three restored Victorian seaside villas comprise the Queen Victoria which is located one block from the ocean in the center of the Historic District. There are twenty-three guest rooms which feature hand-made quilts, ceiling fans, and private baths. Each room offers air conditioning, and several have fireplaces or whirlpool tubs. Use the inn's bicycles to tour historic sites, antique shops, and the town center. Area attractions include restaurants, specialty shops, tennis, fishing, boating, swimming, and biking. Hosts speak English and French. Full breakfast. Facilities available for small weddings and meetings.

Guests write: *"Our room was beautifully decorated in period Victorian and were spotlessly clean. The room and bath were large with modern conveniences (refrigerator and firm mattress). There were lots of complimentary toiletries and chocolates on the pillows at night. In the common rooms were complimentary sherry, candies, popcorn, selection of soft drinks, tea, and coffee." (F. Harris)*

"Our room was bright, cheery, airy, and very comfortable and clean. The bath had a Jacuzzi and came with bath crystals, shower cap, shampoo, and conditioner. At night

your bed is turned down, you are given fresh towels, and a large piece of chocolate is placed on each pillow. Hospitality is outstanding. With all the pampering and little extras, the hosts make you feel as if you are their only guest." (S. Hartman)

"Our suite oozed charm. We had a sitting room which stepped into a bedroom which took us back to the Victorian days. We have stayed in many B&Bs and this Queen Victoria has topped them all. This was our first Christmas in thirty-nine years away from our children and family. Joan and Dane and all of their guests made Christmas 1991 one to remember and we would do it again." (N. Martin)

"The first thing we noticed was that the grass and walks were extremely well-manicured. We liked the location within walking distance to so many things and the ocean. I could not believe it when they emptied the wastebaskets twice a day and turned down the bed with chocolates on each pillow. We could get really spoiled at the Queen Victoria." (R. Mylod)

"We were very impressed with the booklet of information they provided for each guest. One other extra they provided that we really enjoyed was the free use of their bicycles for touring the city. Theirs was the 7th B&B we have reviewed but while we enjoyed all of them, the Queen Victoria had the most to offer and left us with the most pleasant memories of hospitality." (K. Sasdelli)

Chatham

Parrot Mill Inn
47 Main Street
Chatham, NJ 07928
(201) 635-7722
Innkeeper: Betsy Kennedy

♛♛ Rating: B+
Rates: Double/$95
Credit Cards: AE, MC, V

Large Gambrel-roofed home built around 1780, is located three miles from Route 78. Choose from eleven guest rooms, each with private bath. Relax before the fireplace in the keeping room. Area attractions include New York City, museums, shopping, hiking, and bicycling. Continental breakfast. Families welcome.

Guests write: "The Parrot Mill Inn was a home away from home for five weeks during our relocation from South Carolina. Our stay was a vacation as Betsy and *her staff were so warm, friendly, and helpful. The room was delightful and her breakfasts most enjoyable. Thanks to them our move has been much easier than we would have thought possible." (L. Spieth)*

Frenchtown

The Hunterdon House
12 Bridge Street
Frenchtown, NJ 08825
(908) 996-3632 or (800) 382-0375
Fax: (908) 996-2921
Innkeeper: Gene Refalvy

♛♛ Rating: B
Rates: Double/$85-14.
Credit Cards: AE, MC, V

Constructed in 1864, this classic Italianate Victorian mansion is listed on the National Register of Historic Buildings. The formally landscaped property, only half a block from the Delaware River, is located 50 miles north of Philadelphia. Visitors may choose from seven large double rooms, each with its own private bath. Period furnishings and antiques are everywhere. Sherry is offered each evening in the downstairs parlor, and an old-fashioned breakfast is served each morning in the dining room. Browse through the many specialty shops right on Bridge Street for a taste of the local artists and craftsmen. Recreational activities include fishing, boating, tubing, biking, and hiking. Wedding and meeting facilities available. No smoking.

Hacketstown/Hope

The Inn at Millrace Pond
RT. 519
Hope, NJ 07844
(908) 459-4884 or (800) 7-InnHope
Innkeeper: Charles Puttkammer

♛♛♛ Rating: A-
Rates: Single or Double/$85-150
Senior, corporate, and auto club discounts
Credit Cards: AE, MC, V

Restored Colonial inn situated on 23 acres along Beaver Brook is comprised of the Millrace House, the Grist Mill, and Wheelwright's Cottage and is located approximately 65 miles west of New York City. Antique furnishings, wide board flooring, Oriental rugs, and period furnishings accent the Colonial decor found in each of the seventeen guest rooms with private baths. Explore the 1760s Grist Mill which is now a restaurant that features a millrace chamber, open staircase, and massive stone wall. Area attractions: The Delaware Water Gap National Recreation area, Waterloo Village, music festivals, crafts show, winery tours, and antique shopping. Bike along country roads, hike golf, play tennis on the premises, or go canoeing on the nearby Delaware River. A hearty continental breakfast offers homemade pastries and fresh fruit. Small wedding meeting facilities available. Families welcome.

Lamertville

Chimney Hill Farm Bed & Breakfast
207 Goat Hill Road
Lamertville, NJ 08530
(609) 397-1516
Innkeepers: Terry Ann and
Richard Anderson

♛♛   Rating: B+
Rates: Single or Double/$75-150
Auto club, senior, corporate, and
government discounts
Credit Cards: AE, MC, V

Stone manor home set on an eight acre estate is surrounded by lush greenery and abundant wildlife and is located 30 minutes north of Philadelphia and 15 miles east of Princeton. Choose from eight guest rooms with private baths: The Hunt, Cottage, Tapestry, Renaiisance, Garden, Library, Treetops, or Vincent's Hideaway room. Lambertville village, nearby New Hope and Lahaska offer interesting shops, pubs, entertainment, and theater. Area attractions: Belle Mountain Ski Resort, Howell Living Farm, Delaware River tubing and rafting. wineries, Washington Crossing State Park. Continental breakfast featuring homemade muffins is served in the sun room constructed entirely of stone, in the original 1820 dining room, or garden patio. Meeting facilities available. Fax, copier, and secretarial services available. Wheelchair accessible. No smoking.

Spring Lake

Sea Crest By the Sea
19 Tuttle Avenue
Spring Lake, NJ 07762
(908) 449-9031
Innkeepers: John and Carol Kirby

♔♔♔ Rating: A
Rates: Double/$92-239
Credit Cards: MC, V

Thirty-five room Victorian mansion is situated a half block from the ocean and located 5 miles east of the Garden State Parkway at exit 98. Choose from eleven individually decorated guest rooms or one two-room suite, each with private bath. Two rooms offer a fireplace. Play croquet in the yard or borrow a bicycle to explore the town with its charming Victorian homes, lovely beaches, restaurants, antique shops, and boutiques. Golf, tennis, sailing, Garden State Art Center, and Monmouth race tracks are also nearby. Buffet breakfast features scones, fruit tarts, carrot cake, and home-baked bread. Restricted smoking.

Guests write: *"Parking is ample, the innkeepers are friendly and the facilities are meticulously kept. While many Jersey Shore inns and B & B's can claim such amenities, the Sea Crest remains a cut above the others. First, the Sea Crest is one-half block from the boardwalk and beach. Beyond is the Atlantic Ocean surf, pleasure crafts and distant freighters. The Sea Crest provides beach passes, mats, towels and sand chairs. Second, the Sea Crest is located in the quintessential Jersey Shore community."* (J&R Rodriguez)

"The Sea Crest is our escape from the hustle, bustle world we all live in. We have been regulars sine the year John and Carol opened and try to visit often. We always start our 'holiday season' in December at the Sea Crest. The house is decorated so perfect, and it is so relaxing—before we all get swept away with everything that goes with the holidays and the preparation." (J. Zacco)

"We arrived at the Sea Crest by the Sea during a snow storm but were immediately warmed and comforted by the gracious welcome of John & Carol. They soothed our frozen nerves with a wonderful afternoon blend of tea and scrumptious cheesecake. Our room was softly aglow with the warmth of a fireplace which framed the antique furnishings and delightfully elegant appointed room. Morning brought bright sunlight and the opportunity to walk the boardwalk after an elegant candlelit breakfast with homemade breads, scones (with raspberry butter!) and Carol's fabulous 'feather bed' eggs." (S. Morrison)

Additional information on B&Bs in this state is available from the following B&B reservation agency: Mi Casa Su Casa (800) 456-0682.

Albuquerque

Casas de Suenos Old Town Bed & Breakfast Inn
310 Rio Grande Boulevard S.W.
Albuquerque, NM 87104
(505) 247-4560 or (800) CHAT W/US
Innkeeper: Robert Hanna

♛♛   Rating: B
Rates: Single/$85-200; Double/$85-250
Credit Cards: AE, MC, V

Casas de Suenos is a Southwestern garden compound built in 1930 with a main house and fourteen small "casitas" or cottages. Originally built as an artist's colony, the inn is located one block from over a hundred Old Town shops and restaurants. Entrance to the inn is beneath a contemporary structure added recently by world famous architect, Bart Prince. Each of the fourteen guest rooms offers a private bath and eclectic blend of Southwestern decor and furnishings with European antiques, American Indian rugs, thick down comforters, and original art. There are two large common rooms as well as several patios and secluded garden areas including waterfalls. From the inn it's a short walk to museums, galleries, restaurants, nature park, and historic sites. Popular attractions include wineries, the world's longest aerial tram, ancient ruins, and archaeological sites. Full breakfast includes a hot entree and home-baked goods. Function rooms are available. Restricted smoking. Wheelchair access.

Guests write: *"We really enjoyed the Kachina Suite decorated in a southwestern style with a skylight over the king bed. It was lovely to have a gourmet breakfast surrounded by the flowers of their beautiful gardens." (W. Miller)*

"The casitas are so comfortable and complete, with sitting room and garden, that we consider Casa de Suenos our home in New Mexico. Each suite we visit becomes our favorite. La Miradora for the elegance with its Chinese silk rug and antique furniture or the Taos suite with its built-in adobe headboard and pueblo-like atmosphere. The birdsongs in the garden and the gas lamps at night make this a magical world of its own." (J. Cassidy)

Farmington

Casa Blanca
505 East La Plata Street
Farmington, NM 87401
(505) 327-6503
Innkeeper: Marti Wilden

👑👑   Rating: B+
Rates: Single/$40-70; Double/$50-100
Credit Cards: V

Casa Blanca is located in the geographical center of the four states of Colorado, Arizona, Utah, and New Mexico just 45 minutes southwest of Durango, Colorado. The white brick Mediterranean style home with red clay tile roof boasts Spanish wrought iron grillwork on major windwos and front entry. The front yard is landscaped with native plants and the backyard provides a private patio with brick retaining walls. Others features include garden statuary, gazebo, and hot tub. Three guest rooms and a suite are available, each with private bath. Amenities include refreshments, TV with VCR, video library, bathrobes, and telephone. The living room with antique Spanish decor theme has tapestry and leather furniture. A large stone fireplace dominates the den with a terra cotta ceramic floor, Tuscan game table and chairs, Navajo rugs and art, library, and comfortable furniture. Area attractions: mountains, Indian ruins, canyons, golf, fishing, lakes, scenic train rides, restaurants, and skiing in Durango, a 45 minute drive. Continental breakfast includes fresh fruit, juices, cereals, and a tea, cereals, fresh baked items, and regional specialties. Wedding and meeting facilities available. Wheelchair access. No smoking.

Jemez Springs

Jemez River Bed & Breakfast Inn
16445 Highway 4
Jemez Springs, NM 87025
(505) 829-3262
Fax: (505) 829-3262
Innkeepers: Larry and Roxe Ann Clutter

👑👑   Rating: A
Rates: Double/$60-120
Credit Cards: AE, MC, & V

Jemez River Bed & Breakfast Inn is 40 miles NW of Albuquerque, NM, on

State Scenic Highway 4. Adobe-style home with eighteen foot wood-beamed ceilings and an entrance of adobe archways is surrounded by mountains. Behind this bed and breakfast, enjoy the Jemez River or visit the two plaza areas with peach trees and 600 gallon bird bath/pond. Six air-conditioned guest rooms with private baths are available. Each room is individually named and decorated with Southwestern Indian tribes' and pueblos' authentic artifacts, pottery, rugs, paintings, arrowheads, and kachina dolls. The rooms surround the large outdoor garden plaza filled with birds. Other amenities include telephone, television with VCR, hot tub, small gym, and "welcome" fruit or beverage. Views of the Mesa can be seen from grand, picturesque windows that encompass a sizable breakfast area. Within walking distance is cross country skiing, Indian Pueblos and culture, fishing, national forests, national historic sites, hiking, hot baths, and camping. Area attractions: Gillman Tunnels, Jemez River Falls, Virgin Mesa, Red Rocks, the Soda Dam, Battleship Rock Park, Dark Canyon, Fenton Lake State Park, and Valle Grande State Park (world's largest crater), and Jemez State Monument. Full breakfast, served on a large southwestern style table with Navajo placemats, includes pancakes, sausage, bacon, hash browns, Canadian bacon, eggs to order, omlettes, huevos rancheros, breakfast tacos and burritos, waffles, cereal, cinnamon toast, French toast, muffins, biscuits, homemade breads, bagels, fresh fruit, juice, coffee, tea, herbal tea, and soft drinks. Wedding and meeting facilities. Wheelchair Access - two rooms. Families welcome. No Smoking.

Guests write: "*New Mexico is relished as the Land of Enchantment… Jemez River B&B could easily be a major contributor to that enchantment. It's haciena-style living combined with absolutely gorgeous vistas will rival any travel experience of all the Southwest sights to be visited.*" (*W&S Beierman*)

"*All the rooms open onto a beautiful courtyard filled with hummingbirds and a close-up view of the Jemez Mountains. The rooms are provided with every amenity you can think of. Breakfast is made to order form a delicious menu. The entire inn is filled with American Indian art and artifacts that are fascinating.*" (*J. Colrain*)

"*Breakfast is a feast for all the senses: fresh-made waffles with fruit, whirring hummingbirds, morning sunlight glistening from cottonwoods beneath the volcanic cliffs.*" (*L. Berger*)

"*The breakfast was exceptionally delicious! I've had numerous breakfast burritos but this one tops them all! I work at an interior design firm and I found the decorations were unique, yet simple. We especially loved the water fountain and hiking trails out back.*" (*T. Ray*)

Los Ojos

Casa de Martinez
P.O. Box 96
Los Ojos, NM 87551
(505) 588-7858
Innkeeper: Clorinda Sanchez

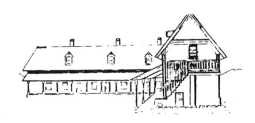

♛♛♛ Rating: A-
Rates: Single or Double/$55-90
Senior discount

Historic Spanish adobe inn built in 1861 has been in the same family for several generations and is located in a rural area 13 miles south of Chama on old US-84 in the small community of Los Brazos. Choose from six guest rooms decorated with antique furniture and local crafts; four offer a private bath. One large first-floor guest suite offers a private bath and fireplace. The inn, hosted by the great-granddaughter of early settlers in the area, has views towards the famous Brazos waterfall named El Chorro. Popular attractions in the area include fishing, hunting, cross-country skiing, and train rides over the Rocky Mountains. Full breakfast is served. Families welcome. The newest addition to the inn is a small conference room and gift shop. Wheelchair access. No smoking. Open February through October.

Guests write: *"Clorinda's special breakfast meals are worth the drive to Casa de Martinez. She and her husband are both interesting to talk to as well as informative about the area."* (D. Crone)

"We enjoy the romantic atmosphere on our annual winter get-away." (J. Ghahate)

"This is a great and pleasant place with wonderful hospitality." (B. Cherin)

"I enjoyed my stay very much since it was such a warm and cozy atmosphere. I will be back." (S. Gonzales)

Santa Fe

Inn on the Alameda
303 East Alameda
Santa Fe, NM 87501
(800) 289-2122
Innkeeper: David Oberstein

♛♛♛   Rating: A+
Rates: Single/$145-320; Double/$155-330
Senior, auto club, business travel, and family discounts
Credit Cards: AE, MC. V

Large adobe and Spanish-Colonial inn is located 5 miles north of I-25, exit
289 in downtown. The inn has sixty-six guest rooms or suites, each with
private bath, fireplace, TV, and phone. Many rooms offer a Kiva fireplaces,
patio, balcony, and Southwest-style French doors. Relax in the main library or
Agoyo Room Lounge with full bar. There is also an on-site spa, fitness center,
massage room, and guest laundry room. Area attractions: Southwest Center for
the Arts, Native American and Spanish cultural sites, desert wilderness,
tennis, fishing, hiking, and skiing. Hearty continental breakfast is served in
the Agoyo Room or out in the courtyard and offers a choice of Kona coffee,
breads, pastries and seasonal fruits. Families welcome. Wheelchair access.

Santa Fe

Pueblo Bonito Bed & Breakfast Inn
138 West Manhattan
Santa Fe, NM 87501
(505) 984-8001
Innkeepers: Herb and Amy Behm

♛♛   Rating: B
Rates: Single/$65-115; Double/$75-125
Credit Cards: MC, V

Historic adobe estate is located in downtown Santa Fe, three blocks south of
the Plaza. Choose from fifteen guest rooms, each with private bath, unique
corner fireplace, and foot-thick adobe walls and window sills. While there is a
variety of size, decor, and amenities throughout the rooms, each has been
furnished with native antiques, Indian rugs, sand paintings, and works of local
artists. Area attractions include historic downtown sites, museums, Indian
pueblos, and specialty shops. Continental "create your own" breakfast buffet
offers a variety of fresh fruits, Danish, muffins, and croissants.

Taos

Casa Europa Inn and Gallery
157 Upper Ranchitos Road
Taos, NM 87571
(505) 758-9798
Innkeepers: Rudi and Marcia Zwicker

👑👑👑 Rating: A
Rates: Single/$60-100; Double/$80-110
Credit Cards: MC, V

Historic Southwestern adobe has been completely restored with modern European finishing and has a rural setting outside the city. There are six guest rooms that vary in size, decor, and amenities but all have a selection of interesting antiques and a private bath. Several offer a fireplace or wood stove and full-size Jacuzzi. There are several common areas throughout the inn offering quiet places for reading, conversing with other guests, or viewing the traditional or contemporary crafts and paintings of native American artists. A quiet courtyard offers a Swedish sauna and hot tub. A ski area is nearby as are Indian pueblos and white-water rafting. Full breakfast and afternoon refreshments served daily. Families welcome. Restricted smoking.

Taos

La Posada de Taos
309 Juanita Lane
P.O. Box 1118
Taos, NM 87571
(505) 758-8164 or (800) 645-4803
Innkeepers: Bill Swan and Nancy Brooks-Swan

👑👑👑 Rating: B+
Rates: Single/$65-105; Double/$75-115

Adobe walls and a latilla fence encompass this 1907 adobe brick inn and its surrounding property in the secluded historic district. Located one hour north of Santa Fe, this one-half acre property is only blocks from the downtown plaza yet offers a view of the mountains that surround the town. All rooms have beam ceilings, or vigas. The six guest units are individually decorated with country pine antiques and each has a private, tiled bath. Five of the rooms are in the inn itself; while the sixth is a separate honeymoon house across the courtyard. The large living room, with a fireplace and bookshelves, is decorated with English country pine antiques. A dining room that seats 12 has French doors opening towards the mountains. Winter recreation includes both downhill and cross-country skiing from three ski areas—Taos Ski Valley, Rio Costilla, and Angel Fire. Summer travelers can ride the whitewater, go fishing in the Rio Grande, ride horseback into the Sangre de Cristo mountains, or visit the Indian pueblos. Taos is also a world-famous artist colony. There are many art galleries, museums, and shops within walking distance. Full breakfast served, with specialties such as lemon bread and Eggs a la Goldenrod. Meeting facilities available. Restricted smoking.

Guests write: *"We felt at home at La Posada de Taos from the moment we walked in the front gate. The decor is homey and each room has its own unique charm. We stayed in the most unique room away from the main house and had a two-story bed where you climb a three-stair ladder and sleep under a skylight!"* (D&R Flade)

"Breakfast was beautifully served each morning on well-appointed table and consisted of different menu each of our nine-day stay. Nancy and Bill were very helpful in sharing the area's many activities and historical sites. The inn was filled with lovely English cottage antiques which were nicely blended with Southwestern furniture and decor." (I. Jeffers)

"The amenities included: antique quilts on the bed, plush, oversized bath towels, good reading lamps placed over the bed for excellent light; electric blankets available, cozy individual stoves, lighted fireplace going constantly in the living room; a good library with great books on Southwestern art; breakfast strada topped with homemade salsa; daily weather report; knowledgable innkeepers." (J. Rheams)

"Located conveniently to all the attractions offered in town, it's a pleasure to walk back to the charming rooms which afford comfort and spaciousness, mountain views, and fireplaces." (J. Bell)

Additional information on B&Bs in New York is available from the following:
Abode B&B (212) 472-2000 or Bed & Breakfast & Books (212) 865-8740

Albany/Dolgeville

Adrianna's Bed & Breakfast
44 Stewart Street
Dolgeville, NY 13329
(315) 429-3249 or (800) 335-4233
Innkeeper: Adrianna Naizby

♛♛   Rating: B+
Rates: Single/$45; Double/$55-58

Modern raised ranch home is located 6 miles north of exit 29-A off I-90 on
the New York Thruway. There are three air conditioned guest rooms that share
two baths and have been decorated with comfort in mind. Relax in the
swimming pool or visit the local golf course. A living room on the main floor
offers a fireplace, TV, and comfortable seating. Nearby attractions include
Saratoga Raceway and Performing Arts Center, Herkimer Diamond Mines,
Herkimer Home, Daniel Green Slipper Outlet, Erie Canal in Little Falls, and
the Lyndon Lyon Greenhouses which specialize in violets. Full traditional
breakfast served. Families welcome. Restricted smoking.

Guests write: *"The accommodations are very comfortable and spacious. Adrianna
serves a terrific breakfast and is an informed and hospitable hostess."* (G. Romanic)

*"Our trip to Dolgeville was for my Dad's funeral. The funeral director suggested
Adrianna's. She didn't know us from Adam but she made us feel like her home was
ours and we almost felt like family when we left. The decor was very tastefully done
throughout. The food was wonderful and the setting and service just beautiful. In
each of the bedrooms was a tastefully selected library that made me want to stay for a
month to read, read, read."* (B. Luft)

*"At no place we have been - motels, hotels, B&Bs - have we received hospitality,
cordiality and accommodations akin to Adrianna's B&B. Hers is tops on our list."*
(F. Belford)

*"Our brief stay was more than a wonderful night's rest followed by a delectable
breakfast, it was an experience in friendship. Never before have we met a stranger
who immediately by her friendliness and warmth, was transformed into a charming
friend."* (G. McCloskey)

Barneveld

Sugarbush Bed & Breakfast
RR 1, Box 227, Old Poland Road
Barneveld, NY 13304
(315) 896-6860 or (800) 582-5845
Innkeepers: William and Maryann Mahanna

👑👑 Rating: B+
Rates: Single/$40; Double/$55-80
Credit Cards: MC, V
Senior, family, business, and auto club discounts

Historic Colonial home is nestled among old maple trees and located twelve miles north of Utica off Route 12. There are five guest rooms on the first or second floor; two offer a private bath. The rooms differ greatly in size and amenities, but all have seating areas and fresh flowers. A large guest suite on the first floor offers a private bath, bedroom and sitting room. There are several common rooms including a living room with fireplace and views of the countryside. Area attractions include Adirondack Park with skiing and water sports. Full breakfast includes eggs, bacon, and waffles topped with New York state maple syrup. Afternoon refreshments are offered and additional meals are available upon request. Families welcome. Restricted smoking.

Canandaigua

The Acorn Inn
4508 Bristol Valley Road, Bristol Center
Canandaigua, NY 14424
(716) 229-2834 or (716) 394-5260
Innkeepers: Joan and Louis Clark

👑👑👑 Rating: A+
Rates: Single or Double/$75-150
Credit Cards: MC, V
Senior and auto club discount

1795 Federal Stagecoach inn has been renovated to reflect 18th-Century style and is located eight miles west of Canandaigua, 30 miles south of Rochester. Choose from four air-conditioned guest rooms with sitting areas and private baths; one with whirlpool. Each room has been furnished with antiques, queen canopy beds, and luxury linens. There is nightly turn-down service with chocolates and ice water provided. Afternoon tea is served in front of the large colonial fireplace outfitted with antique crane and hanging iron pots. There are extensive private gardens perfect for a quiet stroll. Area attractions: Canandaigua Lake, Sonneneberg Gardens, Bristol Harbor Golf Club, Bristol Mountain skiing, Finger Lakes Performing Arts Center, and the Cumming Nature Center. Bristol Blueberry Surprise, spinach strata and artichoke frittata are some of the specialties served at the full country breakfast. No smoking.

Guests write: *"We wrote in the visitors' book that this was the finest B & B we have ever stayed in, whether in North America, England, or Europe. Our stay was indeed memorable also because of our warm and friendly host and hostess."* (M. Lacey)

"After two visits we have come to feel very much at home at the Acorn Inn. No wonder you are rated 'excellent' by the ABBA. You have a very special place. We enjoyed our stay—everything was wonderful—the beds, the breakfasts (especially the blueberry dish with sausages and syrup with blueberries), and the Pop-ups on Tuesday morning were delicious." (P. Ivers)

Canandaigua

Morgan-Samuels Inn
2920 Smith Road
Canandaigua, NY 14424
(716) 394-9232 or Fax: (716) 394-8044
Innkeepers: Julie and John Sullivan

♛♛♛ Rating: A+
Rates: Single/$60; Double/$99-195
Credit Cards: MC, V
Corporate discount

Stone mansion built in 1810 sits at the top of a hill in a rural setting in the Finger Lakes area of west-central New York. Six guest rooms are available and each has distinctive decor and air conditioning. All guest rooms in the house provide fireplaces. The Morgan Suite and Victorian Room offer a Jacuzzi. There are several common rooms throughout the inn and four individual patios overlooking the countryside. The property has forty-six acres of fields and woods to explore as well as a tennis court. Popular attractions in the area include lake recreation, wagon rides, skiing, wineries, antique shops, and outdoor theaters as well as Sonnenberg Gardens, Bristol Mountain, Granger Homestead, and the Radio Museum. Full gourmet breakfast is served by candlelight and an afternoon tea is offered daily. Dinner is available by advance reservation. No smoking.

Cazenovia

The Brewster Inn
6 Ledyard Ave. P.O. Box 507
Cazenovia, NY 13035
(315) 655-9232
Innkeepers: Richard and Catherine Hubbard

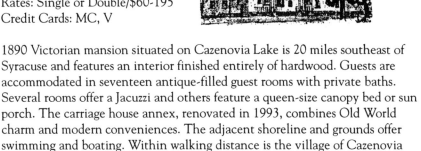

♛♛♛   Rating: A+
Rates: Single or Double/$60-195
Credit Cards: MC, V

1890 Victorian mansion situated on Cazenovia Lake is 20 miles southeast of Syracuse and features an interior finished entirely of hardwood. Guests are accommodated in seventeen antique-filled guest rooms with private baths. Several rooms offer a Jacuzzi and others feature a queen-size canopy bed or sun porch. The carriage house annex, renovated in 1993, combines Old World charm and modern conveniences. The adjacent shoreline and grounds offer swimming and boating. Within walking distance is the village of Cazenovia with its historic homes and Lorenzo, the 18th century estate of the founder of the village. Take day trips to Cooperstown, Chittenango Falls State Park, and to the Finger Lakes/Wine country. A continental breakfast is offered. Wedding and meeting facilities available. Families welcome.

Guests write: *"Outstanding building and grounds. Spacious, beautifully restored and decorated rooms. Homey feeling with fireplaces and friendly staff. Excellent value with reasonable prices. A wonderful, relaxed feeling. The nicest inn that I've stayed in."* (D. Goverts and P. Kanz)

"Our room was spacious and yet very warm and cozy but the staff is what would make us come back. We were snowed in for the storm of '93 and they were bending over backwards to make it as pleasant as could be under the situation. You will also never go wrong with any meal you order. It was fabulous." (D. Greene)

"The Brewster Inn in beautiful Cazenovia is the ideal place. It is truly a winter wonderland. Every member of the staff at Brewster Inn is most friendly and helpful!" (M. Barreras)

Chazy

Grand-Vue Bed & Breakfast
2237 Lake Shore Road
Chazy, NY 12921
(518) 298-5700 or (518) 846-7857
Innkeeper: Rita-Rae Laurin

♛ Rating: C
Rates: Single$35-45; Double/$ 50-60.

Brick Federal-style house built in 1867 is a country farmhouse located on a working dairy farm overlooking Lake Champlain and the Green Mountains of Vermont. Choose from four guest rooms, one with private bath, all decorated with family heirlooms and collectibles. Walk along the private shoreline along Lake Champlain. Relax on the glider under the ash trees, visit calves and chickens on the farm, or explore Chazy township with its apple orchards, the Alice T. Miner Colonial Collection and the Miner Research Institute. Area attractions: year round fishing, swimming, sailing, golfing, hiking on nature trails, bicycling, skiing, maple sugaring, and boating. Within driving distance are Montreal Canada and Vermont attractions. A full breakfast offers country specialties such as quiche, sausage casserole, or pancakes with local syrup accompanied by home made muffins and fresh fruit. Afternoon tea is offered. Small meeting facilities available. Families welcome. Restricted smoking.

Guests write: *Seven of us stayed at Grand-Vue and Rita Rae did everything to make the stay pleasurable. She served breakfast at the time we suggested each morning. The three breakfasts we had were so substantial, we did not want to eat again until evening. How could we with fruit, breakfast casserole, pancakes with maple syrup, gravy, muffins — and all served so attractively."* (M. Rob)

"My husband and I have stayed at many B&Bs all over the U.S. and I have yet to meet a hostess as accommodating, friendly as Rita Rae. The farmhouse is comfortable, quiet, warm, and bright, and we were told to use things, not just look at them. My four-year-old daughter has enjoyed miling the cows and feeding a newborn calf a bottle of milk." (S. Fairchild)

"We were stuck at Canadian immigration due to a technicality and had to wait overnight in the United States. We called Grand-Vue. They picked us up, gave us a simple dinner, and were the sweetest, most genuinely nice people we've ever met. I loved being next to a dairy farm with fresh milk and fruits." (S.K.)

Cooperstown

Angelholm
14 Elm Street, Box 705
Cooperstown, NY 13326
(607) 547-2483
Fax: (607) 547-2309
Innkeepers: Jan and Fred Reynolds

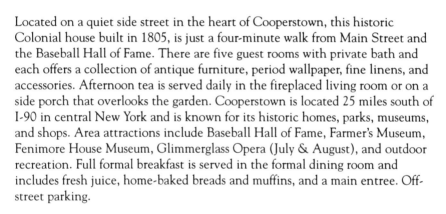

♛♛♛ Rating: A+
Rates: Single or Double/$70-90
Credit Cards: MC, V

Located on a quiet side street in the heart of Cooperstown, this historic Colonial house built in 1805, is just a four-minute walk from Main Street and the Baseball Hall of Fame. There are five guest rooms with private bath and each offers a collection of antique furniture, period wallpaper, fine linens, and accessories. Afternoon tea is served daily in the fireplaced living room or on a side porch that overlooks the garden. Cooperstown is located 25 miles south of I-90 in central New York and is known for its historic homes, parks, museums, and shops. Area attractions include Baseball Hall of Fame, Farmer's Museum, Fenimore House Museum, Glimmerglass Opera (July & August), and outdoor recreation. Full formal breakfast is served in the formal dining room and includes fresh juice, home-baked breads and muffins, and a main entree. Off-street parking.

Guests write: *"Janet and Fred make their guests feel like they are visiting old and dear friends. The breakfasts are outstanding. The hosts enjoy answering questions about Cooperstown and the surrounding area."* (J. Sloan)

Croton on Hudson

Alexander Hamilton House
49 Van Wyck Street
Croton on Hudson, NY 10520
(914) 271-6737
Innkeeper: Barbara Notarius

♛♛♛ Rating: A+
Rates: Single/$75-100; Double/$95-250
Credit Cards: AE, MC, V

Historic 1889 Victorian home situated on a cliff overlooking the Hudson

River, is located four blocks east of Route 9. Choose from nine individually decorated and air conditioned guest rooms, three with private bath. The home has many period antiques and collections and offers several accommodation options for guests: a queen suite with fireplaced sitting room; a double bedded suite with fireplace and small sitting room; two large queen bedded rooms. The master suite has a fireplace, picture windows, stained glass, Jacuzzi, and river views. The newly opened Penthouse Bridal Chamber features king bed, skylights, private bath with Jacuzzi, and fireplace. Guests are invited to use the in-ground swimming pool and outdoor patio with gas grill. Area attractions: West Point, Sleepy Hollow restorations, Lyndhurst, Van Cortlandt Manor, Teatown Reservation, and easy train access to New York City sights. Full breakfast. Families welcome. No smoking.

Elizabethtown

Stony Water Bed & Breakfast
R.R. 1 Box 69
Elizabethtown, NY 12932
(518) 873-9125
Innkeeper: Sandra Murphy

♛♛♛   Rating: A
Rates: Single/$55; Double/$65-75
Credit Cards: MC, V

Italianate house built around 1870 is situated on 87 acres of fields and woodlands and located 30 minutes from Lake Placid, midway between Albany and Montreal. The four guest rooms offer views of the surrounding countryside, antique furnishings, and a private bath. One room features French doors that open onto the swimming pool and woodlands. Enjoy afternoon tea or sit by the fireplace in the library, bicycle along scenic country roads, play the baby grand piano in the parlor, swim in the pool, or relax in the hammock. Hike the well-maintained trails of the Adirondack High Peaks or ski Whiteface Mountain or the nearby Olympic downhill ski venue which are all an easy drive from the inn. Go cross-country skiing, bobsledding, or take a luge run at Mt. Van Hoevenberg. Area attractions include the John Brown Farm and many Revolutionary War sites. A full breakfast entree is accompanied by home-made breads, muffins, and fresh fruit. Small meeting facilities available. Families welcome. Wheelchair access. No smoking.

Guests write: *"The spirit of the house has been warmed by the hosts who prepared us for our hike and made us look forward to coming out of the woods (something that we usually do reluctantly)."* (A. Stidfole)

"In all seasons the drive up the road to the beautiful B&B expands the heart and readies us for a great trip. We love the warmth and comfort of the hearth and library, the delicious, wholesome food, the relaxed innkeepers who impose no rules (not even as to the time of breakfast), and the special Adirondack setting." (N. Gershon and B. Fried)

"The loft above the garage overlooking the hills & meadow is superb — what serenity." (M. Meade)

"The lovely room, the fresh flowers, the good food, the cozy fire, and the warm hospitality made my stay so delightful." (M. E. Cornell)

Hammondsport

The Blushing Rose Bed & Breakfast Inn
11 William Street
Hammondsport, NY 14840
(607) 569-3402 or 569-3483
Innkeeper: Ellen Laufersweiler

♛♛♛ Rating: A-
Rates: Single/$65-75; Double/$75-95
Corporate, and auto club discounts

Small Victorian-Italianate home is located at the southern tip of Keuka Lake in the Finger Lakes region, about twenty-five miles west of Corning in the heart of Western New York state and wine country. There are four guest rooms on the second floor. Each offers a private bath, air conditioning, and individual decor with special touches such as handmade quilts, stenciled walls, lace canopy beds, and white wicker furnishings. Explore the quaint historic village and hiking, bicycling in the area. Popular attractions: Curtiss Museum, Corning Glass Museum, Watkins Glen auto racing, and lake activities. Full breakfast specialties include baked French toast, lemon poppy seed waffles, and strawberry bread. No smoking. 1/$65-75; 2/$75-95.

Guests write: *"Ellen and Buck Laufersweiler greeted us with warm and friendly smiles and welcomed us into their home with open arms. From that moment on, we both knew it was going to be a very special weekend. Our accommodations were everything we had hoped for...antiques and lace nestled among a cozy Victorian decor, flowers, candies and Buck's cookies for our pleasure, breakfasts of heart-shaped waffles and homemade granola and most importantly an atmosphere that lent itself to 'rest and relaxation.' We enjoyed ourselves so much that first year that we have made it an annual Valentine's weekend tradition."* (C&A Weiler)

"Buck & Ellen are innkeepers who have a genuine interest in their guests. We like to stay in their coziest room, Moonbeams. With its sloping ceilings you have to watch your head! We like the skylight in the room, and we always hope for rain—it makes a nice, hypnotic tapping against the window. Breakfast is delicious and filling. Ellen's French toast is so rich it resembles bread pudding." (L. Armstrong)

"The atmosphere is the homey. Both hosts are entertaining and relaxed. They are 'family.' I'll leave the decor to the experts, but everything fit a design. The breakfast of baked French toast and a wide assortment of fruits is filling and tasty." (R. Powell)

"Romantic B & B , 25 steps to Keuka Lake. The 'Burgundy Room' had a king bed with a lace wall canopy. It also had a nice sitting area with plenty of interesting magazines. The inn is furnished with antiques and has a very cozy atmosphere. The inn also has a coffee maker in each room with assorted teas. Outside each room is also an iron and a basket full of those things everybody forgets; such as, toothpaste, deodorant, and sewing things." (L&G Fabian)

Hamptons — (also see the listing under Westhampton, NY.)

Hamptons/Bellport

The Great South Bay Inn
160 South Country Road
Bellport, NY 11713
(516) 286-8588
Innkeeper: Judith Mortimer

♛♛♛   Rating: A-
Rates: Single/$50; Double/$70-120
Senior discount

Restored, late 19th-Century Cape Cod inn is located on Long Island's South Shore. It is in close proximity to the Hamptons and 8 miles southeast of exit 64 of the Long Island Expressway. Each of the six guest rooms are furnished in period antiques and feature the original wainscoting. Two offer a private bath. Stroll Bellport's historic shopping district and view the old historic homes or dine at a variety of fine restaurants. A town ferry is available to take you across to the village's private beach on Fire Island. Homemade scones, cereals, and breads are featured in the continental breakfast and lunch is available. The garden accommodates small weddings and gatherings. Families welcome. Restricted smoking.

Lake George/Warrensburg

House on the Hill Bed & Breakfast
P.O. Box 248 Route 28
Warrensburg, NY 12885
(518) 623-9390 or (800) 221-9390
Innkeepers: Joe and Lynn Rubino

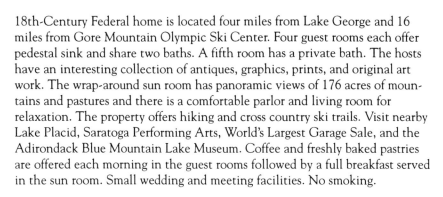

 Rating: B+
Rates: Single/$65; Double/$85-109
Credit Cards: MC, V
Senior, family, corporate, and auto club discount

18th-Century Federal home is located four miles from Lake George and 16 miles from Gore Mountain Olympic Ski Center. Four guest rooms each offer pedestal sink and share two baths. A fifth room has a private bath. The hosts have an interesting collection of antiques, graphics, prints, and original art work. The wrap-around sun room has panoramic views of 176 acres of mountains and pastures and there is a comfortable parlor and living room for relaxation. The property offers hiking and cross country ski trails. Visit nearby Lake Placid, Saratoga Performing Arts, World's Largest Garage Sale, and the Adirondack Blue Mountain Lake Museum. Coffee and freshly baked pastries are offered each morning in the guest rooms followed by a full breakfast served in the sun room. Small wedding and meeting facilities. No smoking.

Guests write: *"The Rubinos got us hooked for life on the B & B concept. They cured my 'motel mentality'. In over 25 years 'stayed in a motel' comments, we have never met people who made us more welcome in our lives. I would recommend this great place to anyone. You will not find better people." (R&B James)*

"We've been telling everyone that the best part of our vacation was definitely where we stayed — The House on the Hill. The kindness and more-than-friendly hospitality made us feel so comfortable. The advice on attractions to see was well appreciated. The breakfast was like no other and our morning conversations were interesting and enjoyable." (Amy Berthiaume)

"Hospitality, great stories, and a great stay in Lake George!" (N. Schandler)

Lisle

Dorchester Farm
RD 1, Box 162, Keibel Road
Lisle, NY 13797
(607) 692-4511
Innkeepers: Carolan and Scott Mersereau

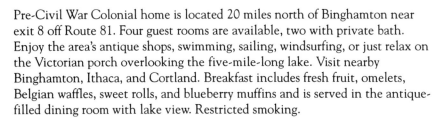

♛♛♛   Rating: A-
Rates: Single or Double/$65-85
Credit Cards: MC, V

Pre-Civil War Colonial home is located 20 miles north of Binghamton near exit 8 off Route 81. Four guest rooms are available, two with private bath. Enjoy the area's antique shops, swimming, sailing, windsurfing, or just relax on the Victorian porch overlooking the five-mile-long lake. Visit nearby Binghamton, Ithaca, and Cortland. Breakfast includes fresh fruit, omelets, Belgian waffles, sweet rolls, and blueberry muffins and is served in the antique-filled dining room with lake view. Restricted smoking.

Guests write: *"I have to say that this was one of the most unique and beautiful B&Bs I have been to. I could spend all day looking at her great antique collections of kitchenware, Teddy Bears, and furniture. The suite with its magnificent view of the lake was breathtaking and I felt very at home with my favorite Crabtree and Evelyn amenities which were so specially arranged in the bathroom."* (M. Vorhies)

"This was our first B&B experience. Any in the future will have a hard time measuring up to the charm and hospitality here." (L. Harwood)

"Everything was super. The house is beautiful, food delicious, gracious hosts. I was completely fascinated by the home." (E. Stiering)

"This is a 150 year old farmhouse that has been restored and is absolutely wonderful in every respect. But more important than the decor (which is extraordinary), the full delicious homemade breakfast and the lovely touches, is the warmth and entertaining side of the hosts." (J. Watso)

"We arrived at Dorchester at night greeted by a blazing fire. The next morning, we woke with a view of mist rising over the lake below our window. The feather-bed mattress and Laura Ashley quality linens almost made it impossible to get out of bed. Before exploring the gigantic turn-of-the-century barn and swinging in the chair above the lake, we feasted on a glorious breakfast of homemade muffins and breads, eggs, sausage, and a hot apple crisp to die for. I still dream about this apple crisp." (H. Else)

New York City — See listings under Croton-on-Hudson and Staten Island.

Plattsburgh

The Marshall House
115 Court Street
Plattsburgh, NY 12901
(518) 566-8691
Innkeepers: Harriette Walker
& Donna Corodimas

 Rating: B+
Rates: Single/$50-70; Double/$60-80

Slate-roofed Queen Anne Victorian painted in greens, gold, fuchsia, and brown has a hooded wrap-around porch and turret and is on a corner lot bordered in cedar hedges and a traditional garden of perennials. Choose from four guest rooms, two with private baths, featuring old quilts, cypress flooring, king or queen-size beds, and period furniture and wallpaper. Relax in the turret shaped parlor with fireplace, piano, books, and television or in the dining room with bay window seating and mahogany inlaid floors. Relax in the swing on the wrap-around porch. Walk to shops, museums, and art galleries. Four-season recreation includes cross-country and downhill skiing, fishing, boating, and hiking in the Adirondacks. Vermont, Lake Placid and Montreal are just a short drive away. Full breakfast features specialities such as orange-chocolate muffins and French toast made with homemade bread. Meeting facilities available. No smoking.

Guests write: *"The other B&Bs at which I've stayed were all in England or Ireland. Let me list a few of the features I enjoyed at the Marshall House, which I did not find at any British B&B: a key to the house itself, rather than just my room; a private bathroom; breakfast served at my convenience; my tastes were consulted in preparing the breakfast menu; an afternoon snack was served every day, left in my room, including fresh fruit and homemade cookies; my own map of the area was also left in my room and extensive advice was given about local attractions; the local paper was ready at the breakfast table; a wonderful supply of paperback novels available included detective novels as well as more highbrow literature."* (L. Kiefer)

"We were extremely pleased with Marshall House. The house itself is a Victorian masterpiece with handsome woodwork, a beautiful central stairhall, and comfortable bedrooms furnished in ways that make one feel at home. Breakfasts are by no means routine; the fare is imaginative, abundant and very good. Above all, the hosts are friendly, easy-going, and attentive to all one's needs." (C. Olds)

Rochester/Fairport

Woods Edge Bed & Breakfast
151 Bluhm Road
Fairport, NY 14450
(716) 223-8877 or (716) 223-8510
Innkeeper: Betty Kinsman

 Rating: B+
Rates: Single/$60-95; Double/$75-95.

Woods Edge B&B is a contemporary home in a secluded setting located 20 minutes from downtown Rochester. Two antique-filled guest rooms with private baths are available. The private guest house features a living room with fireplace, dining area, fully equipped kitchen, bedroom with queen-size bed, and private bath with washer and dryer. Nearby museums, colleges, parks, the Erie Canal, and the Finger Lakes region offer many activities such as swimming, skiing, golfing, sailing, and sport fishing. Full breakfast is served with homemade specialties such as Dutch pancakes, fruit salad, or heart-shaped waffles. Families welcome. No smoking. Resident cat.

Staten Island/New York City

Victorian Bed & Breakfast
92 Taylor Street
Staten Island, NY 10310
(718) 273-9861
Innkeeper: Danuta Gorlach

Rating: B
Rates: Single/$50; Double/$60-75
Credit Cards: AE
Senior and auto club discount

Italianette Victorian built in the 1860s is just three miles west of the Staten Island Ferry to Manhattan and is located on the north shore of Staten Island in the town of West New Brighton. Four guest rooms share two baths. Many furnishings are original to the house and every room in the house has a marble fireplace and mantel. Afternoon tea with baked pastries is served in the dining room or on the verandah. Explore the nearby Early American village or Snug Harbor Cultural Center. New York City's famous attractions are just twelve minutes away by ferry. A full breakfast includes hearty entrees such as egg dishes, fruit pancakes, or blintzes. Families welcome. No smoking.

Syracuse/Baldwinsville

Pandora's Getaway
83 Oswego Street
Baldwinsville, NY 13027
(315) 635-9571 or 638-8660
Innkeeper: Sandra Wheeler

♛♛   Rating: B-
Rates: Single/50; Double/$80
Credit Cards: MC, V

Restored Greek Revival home set high on a hill with sloping lawns is listed on the National Historic Register and located twenty minutes from Syracuse. Choose from four guest rooms, one with private bath. Each room has individual decor and amenities such as a fireplace, color TV, or panoramic views. Relax on the front porch or in the large living room. Area attractions include nearby Finger Lakes, Lake Ontario, and nature center. Baked French toast is often on the full breakfast menu served in the formal dining room. Wedding and meeting facilities available. Families welcome. Restricted smoking.

Guests write: *"We enjoyed the rooms, especially all of the cat decor—as animal lover and 'parents' to 7 felines, we felt at home. The breakfasts were absolutely delectible—the fresh fruits and baked muffins made our day and sent us on our way deliciously satisfied."* (B&V Carfagn)

"Sandy's cooking was just right for us since we are interested in good nutrition—plentiful local fruits in season. The home's setting is delightful—high on the bank of a hill in a quaint, friendly town." (J. Hillier)

"We have stayed at Pandora's Getaway on several occasions. Each time we have enjoyed our spacious room with fireplace, king-size bed, private bath and antique furniture. The common area of the inn always offers us a cozy home-like atmosphere accented with antiques and lots of interesting artifacts. Breakfast is always special—homemade breads and muffins, fresh fruit, coffee, juice and a special main dish. My favorite is the Breakfast Casserole." (J. Fiorini)

"Pandora's Getaway was our first encounter with a B&B. There were no hotels available so we thought we would give it a try. We stayed there out of necessity but it turned out to be a treat! Now our first preference would be a B&B. The food was homemade, delicious, and plentiful. The room was large with a fireplace all ready for us to use. The antiques added a quaint charm. The owners were very pleasant, gracious, and helpful." (S. Amato)

Watkins Glen/Dundee

South Glenora Tree Farm Bed & Breakfast
546 South Glenora Road
Dundee, NY 14837
(607) 243-7414
Innkeeper: Joseph Sullivan

♕♕♕ Rating: A-
Rates: 1/$55; 2/$65
Credit Cards: MC, V

Gambrel roof barn is now an inn situated on an active tree farm of 140 acres that is located in the Finger Lakes region of New York near Seneca Lake. Five guest rooms feature a private bath, air conditioning, queen-sized beds, rocking chairs, and handmade quilts and drapes. Relax in the sixty-five foot common area which features a library, lounge, dining room, and guest kitchen. Surrounding wooded hills and fields offer acres to walk or hike. Area attractions: wineries, wildlife reserves, Corning Glass factory, Grand Prix Raceway, and Watkins Glen. Outdoor recreation nearby includes fishing, swimming, and boating and the area is full of fine restaurants, gift stores, and antique shops. A continental plus breakfast is often served on the wrap-around porch and features home-baked goods and pastries. Families welcome. Wheelchair access. Restricted smoking.

Guests write: *"The bed and breakfast was very well kept, provided accessibility, via ramps and an adapted room and bath, information on the local events and places to enjoy. Use of their kitchen is provided at any time. Very 'country' and removed from the main highway, and simple/healthy breakfast foods." (A&G Hill)*

Westhampton Beach

Seafield House
2 Seafield Lane, P.O. Box 648
Westhampton Beach, NY 11978
(516) 288-1559
Innkeeper: Elsie Collins

♛♛♛ Rating: A-
Rates: Double/$100-195

Historic Victorian home built in 1880 is situated in town near shops and restaurants and located 3 miles south of Route 27, exit 63, or ninety minutes from Manhattan. There are two spacious guest suites with private bath, sitting room, antiques, and family treasures. Enjoy the warmth from the 1907 Modern Glenwood pot-belly stove or the fireplace in the parlor. An enclosed porch overlooks the tennis courts and swimming pool on the property. The beach as well as the shops on Main Street are just a short walk away as are local attractions such as historic homes, antique shops, golf, fishing, swimming, hiking, and bicycling. Full breakfast features home made goodies. No smoking.

Guests write: *"We just returned from an exceptional stay at 1880 House. From start to finish it was a warm, personal, comfortable, special stay. We had a tour of the home which was clean, beautifully decorated and of an era past. Hot tea, wine and biscuits were all set up. Breakfast was served on fine china and crystal in the dining room. We had fresh strawberries, melon to start and fresh orange juice. Even the water goblet contained a slice of fresh lemon. Homemade muffins and croissants were served with an excellent cheese and egg quiche. Our coffee cups were constantly filled." (M&T Kemper)*

"A wonderfully romantic, colonial decor. The breakfast and personality of Elsie, the hostess, are like sunshine in the morning. Every detail for our comfort was subtly addressed, from the bedside candy to the afternoon tea and sherry." (L. Donnelly)

"The breakfasts were marvelous, home-baked blueberry muffins were served with fruit (strawberries, grapefruit, cantaloupe) delicious homemade French toast and fresh squeezed orange juice, all enjoyed on her beautiful sunny porch with daily complimentary copy of the 'New York Times.' The Little Red Barn is a very comfortable bedroom with kitchen area, sleigh-style wooden bed—handmade quilts on walls and ceilings, all very beautiful." (E. Bru)

"The perfect bed and breakfast —everything you could ask for and more. The best 24 hours I ever spent at a hotel/inn." (L. Katz)

Aberdeen/Pinehurst

Inn at the Bryant House
214 North Poplar Street
Aberdeen NC 28315
(910) 944-3300 or (800) 453-4019
Fax: (910) 944-8898
Innkeepers: Bill and Abbie Gregory

♛♛   Rating: B
Rates: Single or Double/$45-70
Credit Cards: AE, D, MC, V
Senior, auto, and corporate discount

Colonial revival with a large, wrap-around porch and white pillars built in 1913 and completely restored. Situated in the historic district 30 miles west of Fayetteville, this inn is listed on the National Register of Historic Buildings. Guests have eight rooms from which to choose, six with private baths. The formal living room has a fireplace and piano. More casual are the TV room and the Green Room, which is the reading room. The Paisley Room is for dining, but there is also space for eating in the Garden Room, an enclosed porch decorated in a garden motif. Finally, there is a sitting room. Main attractions include golf and NASCAR racing. Tennis courts and antique shops are within walking distance. Other attractions, accessible by car, are championship golf courses, Fort Bragg/Pope AFB, and Lake Jordan. An expanded continental breakfast is served each morning. Wedding and meeting facilities available. Computers, fax and secretarial services available. Families welcome. Restricted smoking.

Guests write: *"The Inn at the Bryant House is like being in a large, friendly home. My sons and I stayed in a room with furniture that was original to the inn. The rooms are airy and I sat on a rainy evening in the upstairs sittting area with hot chocolate and my favorite book."* (K. Miller)

Asheville

Beaufort House Victorian Bed & Breakfast
61 North Liberty
Asheville, NC 28801
(704) 254-8334 FAX: (704) 251-2082
Innkeeper: Robert & Jacqueline Glasgow

♛♛♛ Rating: A+
Rates: Single/$65-95; Double/$ 75-150

Completely surrounded by trees, this two and a half story , grand Queen Anne
-style inn with wraparound "gingerbread" porch, and large bay windows is 80
miles north west of Columbia and 100 miles west of Charlotte. Choose from
four guest rooms, all with private baths, and featuring Victorian decor,
antiques, television, VCR, and telephone. Some have Jacuzzi, garden views, or
mountain views; all have fireplaces. Relax in the parlor with games and books
or in the lounge room with television, games, and tables. Borrow movies to
watch on in-room VCR or use the inn's bicycles, badminton, and croquet sets.
Stroll the brick paths through the gardens. Area attractions: Biltmore Estate,
Thomas Wolfe House, Pack Place, Chimney Rock, Blue Ridge Mountains, and
Lake Lure. "White linen" full breakfast includes waffles, French toast, or
omelets served with home baked muffins, biscuits, breads, homemade preserves, specialty coffees, and fresh fruit. Evening tea and sweets are offered
daily.

Asheville

The Colby House
230 Pearson Drive
Asheville, NC 28801
(800) 982-2118 or (704)253-5644
Innkeepers: Everett and Ann Colby

Millikan

♛♛♛ Rating: A+
Rates: Single or Double/$80-110
Credit Cards: MC, V

Dutch Tudor built in 1924 is situated on quiet, hilly residential street in the
historic district of Asheville. All of the four guest rooms feature a private bath
and each room has been individually decorated with a special emphasis on
color and a little "whimsy". Individual features include a four-poster bed,
writing desk, fireplace, or balcony. Enjoy the surrounding gardens in both the

front and the back of the inn. Visit with other guests in the library with its fireplace, game table, and books. Sit on the side porch with rocking chairs or in the parlor where wine and cheese are served in the evening. Raid the Butler's Pantry for baked goods provided both day and night. Area attractions include the Biltmore House, Blue Ridge Parkway, Smokey Mountains National Park, and Connemora. Full gourmet breakfast includes specialties such as eggs Benedict, soufflés, waffles, blueberry pancakes, various coffee cakes, and muffins as well as home-made banana bread. No smoking.

Guests write: *"What makes the Colby House so special? The exceptional attractive exterior, the luxurious appointments in the library and dining room, the warmth and comfort of the beautiful bedroom, the delicious breakfast and perhaps most important, the Colby's personalities." (J. O'Connor)*

"We enjoyed the Foxfire Room. The fireplace provided a warm and romantic setting which was just what we were looking for." (M. Plonk)

"All the special little touches, from the warm fire, to the sherry decanter, to the coffee in the morning. All contribute to a making the Colby House a delightful place to stay." (J. G. Boozer)

"It was so wonderful to come home after a lot of sight-seeing and enjoy some delicious home-made cookies and a drink and then a nice glass of wine later in the day. We really appreciated the input on things to do in Asheville." (L. Tarvin)

Asheville

Richmond Hill Inn
87 Richmond Hill Drive
Asheville, NC 28806
(704) 252-7313 or (800) 545-9238
Innkeeper: Amie Nance

♛♛♛♛   Rating: AA
Rates: Double/$130-350
Credit Cards: AE, MC, V

Victorian country inn with restaurant was built in 1889 and sits majestically atop a hill overlooking the city which is three miles away. There are twelve guest rooms in the mansion and nine rooms in charming cottages situated around a croquet courtyard. The Victorian style garden rooms provide sixteen additional guest accommodations with individual porches and views of the gardens, mountain brook with a series of seven descending waterfalls, or the mansion. Each of the 37 guest rooms has a private bath and many have fireplaces. Special appointments include Victorian furniture, Oriental rugs, and draped canopy beds. Savor American and nouvelle cuisine in the gourmet restaurant. Play croquet or visit the nearby Biltmore Estate, Blue Ridge Parkway, and downtown Asheville. Full breakfast may feature omelets or egg dishes, as well as fresh baked muffins and breads. Facilities are available for weddings, social events, and small business conferences. No smoking.

Guests write: *"We spent two weeks in the mountains of Virginia, North Carolina, and Tennessee. We did not stay exclusively in B&B inns but Richmond Hill Inn was by far the nicest of the B&Bs we visited and superior to any motel or the condo we visited. They truly deserve 1st class status."* (F. Forehand)

"Richmond Hill Inn is a treasure and certainly worthy of comment. Clean and neat goes without saying, but how many forget the setting which is so essential to doing business. Only love can describe the way in which the finest cuisine here is served." (L. Brain)

"Everything is so well done. Our dinner was excellent and the gown I left behind was in the mail to me before I even called to inquire about it."(M. Rogers)

"The food was outstanding. This renovation of a Victorian mansion was remarkably well planned. The insulation in the walls provided great quiet" (R. Lee)

"This was our first stay in the new cottages. They are terrific! These folks do an absolutely first-rate job. Thanks to all the crew who keep the rooms and grounds so clean." (R. Spuller)

Asheville

The Wright Inn
235 Pearson Drive
Asheville, NC 28801
(704) 251-0789 or
(800) 552-5724 ext. 235
Innkeepers: Art and Carol Wenczel

♛♛♛   Rating: A
Rates: Double/$75-110; Carriage house/$175
Credit Cards: MC, V

Historic Queen Anne home is situated in a neighborhood of stately Victorian homes in Asheville located seven blocks off I-240. There are nine guest rooms. Each has a private bath, turn-of-the-century decor, cable TV, and telephone; two have fireplaces. The Carriage House is a separate building on the grounds which is especially suited for families or small groups traveling together. It offers three bedrooms, full kitchen, two baths, living room, and dining room. Popular attractions in this area include Blue Ridge Parkway, Biltmore House and Gardens, Smokey Mountain National Park, Thomas Wolfe Home, and Cherokee Indian reservation. Full breakfast is served in a formal dining room and is not included in carriage house rates. No smoking.

Guests write: *"Of the more than 30 B & B's we've stayed in, this is the nicest one we've found. Excellent and varied food, exquisite decorating. Impeccably maintained. Phones in the rooms (important for business people). Lovely hostess and staff. Lots of parking!" (J. Eidsvoog)*

"We were married at the Wright Inn in a simple and very elegant ceremony. It was exactly as we would have dreamed — only true to life. Betty, Gary and Sandra were all warm and very hospitable hosts who helped make this truly the happiest day of our lives." (S. Talbot)

"The room was very nice and clean. The bed had a big soft down comforter. There was a little basket of candy kisses and bon-bons. The sheets and towels were trimmed in white lace. Breakfast was very good with a fruit cup, juice, coffee, hot tea, eggs, gravy, biscuits, link sausage, homemade preserves, and a friendship cake to top it off. Everything was delightful!" (C. Hayes)

"The breakfasts were wonderful! What did I like best? The attention to detail of Betty, the innkeeper." (K. Carpenter)

Balsam

Balsam Mountain Inn
Balsam Mountain Inn Road
P.O. Box 40
Balsam, NC 28707
(704) 456-9498
(800) 224-9498 (within NC only)
Fax: (704) 456-9298
Innkeeper: Merrily Teasley

♛♛♛ Rating: A-
Rates: Single/$75-130; Double/$80-135
Senior, government, and corporate discount
Credit Cards: MC, V

Just one mile from the Blue Ridge Parkway 35 miles southwest of Asheville reigns Balsam Mountain Inn from high atop a ridge. It is situated on 26 acres of forests and meadows, with springs, a creek, and a pond. Originally opened in 1908, Balsam Mountain Inn is listed on the National Register of Historic Buildings, so recent extensive restoration closely followed U.S. Department of the Interior guidelines for historic buildings. Standing two and a half stories tall, it has a mansard roof that is pierced by numerous dormer windows. Stretching across the front is a two-tiered porch with white pillars, anchored on each end by three-story towers with pyramidal roofs and lined with antique rocking chairs. The thirty-four guest rooms with private bath, including three suites, all have bead-board walls and are furnished with antiques. There are several common areas—a large lobby, which is bright and airy thanks to its 16 windows, a library filled with over 2000 books, and a game room. The main dining room is spacious enough to accommodate 100 guests; a private dining area seats 24. Popular attractions are the Blue Ridge Parkway, the Smoky Mountains National Park, and Smoky Mountains Scenic Railroad, and historic Dillsboro. Enjoy whitewater rafting on the Nantahala River, hiking, skiing, trout fishing, or gem mining. Full breakfast, with specialties such as poppyseed muffins and Elizabethan eggs. Lunch and dinner also available. Wedding and meeting facilities available. Fax and copier services available. Wheelchair accessible. Families welcome. Restricted smoking.

Beaufort

Captains' Quarters of Beaufort, Inc.
315 Ann Street
Beaufort, NC 28516
(919) 728-7711
Innkeeper: Captain Dick Collins

👑👑👑 Rating: A
Rates: Single/$50-80; Double/$60-100
Credit Cards: MC, V

Historic turn-of-the-century Victorian home has been completely restored and is situated one block from the waterfront in the heart of the Historic District. There are three guest rooms on the second floor. Each has a private bath, family heirlooms, and antique furnishings. Take part in the inn's tradition to "toast the sunset" on the verandah or by the parlor fireplace and celebrate the day with wines and fresh fruit juices. Explore the nearby Outer Banks or walk to Maritime Museum, Old Burying Grounds, shops, and restaurants. Airport transportation is available. Continental plus breakfast includes fresh fruits and homemade breads featuring Ms. Ruby's "Riz" biscuits. Restricted smoking.

Guests write: *"The Captains' Quarters Bed and Breakfast and gracious owners, changed our way of traveling completely. We found them by accident on Valentine's weekend, 1993, when we naively ventured off to have a romantic weekend without reservations. Luckily, our first attempt to find lodging found us at Capt. Dick's door. He welcomed us like old friends."* (R&E Williamson)

Belhaven

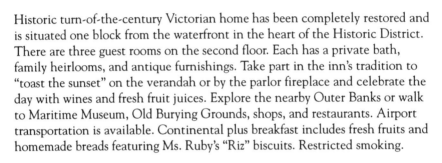

River Forest Manor Inn and Marina
600 East Main Street
Belhaven, NC 27810
(919) 943-2151 or Fax: (919) 943-6628
Innkeeper: Melba Smith

👑👑 Rating: B
Rates: Single or Double/$48-85
Credit Cards: MC, V

Historic riverfront mansion built in 1900 is located on the Pungo River just east of Route 264. There are nine guest rooms throughout the inn and each has a private bath and selection of Victorian antique furnishings; one room is designated as non-smoking. The mansion has retained all of its original architectural treasures including leaded glass doors, Ionic columns, elaborately carved oak fireplaces, ornate plaster ceilings, leaded and stained-glass, and crystal chandeliers. Tennis courts, swimming pool, hot tub, and boat marina are on the premises as well as a restaurant and river room lounge. Guests who arrive by boat can borrow golf carts equipped to run on regular city streets. Continental breakfast. Dinner and smorgasbord available in the restaurant. Facilities available for meetings and social functions.

Burnsville

NuWray Inn
Town Square
P.O. Box 156
Burnsville, NC 28714
(704) 682-2329 or (800) 368-9729
Innkeeper: Chris and Pam Strickland

♛♛ Rating: B
Rates: Single/$60-80; Double/$70-110
Government discount
Credit Cards: AE, MC, V

Nestled in the Blue Ridge Mountains 30 miles northeast of Asheville is the NuWray Inn, offering southern hospitality since 1833. This three-story white clapboard Colonial revival is listed on the National Register of Historic Places. Twenty-six guest rooms, including five suites, each have a private bath and are individually decorated with antiques spanning several periods. The main lobby, featuring a stone fireplace, pine paneling, and wrought-iron railings and fixtures, is furnished with handmade antiques. The Music Parlor has a rare Steinway baby grand piano and combines French and American furniture from the turn of the century. There is a parlor upstairs with a predominately Victorian decor. Anchoring the Town Square, the inn is within easy walking distance of antique shops, art galleries, and craft studios. Take a drive on the Blue Ridge Parkway, go to Mount Mitchell State Park, or visit Crabtree Falls, Linville Falls and Caverns, or the famed Biltmore Estate. Complimentary tea is offered in the afternoon. Full breakfast includes eggs, country ham, sausage, and grits. Arrangements can be made for a picnic lunch. In the evening the dinner bell calls you to a nationally famous, family style dinner that presents a choice of several entrees, vegetables, homemade breads, and desserts. Private dining is also available by special arrangement. Wedding and meeting facilities available. Wheelchair accessible. Families welcome. Restricted smoking.

Clyde/Asheville

Windsong: A Mountain Inn
120 Ferguson Ridge
Clyde, NC 28721
(704) 627-6111 or (704) 627-8059
Fax: (704) 627-8080
Innkeeper: Donna Livengood

♛♛♛   Rating: A+
Rates: Single/$81-85; Double/$95-99;
Guesthouse/$120-140
Credit Cards: MC, V

Contemporary log inn situated in a rural mountain setting is 4.5 miles off I-40 exit 24, and 36 miles west of Asheville. Choose from four large guest rooms, each with private bath, Jacuzzi, high beamed ceiling, light pine log walls, Mexican tile floors, and a delightful decor scheme. There is an extensive videocassette library, piano, billiard table, swimming pool, and tennis court for guest's enjoyment. A new two-bedroom guest house built in 1992 offers complete privacy. Hosts raise llamas on the property and offer dinner treks at the inn and wilderness llama treks. Among area attractions are Great Smoky Mountain National Park, Appalachian Trail, Cherokee Indian Reservation, Biltmore House, Blue Ridge Parkway, hiking, skiing, and white-water rafting. Full breakfast. Facilities available for small group meetings. No smoking.

Flat Rock

The Woodfield Inn
Box 98
Flat Rock, NC 28731
(704) 693-6016 or (800) 533-6016
Innkeeper: Jean Eskew

♛♛   Rating: B
Rates: Single or Double/$45-100
Credit Cards: MC, V
Senior, family, business, and auto club discounts

Historic ante-bellum inn situated on twenty-five acres was built in 1850 and has been in continuous operation for 140 years. There are twenty guest rooms available. Each is decorated in the Victorian period with antique furnishings and hand-crafted coverlets. Most rooms offer a private bath and several have fireplaces. There are several common rooms on the property including a wine room, restaurant dining rooms, a parlor filled with antiques and collectibles, and a secret room where Confederate soldiers hid valuables during the Civil War. Area attractions include Flat Rock Playhouse, Carl Sandburg estate, Kenmure golf course, and Flat Rock historic sites. Continental breakfast. Function facilities include the gazebo and pavilion. Families welcome.

Hiddenite

Hidden Crystal Inn
Sulphur Springs Road
Hiddenite, NC 28636
(704) 632-0063
Fax: (704) 632-3562
Innkeepers: Eileen Sharpe and Lynn Hill

♛♛♛♛   Rating: AA-
Rates: Single or Double/$85-150
Corporate discount
Credit Cards: AE, MC, V

Hidden Crystal Inn is located twelve miles off I-40, exit 150 in an area known as the "Gateway to the Blue Ridge". Nestled among extensive gardens, the inn sits next door to the Lucas Mansion Museum (founded by the inn's owner), and a half mile from an emerald mine open to the public. The manor house offers eight guest rooms and five additional rooms are in the Crystal Cottage. Each is named for a mineral or gemstone found in the area and all feature antiques, original arts and crafts. The Golden Topaz suite offers a two-person whirlpool, stocked refrigerator, sitting area, and entertainment center with VCR. Several common areas are located throughout the inn which frequently holds weddings and small conferences. Croquet, badminton, paddle tennis or volleyball on the lawn may be enjoyed; or stroll in the English country garden, complete with gazebo. An in-ground pool and surrounding landscaped patio is an inviting setting for lounging or conversing with other guests. Area attractions: Alexander County, Brushy Mountain Golf Course, Hiddenite gems at Emerald Hollow, Lucas Mansion Museum and Hiddenite Center for Folklife and Cultural Arts, Linney's Mill, Alexander Railroad, bike trails, hot air ballooning, Rocky Face Mountain, Taylorsville and Taylorsville Beach. Full breakfast includes fresh brewed coffee and special entree such as banana pecan buckwheat pancakes made from flour ground at the nearby Linney's Mill, an "old timey" grist mill. Additional meals are available upon advance reservations. Families welcome.   (Continued)

commitment to seeing that comfort is the number one priority is very evident when you walk through the front doors." (S. Ratcliff)

Highlands

The Highlands Inn
4th & Main Street
Highlands, NC 28741
(704) 526-5036
Innkeepers: Rip and Pat Benton

♕♕♕   Rating: A
Rates: Single or Double/$79-89
Credit Cards: AE, MC, V

Three-story wooden Colonial building on the National Register of Historic Places is located in the heart of a small mountain town 60 miles southeast of Asheville. Choose from twenty-nine guest rooms decorated in either a country or traditional decor. Each has a private bath. Area attractions include auction galleries, antique shops, Highlands Playhouse, tennis courts, swimming pool, horseback riding, Dry Falls, Glenn Falls, and Bridal Veil. Extended continental breakfast features home-made sweet rolls, biscuits, and fresh fruit served in the dining room accented with Southern pottery. The Theater Room is perfect for meetings or special events. Wheelchair access. Restricted smoking.

Guests write: *"For the past eight to ten years, during the Spring, Summer, and Fall, we have on many occasions enjoyed the hospitality, accommodations, food, and people at the Highlands Inn and the Old Edwards Inn. Each time we leave, we look forward to our next trip and we have never been disappointed. The natural charm of the place, accented by the care and concern of owners, Rip and Pat Benton and their staff, makes every visit more enjoyable than the last visit." (E. Baldwin)*

Highlands

The Old Edwards Inn
4th & Main Streets
Highlands, NC 28741
(704) 526-5036
Innkeepers: Pat and Rip Benton

👑👑👑 Rating: A-
Rates: 1 or 2/$69-89
Credit Cards: AE, MC, V

The Old Edwards Inn, a sister inn to the Highlands Inn across the road, consists of the original 1878 building known as The Central House with a connecting brick building constructed in 1931. Reminiscent of a turn-of-the-century mountain town inn, it is surrounded by hemlocks and gardens and is 60 miles southeast of Asheville. The inn was added to the National Register of Historic Places in 1992 and offers nineteen refurbished rooms with paints, stencils, and wallpapers true to the Victorian/Country home period. Most rooms have a queen-size bed and all offer a private bath. The Moose Room, with its large moose head over the stone fireplace, invites guests to gather, converse, watch TV, or enjoy board games. An extended continental breakfast is served in the dining room of the Highlands Inn across the street and includes fresh fruit, cereal, biscuits, and home-made cinnamon buns. Restricted smoking.

Kill Devil Hills

Cherokee Inn Bed & Breakfast
500 North Virginia Dare Trail
Kill Devil Hills, NC 27948
(919) 441-6127 or (800) 554-2764
Innkeepers: Kaye and Bob Combs

👑👑 Rating: B
Rates: Single or Double/$60-90
Senior discount
Credit Cards: AE, MC, V

Cherokee Inn is a traditional beach house located 500 feet from the water on Highway 12 in the Nags Head area, 65 miles south of Norfolk, Virginia. Six guest rooms are available, each with private bath, color TV, soft cypress interior, white ruffled curtains, and ceiling fan. Some rooms offers an ocean view and others overlook the Wright Memorial. Relax on the wrap-around porch with picnic table, settee and lounge chairs, or in the sitting room. Access to a public beach is directly across the street from the inn. Popular attractions in the area include Wright Brothers Memorial, Fort Raleigh, Cape Hatteras National Seashore, and seashore activities. Continental breakfast buffet includes fresh-baked pastries, coffee, and juice.

Guests write: *"Lovely home! We've never had room service at a B&B before."* (S. Hallinan)

"This inn is neat, extremely clean and thoroughly enjoyable." (P. Elliot)

"My son felt it was just like Grandma's home." (W. Brooks)

"We had a very enjoyable stay as it was quite comfortable. It was pleasant to wake to the smell of delicious brewing coffee - like being at home." (L. Kulic)

"The inn was rustic and one block from the ocean so you could smell the sea air. I loved my room - feminine with lots of pillows. The night I arrived there was a storm. The next day I wanted to go for a walk on the beach. They lent me a rain proof jacket and boots which I lived in. I was able to go out and have a great time." (J. Dail)

Manteo

The Tranquil House Inn
405 Queen Elizabeth Street
Manteo, NC 27954
(919) 473-1404 or (800) 458-7069
Fax: (919) 473-1526
Innkeepers: Don and Lauri Just

♛♛♛ Rating: A
Rates: Single or Double/$79-149
Senior, auto club, military, corporate, and government discount
Credit Cards: AE, MC, V

Located on the waterfront just five miles from Nags Head, the Tranquil House Inn was constructed in 1987 near the sight of the original house, circa 1890, which burned in 1932. Built in the style of the stately Outer Banks inns of the past century, it offers 20th century conveniences. The revived inn has cedar shingle siding, gables, and open breezeways. Each of the 25 guest rooms with private, tiled bath and spacious balcony, are uniquely designed and decorated. Choose from a variety of rooms with canopied, four-poster bed or a suite with a kitchenette. The inn's interior features custom cypress woodwork, bevelled glass doors, and stained glass. A lookout room on the top of the inn offers a sweeping view of the Roanoke Sound and Outer Banks. The restaurant on-site offers gourmet food. Nearby attractions include the Queen Eizabeth II, Fort Raleigh National Historic Site, Elizabethan Gardens, North Carolina Aquarium, Wright Brothers Museum, and Lost Colony Outdoor Drama. Enjoy the beautiful beaches, biking, windsurfing, and Atlantic Gulfstream fishing, or take the Manteo Walking Tour. Drive to Corolla to see its lighthouse and wild horses, visit the Pea Island National Wildlife Refuge, or the Bodie Island wildlife Refuge and lighthouse. Continental breakfast. Wedding and meeting facilities available. Computer, fax, copier, and secretarial services available. Wheelchair accessible. Families welcome. Restricted smoking.

Guests write: *"We arrived by boat from Jacksonville after battling the Albemarle Sound. Tranquil House was what we were in need of desperately. As soon as we docked out front and approached the inn we felt so welcome — not only by the outdoor chairs and tables set for the afternoon tea and snacks but by the friendly people all around." (R. Ray)*

"My at at the inn was great. Although I was on business each day it was relaxing and restful. The rooms are such that I felt at home and extremely comfortable. The staff was far beyond excellent when it came to courtesy and service." (P. Thomas)

"How gratifying to find there still remains the old world charm and serenity in a spot so close to our home. When things get too hectic in our everyday life, the inn becomes our refuge for a weekend getaway." (L&E Williams)

Nags Head — (Also see Kill Devil Hills)

Nags Head

First Colony Inn
6720 South Va. Dare Terrace
Nags Head, NC 27959
(919) 441-2343 or (800) 368-9390
Fax: (919) 441-9234
Innkeeper: Camille Lawrence

♛♛♛ Rating: A+
Rates: Single or Double/$120-200
Credit Cards: AE, MC, V

Historic inn on the Outer Banks has undergone extensive rehabilitation and is now listed on the National Register of Historic Places. The inn has a two-story encircling verandah and is a short walk to the beach. Each of the twenty-six guest rooms is decorated with traditional furniture and English antiques and features a telephone, individual climate control, refrigerator, and a private bath with heated towel bars and imported toiletries. Some rooms offer Jacuzzis, VCRs, four-poster beds, wet bars with microwave or kitchenette, and balconies. There is an upstairs library with books, games, fireplace, and a pump organ. Explore the five acres of landscaped grounds, relax by the pool with sun deck, or walk along the boardwalk to the gazebo on the dune which overlooks the beach. Nearby is Cape Hatteras National Seashore, Wright Brothers Memorial, Fort Raleigh, The Lost Colony, Elizabeth II, and the Pea Island Wildlife Refuge. Continental breakfast buffet includes specialties such as fruit breads and juice cordial. Wine, beer, and fruit & cheese baskets available. Small wedding and meeting facilities available. Families welcome. Wheelchair access. No smoking.

Guests write: *"The delightfully pleasant library/game room reminded me of a favorite aunt's upstairs sitting room — a nice place to reminisce during the Christmas holidays and tastefully decorated for the occasion too." (S. Garner Rodgers)*

"The owner and her staff were willing to go out of their way to make our stay comfortable as well as giving us a feeling of 'home'. Even though we had reservations for one particular room, when possible, we were given a tour of all the other rooms. They are exquisitely decorated with antiques. We especially enjoyed tea and

refreshments in the afternoon. The First Colony is located in a perfect setting, convenient to the ocean, to shopping, and yet is a private retreat. The breakfast was more than ample with lovely table settings, fresh fruit, pastries, and lots of coffee. A thoroughly wonderful experience." (M. Hoff)

"What a remarkable place this is! A real aura of history permeates the old building which is a truly superb blend of modern comfort with yesteryear. A rare and wonderful treat." (E. Gwynn)

"Our room was extremely comfortable, large, and airy. I was most grateful for the firm mattress on the bed. There were so many small things which were so pleasant it's hard to name them all. My husband and I would recommend it to the most experienced, worldly traveler without hesitation." (J. Van Egmon)

"The First Colony Inn is the most interesting accommodation I've stayed in from San Francisco to Moscow. My room (#26) was the cleanest I've ever seen. I will send everyone I know to First Colony Inn for 1st class service and comfort." (E. Woodall)

New Bern

Harmony House Inn
215 Pollock Street
New Bern, NC 28560
(919) 636-3810
Innkeepers: A. E. and Diane Hansen

👑👑👑 Rating: A
Rates: Single/$55; Double/$85
Credit Cards: AE, MC, V

Historic Greek Revival inn built in 1850 is located two hours north of Wilmington in a town steeped in history. There are nine guest rooms with private bath. Each features antique furnishings and hand-crafted furniture by local artisans. Popular attractions in the area include Tryon Palace, Trent and Neuse Rivers, antique and specialty shops, and museums. Full breakfast includes a hot entree and homemade granola. Families welcome. No smoking.

Southport

The Indian Oak Inn
120 West Moore Street
Southport, NC 28461
(910) 457-0209; Fax: (910) 457-5009
Innkeepers: Norma & John Kluttz

♛♛   Rating: B+
Rates: Single or Double/$65-75
Credit Cards: MC, V

Two story 1886 Victorian with large bay windows and side and front porches
was named after the 800 year old oak which stands across the street. The inn is
one block form the Cape Fear River at the mouth of the Atlantic Ocean; 30
miles Wilmington, NC and 45 miles outside of Mrytle Beach, SC. Four guest
rooms, two with private baths offer special features such as a large bay window
overlooking the park, oak queen bed, bird and vase pewter bed, wedding ring
quilt, or iris cast iron twin beds. The parlor has oak hardwood floors covered
with a historic collection of oriental rugs and a writing table near the conversation seating area. Guests are invited to enjoy coffee and cookies in the
evening in the Utility Room where glassware and dishes are made available
during their stay. Relax in the picket fenced backyard with flower beds and
bird baths or sit on one of the porches complete with rocking chairs and porch
swings. Walk to historical points of interest including Fort Johnson, Franklin
Park, Keziah Park, Old Smithville Burial Ground, art galleries, the Waterfront
Park and The Maritime Museum. Area attractions: Fishing, historic walking
tours, antiquing, golfing, Fort Caswell, the Oak Island beaches, the Lighthouse
at Caswell Beach, and Brunswick Town and Orton Plantation. Full breakfast
may feature vanilla orange juice, ham strada, blueberry buttermilk pancakes
with strawberry syrup, eggnog French toast, or raisin bran muffins. Small
meeting and wedding facilities. Families welcome. Meeting and wedding
facilities.

Guests write: *"Not only is the Indian Oak Inn one of the most handsome
restorations we've seen, its owners, Norma and John, know exactly how to make a
visitor feel. Our first stay was perfect and when we returned, we felt as if we were
visiting long-time friends."* (C&F Kime)

*"An early evening treat of homemade chocolate chip cookies and coffee are left out
for guests to help themselves. Ice and a refrigerator are available to use for soda,
juice, or fruit. There are baskets of brochures on local restaurants, tours, and 'goings
on'. Norma was a most gracious and helpful hostess without being intrusive. A 'Blue
Ribbon' place for sure."* (J. Glacken)

"A home away from home. That's the feeling imparted by this gracious hostess and her home. As one approahces the house with its welcoming sign, fresh paint, and inviting porches, one feels that the interior is going to be comfortable and attractive. As the front door is opened, one glance is enough to confirm your impression." (B. Brown)

Wilmington

Catherine's Inn
410 South Front Street
Wilmington, NC 28401
(800) 476-0723 or (910) 251-0863
Innkeeper: Catherine Ackiss

Rating: Unrated at press time due to new location of inn
Rates: Single/$65-70; Double/$75-79
Additional Person $15
Corporate discount

Historic home built in 1883 overlooks the Cape Fear River and is situated in the historic downtown area, just minutes from fine beaches. Choose from three guest rooms, each with private bath, air conditioning, ceiling fan, cotton robes, and fresh linens daily. The library offers cable TV/VCR and there is a wrap-around porch with river views. Full breakfast and complimentary refreshments served daily. Airport pick up available as well as space for small weddings and meetings. Special fishing and golf packages are available.

Guests write:"This wonderful Victorian historic home is a real home. Catherine, the innkeeper, is gracious and hospitable. Everyone should experience it and everyone should have the privilege of feeling so at home." (K. Nenninger)

"Wonderful treats included coffee outside our door first thing in the morning, walking distance to all of downtown historical Wilmington attractions. Catherine herself is personable and attentive without being pushy. The inn itself is a grand Victorian." (C. Pitt)

"Never having been in Wilmington before, as well as traveling on my own, made Catherine's hospitality and friendliness heartwarming! I felt like an honored guest, yet at the same time I felt very much a part of the family. She shared information about Wilmington and her love for the area that made me feel less like a stranger." (K. Gray)

Wilson

Miss Betty's Bed & Breakfast Inn
600 Nash Street, NE
Wilson, NC 27893-3045
(800) 258-2058 or (919) 243-4447
Innkeepers: Betty and Fred Spitz

♛♛♛ Rating: A-
Rates: Single/$50-65; Double/$60-75
Credit Cards: AE, MC, V

Miss Betty's B&B Inn consists of four buildings, including three restored Victorian homes. The main house (circa 1858) is listed on the National Register. The inn is situated in the downtown historic area and located 6 miles off of I-95, 45 miles southeast of Raleigh. Guest rooms in the main inn and adjacent homes each offer a private bath, remote control cable TV, heating/air conditioning with individual controls, alarm clock, and private phone. The innkeepers have an antique shop on the premises. There are four golf courses, numerous tennis courts, and an Olympic sized swimming pool nearby. Tour the historic district, visit antique shops, the Tobacco Farmer's and Country Doctor's Museums. Home-made pastries, eggs, hot cakes, Wilson sausage, bacon, and fresh fruits and juices are some of the house specialties served at the full breakfast. Small weddings and catered receptions are available. Wheelchair access. No smoking.

Guests write: *"My stay at Miss Betty's was most enjoyable. Service was always exceptional and the owners were friends." (S. Palmer)*

"I cannot praise Miss Betty's (Betty and Fred) highly enough. It's gorgeous, clean, homey...the hospitality is outstanding and we all (about 10 of us) had a marvelous stay while attending a family wedding." (D. Tessitore)

Luverne/Fargo

Volden Farm B&B
R.R. 2, Box 50
Luverne, ND 58056
(701) 769-2275
Innkeeper: JoAnne Wold

♛♛♛ Rating: A-
Rate: Single/$40; Double/$50-75

Wood farmhouse with a Scandinavian and Russian atmosphere is located 38 miles northwest of exit 302 off I-94. Choose from two guest rooms which share a private guest bath in the main house or the newly renovated "Law Office" which is a private cottage a few yards from the main house. The rooms, with views of the prairie from every window, have a country decor and feature a lace-canopy or metal bed. Nooks and crannies abound, filled with objects d'art from the host's tour in Russia and travels in Scandinavia. There are several common areas in the house which offer private areas for reading, sitting in front of a fireplace, playing a game of pool, or conversing with other guests. The farm has several acres inviting exploration and a small playhouse and swing set are available to delight children. Full breakfast specialties include Swedish pancakes or Danish Aebleskiver with fresh farm produce. Families welcome. Smoking permitted on porches.

Guests write: *"Joanne's attention to detail was great. She thought of everything (even a light over the bathtub to read by). I travel a great deal and this is one of the nicest places I have stayed in."* (M. Scholz)

Additional information on B&Bs in this state is available from the following B&B reservation agency: Private Lodgings (216) 321-3213.

Carpenter

Carpenter Inn & Conference Center
39655 Carpenter-Dyesville Rd
Carpenter, OH 45769
(614) 698-2450
Innkeepers: Pnina Sabel & Renee Gremore

♛♛　Rating: B
Rates: Single/$45-55; Double/$55-65
Credit Cards: MC, V

With a view of the countryside, this one-hundred year old early American two-story sits on 250 acres of open land and forest and is conveniently located near Ohio University, 16 miles west of Athens. Eight guest rooms and one suite are available. Some of the features include early American decor with hand-made quilts and antique furniture. The common rooms, decorated in early American, consist of a living room with an open kitchen. A fireplace can be enjoyed on cool evenings, and three couches and comfortable chairs can be used for reading or quiet conversation. The dining room has a large table which comfortably seats eight. Enjoy the sunrise while sipping a cup of herbal tea on the wicker decorated front porch. After a sauna or soak in the outdoor hot tub, relax on one of several decks or on a bench in the garden. Extensive herb gardens are maintained around the house and nearby are nature trails for hiking and a pond for fishing. Area attractions: Old Man's Cave, Ash Cave, Rock House, scenic railway in Nelsonville, Lake Hope and Lake Alma State Parks, covered bridges, Hocking Hills Regions, Hocking Valley Artisan Mall, Noah's Ark Animal Farm, fishing, Wahkeena Nature Preserve, and the Wayne National Forest. Full country breakfast (with a vegetarian option) includes fresh fruit or juice, homemade granola, assorted homemade rolls and muffins, herbal teas and coffee is served each morning and a complimentary snack is provided in the evening. Facilities available for weddings, meetings, and conferences and a wide variety of workshops are held on a regular basis. Restricted Smoking

Guests write: *"Having never been in this area before nor having any recommendations from anyone, we were very surprised by what we found. Certainly much more than what we expected. A beautiful old farmhouse decorated with antique farm decor mixed with modern conveniences. The hostess was very pleasant and accommodating."* (M. Davis)

"*The best part of this B&B is the innkeeper. She welcomed us with the warmth of an old friend. She prepared a beautiful breakfast each morning of fruit from the area, homemade granola, delicious coffee, excellent potato pancakes with cayenne pepper, eggs — the works! The room was cozy and private. The hot tub was unmatched as was the gorgeous country setting.*" (A. Hubben)

"*Our family is fairly new to B&Bs. We came to Athens for a wedding and the inn was highly recommended. Our expectations were surpassed! The accommodations were quaint and comfortable. The service and overall hospitality was outstanding.*" (C. Auberger)

Fredericktown

Heartland Country Resort
2994 Township Road 190
Fredericktown, OH 43019
(800) 230-7030
Innkeeper: Dorene Henschen

♕♕♕   Rating: A
Rates: Single/$70-120; Double/$80-150
Credit Cards: MC, V

Heartland Country Resort is 40 minutes northeast of Columbus and 5 miles off I-71, Exit 151 (just south of Chesterville, OH). 1878 restored farmhouse has a serene country setting with hills, woods, pastures, fields, wooded trails, barns, horse stables, and riding arenas. One guest room in a new addition offers a spacious bathroom with private Jacuzzi while another, on the second floor, has a private stairway and bathroom. A two-bedroom suite on the second floor of the original section of the house offers five beds, a sitting room and bathroom. Relax in the living room with vaulted ceiling and woodburning stove. There you will find books, games, and quiet corners with comfortable seating. A large recreation room provides a billiard table and entertainment center with TV and VCR. Breakfast can be enjoyed in the dining room which features wide plank flooring and large fireplace, or in one of the several quiet nooks located throughout the farmhouse. Horseback riding, hiking, relaxing in a heated outdoor swimming pool, cross-country skiing, hay rides, bonfires, playing basketball, horseshoes, Ping-Pong, billiards, and a petting zoo can all be enjoyed on the grounds of the resort. Area attractions: two downhill ski resorts, Mid-Ohio race track, fishing, boating, canoeing, hiking, sky diving, Mohican State Park & Forest, golf courses, Kingwood Center (gardens), Amish settlements, antique shops, and Country Music Park. Continental candlelit breakfast features fresh fruit, breads, muffins, coffeecake, cereals, juices and coffee or tea. A full country breakfast, picnic lunch, and dinner are available upon request. Meeting facilities. Families welcome. No smoking.

Guests write: *"Our favorite part of our visit was the individual attention we each received while horseback riding. The trainers are special people who have lots of patience with children. We each rode at our own pace but under the watchful eye of the trainers. My daughters loved the breakfast bacon from the local market, the blueberry muffins, and we all enjoyed the fresh sour cream coffee cake."* (D. Torres)

"Dorene and Ben made us welcome form the moment we arrived. Their home is beautiful and quite comfortable. We felt very at home and that is the thing that we miss the most when we travel. cooking like you have at home and most of the comfort of the bed. The staff was very nice and were doing a good job. " (G. Beard)

" The Heartland Resort offered a wide variety of activities, all engulfed in beautiful, natural scenery. We rode the horses on a few of the nature trails which wind through the nearby woods. The local towns provide plenty of 'old fashioned' hospitality, culture and good dining (although nothing beats the Heartland's home cooked breakfasts) The resort's luxuries include a master bedroom suite which sports a Jacuzzi !! Great way to relax after horseback riding. " (M. Miller)

Oklahoma

Additional information on B&Bs in this is available from the following B&B reservation agency: Ozark Mountain Country B&B (800) 695-1546.

Oregon

Cloverdale

Sandlake Country Inn
8505 Galloway Road
Cloverdale, OR 97112
(503) 965-6745
Innkeeper: Margo Underwood

♕♕♕   Rating: A
Rates: Single/65-110; Double/$70-115
Credit Cards: MC, V

Two-story farmhouse built in 1894 is nestled on 2.5 acres just off the Three

Capes Scenic Loop, 16 miles south of Tillamook. Three guest rooms in the main house offer fresh flowers, antique furnishings, and collectibles. A Honeymoon suite with four rooms on the second floor features a deck overlooking the garden, private dining room with refrigerator and claw-foot tub. The small, modest looking cottage is a treasure inside with a private bedroom, luxury bath with whirlpool tub for two, living room with black marble fireplace, and full kitchen. Popular attractions in the area include Netarts Bay, Cape Lookout State Park, Tillamook cheese factory, and beaches. Full breakfast with home-baked goods. Special gourmet picnic baskets are available at an additional cost for those arriving late at night, or for day trips in the area. No smoking. The Timbers cabin is wheelchair accessible and has closed-captioned TV for the hearing impaired.

Guests write: *"The inn is nestled along the Oregon coast in a very secluded and wooded area. We could walk in the woods or traipse across an open meadow. We had the entire 2nd floor of this beautiful farmhouse to ourselves and enjoyed being pampered."* (B. Earl)

"We were given a warm welcome and tour of the home… the Jacuzzi, outdoor lawns and swing, books, magazines, TV, VCR, radio, tape player, and our living quarters. The tour was complete but short. Then we were promised privacy and we were given it! Everything I ate intrigued my taste buds." (S. Fleischmann)

"We have stayed at the inn twice, each time in a different room. They were both exquisitely decorated in a very romantic style." (D. Pettijohn)

"Sandlake Country Inn is a peaceful retreat. My husband always said he would never set foot in a B&B but he took us back four times last year. The privacy, personal attention, and food have made it a place we will return to at least once a year." (E. Doyle)

"It's the last morning of our stay at Sandlake. I've lit a fire and am curled up on the sofa reflecting on the past few days. This has been a special time for us because it is the beginning time for dreaming, setting goals, and time for us alone. I don't think we could have found a more perfect place to do that and more." (J. Marcotte)

"From the moment we arrived and saw the heart cookie inscribed with our names and "eleven" for our 11th anniversary, we knew we chose the right place to celebrate. The beautiful room, the relaxing tub, the quilt, and luscious breakfasts all combined to create a perfect weekend." (J. Edbert)

"Last summer my husband and I made a tour of the B&Bs on the Oregon coast, only to discover that our initial judgment had been correct. The Sandlake Country Inn is by far the best. It is secluded, yet within easy driving distance of many points of interest and forms of entertainment." (D. Grier)

Seaside

Gilbert Inn Bed & Breakfast
341 Beach Drive
Seaside, OR 97138
(503) 738-9770
Innkeepers: Dick and Carole Rees

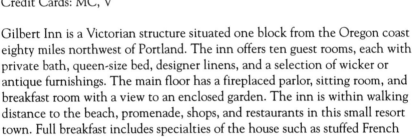

♛♛♛   Rating: A
Rates: Single/$75; Double/$85-120
Credit Cards: MC, V

Gilbert Inn is a Victorian structure situated one block from the Oregon coast eighty miles northwest of Portland. The inn offers ten guest rooms, each with private bath, queen-size bed, designer linens, and a selection of wicker or antique furnishings. The main floor has a fireplaced parlor, sitting room, and breakfast room with a view to an enclosed garden. The inn is within walking distance to the beach, promenade, shops, and restaurants in this small resort town. Full breakfast includes specialties of the house such as stuffed French toast with apricot sauce. Families welcome. No smoking.

Pennsylvania

Additional information on B&Bs in Pennsylvania is available from the following B&B reservation agencies: B&B Connections/B&B Philadelphia (800) 448-3619 (Outside PA); Hershey B&B Reservation Service (717) 533-2928; Rest & Repast B&B Reservation Service (814) 238-1484.

Akron

Boxwood Inn
P. O. Box 203
Diamond Street and Tobacco Road
Akron, PA 17501
(717) 859-3466 or (800) 238-3466
Fax: (717) 859-4507
Innkeepers: June & Dick Klemm

♛♛♛   Rating: A
Rates: Double/$75-135
Credit Cards: MC & V
Boxwood Inn is located in Lancaster County, about 8 miles from Lancaster

City and 3 miles from Ephrata where there is abroad expanse of farmland dotted with one-room school houses and covered bridges. The inn is a classic stone, two-story farmhouse, built in 1768 by Mennonite settlers, sits on 3.5 acres overlooking adjacent Amish/Mennonite farms. The property sits high with rolling lawns and has a grove of English walnut trees, fruit trees and a small garden. Outbuildings include an ice-house, greenhouse, herb shed and carriage house. Each of the uniquely decorated guest rooms includes private baths. The *Hunt Room* features a whirlpool, and *The Carriage House* provides a whirlpool, fireplace, barsink with refrigerator, and private balcony. Enjoy the large glassed-in room overlooking the gardens, patio, and horse and buggies passing by, or relax in the spacious living room with fireplace, television, and two seating areas suitable for small conferences. The dining room comfortably seats twelve. Walk to local farm country, or visit Martins hand-twisted pretzel bakery and take the tour. Area attractions: auto and bicycle trips through Amish farm country, local crafted furniture, quilts, arts and crafts, museums, including Ephrata Cloister and Landis Valley, farm and antique auctions, Sunday antiquing in Adamstown, visits to Hershey, Gettysburg, and Brandywine Country. Enjoy a full breakfast served on a banquet-sized table with imported china and sterling silver place settings. This includes fresh muffins and breads and entrees such as crepes Lorraine. Afternoon tea is served with special treats and house specialties. Meeting facilities. No smoking. Families Welcome.

Guests write: *"These are two of the most friendly, gracious innkeepers you'll ever meet. The Early American decor was lovely with handmade Amish quilts on each bed. Breakfast was corn fritters with sausage and homemade muffins the first day. Mushroom and cheese omelet with tomatoes (picked that morning) and homemade muffins the second day."* (B&K Eppensteiner)

"Far and away the finest B&B we've been in. Excellent food, very clean rooms, great owners, nice surroundings— and priced right! " (M. Bartlett)

"Our host prepared our own map of a round trip to take from the B&B that would take us past an old school house, Mennonite Church, covered bridges, Amish quilter's shop and more. Tea in the afternoon is a nice touch and breakfasts are delightful— fabulous muffins along with French toast or egg casserole— yummy!" (S. Brooks)

Allentown

Coachaus Inn
107-111 North Eighth Street
Allentown, PA 18101
(610) 821-4854 or (800) 762-8680.
Fax: (610) 821-6862
Innkeeper: Barbara Kocher

♛♛♛   Rating: A-
Rates: Single/$68-125; Double/$78-135
Family, weekly, and monthly rates available
Credit Cards: AE, MC, V

Victorian European-style urban inn has been completely restored and is located in downtown Allentown, 1.5 miles south of US-22 and 3.5 miles from I-78. There are twenty-four guest rooms that vary in size, decor, and amenities including rooms, apartments, and townhouses. Each bedroom has a private bath, cable TV, telephone, and air conditioning. Walk to fine dining, boutiques, antique shops, Old Allentown Historic District, and the Liberty Bell Shrine from the inn. Recreation nearby includes Dorney Amusement Park, skiing, antiquing, hiking, white-water rafting, and biking. Full breakfast and evening refreshments offered daily. Families welcome.

Allentown/Fogelsville

Glasbern
2141 Packhouse Road
Fogelsville, PA 18051
(610) 285-4723
Innkeepers: Al and Beth Granger

♛♛♛♛   Rating: AA-
Rates: Single/$85-105; Double/$100-230
Credit Cards: AE, MC, V

This original 1800's Pennsylvania barn has been refurbished into an inn with exposed timber, cathedral ceilings, and many windows. It is situated on one-hundred acres near Allentown, 2 miles northwest of the intersection of Routes I-78 and 100. Choose from twenty-three guest rooms with a mix of contemporary and antique furnishings, private bath, refrigerator, phone, TV, VCR and radio. Sixteen rooms have whirlpool baths, several also have a fireplace or wood-burning stove. Popular activities in the area include bicycling, parks, wildlife sanctuaries, wineries, antique markets, and covered bridge tours. Tennis, fishing, hiking, and skiing are nearby. Full breakfast. American contemporary dining is available in the restaurant every evening. Tuesday through Saturday. Facilities available for meetings and social functions. Wheelchair access.

Guests write: *"Talk about a stress release! From the moment you enter you are received like royalty. The rooms are well kept and of the Early American design. You have your own VCR, and the television also has a stereo radio. We took the accommodations with the Jacuzzi. The morning breakfast was very abundant from the bottomless cup of coffee, to the large varieties of fresh and different breads for pleasure."* (B. Sheerin)

"At present we have two children under five years of age. Consequently, when we venture away from home, we want something relaxing and special at the same time. The Glasbern Bed and Breakfast has become both of these. Upon entering the establishment, you are greeted with smiles and warmth. One feels as though you are entering into an old friends home. At any price range, the accommodations are exceptional—the cozy wood-burning fireplace, the fluffy comforter, and luxurious Jacuzzi. The meals are sophisticated but easy on the palate. My husband is a 'meat and potatoes' man; however, the menu is varied enough to please all. The complimentary breakfast allows for those with more fancy tastebuds, and also the simple eaters to feel satisfied. Everything is served with a warm smile and a sincere wish for a happy day." (M&C Gano)

"Glasbern has a very enjoyable and relaxed atmosphere, the food is excellent, and hospitality superb. We had our small wedding in front of the fireplace in November 1991 and dinner afterwards. The day could not have been more beautiful." (A. Xander)

"We thoroughly enjoyed our stay at Glasbern. The service was excellent, atmosphere and decor of the rooms and lodge was outstanding. It was just what we needed after having a baby three months before." (D. Butler)

"They made our 34th Anniversary so special! Everything is already excellent and no improvement is necessary." (C. Kampmeyer)

Allentown/Emmaus

Leibert Gap Manor Bed & Breakfast
4502 South Mountain Drive
Emmaus, PA 18049-623
(800) 964-1242 or (610) 967-1242
Innkeepers: Wayne and Pauline Sheffer

Millikan

♛♛♛ Rating: A
Rates: Single/$75-115; Double/$85-125
Senior, corporate, and auto club discounts
Credit Cards: AE, MC, V

Nestled on 17 acres in South Mountain near the cities of Allentown and
Bethlehem, this 1980s Williamsburg-style manor is comprised of Mt. Vernon
brick combined with a log cabin. It is hidden in the deep forest just minutes
away from downtown Emmaus. Two upper level guest rooms decorated with
canopy beds and antiques feature a widows walk with panoramic views of the
Lehigh Valley. The two main level guest rooms are decorated with Colonial
furnishings. All rooms offer a private bath. Throughout the house, random
width board floors and Oriental rugs are accented with antiques and collectibles. The solarium provides guests with space in which to read, have tea,
and bird watch. Sit in front of the fireplace in the keeping room, play pool in
the game room on the 19th-Century pool table, explore the groomed hiking
trails, or borrow a bike from the innkeepers. The inn is just minutes away from
public swimming, tennis courts, and three public golf courses. A wide variety
of area attractions include the Allentown Fair, historic Bethlehem, cultural
events, the Musicfest, Celtic Classic, art centers, museums, antique shopping,
restaurants, and many sports activities. Full breakfast includes baked goods,
fresh fruit plates, and a specialty entree. Small wedding and meeting facilities
available. No smoking.

Guests write: *"We had never stayed at a bed and breakfast before. We both enjoyed
the personal touch of our host and hostess's hospitality. The way the Leibert Gap
Manor is decorated let us step back in time when life was not so complicated and
truly relax during our stay. The food was excellent in taste and appearance."* (J.
Schlaner)

*"Leibert Gap Manor was the host of our wedding reception (60 people). We had the
affair catered (hors d'oeuvres and cocktails). We also had a pianist play the piano. It
was by far the most elegant wedding reception ever. The atmosphere was relaxed,
and my guests took full advantage of the two gazebos, tea house, and walking trails.
My husband and I will return every year on our anniversary."* (R&C Schlener)

"*The perfect blend of elegance and comfort. Immaculate, serene, yet cheerful and welcoming ambiance. I especially appreciated and enjoyed a beautiful fresh fruit breakfast prepared to meet my special dietary needs. My room was quiet, the bed as comfortable as my own at home.*" (M. Saylor)

"*We celebrated our 10th Anniversary in the peaceful, secluded home of Pauline & Wayne Sheffer. We appreciated the care they took in preparing our breakfasts, including a special place setting on the morning of our Anniversary. The Early American beds and furniture added to the charm of our room.*" (G. Farnham)

"*We had a thoroughly enjoyable two night stay at Leibert Gap Inn. Our accommodations were beautiful and immaculate and our breakfasts were fantastic. We were happily impressed with the hospitality of our hosts and greatly appreciated their knowledge of the area.*" (B. Stellwagon)

"*Our two night stay was delightful. We were treated like royalty in a spotless, comfortable and spacious inn. Our hosts were especially helpful in giving us directions and pointing out local events of special interest. Breakfasts were pleasurable experiences and not only delicious but attractive. Bird-watching and hiking were added attractions.*" (D. Dice)

Allentown/Bethlehem

Wydnor Hall
Old Philadelphia Pike
Bethlehem, PA 18015
(610) 867-6851 or Fax: (610) 866-2062
Innkeeper: Kristina Taylor

♛♛♛ Rating: A
Rates: Single/$75-115; Double/$85-125
Corporate services and discounts
Credit Cards: AE, MC, V

Wydnor Hall is a restored late-Georgian fieldstone manor, located 3 miles south of Bethlehem on historic Old Philadelphia Pike. Guest rooms have been furnished in the manner of an English country house hotel with heirloom antiques and quilts. All rooms offer private baths. Afternoon tea is served daily by uniformed staff in an elegant and comfortable sitting room. Area attractions include historic sites in Bethlehem, Lehigh University and Moravian and Lafayette Colleges, Bach Festival, Musikfest, and Celtic Classic Highland Games. Full breakfast on weekends offers choices from a varied menu. Continental breakfast is delivered to guest rooms during the week. A morning coffee tray and newspaper are also available upon request. Restricted smoking.

Guests write: *"My husband and I stayed in the double room named 'Noodles,' and the couple we were traveling with stayed in 'Chester.' The rooms were beautifully appointed with breathtaking window treatments, beautiful linens, and luxurious towels in the bathroom. The innkeeper was extremely gracious and hospitable! He helped us chart our course for our next day's travel and recommended a perfect spot for dinner. Breakfast was coffee, orange juice, blueberry muffins, rolls and jam, a very elegant presentation."* (J. Montanus)

"We have visited Wydnor Hall several times over the past few years. The surroundings are beautiful. The breakfast is always sumptuous and varied (all homemade goodies)! The interior of this lovely stone Pennsylvania inn is appointed with elegant antiques and beautiful original art (pottery and paintings). The hosts are warm and friendly and make an extra effort to always make our stay very comfortable and special." (L&R Lynch)

"The owners have created an atmosphere of quiet elegance. Upon entry to the very well-appointed and spacious parlor, I immediately feel a sense of calm and the urge to simply sit and relax, to perhaps browse through any of the myriad reading materials available—essentially to yield to the slowing of time. In summary, Wydnor Hall is perfect for both a business and pleasure stay and is a very welcome relief and change from the sameness of larger hotel establishments." (E. Brady)

"Wydnor Hall resembles a small European hotel with all the accompanying assets. They excel at service and amenities. I think the Wydnor would appeal to the sophisticated traveler. The best thing about the Wydnor is that you are only a stranger once. They remember you on subsequent visits, as well as your likes and dislikes." (P. Fay)

"Our weekend stay at Wydnor Hall was similar to being the guest at a very grand and well-staffed home. The quality of the surroundings, the service, and the food was superb. From the coffee tray in the morning with newspaper, through the superb breakfast and afternoon tea (and wine), the comfort of the service and surroundings is on a par with a fine European hotel." (P. Kuyper)

"The attention to detail here is 'beyond the call of duty'. We arrived late (due to Pacific Time change) and assumed that we would miss breakfast as we slept beyond the posted 10:00 am posted time. To our surprise, the management called to say the would be glad to give us breakfast and served us after 11:00. I appreciated the immaculate condition of the bathrooms and when I set out my array of cosmetics on the dressing table, I later found them set on a special tray just the right size." (E. Little)

Bethlehem/Bucks County

Lightfarm
2042 Berger Road
Kintnersville, PA 18930
(610) 847-3276 or (610) VIP-FARM
Innkeepers: Max and Carol Sempowski

♛♛♛ Rating: A
Rates: Single/$85-95; 2Double/$95-105
Extended stay, senior, and corporate discounts
Credit Cards: MC, V

Georgian Federal with Greek Revival influences is fifty miles north of Philadelphia on a rural road between Bethlehem and New Hope. Choose from three guest rooms with private bath that have been decorated with period furnishings to honor the 18th-Century founding family of the Lightfarm. Explore the 92-acre working farm with sheep, flowers, and rich history. Enjoy afternoon tea, take a nature walk, or help with the farm chores. On-location archaeological site offers opportunities for learning about early days of American farm life and it is known as a Bucks County historical site and significant natural area with excellent country bike trails and park trails. Visit Nockamixon State Park, Delaware River Country, and many antiques stores nearby. Pennsylvania Dutch full breakfast is served in the enclosed porch or formal dining room. Outdoor wedding facilities available. Families welcome. No smoking.

Guests write: *"The queen size bed with four posters was turned down and decorated with candy for us. This was like our own intimate cruise ship! Fresh flowers and clean towels before bed was a special touch!"* (B. Carr)

"I honestly knew nothing about Lightfarm prior to my arrival. From then on, every aspect of my stay was a delightful surprise. The farm food, company, care and accommodations were great." (P. Simpkins)

"We really enjoyed the warmth and hospitality of our hosts. The ambiance was wonderful as were the animals and the beauty of the land. The food was delicious." (L. Kinius)

"I was really impressed with the 'little things,' to make you feel right at home: flowers in the rooms, candy here and there, the warm hospitality and the great food." (M&L Anthony)

Chambersburg

Shultz Victorian Mansion Bed & Breakfast
756 Philadelphia Avenue
Chambersburg, PA 17201
(717) 263-3371
Innkeeper: Joseph & Doris Shultz

♛♛   Rating: B
Rates: Single /$55-73; Double/$60-78

Located on a tree-lined street in the north end of Chambersburg, this 1880 Victorian style home has an onion-topped turret, red brick exterior , and elaborate wood carving in foyer open hearth and open stairway. It is found along Route 11 which runs parallel to I-81, 24 miles north of Hagerstown. Choose from five guest rooms with private baths and air conditioning ; most rooms decorated with antiques and oriental rugs .Relax by the open hearth in winter or enjoy porches, balcony, and lawn area. The living room and dining room are available for reading or chatting. Walk to historic old jail museum, Wilson College, or go sightseeing in the neighborhood. Area attractions: Gettysburg, and Antietam Historic Battlefields, Ski Liberty, Whitetail Ski Slopes, Mercersburg Academy, Dickenson College, Carlisle Antique and Car Shows, Caledonia and Cowan's Gap State Parks, and Totem Pole Playhouse. Full breakfast might include apricot-stuffed French toast, Apple pancakes, or pecan buttermilk waffles served on a full table setting with crystal, silver, fresh flowers, and candlelight. Small meeting and wedding facilities available. No smoking.

Guests write: *"As a student at Wilson College, I often walked into town along Pennsylvania Avenue and admired this gracious Victorian mansion. I even dreamed of living in one. It has been over forty years since I graduated but my dream has in great part come true for my husband and I often stay at Shultz Victorian Mansion B&B. We sleep in the turret room which is filled with light from five floor-to-ceiling windows." (A&B Foreman)*

"Everything was lovely. Doris gives her B&B a very personal touch and she is a very friendly hostess. She is also well informed of the area. We certainly enjoyed our stay and delicious breakfast." (J&J Bloomfield)

"The rooms are decorated with lovely Victorian antiques. Each breakfast has been delicious and served with special care taken for appearance and taste. My favorite is the French toast with wonderful orange sauce." (B. Hazzard

Eagles Mere

Eagles Mere Inn
Mary & Sullivan Avenues
Eagles Mere, PA 17731
(717) 525-3272
Innkeepers: Susan and Peter Glaubitz

♛♛ Rating: B
Rates: Single/$85-125; Double/$125-195
Credit Cards: MC, V

Inn built high on Eagles Mere in the "Endless Mountains" of Northeastern Pennsylvania is 45 miles northwest of Wilkes Barre in a small, old-fashioned Victorian resort. Guests are accommodated in the 1878 Victorian inn and Garden House that offer a total of fifteen guest rooms with private bath. Stroll along the path of the mile-long Eagles Mere Lake, take a toboggan ride down the ice slide, explore the nearby forests, or go cross country skiing on the local trails. Four-season activities in the area include nature hikes on well marked trails, swimming and boating on private lake and beach, antiquing at shops and auction houses, and skiing, skating, and sleighing around the lake. Full breakfast specialties include French toast with raspberry brandy sauce or real maple syrup. Wedding and meeting facilities available. Families welcome. Restricted smoking. Rates include breakfast and gourmet dinner.

Guests write: "*I commend them both on their hospitality. The food was impeccable and they were so friendly, charming, and helpful during our stay. We had not been recommended to them and just took a chance seeing there was an inn near the toboggan run. We truly had a much needed relaxing, yet elegant and casual weekend. It really met our needs.*" (L. Mease)

"*All the little things they did to help us with our daughter made it pleasant for us. It was such a nice feeling to come down and have the highchair and toys already set for us at the table. We enjoyed the warmth we felt there.*" (D. Shawson)

"*We will always remember our 41st Anniversary as extra special. The warm hospitality, wonderful food, and the charming decor of our room and the entire inn more than lived up to our expectations.*"(M. Jereb)

"*The town was charming, low-key, and relaxing in a way some of us really need! But to find the warm hospitality and creative dining makes the community perfectly complete. We hope to be back in winter for a sled run across the lake in winter.*" (E. Miller)

Erie

Spencer House Bed & Breakfast
519 West 6th Street
Erie, PA 16507
(814) 454-5984 or (800) 890-7263
Fax: (814) 456-5091
Innkeeper: Pat Hagenbuch

♛♛   Rating: B
Rates: Single/$60-90; Double/$65-95
Government and corporate discount
Credit Cards: AE, MC, V

Restored 1876 three-story Eastlake Victorian mansion has many distinguishing characteristics, among them a slate mansard roof and a 36-foot tower on the front of the house. It is located in the heart of Erie along what once was known as "Millionaires Row" and where many lovely mansions still stand. Five individually decorated guest rooms with private bath, cable TV, private telephone, and air conditioning are available. Several of these rooms have a fireplace and contain antiques, some original to the house. Original, restored woodwork is one of the most eye-catching features of the interior and five common rooms. The parlor, library, and dining room each have 12-foot ceilings and a fireplace, with the parlor also boasting a baby grand piano. A solarium on the second floor houses many plants and white wicker furniture. There is also a sitting room with a small library on the third floor. Nearby attractions include Presque Isle beaches, picnic areas, and amusement park, downtown Erie, antique shops, art galleries, the Erie Bayfront, the Erie Historical Museum and Planetarium, and the Erie Art Museum. Guests can also enjoy golf, bicycle riding, hiking, fishing, and boating. Wine country tours, a large shopping mall, and both downhill and cross-country skiing are all a short distance away. Start your day with a full breakfast including fresh baked muffins and, in season, strawberry and blueberry pancakes. Enjoy afternoon tea on the wrap-around porch. Wedding and meeting services available. Fax available for guest use. Restricted smoking.

Franklin/Oil City

Quo Vadis Bed & Breakfast
"Whither Goest Thou?"
1501 Liberty Street
Franklin, PA 16323
(814) 432-4208
Innkeepers: Janean and Allan Hoffman

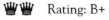 Rating: B+
Rates: Double/$48-70 plus tax
Credit Cards: AE, MC, V

1867 Queen-Anne Victorian home accented with terra cotta is located near the junction of Routes 8, 62, and 322, halfway between Pittsburgh and Erie near the Ohio line. Six guest rooms each offer a private bath, high ceilings, detailed woodwork, quilts, embroidery, and lacework, as well as furniture that has been acquired by four generations of the same family. Area attractions: Historic District with Victorian homes, DeBence Antique Music Museum, antique malls, unique gift shops and galleries, Drake Well Museum and Park with its 2.5 hour train trips, and outdoor recreation. Visit the newly restored Barrow Civic Theater or hike the extended Samuel E. Jurstus Recreational trail. Full breakfast includes fresh fruit, home-baked goods, croissants, and varied specialties on weekends such as quiche, repes, waffles, popovers, or egg in a basket. No smoking.

Guests write: *"We are repeat customers, many times over. I am always amazed that the breakfast is never a repeat. The house is a home. It is filled with beautiful antiques that have always been in the same family. I cannot compare Quo Vadis with other B & B's since this is the only one we frequent. I am almost afraid to venture out because I am sure no other could measure up!"* (B. Umbaugh)

"When we stay at the Quo Vadis, it's as though we are in the early 19th century, with the high ceilings, detailed woodwork, and unique furniture. Handmade quilts, embroidery and lace work adorn each room." (P. &B. Gilfoyle)

"A working hand-crank Victrola with a generous record collection, bookcases of interesting rarities, games and magazines are among the amenities that lend atmosphere to this exquisitely restored mansion. The hosts were accommodating to my dietary preferences, so breakfast was a treat as well, with fresh fruit supplementing such delicacies as eggs baked in pastry puffs. The service at this B & B was notably cheery." (D. Kamin)

Gettysburg

Baladerry Inn
40 Hospital Road
Gettysburg, PA 17325
(717) 337-1342
Innkeepers: Tom and Caryl O'Gara

♛♛♛ Rating: A
Rates: Double/$65-95.
Senior, corporate, and auto club discount
Credit Cards: AE, MC, V

1812 Federal-style red brick home in a country setting at the edge of the battlefield and once served as a hospital in the Civil War. The inn was renovated with an addition in 1977 and again in 1992, and is located 50 miles northwest of Baltimore, Maryland and 60 miles northwest of Washington, DC. Five guest rooms feature newly tiled private baths, queen or twin beds, and traditional furnishings. Read, chat, and relax in the great room with massive fireplace, sitting area, game/library area, and three sets of French doors that open onto a brick terrace. Relax on the terrace overlooking the surrounding four acres or escape to the calm of the gazebo. Play tennis on the inn's court or go biking. Visit nearby Gettysburg National Military Park, Eisenhower Farm, National Riding Stable, National Apple Museum and fruit orchards, and Ski Liberty. Enjoy the area's many restaurants, antique shops, wineries, colleges, and four golf courses. Full breakfast might include poached eggs or pancakes served with bacon or sausage and accented with a fresh fruit plate. Restricted smoking.

Guests write: *"We will remember this perfect place—the restful sleep and delicious breakfast—the music indoors and sweet birdsong out of doors—sunlight shining on yellow tulips in a sparkling glass vase—what a great pleasure it was to have been welcomed here."* (N. Perez)

Gettysburg

The Herr Tavern and Publick House
900 Chambersburg Road
Gettysburg, PA 17325
(717) 334-4312 or (800) 362-9849
Fax: (717) 334-3332
Innkeeper: Denise Clark

♛ ♛ ♛   Rating: A-
Rates: Double/$65-170
Credit Cards: AE, MC, V

Surrounded by gardens in a country setting with views of the first day's battle at Gettysburg, this two-story, brick Federal was built in 1815. Five guest rooms offer private baths. The inn's porches invite guests to sit and relax and the brick patio is available for outdoor dining. An "in-the-works" jigsaw puzzle is in the sunroom for guests as are books, snacks, television, and stereo. Area attractions: Gettysburg Battlefield, museums and tours, antique shops, Gettysburg College, golf courses, and skiing. A full breakfast, set with fresh flowers, is served on white stoneware and includes fresh fruit plate, homemade pastries, and entree of the morning. Weddings and meeting facilities available. Restricted smoking.

Guests write: "We walked across the wide planked wooden floor toward our canopy bed. The warm glow of the fireplace cast a romantic light on the beautiful country decor. The oak washstand, the coal oil lamp topped wooden table, plank bottom chairs, and shaker peg coat rack all helped to create a cozy Colonial ambiance. After our relaxing in-room Jacuzzi bath, we retired to our quilt-covered canopy bed. We awoke to a bountiful country breakfast of fresh fruit, warm sticky buns, and ham and eggs. A meal General Meade himself would have fought for." (T&S Lovelace)

"We are especially impressed with the decor of the Elizabeth Room which was warm and spacious. Breakfast was served in the sunroom. We had a delicious fruit plate, healthy servings of French toast and ham. Denise came in dressed as Santa (December 21st), and spent time explaining the history and renovations of the tavern, which we all enjoyed hearing." (C&D Handshue)

"The employees of Herr Tavern go above and beyond to make you feel welcome. We chose the Elizabeth Room with canopy bed, fireplace, and antique bathroom, just what we love. The room was clean and always kept tidy whenever we left for touring in town. On the second day, the staff found out we were newlyweds, so when we left for dinner they surprised us by leaving champagne and flowers. What a beautiful touch!" (T&K Newmann)

Gettysburg

The Tannery Bed & Breakfast
449 Baltimore Street
Gettysburg, PA 17325
(717) 334-2454
Innkeepers: Julius and Charlotte Swope

♛♛   Rating: B+
Rates: Single/$50; Double/$65-85
Credit Cards: MC, V

Historic Gothic inn rich with Civil War history is located four blocks south of
the center of town. Five large guest rooms each feature a private bath and
traditional furnishings. A large activity room offers games and a collection of
books on the Civil War. Afternoon refreshments are often served on the
spacious front porch. The Gettysburg tour buses are headquartered one block
from the inn and well-known landmarks are within walking distance as well as
shops and restaurants. Continental breakfast. Restricted smoking.

Harrisburg/Carlisle

Kanaga House
6940 Carlisle Pike
New Kingston, PA 17072
(717) 697-2714 or 766-8654
Innkeepers: Mary Jane and Dave Kretzing

♛♛♛   Rating: A
Rates: Double/$75
Credit Cards: MC, V

Built in 1775 by one of the earliest settlers to the area, this limestone manor
house is surrounded by three acres of trees and landscaped garden, midway
between Harrisburg and Carlisle on US 11; near PA Turnpike exit 16. The five
guest rooms with private baths and air-conditioning are accessible from a
sitting room with wet bar and have been individually furnished with antiques
and queen size canopy beds. The Bridal Suite features a working marble
fireplace. Relax in the ambiance of the restored mansion with antiques and
fireplaces throughout or stroll the grounds to the gazebo and patios. Area
attractions: antique shops, historic Carlisle, Carlisle Production car show and
antique shows, Dickinson College, Harrisburg, Gettysburg, Hershey, and the
Dutch Country. Go fishing, hiking, golfing, and skiing. Full breakfast includes

a specialty such as stuffed French toast or cheese and bacon frittata, along with fruit medley and pastries home made daily. Enjoy breakfast in the fireplaced kitchen, formal dining room, or intimate Williamsburg Tavern room. Wedding and meeting facilities available. No smoking.

Guests write: *"We often stay in B&Bs, so we feel qualified to make comments. We have stayed here four wonderful nights and find the food excellent and the hosts and history make the stay very special."* (R. Mikkelson)

"This is a unique blend of antiques, hospitality, and charm. Each room has its own unique decor. Breakfast is always tastefully done with English china, fresh fruit, and enough selection to satisfy adults and younger folk." (S. Kudlacik)

"The Kanaga House is the quintessential B&B with elegant decor and friendly hospitality. The host make you feel welcome as you would at your grandparent's house. The breakfast is served with kindness and attention to your individual requests." (J. Colina)

Harrisburg/New Cumberland

Farm Fortune
204 Limekiln Road
New Cumberland, PA 17070
(717) 774-2683
Innkeeper: Phyllis Combs

♕♕♕   Rating: A
Rates: Double/$65-85; Suite/$110
Credit Cards: AE, MC, V

Limestone farmhouse built in the 1700's is situated on a hill overlooking the Yellow Breeches Creek just off Route 83 at exit 18-A. Each of the four guest rooms offer a double or twin beds, antique furnishings, and comfortable seating with good lighting. Two rooms offer a private bath and large porch area. Popular activities here are trout fishing on the property, sitting on the porch or terrace, and bird watching while enjoying the scenic view. An antique shop called the "Honeycomb Shop" is on the premises. Area attractions include historic homes, museums, antique shops, ski areas, and hiking. Hershey, York, Gettysburg, and Lancaster County are a short drive away. Full breakfast. Function rooms are available for small meetings and weddings.

Guests write: *"Exquisite antiques in every room are complemented by fine reproductions and harmonized to perfection without sacrificing comfort or*

convenience." (J. Fambrough)

"I discovered Farm Fortune B&B quite by accident while on a business trip. Since then I have become one of the many regulars who view the Farm Fortune and Chad and Phyllis Combs as extended family. I have had the pleasure of staying in every bedroom of the inn and each one is quite unique although the room with the private bath and balcony with rocking chairs and porch swing is my favorite. Phyllis prepares an excellent breakfast that is as pleasing to the eyes as it is to the taste buds and is always served on collectible dinnerware. While the house and the antiques are worth the trip, the best part of Farm Fortune is Chad and Phyllis and their hospitality. Farm Fortune has become a home away from home for me and many others." (R. Rice)

"Our room was cheerful and pleasing to the eye. Very relaxing with a lovely view. Bathrooms was bright and clean! The food was luscious and presented beautifully. Everything served looked like a picture. The family dog was as friendly and welcoming as the lambs. It was a fantastic weekend that we'll remember for many years to come."(C. Carson)

Harrisburg/Elizabethville

Inn at Elizabethville
30 West Main Street
Elizabethville, PA 17023
(717) 362-3476 or Fax: (717) 362-4571
Innkeeper: Jim Facinelli

 Rating: B
Rates: Single/$55; Double/$60
Business travel and long-term discounts available
Credit Cards: MC, V

Small Victorian inn located in the heart of the state is one block west of the intersection of Routes 225 and 209. Built in 1883, the inn offers seven guest rooms with private bath and is decorated in Mission Oak and Arts & Crafts styles. Guests are welcome to use the dining, living, and conference rooms, as well as the kitchen, porch, and sun parlor. Area attractions include the Millersburg Ferry, an 18-hole golf course, Appalachian Trail hiking, hunting, fishing, and country auctions. Buffet self-serve continental breakfast features cereals, juices, English muffins, coffee, and tea. Small meeting facilities available. Families welcome. No smoking.

Harrisburg/Lewisberry

The Dutch Country Inn- A Bed & Breakfast
301 Market Street
Lewisberry, PA 17339
(717) 938-8191
Fax: (717) 932-8024
Innkeeper: Stacy Miller

♛♛♛   Rating: A-
Rates: Single/$85; Double/$100
Corporate and senior discount and ski packages
Credit Cards: MC, V

Renovated two story traditional Pennsylvania Farmhouse with Victorian gingerbread facia, tin roofs, and large open porches with wicker furniture is located on the town's Market Square, near the Town Hall and library. The house and barn are surrounded by rose gardens with pine, maple, and locust trees. Atop the authentic two-turn Farmhouse staircase, guest suites adjoin the Victorian Sitting Room where morning coffee, tea, and juices are served with wake-up calls. Both suites offer private baths with the Country Suite featuring antique furniture from the original home, country stenciled walls accented with Amish quilts, and private sitting area. The Dutch Suite offers antique iron bed with Dutch blue accents and Amish quilts as well as a sitting room with king-size wing-back chairs and an enamel trundle bed that expands to a king or two twin beds. Relax and watch television or videos or listen to music near the wood stove in the downstairs parlor or enjoy a game of chess by the fireplace in the main Living Room. Walk to the historic school house and 19th-Century Methodist church. Area attractions: Hershey Park, Gettysburg, Lancaster, Harrisburg, Ski Roundtop, Gifford Pinchot State Park and numerous hunting and fishing locations. Full gourmet breakfasts and weekend brunches feature house recipes such as tomato Dill Soup in puff pastry and butter basted eggs over Poached Salmon with creamed dill sauce or cold apricot soup with sour cream and rosemary lamb quiche. Afternoon refreshments feature fresh baked goods and assorted teas. Evening desserts offer treats such as champagne hazelnut cheesecake. Weddings and meeting facilities available. Families welcome. Restricted smoking.

Guests write: *"The innkeepers at this clean, small, and carefully appointed inn is ever mindful of the comfort of his guests. Breakfast is a memorable feast interlaced with seasonal foods. Coffee is left on a tray in the sitting groom upstairs for early risers. Directions to the many scenic and historic attractions nearby are given helpfully. Enthusiasm and thoughtfulness abound at this B&B." (J. Winant)*

Lancaster/Bird In Hand

The Village Inn of Bird-in-Hand
Box 253
2695 Old Philadelphia Pike
Bird-in-Hand, PA 17505
(717) 293-8369
Innkeeper: Richmond Young

♛♛♛   Rating: A
Rates: Double/$74-139; Suite/$140-170
Credit Cards: AE, MC, V

Mid-Nineteenth Century Victorian inn is 7 miles east of Lancaster on Route
340. Each of the eleven guest rooms has its own private bath and down-filled
bedding. Four of the rooms are suites, some with king-sized beds, whirlpool
baths, and one with a working wood stove. Enjoy a complimentary tour of the
Dutch Country or visit the adjacent farmer's market, country store, family
restaurant, bakery, and number of quilt and craft shops. Just a few minutes
away are Lancaster County attractions including museums, outlet shops, golf
courses, and farmlands. Continental breakfast and light evening snacks served
daily. Restricted smoking.

Lancaster/Elizabethtown

West Ridge Guest House
1285 West Ridge Road
Elizabethtown, PA 17022
(717) 367-7783
Innkeeper: Alice Heisey

♛♛♛   Rating: A+
Rates: Double/$60-85
Credit Cards: MC, V

Tucked midway between Harrisburg and Lancaster, this European Manor can
be found 4 miles off Route 283 at the Rheems-Elizabethtown exit. Nine guest
rooms with private bath are each decorated to reflect a different historic
period. An exercise room with hot tub and large social room are in the
adjacent guest house. Fish in one of two ponds or travel 20-40 minutes to local
attractions such as Hershey Park, Lancaster County Amish farms, outlet
shopping malls, Masonic homes, and Harrisburg State Capital. Full breakfast
offers the choice of eggs, pancakes, or French toast. Wheelchair access. No

smoking.

Guests write: *"Being a disabled veteran, I appreciated the ample access to the guest house and spacious parking. I had a large room, luxurious bathroom, all linens were changed every day, snacks and newspapers were available outside the bedroom door. The exercise room and hot tub were just across the hall and you can get full value in the breakfast alone. I stay in the Ritz Hotel in London, the George V Hotel in Paris, and the Waldorf in New York, but I always request accommodation at West Ridge Guest House in this area and I plan on accommodating and entertaining my guests here."* (R. Roberts)

Lancaster/Ephrata

The Smithton Inn
900 West Main Street
Ephrata, PA 17522
(717) 733-6094
Innkeeper: Dorothy Graybill

♛♛♛   Rating: A-
Rates: Single/$55-125; Double/$65-135; Suite/$140-170
Credit Cards: AE, MC, V

Classic stone inn that first opened in 1763 stands in the historic part of the village on Highway 322, 2.5 miles west of access Highway 222. The inn's seven guest rooms and suite each offer a private bath, canopy and four-poster bed with Pennsylvania Dutch quilts, working fireplace, and comfortable sitting area. All rooms have a refrigerator, phone jack, chamber music, night shirts, fresh flowers, optional candle lighting, and several rooms have whirlpool tubs. Lancaster County's Old Order Amish and Mennonite people, still farming with horses and living the life of our ancestors, make this area a fascinating place. Attractions include farm tours, historic sites, handicrafts, daily auctions, farm markets, and the largest antique market in the East. Full breakfast with all-you-can-eat waffles, pastries, and fruit. Families welcome. Wheelchair access. No smoking.

Guests write: *"Our room, with its own fireplace (started with wood each day) is an excellent example of Pennsylvania Dutch craftsmanship. From the four-poster bed with handmade quilt to the painted chest and braided rugs, we took a giant step back in time to a gentler America."* (J. Pulvermacher)

Mercersburg

The Mercersburg Inn
405 South Main Street
Mercersburg, PA 17236
(717) 328-5231 or Fax: (717) 328-5403
Innkeeper: Fran Wolfe

♛♛♛   Rating: A
Rates: Signle or Double/$110-180
Corporate rates
Credit Cards: MC, V

Restored early 1900s Georgian Revival was originally a part of the six-acre estate of a prominent business man. The brick and slate mansion, listed on the National Resister of Historic Buildings, is 90 miles northwest of Washington, DC. Choose from fifteen rooms filled with either locally made furnishings or restored antiques. Each has a private bath and ten offer king-size four-poster beds with hand-knotted canopies. Enjoy panoramic views of the Tuscaroroa mountains of the Alleghenies and the rolling farmlands that surround the area. Visit Whitetail Ski Resort, Gettysburg, Harper's Ferry, or Antietam. Antique shops, hiking, and golfing are nearby. Home baked breakfast breads, sausage and egg casserole, and home-made sticky buns are often featured at a full breakfast. Six-course dinners are available. Wedding and meeting facilities available. Families welcome. Wheelchair access. Restricted smoking.

Mercer

The Magoffin Inn
129 South Pitt Street
Mercer, PA 16137
(412) 662-4611 or (800) 841-0824
Innkeeper: Eugene Slagle and Jacque McClelland

♛♛♛   Rating: A-
Rates: Double/$85-110
Credit Cards: AE, V, MC

Three-story Queen Anne Victorian brick home at the edge of a residential neighborhood is near the county courthouse in the heart of town and located

60 miles north of Pittsburgh and 70 miles south of Erie. Choose from five guest rooms, each with working fireplace, private bath, and antique decor. The Bridal Suite offers a high Victorian walnut bed with matching dresser and wash stand and a clawfoot tub with shower. The Amish suite has two levels and includes a sitting room and bedroom loft. Relax in one of the three dining and sitting rooms or walk to the nearby museum, courthouse, and variety of shops. Area attractions: antique shops, Amish community, golf courses, state parks, and museums. A full breakfast may include sausage egg bake, fresh fruit, juice, muffins and croissants. Lunch and dinner are available by advance reservation. Small meeting and wedding facilities. Families welcome. No smoking.

Milford

Black Walnut B&B Inn
R.D. 2, Box 9285
Milford, PA 18337
(717) 296-6322 or (800) 866-9870
Innkeepers: Stewart and Effie Schneider

♕♕ Rating: B
Rates: Double/$60-150
Credit Cards: AE, MC, V

160-acre estate with Tudor-style mansion is located 2 miles southeast of I-84 exit 10. There are twelve guest rooms and one suite available with antique furnishings and brass beds; eight offer a private bath. Popular activities at the inn include swimming in the small lake and paddleboat rides. There are several common areas including a front porch with wicker furniture and dining area that overlooks the pond. Area attractions include fishing, swimming, rafting, canoeing, skiing, golf, horseback riding, and hiking. Full buffet breakfast is served overlooking the lake. A la carte dining room overlooking the lake is open for dinner. A wrap-around deck is available for group get-togethers. Restricted smoking.

Montgomeryville/North Wales

Joseph Ambler Inn
1005 Horsham Road
North Wales, PA 19454
(215) 362-7500
Innkeepers: Steve and Terry Kratz

♛♛♛　Rating: A-
Rates: Single/$85; Double/$140
Auto club discount
Credit Cards: AE, MC, V

Colonial country inn situated on a twelve-acre estate of rolling countryside is 40 miles from Philadelphia near the intersection of Routes 202 and 309. Twenty-eight guest rooms are available in the main inn or the converted barn. Each room provides a private bath, antique furniture, four-poster bed, and Oriental rugs. Enjoy a stroll on the grounds or relax in three living rooms, one with massive, walk-in fireplace. Area attractions include Valley Forge, Peddler's Village, Skippack, picturesque New Hope, and historic sites of Philadelphia. Full breakfast. A restaurant on the premises offers dining. Families welcome. Facilities available for meetings and social functions.

Guests write: *"I stayed at the Ambler as a business traveler. The employee staffing the check-in left her station and led me to the room (Penn) in the original house, explained the floor plan and showed me the unique features of the room. The Penn is a second floor end room with a view of the grounds on three sides. Guests enter the room into a private bath and descend two steps down into the bedroom. The French toast was excellent and the buffet fruit bar with baked goods was a treat also." (S. Fortner)*

"Spending the night here at the inn was a unique and interesting experience—a wonderful way of celebrating our 51st anniversary." (E. Hoch)

"We were treated to our stay in celebration of our 40th anniversary and will certainly return and recommend others to do the same. The room was immaculate and charming, with authentic or reproduction furnishings."(B. Griliches)

"Everything here was excellent—room, service, food, staff, etc. Would come here again and would not hesitate to recommend Joseph Ambler Inn to anyone." (R. March)

Philadelphia

Thomas Bond House
129 South 2nd Street
Philadelphia, PA 19106
(215) 923-8523 or (800) 845-BOND
Innkeeper: Thomas F. Lantry

♛♛♛ Rating: A
Rates: Double/$80-150
Business travel discount
Credit Cards: AE, MC, V

Brick Federal inn built in the 1700's is located one mile off I-95 in the
Independence National Historic Park and was the former residence of an early
Philadelphia physician. There are twelve distinctive guest rooms with private
bath, period furnishings, TV, and telephone. Two rooms offer queen-size beds,
sofa beds, working fireplaces, and whirlpool baths. Reproduction furniture,
maps, and accessories are offered in the Key and Quill gift shop located in the
inn. Continental breakfast is served weekdays and a full breakfast on weekends. All baking is done on premises. Enjoy evening wine and free soda and
coffee as well as turn-down service with cookies. Facilities are available for
meetings and social functions.

Slippery Rock

Applebutter Inn
152 Applewood Lane
Slippery Rock, PA 16057
(412) 794-1844
Innkeeper: Kimberly Moses

♛♛♛ Rating: A+
Rates: Single$55-81; Double/$69-115
Credit Cards: MC, V

Federal Colonial inn built in 1844 is nestled in the rolling green meadows of
rural Western Pennsylvania, 3 miles southeast of I-79 exit 30. Choose from
eleven guest rooms, each with unique decor, antique furnishings, and private
bath. Special features of the inn include 12-inch brick walls on a hand-cut
stone foundation, exposed brick fireplaces, and original chestnut and poplar
floors. The main floor offers a relaxing sitting room and parlor with fireplace.
Area recreation includes golf, bicycling, jogging, and country walks. Full

breakfast served daily. A cafe on the premises is open to guests and the public and serves lunch and dinner seven days a week. Full breakfast served daily to overnight guests. Families welcome. No smoking.

Guests write: *"First of all, I was kidnapped by my wife and brought here for our 12th anniversary. It's a lovely place to stay. The room was clean and all the facilities were perfect. My wife and I love this type of interior decor. Everything about the stay was perfect. I will be back again (with my wife, of course). If all kidnappings were like this, we wouldn't need the FBI."* (P. De La Torre)

"In the last few years, my husband and I have stayed in many B&Bs and country inns in the USA, Applebutter Inn is one of our favorites because we believe everything about it is first class. The rooms are beautifully decorated, and eating at the Schoolhouse Cafe is a real dining experience." (V. Luthans)

"It is immaculate in every sense of the word! What a pleasant assault to one's senses: beautiful quilts, stencils, and wall hangings to be seen; softly scented potpourri, candles, and soaps to be smelled; antiques, photos, and bric-a-brac to be touched; the relaxing, muffled sounds of guests quietly treading the carpeted stairs or hardwood floors to be heard; and delectable treats including homemade lemonade to be tasted. An added touch is the unique Wolf Creek Restaurant (a transplanted one-room schoolhouse filled with school memorabilia) which is adjacent to the beautifully manicured landscape." (J. Wingenroth)

"Applebutter Inn provided probably the most wonderful weekend that my husband and I have shared in our 22 years together. It was a journey into an era of simple, restful, quiet appreciation of grace and beauty. Our room was so beautiful with a cozy fire casting shadows on the carefully appointed pastel wall coverings. The four-poster net canopy bed, baskets of wild flowers, candles glowing in each window, wonderful goose-down comforters — each of these things added to such an unforgettable weekend. We came to the Applebutter to celebrate my birthday but in addition to that were able to renew our spirits and our love, and we'll be forever grateful for that." (J. Raimondi)

"Applebutter Inn is charming! Each room has a name and that theme is carried out in the decor. There are beautiful antiques in each room, lovely quilts, and decorations. Each room has a guest book for comments. Breakfast is bountiful and delicious! It is served in an adjoining old school house where you can also get lunch or dinner if you don't want to stray far." (B. Rankin)

"The gracious hospitality and warmth of the inn staff and the inn itself was second to

none. My room was a treasure of charm and comfort and the view spectacular of the rolling Pennsylvania farmland. I would enthusiastically welcome a chance to go back and recommend it to all looking for an inn filled with warm ambiance and gourmet, delectable fare." (C. Dayle)

Somerset

The Inn at Georgian Place
800 Georgian Place Drive
Somerset, PA 15501
(814) 443-1043
Fax: (814) 445-3047
Manager: Jon Knupp

♛♛♛♛ Rating: AA-
Rates: Double/$85-165
Credit Cards: AE, MC, V

Turn-of-the-century Georgian revival mansion sits atop a hill overlooking the town, Lake Somerset, and the Laurel Mountains. It is 60 miles east of Pittsburgh off Exit 10 of the Pennsylvania Turnpike. Eleven guest rooms, each with private bath, feature special touches such as king-size sleigh bed, cherry paneled fireplace, four-poster rice carved bed, and Victorian wicker. Watch TV, read, or play cards in the oak paneled living room with concert grand piano, bookcases, and fireplace or enjoy a sunset view from the bow front window in the Zimmerman family breakfast room with cherry paneled walls. The dining room, sunroom, and drawing room all offer views of Lake Somerset. Walk to Georgian Place outlet shopping center with over 50 manufacturer's stores. Area attractions: Somerset Historical Center, Johnstown Flood Museum, Fallingwater, and Hidden Valley. A full breakfast is served at a formal table setting with white linens and fresh flowers. Sample menu entrees may include Finish pancake with fruit, Italian fritatta, or blueberry pancakes. Afternoon tea features a variety of sandwiches and desserts. Meeting and wedding facilities.

Guests write: "This is one of the most elegant, comfortable, delightful places I have ever stayed in. It was truly a dream weekend with beautiful decor and a gracious host." (L. Lau)

"We have had a B&B in our home for 7 years and have used B&Bs every chance we can get for travel. This is by far the best. The staff is efficient and pleasant and the food was 'four star' and served with grace." (J. Hartwell)

Somerset

Glades Pike Inn
RD 6 Box 250
Somerset, PA 15501
(814)443-4978
Innkeeper: Janet Jones

👑👑 Rating: B
Rates: Single/$40-70; Double/$50-80
Credit Cards: AE, M, V

Glades Pike Inn, a mid 19th-Century Colonial, once served as a stagecoach stop and is located 6 miles west of Somerset and 13 miles east of Donegal. The inn was remodeled in 1987 and features exposed wood floors, high ceilings, and brick construction. Each of the five guest rooms offers a double bed and three rooms have a private bath and woodburning fireplace. Relax in one of the large chairs in front of the fireplace in the living room or visit with other guests at the wine and cheese social offered on weekends. Area attractions include the Laurel Hill Hiking Trail, Hidden Valley and Seven Springs, resorts for skiing, Ohiopyle State Park for fishing and white water rafting, and many historic sites. Apple soufflé pancakes are a house specialty often featured at the full breakfast. Families welcome. Restricted smoking.

State College/Pine Grove Mills

Split-Pine Farmhouse B&B
P.O. Box 326
Pine Grove Mills, PA 16868
(814) 238-2028
Innkeeper: Mae McQuade

👑👑👑 Rating: A-
Rates: Single/$50; Double/$65-100
Credit Cards: MC, V

Simple Federal home built in the mid-19th Century is set in a rural area just minutes from Pennsylvania State University and State College, two hours west of Harrisburg and four hours outside of Philadelphia. Choose from five guest rooms with country views which feature an international collection of vintage and antique furnishings. One room offers a private bath. Other rooms are shared by no more than two guest rooms. Relax in the formal sitting room with fireplace, baby grand piano, and French Liqueur Cabinet. Explore the surrounding acres of lawns and flowers with views of mountains and fields. Hiking, fishing, water sports, cross country skiing, and antiquing are all nearby. Area attractions include the Pennsylvania Arts Festival, Bellefonte Victorian Christmas, the Amish Market at Belleville, and the Dinner Train from Bellefonte to Tyrone. A full breakfast served at the dining room's mahogany table might feature ham crepes with Florentine sauce, mushroom strudel, breakfast kabobs, nutty French toast or Santa Fe strata. Dinners, luncheons, teas, and receptions can be arranged. Restricted smoking.

Guests write: *"My colleagues and I have had retreats at the Split-Pine Farmhouse B&B for the past two years, and look forward to making it an annual event. The house is beautiful, an old farmhouse in a historical area with furnishings and accessories that come from all over the world and are presented in an elegant and unique way. The environment is private and restful. Mrs. McQuade is the perfect hostess, anticipating our needs and providing extra touches throughout the weekend. The breakfasts are bountiful and beautiful, with special cakes and breads, casseroles, and fruit combinations that are unusual and delicious."* (C. Epp)

"The room I stayed in (Black & White Room) was spacious and decorated in a funky way. The other rooms were much more formal and beautiful, but the Black & White Room was youthful and fun. The B & B was surrounded by cornfields and there were cows nearby. I just loved the atmosphere. It was relaxing and luxurious." (E. Belansky)

"Our 3rd floor room was very enjoyable. It was large enough to allow one person to snuggle up and read on the corner sofa while the other slept or watched TV from the bed. The eclectic decor included antiques, collectibles, and interesting objects. I enjoyed the variety of books available. I really liked the sketches of country scenes which covered the stairwell from the second to third floors. Our hostess was very attentive and provided hot beverages at our door each morning and whenever we returned from our winter outings." (A. Malkis)

"Split Pine Farmhouse B&B has been our mainstay each football weekend for the past eight years. We have enjoyed warm hospitality and excellent food in uniquely original surroundings. Over the years we have stayed in all the bedrooms and find each one has individual charm while meeting high standards for comfort." (M. Bieberbach)

"We loved our first visit for the setting, but especially because of Mae and her gracious manner. Mae truly puts herself out to please her guests. The breakfasts at Split Pine are what I call a 'happening'. Mae is a gourmet at cooking, presentation, and table setting. The anticipation of what our next breakfast will be is great fun!" (M. McGarvey)

Wellsboro

Kaltenbach's Bed & Breakfast
RD #6 Box 106A
Wellsboro, PA 16901
(800) 722-4954 or (717) 724-4954
Innkeeper: Lee Kaltenbach

♛♛♛   Rating: B
Rates: Single/$35; Double/$60; Suite/$125
Credit Cards: MC, V

Flagstone ranch house nestled on 72 acres of rolling hills is in north central Pennsylvania one hour north of Williamsport. Ten guest rooms with king or queen-size beds are available. Six rooms have a private baths and two rooms are honeymoon suites with oversized tubs-for-two. Explore this Tioga County farm with its sheep, pigs, rabbits, and beef cattle. Take a walk through meadows and the forest. Year-round recreation includes skiing at Denton Hill or Sawmill ski areas, cross country skiing and snowmobiling on trails at the farm, hiking, biking, fishing, and hunting. Visit the nearby Grand Canyon of Pennsylvania, Corning Glass Center, Coudersport Ice Mine, Watkins Glen Raceway, or the State Laurel Festival held annually. Full breakfast features eggs fixed five different ways, breakfast meats, and home-made jams, jellies, and baked goods. Wedding and meeting facilities available. Families welcome. Wheelchair access. No smoking.

Guests write: *"The 'Antique Red Room,' which is one of the suites which we stayed in, was absolutely immaculate and romantic, with its brass bed, color TV, direct phone dialing, and of course a hot tub to add that special touch! The town that surrounds the B & B is a perfect choice for antique lovers with its many novelty shops. It's a collector's dream." (C. Koons)*

"Kaltenbach's B & B, nestled in the center of the endless mountains of North Central Pennsylvania, provided us with the peaceful and quiet country weekend getaway. Lee's knowledge and familiarity of the surrounding area is refreshing and reassuring to anyone looking for a small town atmosphere with plenty of activities and events."(T. Benetz)

"The Kaltenbach Farm offers an appealing, rural family atmosphere in which anyone will feel welcome. The home offers large common areas and comfortable, private guest rooms and baths. A farm-style feast describes the usual breakfast, which features farm-raised meats and home-baked blue ribbon breads. Lee Kaltenbach, the owner, proved to be one of the most accommodating, friendly, receptive and interesting hosts that I have encountered during my extensive travels. " (G. Gass)

Wilkes-Barre/Dallas

Ponda-Rowland Bed & Breakfast
R.R. 1, Box 349
Dallas, PA 18612-9604
(717) 639-3245 or (800) 854-3286
Fax: (717) 639-5531
Innkeepers: Cliff and Jeanette Rowland

♕♕ Rating: B+
Rates: Double/$55-85
Credit Cards: AE, MC, V

Mid-nineteenth-century plank frame home with beamed ceilings has a rural setting and is located 10 miles northwest of Wilkes-Barre off Route 309. Four guest rooms and one suite, all with private baths, have been furnished with American Colonial antiques and country accents. Guests are invited to relax on the enclosed front porch or sit in front of the fire in the Great Room. Popular activities in the area include fishing at the family trout fishing park just up the road, local rail tours, Pocono Downs, canoeing, swimming, skiing, horseback riding, and tobogganing. Hay rides are offered on-site as well as visits with the farm's animals. A master timberframe craftsman has a shop on the premises. A hearty breakfast is served by the fire in the Great Room. Families welcome. Restricted smoking.

Guests write: *"As soon as we pulled up the driveway, we felt right at home. Our room was lovely. It is spacious and greatly decorated with antiques. The great room, the fireplace, the sunroom and dining area are all outstanding. Jeanette cooks breakfast from the heart. We started off with a delicious fruit salad and proceeded with a truly great country breakfast. The Rowland Farm is indeed a great farm. With so many friendly animals, all eager to be petted and fed, we felt like kids."* (B&B Murphy)

"The inn lures one back to simpler times with its antique furnishings and memorabilia. The casual country atmosphere connotes comfort and invites relaxation. On each of my visits I stayed in different rooms, which were appointed with different antiques; and each day I discovered something I hadn't noticed previously. At night I snuggled under the homemade quilts with a cool cross breeze of fresh country air wafting over me. Breakfast consisted of delectable visual art. Fresh fruits were served in a variety of arrangements, as were griddle cakes, corn cakes, waffles, French toast, baked eggs, muffins, toast, and homemade jams, jellies and syrups." (M. Holm)

Ceiba

Ceiba Country Inn
Carr # 977 KM 1.2
Ceiba, Puerto Rico 00735
(809) 885-0471
Fax: (809) 885-0471
Innkeeper: Nicki Treat

♛♛   Rating: B
Rates: Single/$45; Double/$60.
Credit Cards: AE, MC, V

Tropical architecture graces this fifteen-year-old countryside inn located on the east coast of Puerto Rico, thirty-five miles southwest of San Juan. There are nine guest rooms washed in white walls with colorful pillows, curtains, and bedspreads. Guests enjoy the palm trees and sea breezes as well as the surrounding ocean views and rolling hills. Visit nearby Luquillo Beach, Seven Seas Beach, El Yunque Rain Forest, and the five marinas that are within twenty miles. Continental breakfast includes home-baked nut breads and a selection of tropical fruit. Function rooms available for small meetings. Families welcome.

Guests write: *"We were in Puerto Rico on business which extended into the Christmas holiday. Our hosts included us into their family circle and with their many friends in the area. Our accommodations were very clean and pleasant, with grapefruit and banana trees just outside our door. We were on a mountain hillside with a beautiful panoramic view of surrounding hills and El Yunque rain forest in distance."* (D&S DuQuet)

"We have thoroughly enjoyed our stays at the Ceiba Country Inn. The view is breathtaking; the rooms are neat and clean, the owners friendly and very accommodating. It is like a home away from home! We love it!" (D&M Gardner)

"The rooms were impeccably clean. The towels were big and of a good quality. The owners were very helpful with providing information on nearby restaurants and places of interest in the area. The breakfasts were of fresh fruits, juice and coffee, a choice of cereal, and baked goods. Our family of five always enjoys our stay and the attention of our host and hostess." (M&M Rios)

Newport

Admiral Fitzroy Inn
398 Thames Street
Newport, RI 02840
(401) 848-8000, or (800) 343-2863
Fax (401) 848-8024
Innkeeper: Judy Rush

 Rating: A-
Rates: Double/$65-150
Credit Cards: AE, MC, V

Admiral Fitzroy Inn, one of four Admiral inns, is listed on the National Register of Historic Places and located in the heart of Newport's waterfront district, 1.5 hours from Boston. Choose from eighteen guest rooms with private bath and unique hand-painted walls. The inn's roof-deck offers views of the harbor. The narrow streets of this old seaport town boast examples of Victorian architecture, Colonial houses, and summer cottage mansions along with Fort Adams, restaurants, art galleries, and shops. A full breakfast includes muffins, hot entrees, fresh fruit, croissants and is served in the breakfast room or taken up to guest rooms. Meeting facilities available. Families welcome. Wheelchair access.

Newport

Spring Street Inn
353 Spring Street
Newport, RI 02840
(401) 847-4767
Innkeeper: Parvine Latimore

 Rating: B
Rates: Single/$40-100; Double/$50-130
Credit Cards: MC, V

Located on historic Spring Street, named by 17th century settlers, this three story Empire Victorian is within walking distance to the many Newport attractions. With furnishings selected to enhance this Victorian home, each of the eight guest rooms have private baths. Rooms on the upper floor boast views of the historic town of Newport. A guest sitting room features antiques, plants, and color cable television. Walk to beaches, the harbor, the historic district, mansions, museums, restaurants, antique shops, and gift stores. Area attractions: sailing, golf, swimming, tennis, fishing, topiary gardens, Norman Bird Sanctuary, Mystic Seaport, Block Island, Martha's Vineyard, and the City of Providence. A full breakfast might include freshly baked muffins served warm, fresh fruit and assorted cereals, and a Savory Cheese Omelet served with toast and hash browns or sausage. Guests with dietary needs provided for. Restricted smoking. Weddings and meeting facilities available .

Guests write: " *The innkeepers were very kind, polite and efficient. They did all they could to make our stay both comfortable and pleasant. Our room was very clean and appropriately furnished. Breakfast was delicious and the hospitality warm and welcoming.* " (*R. Smith*)

"*The owners were more than helpful in telling us the best places in Newport to go to. The breakfast more than I imagined and the rooms were beautiful. It seemed to me that everything was perfect.*" (*L. Newman*)

"*The innkeepers were most willing to make your stay worry-free. Their personal touch made a big difference from my other experiences at other B&Bs. There was complete selection at breakfast from fruit, cereal, to home cooking. All in all, the inn is a great value and I would definitely recommend it to others.*" (*W. Manns*)

"*The aroma of Damian's freshly baked muffins filled the elegant, but not overly formal dining room in the morning. Whoever we came into contact with at the inn was most helpful and courteous. We really enjoyed our trip to Newport and our stay at the Spring Street Inn.*" (*L. Volz*)

Newport

Cliffside Inn
2 Seaview Avenue
Newport, RI 02840
(800) 845-1811 or (401) 847-1811
Innkeeper: Stephen Nicolas

♛ ♛ ♛　Rating: A+
Rates: Double/$125-205
Credit Cards: AE, MC, V

Built in the late 1800s as a summer home for a Maryland governor, this seaside Victorian has been in operation for 22 years and is 35 miles east of Providence. The inn features period furnishings, floor to ceiling windows, and Laura Ashley fabrics. Each of the twelve guest rooms with private bath are decorated with antiques and decorator linens. Some rooms feature a fireplace or whirlpool bathtub. Sit by the fire in the parlor, relax on the porch, or explore Cliff Walk, the city's famous seaside walking trail, just one block away. Take an easy stroll to the beach or to the famous Newport mansions, go sailing, or tour the Old Colonial homes. Full breakfast specialties include walnut pancakes, eggs Benedict, or Chambourd French toast. Afternoon appetizers are offered in the parlor. Restricted smoking.

Guests write: *"We give them high marks for the great muffins and coffee cakes they always hand make and serve along with their wonderful breakfast. Our room was quiet, romantic and so very pretty. As if that wasn't enough, we had all of the beautiful Newport mansions to visit with Annette and Norbert giving us suggestions and also stories about some of the mansions or their owners."* (M. O'Brien)

"We stayed in the Attic Room in December. What a terrific hide-away the inn is. Everything was perfect!" (L. Ilberg)

"It's really a wonderful inn. Beautifully done. You have total privacy, it's near the water, and the innkeepers are especially sweet, kind, and extremely relaxing to be around. " (K. Pendleton)

Newport

Melville House
39 Clarke Street
Newport, RI 02840
(401) 847-0640
Fax: (401) 847-0956
Innkeepers: Vincent DeRico
and David Horan

♛♛   Rating: B+
Rates: Double/$50-110
Credit Cards: AE, MC, V

Historic Colonial home built in 1750 is located in Newport's Historic District, listed on the National Register of Historic Places, and offers off-street parking behind the inn. Choose from seven guest rooms with antique furnishings; five have a private bath and all are decorated in the simple tastes of the early Colonists. Walk to Newport's interesting boutiques and restaurants from the inn as well as the Brick Market, Touro Synagogue, and Trinity Church. Popular attractions in the area include beaches, mansion tours, sailing, Cliff

Walk, and 10-mile Ocean Drive. Breakfast includes homemade muffins, bread, granola stuffed French toast, fruit pancakes, and Johnny cakes. Complimentary evening beverages, tea and biscotti are offered.

Guests write: *"Melville House is so charming and clean. I love the little 'touches,' wallpaper and stenciling which are our decorating ideas too. And that cup of tea after a cold day just hit the spot."* (E. Bailey)

"The Melville House was by far one of the best inns we've been to. Our room's decor was absolutely beautiful. The four-poster bed with flannel sheets made getting out of it next to impossible. Such comfort!! One nights' stay was not nearly long enough." (L. Mikon)

"The Melville House has been a real treat—neat as a pin, two charismatic cats, and beautifully cooked and presented breakfasts. We've had blueberry French toast, lemon squash muffins, and cappuccino-hazelnut biscuits." (J. Benz)

Providence

The Old Court Bed & Breakfast
144 Benefit Street
Providence, RI 02903
(401) 751-2002 or 351-0747
Fax: (401) 272-6566
Innkeeper: Jon Rosenblatt

♛♛   Rating: B
Rates: Single/$95-110; Double/$110-250
Corporate discount
Credit Cards: MC, V

Italianate brick home built in 1863 overlooks the Capitol and downtown Providence and is located on historic Benefit Street. Choose from eleven guest rooms with private bath and modified Victorian beds that are both unique and comfortable. Some rooms offer wet bars, telephone, and air conditioning. All have been decorated to reflect the Victorian period. The breakfast room features nineteenth-century decor with ornate Italian mantelpieces, plaster moldings, and twelve-foot ceilings. Relaxation can be found in the new TV-sitting lounge. Walk to downtown in three minutes or to the nearby campuses of Brown University, Rhode Island School of Design or the city's East Side with its interesting architecture and shops including Benefit Street's collection of Colonial and Victorian houses. Continental breakfast includes homemade breads. Fax machine, private phones, and wedding/meeting facilities available.

Westerly

The Villa
190 Shore Road
Westerly, RI 02891
(800) 722-9240 or Fax: (401) 596-6268
Innkeeper: Jerry Maiorano

♛♛♛   Rating: A-
Rates: Single/$70-170; Double/$75-175
Senior, family, corporate, and auto club discounts available
Credit Cards: AE, MC, V

The Villa was built in 1938 in the Dutch Colonial style with Mediterranean accents such as porticos, archways, and verandahs and is located 20 minutes east of Mystic, 50 minutes west of Newport. Choose from six individual suites, all with private baths. Two suites have a fireplace, sitting area, and private entrance. Another has a private Jacuzzi. Each room offers color TV, refrigerators, and air conditioning. Explore the surrounding one and one half acres of landscaped grounds, gardens, and lawns which include a lovely in-ground swimming pool and outdoor hot tub. Visit nearby Misquamicut Ocean beaches, Mystic Marine Life Aquarium, Foxwoods Casino, Mystic Seaport, and the Newport Mansions. An expanded continental breakfast buffet is served poolside, or in your room, and consists of assorted cereals, fresh fruit, home-made muffins, bagels, jellies and jams. In season, a complimentary Italian dinner is offered to Thursday evening guests. Families welcome.

Guests write: *"I can't stop telling my friends about the romantic weekend we spent here. I was so impressed that my fiancée and I would like to spend a weekend there in April. One night in their pool-house suite and we were hooked."* (L. Kiel)

"The Villa is a very attractive, Mediterranean style house about a mile from the beach. It has a lovely in-ground pool for guest's use. Clean and well maintained. Innkeeper Jerry Maiorano is very friendly and makes delicious baked goods!" (B. Alburger)

Additional information on B&Bs in South Carolina is available through the following B&B reservation agency: Historic Charleston B&B (800) 743-3583.

Charleston

Thirty Six Meeting Street
36 Meeting Street
Charleston, SC 29401
(803) 722-1034 or 723-0949
Fax: (803) 724-6352
Innkeeper: Anne Brandt

♛♛ Rating: B
Rates: Double/$75-125
Credit Cards: MC, V

Georgian home built in 1743 is situated in the heart of the Historic District a block and a half from the Battery. Each of the three guest suites features a private bath, rice bed, kitchenette, and period furnishings. Some suites can accommodate up to five people, great for families. Guests are invited to relax in the garden or to borrow bicycles to tour the Charleston area. Explore the interior of the residence with its examples of Georgian detailing or study the historic architecture of surrounding homes. Continental breakfast is provided in each of the rooms and includes freshly baked breads and pastries. Families welcome. Restricted smoking.

Georgetown

1790 House
630 Highmarket Street
Georgetown, SC 29440
(803) 546- 4821
Innkeepers: John and Patricia Wiley

♛♛♛ Rating: A
Rates: Double/$70-115
Senior and corporate discount
Credit Cards: AE, MC, V

Plantation-style 1790s inn is situated near the downtown business district of this historic port city and one hour away from Charleston. The home maintains many of its original features including a wrap-around verandah facing historic homes and its own gardens. Each of the air conditioned guest rooms, six in all, offer a private bath and Colonial furnishings. Some rooms have a separate sitting room with fireplace, a Jacuzzi tub, or an outside patio overlooking the gardens. Take a walking tour of the historic district, explore museums, shops, beaches, and nearby plantations. Borrow a bike from the inn to explore the downtown area. Recreation nearby includes boating, fishing, golf. Refreshments are served each afternoon. Full breakfast features gourmet specialties accented with home-made muffins and breads and is often served on the verandah. Wedding and meeting facilities available. Wheelchair access. Restricted smoking.

Guests write: *"What a wonderful get-away! The hospitality was so gracious, the food delicious, and the special touches were icing on the cake"* (B. Burgess)

"I have enjoyed the fine accommodations at the 1790 House on two different occasions and John Wiley's friendly hospitality makes me feel like I'm spending the weekend with a good friend. He is sincerely interested in his guests, and in making them feel welcome. An overnight stay at the 1790 House is a special treat." (D. Huggins)

"They pampered us beyond our dreams. We had good conversation with guests and privacy with each other." (S. Erickson)

South Dakota

Additional information on B&Bs in South Dakota is available from the following B&B reservation agency: B&B Western Adventure (406) 259-7993.

Ducktown

The White House Bed & Breakfast
Box 668, 104 Main Street
Ducktown, TN 37326
(800) 775-4166 or (615) 496-4166
Innkeepers: Dan & Mardee Kauffman

♛♛   Rating: B+
Rates: Single or Double/$55-60

Listed on the National Register Of Historic Places, this turn-of-the-century Victorian home is 2 hours north of Atlanta, 90 minutes east of Chattanooga, and 2.5 hours southwest of Asheville. The air-contitioned home offers three guest rooms, one with a private bath. Sit on the front porch on one of the rocking chairs or go exploring in the small town of Ducktown with its population of 535. The inn is convenient to antique shops, flea markets, and golf courses. Three TVA lakes offer water skiing, fishing, swimming, boating, and hiking. Go white water rafting or kayaking on the Ocoee River. This river, just 10 minutes away, is the venue for the 1996 Olympic white-water events. Rafting or floating may also be enjoyed on the Hiwassee River or visit the Ducktown Basin Museum with its exhibits of copper mining and Cherokee Indian Heritage. Baked grits souffle is sometimes featured at full breakfast which is accented with home-made bread and rolls. Restricted smoking.

Guests write: *"Our first night in the White House was most enjoyable—an evening 'snack' of homemade upside-down cake and ice cream was served with coffee before my husband and I retired to our most comfortable and attractive upstairs bedroom. The next morning we were served a very 'Southern' breakfast of fresh fruit compote, juice, baked grits, eggs, bacon, poppyseed bread (homemade, of course) plus fresh biscuits and jelly."* (J. Smith)

"Our recent stay at The White House was our first experience at a B & B, and now we're convinced it's the only way to go! The owners' extensive knowledge of the history of the surrounding area provided us with a valuable background as we toured this beautiful country. Most impressive, however, was the wonderful hospitality we enjoyed. They even drove us around to some special sights they knew we'd enjoy!" (V. McLean)

"This B & B is nestled in a quaint little town in the middle of copper mining country. The house itself is beautifully decorated and offers a comfortable, warm environment. The food is the highlight of this B & B! The operator's previous experience in the restaurant industry is evidenced by the elegant and delicious breakfast." (M.& C. Prinster)

Gatlinburg

7th Heaven Log Inn
3944 Castle Road
Gatlinburg, TN 37738
(800) 248-2923 or (615) 430-5000
Innkeepers: Ginger and Paul Wolcott

♛ ♛ ♛   Rating: A-
Rates: Double/$77-117
Credit Cards: MC, V

7th Heaven Log Home Inn is located on the 7th green of Bent Creek Golf Resort with the Smoky Mountain National Park just across the road. Downtown Gatlinburg is a ten mile drive. Four log and knotty pine guest rooms with private bath open to a common recreation room with stone fireplace, professional billiard table, bumper pool table and fully equipped kitchen. Relax in the log gazebo hot tub that overlooks a creek, pond, and golf course with a view of the Smoky Mountains beyond. Three mountain swimming pools and tennis courts are within a few blocks. Nearby attractions include Dollywood Theme Park, craft and antique shops, indoor ice skating, white water rafting, and hiking trails. Enjoy the scenic aerial tram to Ober Gatlinburg for skiing, indoor ice skating or a ride on the 1800 foot Alpine Slide. Coffee is set outside the guest room door each morning and a full "loosen your belt" breakfast follows.

Guests write: *"We were hesitant to stay at a B & B because we are not comfortable mixing with people we don't know or being in someone else's home. This log home was built specifically to be a B & B and that is proven by the comfort and convenience it provides; such as, private entrance with your own key to house, private bath, complete kitchen with microwave, dishes, etc. The large recreation room is in the center and has a variety of things to entertain you and room enough to be sociable or unsociable, puzzles, two pool tables, VCR, fireplace, etc. Our brochure advertised a seven-course breakfast and that it was!"* (W&M Kramp)

"Their care and hospitality is only surpassed by the incredible, comfortable rooms and the amenities that their beautiful home provides. The pool table, fireplace, separate kitchen and spa are all key elements to a wonderful time. Don't worry about eating lunch during your stay, you will be too full from breakfast! (D. Ames)

"You awake with the smell of coffee brewing and the sound of two jolly chefs upstairs cooking away to make the most delicious breakfast from country gravy and eggs and homemade biscuits to a most delicious cereal with fruits and cream." (R. Wilhoite)

Gatlinburg

Butcher House in the Mountains
1520 Garrett Lane
Gatlinburg, TN 37738
(615) 436-9457
Innkeeper: Gloria and Hugh Butcher

♛ ♛ ♛   Rating: A
Rates: Double/$79-109
Credit Cards: AE, MC, V

The Butcher House is located 40 miles southeast of Knoxville off of I-40, just above the main street of Gatlinburg and the main entrance to the Smoky Mountain National Park. The three-story Swiss Chalet-style home made of cedar and stone has spectacular views of Mt. LeConte and the Smokies. Choose from five guest rooms, each with private bath, floral arrangements, art and collectibles, and antique furniture. Relax on one of the deck swings while overlooking mountain vistas, sit by the wood burning stone fireplace in the Great Room. Area attractions: Smoky Mountain National Park, hiking trails, horseback riding, Ober Gatlinburg, Dollywood, Gatlinburg Passion Play, live theater, factory outlet malls, and Winterfest. A full breakfast is an original creation of the hosts featuring such specialties as eggs Sebastian, crepes Italian, or Eggs Josephine and is served on china. Weddings and meeting facilities available. No smoking.

Guests write: *"Our guest room, like the entire home, is decorated beautifully with many special touches from the dish of candy on the nightstand, coordinating private bath, to the cable TV provided. From our bedroom or the guest porch swing, we could look right out on Mt. LeConte — it's as pretty a view as could be seen anywhere." (B&P Burrows)*

"Staying at this B&B can best be described as staying in the home of dear friends who go out of their way to make your stay a most pleasant one. Upon arrival we were greeted with dessert and hot beverage of choice. Rooms were very clean and charming with antique decor. The view of the mountains is spectacular!" (G. Johnson)

"My husband and I were planning our 10-year anniversary and had never stayed at a B&B before. Breakfasts included exquisite gourmet entrees - a different one each morning. The hosts are a most adorable couple. Each evening, a special dessert was left out for guests to enjoy. The Butchers were most hospitable." (G&D Beckner)

Gatlinburg

Tennessee Ridge Inn
507 Campbell Lead
Gatlinburg, TN 37738
(615) 436-4068
Innkeeper: Dar Hullander

♛♛♛   Rating: A+
Rates: Double: $92-135
Credit Cards: AE, MC & V

Tennessee Ridge Inn is 36 miles from Knoxville via interstate 40, state 66 & U.S. 441. This three-story redwood and stone contemporary, with large expanses of glass, sits on the ridge line of Crockett Mountain, near the top of the sky lift in a wooded area. Views of the surrounding mountains and the city lights of Gatlinburg are dominant. Four guest rooms and one suite, all with private baths and in-room Jacuzzis, are individually decorated with sitting areas in front of stone fireplaces. Other features include private balconies, telephones, and fireplaces. The suite offers a living room, sofa, love seat, reading chair, entertainment center, balcony, and fireplace. Guests enter the Inn through the two-story Great Room. A stone fireplace dominates this room with its deep leather chairs and numerous conversation areas. Adjoining is the dining room with its cathedral ceiling and glass enclosure on three sides. The party/conference room is another large area with a stone fireplace, conversation areas, sports screen television, and conference tables. A covered balcony with chairs and tables adjoins. A swimming pool and meeting facilities are available. Walk to Gatlinburg shops, restaurants, entrance to Smoky Mountain National Park, Convention Center, Space Needle, and Sky Lift, aerial tramway to Ober Gatlinburg. Area attractions: Great Smoky Mountains National Park, hiking, horseback riding, water rafting, fishing, skiing, art galleries, specialty shops, Crafters Community, Cherokee Indian Reservation, Caverns, Newfound Gap, Cades Cove, Pigeon Forge (200 factory outlets), Dollywood, Dixie Stampede, and Music Mansion. Full Breakfast, served with china, crystal and sterling flatware, includes fresh fruit, juice, coffee, tea, homemade biscuits, gravy, scrambled eggs, and sausages. Wedding and meeting facilities. Restricted smoking.

Kodak

Grandma's House
734 Pollard Rd. PO Box 445
Kodak, TN 37764
(800) 676-3512 or (615) 933-3512
Innkeepers: Hilda and Charlie Hickman

♛♛♛ Rating: A
Rates: Single/$50; Double/$65-75
Credit Cards: MC, V

New Colonial home is located right in the center of East Tennessee, two miles off exit 407 of I-40, and is situated off a country lane leading to the French Broad River. Three guest rooms with private bath feature country decor with Hilda's home-made quilts, crafts, and paintings. One extra large room has a bay window and another features grandma's fancy iron bed. Relax in two common rooms with television, VCR, books, magazines, and games. Watch the sunset from the balcony or swing on the front porch. Minutes away are Knoxville, Oak Ridge, Norris, Pigeon Forge, Gatlinburg, and the Great Smoky Mountains. Visit historic sites, factory outlets, caverns, museums, and amusement parks. Full "farm-style" breakfast may include fruit soup, ham and egg puff, or buttermilk biscuits with gravy. No smoking.

Guests write: *"It is a newly built home, yet it has an old-fashion country charm to it. The rooms are decorated with handmade country quilts and crafts, and there are some beautiful antiques that really add charm. We had a great big country breakfast every morning with bacon, sausage, eggs, and some of the best breakfast casseroles I've ever had. There is a big sitting room in the front of the house with two couches, some chairs, a fireplace, and television. It is here that the guests and hosts relax, talk, and watch TV."* (J&T Zaro)

"Our stay at Grandma's House was our first experience with a bed and breakfast. The host and hostess treated us as special guests, inviting us to treat our stay as though we were in our own home. They were warm and congenial without being intrusive. There were unadvertised 'special benefits' such as, an opportunity to participate in a murder mystery (including dinner) which did not require additional cost." (J. Stucki)

"The house was spotless on both of our stays. The food and company were fabulous!! I wouldn't stay in another hotel if I thought all B&Bs were as good as Grandma's House." (T. McCall)

Monteagle/Chattanooga

North Gate Inn
Monteagle Assembly
P. O. Box 858
Monteagle, TN 37356
(615) 924-2799
Innkeepers: Nancy & Henry Crais

♛♛   Rating: B+
Rates: Single or Double/$60-78

North Gate is located approximately a half mile from Exit 134 off I-24. It is 45 miles northwest of Chattanooga and 85 miles southeast of Nashville. The two-story inn built in 1896 (with later additions) dominates the corner of Laburnum and Pine streets. Each of the seven guest rooms has a private bath and is decorated in an individual "flower garden" color accented with fresh flowers. Relax in the living room with wood burning fireplace or visit with other guests in the sun room with French doors and a wall of windows. Glassed-in porch features a blue ceramic wood burning stove and several seating areas. Area attractions: 100 acre scenic Assembly grounds featuring eight-week summer Chautauqua Season (gate ticket required); wilderness hiking, caving, fishing, and hiking trails. The lovely Gothic campus of the University of the South is a six mile drive and offers year-round cultural activities including Summer Music Center and writer's conference. Drive to Savage Gulf Natural area, Foster Falls, Bridal Veil Falls, and South Cumberland State Recreation Area. Full breakfast entrees include house specialties such as apple crepes, Mountain Grits & Sausage, baked eggs Florentine, or Belgian waffles. Small group and meeting facilities available. No smoking. Families welcome.

Guests write: *" Never have I been so impressed with the cleanliness of any place. This inn is a well conceived atmosphere, a place to unwind, relax and remember."* (L&J Wellborn)

" The setting of North Gate is lake a time machine set on 'yesteryear'. Nancy and Henry have a gift for inviting one to feel at home while allowing you the freedom to find whatever you planned from the time spent there." (G&B Berryman)

" Every morning at 8:30 we will think of North Gate Inn and wish we were having breakfast there. The Mountain Sausage & Grits was so good we logged it in our travel diary." (D. Magevney)

Pikeville

Fall Creek Falls Bed & Breakfast
Box 298-B, Route 3
Pikeville, TN 37367
(615) 881-5494
Innkeepers: Doug and Rita Pruett

♛♛♛   Rating: A
Rates: Single/$ 50-65; Double/$63-77

Custom-built brick country manor home located on 40 acres of rolling hillside is just one mile from Fall Creek Falls State Resort Park and 50 miles north of Chattanooga. Guests are accommodated in one of eight, air conditioned guest rooms that have been decorated with a blend of Victorian and Country styles. Six have a private bath. A special "Sweetheart Room" features brass bed and a red, heart-shaped whirlpool. There are several sitting areas on the main floor where guests can visit, read, and relax. The nearby resort park offers tennis, fishing sports, hiking, horseback riding, swimming, and a championship golf course. Drive to nearby recreation areas that offer canoeing, and cave exploring. There are also a number of antique shops near the inn. A full breakfast is served in the country kitchen, dining room, or in the Florida room. Menus vary but might include house specialties such as pecan waffles or grilled muffins Benedict. Restricted smoking.

Guests write: "We did not desire the usual 50th anniversary reception, so our daughters surprised us with reservations at Fall Creek Falls Bed and Breakfast Inn. Our room was 'homey' in many ways—cross-stitched plaques and other homemade, unusual framed pictures, heavy lace curtains, quilt bedspreads, throw covers and furniture of various periods but well-preserved. There were even hand-embroidered scarves for the furniture. The bath had a new and modern shower and tub; the linens were plentiful, and the table beside the lavatory had all of the amenities of home— spray, Q-tips, cotton balls, and toothbrush holder." (J. P. Oliphant)

"One of the rooms has a Jacuzzi that is especially popular with newlyweds who often come to Fall Creek Falls for honeymoons. The sunroom overlooks acres of fields that Doug has planted with forage for the deer and other wildlife. As you look down the rolling fields that fall away toward the Cumberland Plateau, you can also enjoy the many hummingbirds that come to the sun porch feeders, or walk outside to check out Doug and Rita's vegetable garden. Deer and other wildlife are numerous in the park. One day we counted six pair of pileated woodpeckers. Sometimes on Sunday evenings we catch the local musicians picking guitars, mandolins, fiddles, etc. at a local country store two miles from the inn." (F&G Gibson)

Glen Rose

The Lodge at Fossil Rim
RT 1 Box 210
Glen Rose, TX 76043
(817) 897-7452
Innkeepers: Lisa and Artie Ahier

♕♕♕   Rating: A+
Rates: Double/$125-200
Special rates for booking entire lodge
Credit Cards: AE, MC, V

Located on a 3,000 acre Wildlife Center which breeds exotic endangered species, this 3-level Ranch made of stone, cedar, and fir is located 75 miles southwest of Dallas. Choose from five guest rooms at the lodge. Three offer a private bath and fireplace. Other special amenities in some rooms include Jacuzzi, private patio, and king-sized beds. Unusual and antique furnishings accent the entire inn. Guests can relax in front of the large stone fireplace in the common room with cathedral ceiling, stained-glass window, large-screen TV, and beverage bar. The dining room and connecting deck features panoramic views of the countryside and surrounding wildlife. A lovely outdoor swimming pool with unusual natural environment and architecture is near the inn and reached by a short ride in the safari truck. The Center offers many activities to guests at an additional cost including safari rides and a behind the scenes look at the care and breeding of animals. Pecan waffles, breakfast pizza, and smoked turkey quiche are just three samples of entrees served at the full breakfast. Dinner by reservation is available Friday and Saturday evenings. The game room can be used for meeting facilities. Families welcome. Restricted smoking.

Guests write: *"To feel a giraffe, massage the snoot of a rhinoceros and gaze upon the many endangered species, is truly an unforgettable experience. It is not often that one is reluctant to rave over a 'good thing,' since others may then discover this rare find. The Lodge at Fossil Rim is truly work keeping the secret to ourselves, but we know its success is sure to come, after all."* (F&D Laughlin)

"Something not to be missed is the open air jeep tour available in the late afternoon or early in the morning. The tour is available only from the Lodge and lasts about 2 1/2 hours." (J&B Merritt)

Houston

Durham House Bed & Breakfast Inn
921 Heights Blvd
Houston, TX 77008
(713) 868-4654
Innkeeper: Marguerite Swanson

♛♛   Rating: B+
Rates: Single/$55-75; Double/$65-95
Credit Cards: AE, MC, V

Located on a wide boulevard with jogging trails, this historic Queen Anne
Victorian with a turret and cupid weather vane is listed on the National
Register of Historic Places. The inn sits on an oversized urban lot with large
trees and garden gazebo. Choose from six guest rooms, four with private baths.
The second floor carriage house suite features a collection of heart motif wall
decorations. An antique wedding gown adorns the Blue Room, and the Rose
Room has an 1860 walnut Victorian bed and beveled glass window with a view
of tall pecan trees. All bathrooms offer antique clawfoot tubs with overhead
showers. An antique filled parlor features a player pinao for guest use and a
spacious solarium is furnished with white wicker. Area attractions: Galleria
shopping; Astrodome and Astroworld, the largest medical center in the
U.S.A., museums and art galleries, and a walking tour of historic homes. A
full breakfast served daily on formal china and linens includes home baked
choices and individual dietary restrictions are attended to. Weddings, receptions, original murder mystery dinner parties, and meeting facilities available.
No smoking.

San Antonio

Adams House Bed and Breakfast Inn
231 Adams Street
San Antonio, TX 78210
(210) 224-4791
Fax: (210) 223-5125
Innkeeper: Betty Lancaster

♛♛   Rating: B+
Rates: Single/$65-95; Double/$70-100
Government discount
Credit Cards: AE, MC, V

This two-story brick Victorian Italianite, built in 1902, is located in downtown San Antonio in the King William Historic Distance. Three guest rooms are currently available, each with private bath, soon to be expanded to five. All guest rooms are tastefully appointed in matched oak or walnut bedroom sets with beautiful antiques. The Adams parlor has a piano and stereo equipment for your pleasure. The library has a large selection of books and records, some of them rare, and it also includes a law library. Central air and heat, as well as ceiling fans, assure comfort year round. The Adams House is surrounded by many of the city's famous attractions. The famous Riverwalk winds its way through the neighborhood, offering a scenic route to downtown. A short trolley ride will take you to the Alamo, Convention Center, Alamodome, Tower of the Americas, Institute of Texan Cultures, Market Square, Rivercenter Mall, and the Spanish Governor's Palace. Or allow express buses to wisk you to Sea World, Fiesta Texas, the San Antonio Missions, Brackenridge Park, or your choice of several museums. Enjoy a full breakfast, served in the dining room or out on a veranda. Fax, copier, and computer available for guest use. No smoking.

San Antonio

Norton Brackenridge House
230 Madison
San Antonio, TX 78204
(800) 221-1412 or (512) 271-3442
Innkeepers: Carolyn and Nancy Cole

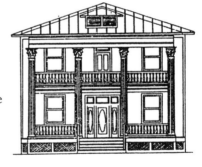

♛♛   Rating: B
Rates: Single or Double/$75-95
Credit Cards: AE, MC, V

Historic Victorian frame house built in the early 1900s is situated in a quiet residential area six blocks from downtown. Choose from five guest rooms on the first or second floor. Each has a private bath and several offer a private entrance. Common rooms are located on the second floor where guests meet to converse or plan their day's activities. Walk to downtown San Antonio's many attractions or visit nearby San Antonio River, Convention Center, the Alamo, Sea World, or Fiesta Texas. A full breakfast often features blintz soufflé or eggs Benedict casserole accented with almond poppy bread or sour cream cake. Restricted smoking.

San Antonio

San Antonio Yellow Rose
229 Madison
San Antonio, TX 78204
(210) 229-9903 or (800) 950-9903
Innkeepers: Cliff and Jennifer Tice

👑👑👑   Rating: A-
Rates: Double/$75-110
Government discount
Credit Cards: AE, MC, V

Victorian two-story built in 1878 by the Charles Mueller family has been recently restored by the current innkeepers and is located only two blocks from Riverwalk. The asymmetrical design of the home allows for a grand staircase and generous common areas on the main floor. A pre-1878 farmhouse attached to the main Victorian structure offers guest accommodations as well as the second floor of the main house. A courtyard and inviting porches invite relaxation. Select from five guest rooms with decor ranging from French Country to Victorian and accessories collected during the hosts' extensive travels. Each room has a private bath, two of which are not connected to the room but are accessed through the hallway. Walk to the Alamo, Mexican Market, and ancient missions. Area attractions: Sea World, Fiesta Texas, German settlements, and great charm in the Texas hill country within a short drive. A full gourmet breakfast is served daily and refreshments are served upon arrival and throughout a guest's stay. Meeting facilities available. Restricted smoking.

Guests write: "*This is a fresh and bright Victorian B&B decorated comfortably but not excessively with antiques. The updated bathrooms, white lace curtains, and comfortably upholstered furniture contribute to make guests feel at home. The delicious breakfast included generous fruit cup and caramel pecan French toast with bacon strips, juice, and coffee. Hosts Jennifer and Cliff Tice seem like old friends.*" (M. Parker)

"*The home was well cared for, clean, friendly and felt like we were ' home away from home'. The host fixed early breakfast for the ministers who had early business meeitngs and for the rest at their conveience. Both host and hostess are a credit to their community and a good advertisement tof continued visits to B&Bs.*" (J. Tow)

Waco

Thornton's Bed & Breakfast
908 Speight
Waco, TX 76707
(817) 756-02707 or FAX: (817) 756-0711
Innkeepers: Davis and Jennifer Thornton

♛♛♛   Rating: A
Rates: Single/$79: Double/$79-89
Credit Cards: MC, V

Traditional redbrick, 1 1/2 story with gabled roof was built in 1921 and is near Baylor University. Four guest rooms with hardwood floors and private baths, are decorated in Country English with some antiques. Relax in the living room in front of the fireplace or walk to Baylor University and museums. Area attractions: water skiing & fishing; Dr. Pepper Museum; Texas Ranger Museum; and Waco 200. A full breakfast is offered. Afternoon tea. Wheelchair access. No smoking.

Guests write: *"Each room is tastefully appointed with a beautiful mixture of antiques and the latest in decorating ideas. From the Tiffany lamps to the grapevine wreaths and attractive window and wall treatments, everything contributed to the warm, inviting atmosphere. The queen-size bed was a dream come true and the bathroom was spotless and well-equipped. When we returned from dinner, we found that our bed had been turned back and mints were placed on each pillow. And when we left, Jennifer gave us the tiny potted plant from our nightstand in honor of Valentine's Day. It remains on my dresser at home as a reminder of a perfect weekend."* (T&A Ownby)

"It's like stepping into one of the most pristine B&Bs in England. Each room has a unique character that is impeccably decorated. Breakfast was a custom blend of healthy contemporary and English food. The proprietors are warm, young, vivacious and made us feel like family. We find ourselves making up special events to justify going back." (T&D Salladay)

Waxahachie

BonnyNook Inn
414 West Main Street
Waxahachie, TX 75165
(214) 938-7207 or (800) 486-5936 (Outside TX)
Innkeepers: Bonnie and Vaughn Franks

♛♛♛   Rating: A
Rate: Single or Double/$70-100
Credit Cards: AE, MC, V

Turn-of-the-century Victorian inn with wide porches and gingerbread accents is located 30 miles south of Dallas on I-35. Five antique furnished guest rooms offer private baths and feature unique antiques such as; a sleigh bed, Belgium antique bed, and 150-year old English bedroom suite. Several rooms have Jacuzzi tubs. Walk two blocks to the historic Town Square with its 1850 Courthouse. Nearby attractions include the largest concentration of Victorian gingerbread homes in the state (many are used as movie sites), as well as many antique shops, malls, and fine restaurants. Full breakfast. Six-course dinners available for an extra fee. Function rooms are available for meetings and social occasions. Families welcome. Restricted smoking.

Guests write: *"As a veteran traveler and devotee of bed and breakfast inns from all across the USA, I was pleased to recently discover the BonnyNook right in my own backyard in North Texas. To me the BonnyNook has captured the essential ingredients found in thebest of the B&Bs — a variety of choice room accommodations in an authentically restored Victorian period residence."* (M. Shelton)

"Our stay was similar to a trip back in time. The elegant furnishings, no TV or phone to distract, and a delicious breakfast of omelets, fruit, coffee and juice. It made us realize how hectic our modern life has become, even with so-called conveniences and progress." (L. McAlister)

"Not only is this bed and breakfast a welcome, safe alternative to staying in Dallas; but it's by far the best decorated and furnished and has an excellent menu." (R. Shelton)

"The room made us feel the romance of the last century and the bubble bath was great. They've added so many unique touches. We'll never forget the delicious breakfasts." (S. Peak)

"I can't think of a better way to spend a birthday than going away with the man you love and have been married to for almost fourteen years and coming to such a wonderful place as BonnyNook. We had a great time relaxing, taking a bubble-bath in the old claw-foot tub and just enjoying each other without the kids." (C. Parga)

"This was a wonderful retreat from the everyday hustle and bustle and we didn't hear a phone ring once!" (B. Burns)

"We ended our Christmas holiday with dinner at the BonnyNook. This stay was our first experience at B&Bs and it's just the prescription for two busy professionals from the big city. BonnyNook allowed us to imagine and experience what life was like when the world wasn't so busy faxing a report or E-mailing a memo. We'll carry the BonnyNook's grace and charm with us as we enter 1992." (P. Borchardt)

"We appreciated all the amenities, the sample menus from local restaurants, the fresh fruit tray, the tea and coffee service, the decanter of wine after our return from dinner, the three-course breakfast, the charming hospitality, and the Frank's Room with the beautiful Jacuzzi tub." (M. Matthews)

Utah

Additional information on B&Bs in Utah is available from the following B&B reservation agencies: Mi Casa Su Casa (800) 456-0682

Alburg

Thomas Mott Bed & Breakfast
Blue Rock Road on Lake Champlain
Route 2, Box 149B
Alburg, VT 05440
(802) 796-3736 or
(800) 348-0843 (US and Canada)
Innkeeper: Patrick Schallert

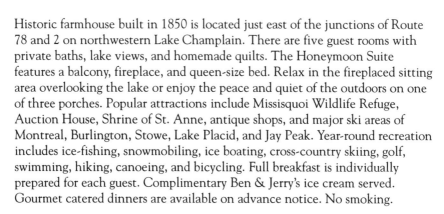

♛♛♛   Rating: A-
Rates: Double/$55-70
Credit Cards: MC, V

Historic farmhouse built in 1850 is located just east of the junctions of Route 78 and 2 on northwestern Lake Champlain. There are five guest rooms with private baths, lake views, and homemade quilts. The Honeymoon Suite features a balcony, fireplace, and queen-size bed. Relax in the fireplaced sitting area overlooking the lake or enjoy the peace and quiet of the outdoors on one of three porches. Popular attractions include Missisquoi Wildlife Refuge, Auction House, Shrine of St. Anne, antique shops, and major ski areas of Montreal, Burlington, Stowe, Lake Placid, and Jay Peak. Year-round recreation includes ice-fishing, snowmobiling, ice boating, cross-country skiing, golf, swimming, hiking, canoeing, and bicycling. Full breakfast is individually prepared for each guest. Complimentary Ben & Jerry's ice cream served. Gourmet catered dinners are available on advance notice. No smoking.

Guests write: *"At the end of August, my husband and I took an eight-day vacation traveling through Vermont, New Hampshire, and Maine. We had our first experience with bed and breakfasts, staying in a different one each evening. I am writing you to express my fondness for one bed and breakfast in particular. That is the Thomas Mott B&B in Alburg, Vermont. Pat made both of us feel very much at home and there was plenty to keep us busy. He offered the use of his canoe and bikes. We could watch television or read a book, of which there were many! (S. Danson)*

"We spent a wonderful 24 hours at the Thomas Mott Homestead. Our suite was perfect and included a full moon on the waters of Lake Champlain. The French toast was superb and the proprietor most accommodating. We recommend a stay for the memory bank." (T&K Riggione)

"I felt as though I was staying at my Grandfather's old log cabin. I found the house very cozy and comfortable and the host, Pat Schallert, was warm and friendly. The location is right on the lake." (W. Passman)

Arlington

Hill Farm Inn
RR 2, Box 2015
Arlington, VT 05250
(802) 375-2269 or (800) 882-2545
Innkeepers: John and Regan Chichester

♛♛   Rating: B
Rates: Single/$55-100; Double/$75-120
Credit Cards: AE, MC, V

Hill Farm Inn has served as a farm vacation for guests for over eighty-five years and is located in the southwest corner of the state on land which was once part of a historic land grant. There are thirteen rooms in the main inn or guest house; eight offer a private bath. The decor of each room captures the simplicity and charm of a traditional New England farmhouse. A large living room offers comfortable chairs, sofas, and a fireplace. Battenkill River borders the farm and is fun for canoeing and fly-fishing. Other attractions in the area include Bennington Museum, Green Mountain National Forest, antique shops, hiking, bicycling, and skiing. Full country breakfast is included in the rates and a four-course dinner is available at an additional charge by advance reservation. Families welcome.

Guests write: *"The guest house is nice if what you are really looking for is peace, quiet, and privacy. When the staff found out that we had gotten engaged, they left champagne and chocolates in our room, showered us with heartfelt congratulations, and even pulled a few strings at a local restaurant to get us last minute dinner reservations. The staff of the Hill Farm Inn worked hard to make sure that our engagement weekend was very special."* (S. Croll)

"We enjoy going to Hill Farm Inn for many reasons, especially the friendly feeling we get every time we go. On our latest visit we brought my parents and also our two children, and they loved their rooms because their beds were so comfortable; and each room is decorated with a little basket of apples or oranges. Their front porch in the fall is so inviting. With a cup of tea and cookies and a good book, you sit on a rocker and look at the mountains all around. It is a very tranquil feeling, one we cannot get enough of." (D&M Desrosiers)

"We drove up the country road past an old graveyard and church from the eighteenth century, wondering if the relaxation we sought would turn to boredom. From the moment we entered the Hill Farm Inn, it felt like we came back to an old family vacation home." (C&L Curtice)

Barre

Woodruff House
13 East Street
Barre, VT 05641
(802) 476-7745 or 479-5190
Innkeepers: Robert and Terry Somaini

♛♛♛ Rating: A
Rates: Single/$50; Double/$70

Historic Queen Anne Victorian home is situated across from a quiet park near the village center and located halfway between Boston and Montreal at I-89, exit 7. There are two guest rooms available with private bath. Each is individually decorated with antiques, eclectic furnishings, and collectibles. There are two large common rooms which offer comfortable seating for viewing TV, quiet nooks for reading or conversing, and a large collection of interesting books. Area attractions include State Capitol, tour of the largest granite quarries in the world, and leaf peeping. Full breakfast is served with fine china, crystal, and silver in the formal dining room. No smoking.

Guests write: *"Robert and Terry prepared tea, crackers, cheese, and sliced fruits for us when we arrived very tired and hungry. They also prepared a late night snack for us before we went to bed. This was our first opportunity to stay at a B&B and we're now convinced if they're all like the Woodruff House we shall be customers for life."* (R. Sunday)

"We are the family of Dr. John H. Woodruff who brought his family back here to visit his brother and family. We were privileged to get to stay in his family home. It had been restored and was in great shape. The whole Woodruff family feels very fortunate to have our house in such beautiful shape and in such friendly hands." (J. Woodruff)

"Bob & Terry's sincere concern for our comfort and pleasure was unmatched by any other experience we've had in a B&B. The table was set with the finest details in this most authentic Victorian home. I stepped back in time." (B. Pivnick)

"After sleeping soundly under down comforters, we enjoyed warm conversation by candlelight over breakfast in an elegant dining room. We would choose this delightful bargain over a hotel or a condominium for any of our Vermont ski vacations." (G. Hills)

Chester

Henry Farm Inn
Green Mountain Turnpike
P.O. Box 646
Chester, VT 05143
(802) 875-2674 or (800) 723-8213
Innkeeper: Jean Bowman

♛♛   Rating: B+
Rates: Double/$37.50-62.50; Double/$50-90
Credit Cards: AE, MC, V

Historic Colonial farmhouse situated on fifty forested acres of foothills was
built in 1750 and is located ten miles from I-91 near Routes 103 and 11. There
are seven guest rooms with private baths. There are two fireplaced sitting
rooms on the main floor for reading, conversing, and relaxation. Area recreation includes skiing, hiking, fishing, golf, and tennis. Full breakfast. Families
welcome. No smoking.

Dorset

Dovetail Inn
Route 30 and Main Street
Dorset, VT 05251-0976
(802) 867-5747 or (800) 4-Dovetail
Fax: (802) 867-0246
Innkeeper: Jean & Jim Kingston

♛♛   Rating: B
Rates: Single/$50- 80; Double/$ 60-125
Credit Cards: V, MC

Federal style inn overlooks historic Dorset Village Green and Spruce Peak on
the main street of a New England village, six miles north of Manchester on
Vermont Route 30. Choose from eleven guest rooms, each with private baths,
sitting areas, and air conditioning. Relax in the Alonson Gray House sitting
room with cable television and butler's pantry or in the Marsha Gray House
Keeping Room where breakfast is served each morning. Walk to the Dorset
Village Library, Historical Society Museum (featuring history on the first
marble quarries in America), antique shops, gourmet market and deli, restaurants, and summer stock theater. Area attractions: Proctor Marble Exhibit, ski
mountains, cross-country skiing, Southern Vermont Art Center, Lake George,

Norman Rockwell Museum, and the Grandma Moses Museum. Shop at upscale designer outlets and quaint boutiques. Attend major seasonal concerts, fairs, and sporting events. Continental plus breakfast buffet includes seasonal fresh fruits or compotes, muffins, coffee cakes, and locally made jams and jellies. Breakfast in bed by request. Afternoon tea offered.

Fairlee

Silver Maple Lodge
RR 1, Box 8
South Main Street
Fairlee, VT 05045
(802) 333-4326 or (800) 666-1946
Innkeeper: Scott Wright

♛♛ Rating: B
Rates: Single/$42-62; Double/$48-68
Credit Cards: AE, MC, V

Historic country inn dating back to the late 1700s is on Route 5, half a mile south of I-91, exit 15. Choose from sixteen antique-furnished guest rooms, fourteen with private bath. Private cottage accommodations offer knotty pine walls and wide board floors of lumber cut on the property. Three cottages have working fireplaces and kitchenettes. Relax on the wrap-around porch or play horseshoes, croquet, badminton, or shuffleboard on the lawn. Visit nearby Lake Morey, Lake Fairlee, Maple Grove Museum, St. Johnsbury, Quechee Gorge, and Saint Gaudens National Historic Site. Local recreation includes golf, tennis, fishing, boating, skiing, hiking, and hot air ballooning. Continental breakfast. Families welcome.

Guests write: *"We have stayed at the Silver Maple for several years and have never had a complaint except that the stay was always too short. The owners really care about their guests and always go out of their way to make us happy. We enjoyed everything immensely - the lovely room, good breakfasts, fabulous weather, interesting people, use of their video, comfortable lawn chairs, perfect location for everything we wanted to do and see."* (B. Solomon)

Jericho

Homeplace Bed & Breakfast
RR 2, Box 367
Jericho, VT 05465
(802) 899-4694; Fax: (802) 899-4883
Innkeeper: Mariot Huessy

♛♛ Rating: B+
Rates: Single/$45; Double/$55

Modern farmhouse is situated on one-hundred acres of woods and located 1.5 miles from Route 15 and 8 miles from I-89, exit 12. Choose from three guest rooms which share two baths and feature crewel-style spreads and embroidered pillowcases. The home is filled with European antiques, Vermont craft work, and a large collection of books. Animals on the farm include horses, sheep, pigs, ducks, chickens, cats, dogs, and donkeys. Explore miles of cross-country or hiking trails. Area attractions include University of Vermont, Shelburne Museum, Stowe ski areas, and Lake Champlain. Full country breakfast may feature eggs, bacon or sausage, home-made rolls, and fruit. No smoking

Killington

Inn at Long Trail
P. O. Box 267
Route 4
Killington, VT 05751
(802) 775-7181 or (800) 325-2540
Innkeeper: Rosemary McGrath

♛♛ Rating: B-
Rates: Single/$46-120; Double/$58-156
Suite/$76-200
Senior, auto club, and family discounts
Credit Cards: MC, V

Traditional New England ski lodge situated in the Green Mountains is located east of Rutland and one mile west of Route 100 North. The McGrath family have been innkeepers here since 1977. There are twenty-two guest rooms or suites each offering a private bath. The suites feature working fireplaces. Popular activities here include relaxing in the living room, choosing a good book from the library, enjoying the hot tub, and watching TV. Area attractions include historic tours, antique shopping, skiing, hiking, horseback riding, and golf. Full breakfast. Function rooms are available for meetings, weddings, retreats, and family reunions. Families welcome. Open Summer, Fall, and Winter.

Londonderry

The Village Inn at Landgrove
RD 1, Box 215, Landgrove Rd.
Londonderry, VT 05148
(800) 669-8466 or (802) 824-6673
Innkeepers: Jay and Kathy Snyder

♛♛   Rating: B
Rates: Single/$50-90; Double/$55-105
Credit Cards: AE, MC, V

Originally a farmstead built in the 1820s and added on to through the years, this "Vermont Continuous Architecture" inn is 80 miles northeast of Albany, New York, and 30 miles southeast of Rutland. Choose from eighteen guest rooms with Colonial decor and individual temperature control; sixteen offer a private bath. Dine by the fireplace in candlelit surroundings, relax in the Rafter Lounge or the whirlpool spa. Cross country ski from one of the marked trails leading from the inn into the national forest. Horse-drawn hay and sleigh rides are available and the stocked fishing pond becomes an ice skating rink during winter months. Play tennis, go golfing, hiking, or visit nearby antique and outlet shops. A full breakfast may feature blueberry pancakes or the "J-bar special-bit of everything". Wedding and meeting facilities available. Families welcome. Restricted smoking.

Guests write: *"Perhaps it's those blueberry pancakes, the delicious soup served as we sit around the wood-burner. It's a true feeling of welcome and being part of their magnificent family"(B. Hill)*

"I discovered the Village Inn as a biker's oasis while peddling along the back roads. The magnetic quaintness of the historic buildings and the genuine friendliness of the proprietor's mother as she presented each room of her 'home' were irresistible. Charm, warmth, home cooking and instant acceptance into a family atmosphere provide a country environment that relaxes and rejuvenates the body and soul." (P. Arnold)

"The Snyder family makes a guest feel like on their own with real old-fashioned service, a warm welcome, and smiles all around. The abundance of fireplaces, charming antiques, country scenery, and architecture can take even city folks back a century or two." (J. White)

"Charmingly nestled in the secluded, but accessible valley. Food is plentiful and tasty- just like Grandma's. It's like coming home." (N. Threlfall)

Ludlow

Echo Lake Inn
P.O. Box 154
Ludlow, VT 05149
(802) 228-8602 or (800) 356-6844
Fax: (802) 228-3075
Innkeepers: Chip Connelly, John
and Yvonne Pardieu

♛ Rating: C
Rates: Single/$40-109; Double/$64-178
Credit Cards: AE, MC, V

Echo Lake Inn is 12 miles from Rutland on Route 100. Historic 1840s country inn that was frequented by such famous visitors as Calvin Coolidge has four stories and a gabled roof. Found on a scenic route near Echo Lake, it is surrounded by lawns and offers a tennis court and swimming pool. The twenty-six guest rooms range from suites to shared and family units and have been individually decorated, some with antiques. Sit by the fire and read a book or relax on one of the antique red rocking chairs on the front porch. Stroll through the fall foliage, play a game of tennis, or take a steam bath before dinner. Take a picnic on Echo Lake in a complimentary canoe or hike, jog, or bike through the woods. There is a Rathskeller and game room, cocktail lounge, and a full service dining room offering gourmet cuisine. Area attractions include the Coolidge birthplace State Park, all types of skiing, horseback riding, fishing, and shopping. Enjoy a full breakfast with an omelet du jour, "eggs your way", Vermont butter milk pancakes, or waffles with sautéed fresh fruits. Restricted smoking. Weddings and meeting facilities available.

Manchester Village

The Battenkill Inn
PO Box 948
Manchester Village, VT 05254
(802) 362-4213 or (800) 441-1628
Innkeepers: Ramsay & Mary Jo Gourd

♛♛   Rating: B
Rates: Double/$70-160
Credit Cards: AE, MC, & V

The historic Battenkill Inn is 130 miles west of Boston on historic Route 7A. This 1840's Victorian farmhouse sits between the Taconic and Green Mountains on seven acres of lawns and pastures, bordered by the Battenkill River, and just four miles south of Manchester Village. The inn's two-story porch offers a mountain view, and the perennial border gardens and small trout pond add tranquillity to this rural setting. Ten distinctive guest rooms, each with a private bath, are decorated with antiques. Four have wood burning fireplaces, and several open onto balconies looking out to the mountains. Relax by the large brick fireplace in the rear sitting room, and enjoy wine and cheese here during the evening. A game of backgammon may be found in the front parlor with marble fireplace and family antiques. Two dining rooms are available, one offering a large Duncan Phyfe table seating ten and another with two tables seating four people each. Fresh cut flowers decorate the breakfast area where you will find fresh fruit, fresh bread and muffins, orange French toast, Italian morning stratta, sausage, cinnamon biscuits, juice, coffee, tea or hot cocoa. Box lunches are available with advanced reservation. Meeting facility. Wheelchair Access. No Smoking.

Guests write: *"It was refreshing to be able to enjoy the surroundings of a large country estate with thematically designed rooms full of antiques. The atmosphere is warm and one in which you feel like you're at home rather than in a museum. The owners do all the special things that spoil you yet allow you enough space so that you feel privacy too."(M&G Hopkins)*

"Our room was beautifully decorated in Victorian style with lace, floral patterns, antiques, and a cozy fireplace and private bath. Each room in the inn provided a comfortable atmosphere of warmth and hospitality. Each breakfast gave true meaning to the words home cooking. The muffins were exceptional!" (M. Henry)

"We stayed in the 'Blue Room'— clean and cozy, the towels were thick, the shower raised two steps, and the balcony overlooking the pond."(S. Evans)

Manchester Village

The Reluctant Panther Inn & Restaurant
PO Box 678, West Road
Manchester Village, VT 05254-0678
(802) 362-2568
Innkeepers: Maye and Robert Bachofen

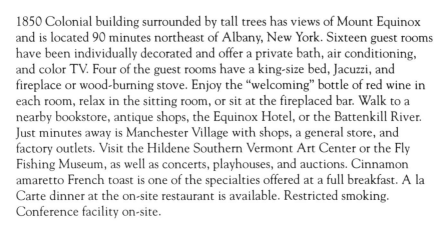

👑👑👑 Rating: A
Rates: Single/$135-255; Double/$175-295
Credit Cards: AE, MC, V

1850 Colonial building surrounded by tall trees has views of Mount Equinox and is located 90 minutes northeast of Albany, New York. Sixteen guest rooms have been individually decorated and offer a private bath, air conditioning, and color TV. Four of the guest rooms have a king-size bed, Jacuzzi, and fireplace or wood-burning stove. Enjoy the "welcoming" bottle of red wine in each room, relax in the sitting room, or sit at the fireplaced bar. Walk to a nearby bookstore, antique shops, the Equinox Hotel, or the Battenkill River. Just minutes away is Manchester Village with shops, a general store, and factory outlets. Visit the Hildene Southern Vermont Art Center or the Fly Fishing Museum, as well as concerts, playhouses, and auctions. Cinnamon amaretto French toast is one of the specialties offered at a full breakfast. A la Carte dinner at the on-site restaurant is available. Restricted smoking. Conference facility on-site.

North Hero

North Hero House
Route 2, Champlain Islands
North Hero, VT 05474
(802) 372-8237
Innkeeper: John & Ann Marie Sherlock

👑 Rating: C+
Rates: Double/$45-110

North Hero House is 35 miles north west of Burlington, VT off of I 89 on Route 2 and is 60 miles south of Montreal, Quebec, Canada. Three story Colonial structure with slate roof was built in 1891 and boasts a view of Lake Champlain and the Green Mountains. Choose from twenty-three rooms, all with private baths, some with lake views. Relax in the lounge or game room with barn siding or in the library or lobby with fireplace and television. Enjoy the beach, swimming area, fishing, boating, and docking. Area attractions: Burlington, University of Vermont, summer home of the White Lipizzan stallions, St. Michael's College Playhouse, and the Canadian Border. Continental breakfast. Meeting and wedding facilities. Families welcome. Restricted smoking

Stowe

Inn at the Brass Lantern
717 Maple Street
Stowe, VT 05672
(802) 253-2229 or (800) 729-2980
Fax (802) 253-7425
Innkeeper: Andy Aldrich

♕♕♕   Rating: A
Rates: Double/$70-150
Credit Cards: AE, MC, V

1810 Colonial farmhouse is located off Route 100, a half-mile from the center of the village at the foot of Mt. Mansfield. Choose from nine guest rooms with private bath, antique furnishings, and handmade quilts. Several of the rooms feature working fireplaces. Each evening, guests are invited to sit by the fire in the living room where tea and dessert are offered. Area attractions include craft and antique shops, buggy and sleigh rides, skiing, fishing, hiking, and golf. Full breakfast. Facilities are available for weddings and small meetings. No smoking.

Guests write: *"We found the Brass Lantern Inn to be very clean and comfortable. The proprietor was very accommodating and eager to be sure our visit was all that we expected. Our breakfasts were served in a timely manner and were delicious, as well as being eye appealing."(D&P Woods)*

Waitsfield

Mad River Inn
P. O. Box 75
Tremblay Road off Route 100
Waitsfield, VT 05673
(802) 496-7900 or (802) 496-6892
Innkeepers: Luc and Rita Maranda

W W W   Rating: A
Rates: Single/$49-95; Double/$59-125
Credit Cards: AE, MC, V

Surrounded by the Green Mountains and in the heart of the Mad River Valley, this Victorian is situated one mile north of Waitsfield off of Route 100. Period fabrics, furnishings, and finishes as well as feather beds are featured in each of the nine guest rooms with private bath. Relax in the Victorian parlor with fireplace. The living room has large picture windows and authentic antiques. The Queen Anne dining room reflects the decor of an English tea room where a complimentary afternoon tea is offered daily. The area is perfect for four-season sports such as golfing, skiing, hiking, and swimming. Ben & Jerry's Ice Cream factory is nearby as is Cold Hollow Cider Mill, Warren Store, Green Mountain Chocolate Factory, and the picturesque Green Mountains. Gourmet breakfast starts with fresh juice and includes harvests from the inn's organic garden. Special dishes include oven baked French toast, Southwestern strata, and fresh fruit crepes. Saturday ski season dinners and group gourmet dinners available as well as wedding and meeting facilities. Families welcome. Restricted smoking.

Warren

The Sugartree, A Country Inn
RR 1, Box 38, Sugarbush Access Rd.
Warren, VT 05674
(800) 666-8907 or (802) 583-3211
Innkeepers: Frank and Kathy Partsch

W W   Rating: B+
Rates: 1/$55-66; 2/$80-135
Credit Cards: AE, MC, V

Saltbox-style inn has an exterior reminiscent of a European hotel and is located thirty miles southwest of Montpelier, 1/4 mile west of the Sugarbush

Ski area. Waverly wallpaper, custom-designed stained-glass, ruffled country curtains, and handmade quilts are featured in the ten guest rooms with private bath. A newly renovated suite offers a gas fireplace. Enjoy biking, golfing, tennis, hiking, swimming, and antiquing as well as leaf watching or exploring covered bridges and white steepled churches. Both alpine and cross country skiing are available in the area. A full breakfast might offer egg and three cheese casserole, waffles, French toast, or pancakes with home-made syrups and butters. Wedding and meeting facilities available. Wheelchair access. No smoking.

Guests write: *"Hosts, Kathy and Frank, were very welcoming—they showed a real interest in us as individuals. They were always willing to suggest places of interest and special events taking place. The inn has been decorated with many antique and country style furnishings. The pump organ in the lounge area actually works! Overall it's very cozy with homemade quilts and chintz drapes. If you like attentive hosts and country comfort in a beautiful setting, this is the place to stay."* (L. Moysey)

"Our room was homey, the beds were very comfortable, pillows fluffy. We were stuffed after breakfast; and our favorites included chocolate chip pancakes and an apple strudel-type, baked French toast. We enjoyed meeting the other guests and spending time with them around the breakfast table." (D. Dickerhoof)

"This little inn reminds me of someplace in the Swiss Alps. It's tucked into a mountainside and is really cozy. It has window boxes brimming with flowers, the rooms are furnished with antiques and canopy beds, and the breakfasts are tasty. You won't go hungry there. There is no traffic, the roads are fun to drive on, and the scenery is right off a calendar." (Mrs. Hughes)

"Two thumbs up! In an era when one is often treated as merely another paying customer, Frank and Kathy have succeeded in creating a mountain retreat where every guest is treated as a treasured visitor. Kathy spoils you with good food and lively conversation on a chilly evening and Frank pampers you with roaring fires in the living rooms. There might be a deadly game of Trivial Pursuit in progress one evening and 15 guests laughing crazily over a game of dictionary the next. This is Vermont as I always hoped it would be." (S. Beck)

"A very clean, charming and warm B&B with charming and accommodating hosts. Great breakfasts!" (B. Mower)

Waterbury/Stowe

Black Locust Inn
RR 1, Box 715
Waterbury Center, VT 05677
(802) 244-7490 and (800) 366-5592
Innkeepers: Anita and George Gajdos

♛♛♛   Rating: A
Rates: Single/$55-79; Double/$65-95
Senior discount
Credit Cards: MC, V

Historic farmhouse built in 1832 is situated in the hills near Stowe and located five miles north of I-89, exit 10. There are six guest rooms which feature brass beds, private baths, antique furnishings, and polished wood floors. A common room on the main floor offers a cozy corner with a wood stove. A game table is situated by a large bay window. Area attractions include major ski areas, Cold Hollow Cider Mill, Ben & Jerry's Ice Cream Factory, and outdoor recreation. Full breakfast is served on linen and snacks are offered each afternoon. No smoking. Open year-round except for two weeks in April and November.

Weathersfield

Inn at Weathersfield
P.O. Box 165, Route 106
Weathersfield, VT 05151
(802) 263-9217 or (800) 477-4828
Fax: (802) 263-9219
Innkeepers: Ron & Mary Louise Thorburn

♛♛♛   Rating: A+
Rates: Single/$120-135; Double/$175-220
Business travel and package discounts.
Credit Cards: AE, MC, V

Large country inn located 5 miles north of Springfield was built in 1795 and is rich in history. Each of the twelve guest rooms offers a private bath, period antiques, working fireplace, and views of the surrounding countryside. There are five common rooms at the inn including the library with a collection of 4,000 books and a game and exercise room on the lower level. The restaurant and lounge on the premises serves a five-course dinner and offers live piano music nightly. A full breakfast and afternoon tea are served in the library or on the sunporch. Recreation in the area includes tennis, fishing, hiking, and skiing. A pond on the premises offers ice-skating in winter. Several function rooms are available for meetings and weddings. Rates include breakfast, tea, and dinner.

West Dover

Austin Hill Inn
Route 100
West Dover, VT 05356
(800) 332-RELAX or
(802) 464-5281
Fax: (802) 464-1229
Innkeeper: Robbie Sweeney

♛♛♛   Rating: A-
Rates: Single or Double/$80-125
Credit Cards: AE, MC, V

Newly renovated Country Colonial inn is located outside the village of West Dover just off Route 100. Choose from twelve guest rooms, each with private bath and individual decor; several offer a private balcony. For moments of relaxation there are several common rooms with a fireplace as well as a heated outdoor swimming pool. Area attractions include fishing, boating on Lake Whitingham, Mt. Snow Ski Resort, golf at Haystack or Mt. Snow championship courses, designer outlet stores, antique malls, and the Marlboro Music Festival. Full New England country breakfast, afternoon tea, and complimentary wine and cheese served daily. Candlelit dinners are available for private parties. The inn specializes in "Murder Mystery" weekends throughout the year. There are several function rooms on-site for meetings and social occasions. No smoking.

Guests write: *"You dream of the perfect New England inn and you come to Austin Hill, and there it is! Roaring fires in cozy, beautifully appointed sitting rooms, country-style bedrooms complete with rocking chairs, afghans, candlelight, and chocolates at bedtime, and a friendly, courteous and eager staff. It all sounds like a movie set and it's like a movie set come to life."* (R. Seider)

"I have grown accustomed to the efficiency of modern hotels but Austin Hill Inn has spoiled me. Their friendly dogs, charming and comfortable appointments, and most of all the gracious warmth of the staff have set better standards." (H. Levy)

"Although our stay at the inn was very brief, for two weary travelers, it brought

needed relief. Their cheery warm welcome as we entered the door was like that of a good neighbor. Who could ask for anything more? With four married children and seven grandchildren, we on occasion look for a hideaway. We'll be back." (B. Ford)

"Another bright star has been added to the twinkling Vermont sky, the Austin Hill Inn. Walk through the door and step into a world of warmth and charm from days gone by. Once you arrive you're treated like a special guest but feel like part of the family." (P. Kerantzas)

Wilmington

Nutmeg Inn
West Molly Stark Trail
Route 9
Wilmington, VT 05363
(802) 464-3351
Innkeepers: Del and Charlotte Lawrence

♛♛♛   Rating: A
Rates: Double/78-210
Credit Cards: AE, MC, V

Early-American farmhouse built in 1777 stands near a mountain brook near the junctions of Routes 9 and 100 in the village center. There are thirteen guest rooms or suites and each offers a private bath, television and VCR, brass or iron beds, quilts, and antique dressers. Nine rooms feature a working fireplace, and one suite has a private balcony overlooking Haystack Mountain and the surrounding meadows. Several of the older rooms feature exposed beams and slanted ceilings which reflect the rich history of the inn. The original carriage house offers a living room with fireplace, TV, and piano, and there is a small library with a collection of books. An extensive plate collection is on display throughout the inn. Recreation nearby includes skiing, leaf peeping, scenic drives, hiking, antiquing, fishing, boating, and golfing. Full breakfast and afternoon or evening beverages served daily. Families welcome. Wheelchair access. Restricted smoking.

Guests write: *"This is the most beautiful and gracious inn we've ever stayed in. Excellent French toast! The inn had all of the luxury of being away, yet the comfort of being home."* (P. Quasius)

Wilmington

Trail's End, A Country Inn
Smith Road
Wilmington, VT 05363
(802) 464-2727 or (800) 859-2585
Innkeepers: Bill and Mary Kilburn

♛♛♛   Rating: A+
Rates: Single/$90-120; Double/$90-170
Credit Cards: AE, MC, V

Rustic country inn in a tranquil setting is located in the heart of Deerfield Valley, a half mile east of Route 100 North. Choose from fifteen guest rooms or suites, each with private bath, individual decor, and family heirlooms. The grounds offer an outdoor heated swimming pool, clay tennis court, stocked trout pond, and English flower gardens. Relax by the fifteen foot stacked-stone fireplace or in the game room. Four-season recreation includes canoeing, horseback riding, hiking, golfing, sleigh rides, and downhill or cross-country skiing. Full breakfast includes homemade granola and a varied choice of entrees such as pancakes, waffles, egg dishes and breakfast meats. Afternoon refreshments are served daily. Families welcome. Facilities available for meetings and social functions.

Guests write: *"Each winter we look forward to visiting this beautiful inn, which is located on a gentle secluded mountain road. The inn has everything to be desired for a romantic weekend, a skiing vacation, fall colors, Vermont shopping, or just a quiet escape from the pressures of the working world. The facilities are first class. Quaintly decorated rooms or larger suites with fireplaces; beautiful parlor with a large fireplace for a drink or snack after a fatiguing day on the nearby ski slopes; large breakfast area where guests meet and exchange ideas and plans for the day's activities; fine dining, skiing, entertainment, and shopping only minutes away."* (B. Lewis)

"Mary and Bill's decor is very pleasing to the eye. A great fireplace is the center of attraction in the living room, a great place to meet new faces after a long day. Or, you can relax in the privacy of your own room, enjoying the fireplace or a Jacuzzi! Great handmade comforters adorned antique bureaus or a beautiful wicker loveseat which made the 'little things' make a big difference. I found the inn quaint, cozy, and yes, romantic!" (C. Radigan)

"My husband and I went to Trail's End on our Honeymoon. We were very impressed with the atmosphere and hospitality. Bill and Mary Kilburn make you feel more like a family than a guest." (K. Bird)

Woodstock

The Canterbury House
43 Pleasant Street
Woodstock, VT 05091
(802) 457-3077
Innkeepers: Fred and Celeste Holden

♛♛♛　Rating: A-
Rates: Double/$85-135
Credit Cards: AE, MC, V

The Canterbury House is located 30 miles from Rutland off I-91 on Route 4. 1880 Victorian Colonial home restored in keeping with historic authenticity is located in the historic village of Woodstock just 2.5 blocks from the town green. Each of the air-conditioned guest rooms has a private bath and has been decorated with such special touches as wicker bedroom furniture, a brass and iron bed, Victorian walnut beds, or antique country pine furniture. The living room is a comfortable place to sit by the fire, watch TV, browse through magazines, and play cards or board games. Walk to the nearby village green, shops, restaurants, art galleries, antique stores and museums. Go downhill skiing at Killington, Pico, or Okemo, game fish on lakes and streams, or borrow the inn's bikes to tour the countryside. Visit the Rockefeller Estate and Billings Farm or sit by one of the town's two rivers. The full gourmet breakfast is served on a reproduction or Victorian dining table. Weddings and meeting facilities available. No smoking. Wheelchair access.

Guests write: *"We could not have had a more perfect 4-5 days in Vermont. We all felt right at home here. And then there are the breakfasts — outstanding! We have a special place in all our family's memories for Canterbury House." (T&L Larson)*

Woodstock

Deer Brook Inn
HCR 68, Box 443
Woodstock, VT 05091
(802) 672-3713
Innkeepers: Brian and
Rosemary McGinty

♛♛♛ Rating: A-
Rates: Single/$50-60; Double/$70-95
Credit Cards: MC, V

Historic Colonial farmhouse built in 1820 was once a working dairy farm and is located on Route 4, four miles west of the village. There are four large guest rooms and each offers a private bath, homemade quilts, and polished wide pine floors. The front porch offers views of the Ottauquechee River meandering by and there's a living room with fireplace for warming up after a day of skiing. Recreation in the area includes skiing, bicycling, golf, hiking, swimming, and fishing. The area is also known for its numerous antique shops. Full breakfast features home baked muffins and is served in the family-style dining room. Families welcome. Restricted smoking.

Guests write: *"Breakfast was wonderful, a one-egg omelet in an individual serving dish accompanied by fresh fruit (melon, grapes, apples). A serving of lemon-blueberry coffee cake was also included (homemade). The dining room was very bright and cheery with a birdfeeder that sits in the window with a one-way mirror type wall so birds can't see into the dining room but guests can see birds feeding. This is our third year in a row we've been back." (T. Jackman)*

"The original pine floors, handmade quilts and stenciling combined to make the room very pleasant. Apple pancakes were delicious—also, muffins, fruit and plenty of coffee." (L. Adrian)

"Our room was warmly furnished with early American pieces and had stenciled walls. Our breakfast was served overlooking a mountainous terrain, with chickadees feeding at our window. The breakfasts of French toast and Featherbed Eggs were a wonderful way to begin our day of skiing." (M. Middleton)

"This was a warm and welcoming place to return to after some rather cold and unwelcoming ski slopes. We've been having breakfast withdrawal since we left! Cereal and grapefruit aren't making it and Gary (my husband) is after me to make quiche." (J. Moffie)

Woodstock

Kedron Valley Inn
Route 106
South Woodstock, VT 05071
(802) 457-1473
Fax: (802) 457-4469
Innkeeper: Max and Merrily Comins

♛♛ Rating: B
Rates: Double/$93-209
Credit Cards: AE, MC, V

The Kendron Valley Inn is 5 miles south of the village of Woodstock, 30 minutes from Lebanon. Two Federal-style, multi-storied buildings comprise the inn which features brick and clapboard, columned porches, and a third building with exposed logs on both the inside and outside. Nestled on 15 acres of foothills of the Green Mountains and surrounded by perennial gardens and country roads, it offers twenty-seven guest rooms and two suites, all with private baths and special features such as fireplaces, antique quilts, queen-size canopy beds, a private deck, and television. Relax on the two white sand beaches of the inn's spring-fed pond, go horseback riding at the nearby 50-horse stable, or take advantage of the area's skiing opportunities in the winter. There are several historic estates as well as antique stores and quaint shops to explore. Take a surrey ride, go golfing, play tennis, or just explore the historic Woodstock area. A full breakfast might offer Eggs Benedict, Italian Fritatta, or Eggs Florentine and is served on the windowed dining patio. Candlelight dinners available in restaurant. Weddings and meeting facilities available. Wheelchair access. Families welcome. Restricted smoking.

Woodstock

Woodstocker B&B
Route 4, 61 River Street
Woodstock, VT 05091
(802) 457-3896 or (800) 457-3896
Innkeepers: Jerry and JaNoel Lowe

♛♛♛   Rating: A-
Rates: Single/$90-115; Double/$100-125
Credit Cards: MC, V

Historic Cape Cod home built in 1830 is nestled at the foot of Mt. Tom and located ten miles from I-89 and I-91 on Route 4. There are nine guest rooms or suites and each offers a private bath and individual decor with a canopy, brass, or iron bed. A comfortable living room on the main floor provides a quiet place for reading, playing board games, watching cable television or VCR movies. The inn is within walking distance of quaint village shops, galleries, restaurants, theater, and the village green park. Area attractions include factory outlets, museums, bicycling, tennis, skiing, hiking, golf, and horseback riding. Full four-course breakfast. Families welcome.

Guests write: *"Innkeepers Jerry and Janoel Lowe have done a superlative job with this circa 1830s house and series of attached barns and sheds. The effect is one of charm and grace, welcome and comfort, the air throughout delicately hung with fragrant potpourri. The public rooms invite guests to sit down to a game of checkers, to read a good book, or to watch a movie from the Lowe's extensive collection on the VCR. Each of the nine guest rooms has been dubbed and decorated to evoke a spirit of tradition. Our large room, Sunflower Dream, featured two comfortable queen-size brass beds, splashed with fine linens and window treatments inspired by Van Gogh's refreshing palette of blue, yellow, and white. An in-suite private bath held plenty of luxurious towels and fragrant house toiletries. Every room or suite of rooms in the inn is equipped with a stereo CD/cassette/AM-FM player. We slept in peace with the gentle glow of window candles for night lights."* (S. Reamy)

"I have stayed in numerous B&B establishments and have found this one to be unique. Perhaps it is the sincere friendliness of the charming host and hostess. This couple is professional and at the same time presents a family-like environment. The accommodations are comfortable, clean, and homey - like a visit to Grandmother's house." (D. Lepor)

Additional information on B&Bs in Virginia is available from the following B&B reservation agencies: Guesthouses Bed & Breakfast (804) 979-7264 and Princely Bed & Breakfast (703) 683-2159.

Champlain

Linden House Bed & Breakfast
P.O. Box 23
Champlain, VA 22438
(804) 443-1170 or (800) 622-1202
Innkeepers: Ken and Sandra Pounsberry

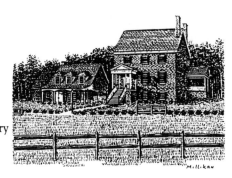

 Rating: A+
Rates: Single or Double/$55-135
Family discount
Credit Cards: MC, V

Historic Colonial inn built in 1750 is listed on the National Register of Historic Buildings and located in rural Essex County on Route 17, minutes from Tappahanock and 35 minutes south of Fredericksburg. There are six guest rooms furnished with antiques. Three provide a private bath and several have sitting areas, fireplaces, Jacuzzi with steam bath, or views of the English Garden and landscaped yard. Relax on one of five porches or the gazebo which overlooks pastures. Explore the two hundred acres of historic surroundings, or take a cruise on the Rappahanock River and view the many water fowl and wild life including bald eagles. Area attractions: Stratford Hall, Wakefield and Westmoreland State Park, antique shops, Wakefield and Tappanhannock. Full breakfast with a Plantation menu vary with the seasons and might include omelets presented with fresh fruit in Pina Colada dip. The English Basement, large patio, and landscaped yard provide space for weddings and meetings.

Guests write: *"The Linden House was everything we were looking for in a quiet little getaway and more! Our objective was to go somewhere alone together and relax without the cats, dog, kids, phone, TV, etc., and not have anything pre-planned. We just wanted to 'go with the flow' and enjoy each other's company. We certainly picked the right spot. One of the things we enjoyed most about our stay was the wonderful ambiance of the home. It was neat, clean, beautifully decorated and had been remodeled a few years ago in an exquisite manner to provide for modern convenience yet retain the flavor and atmosphere of old America. What made our visit complete was the warmth, charm, and friendship extended to us by our hosts."* (R&D Saunders)

(Continued)

"This is the most relaxing B&B to stay at. The plantation-style breakfast is wonderful. The atmosphere is quiet, peaceful and very enjoyable." (C&M Esquibel)

"Linden House was a 'joyful' and 'unique' experience. It was relaxing, comfortable, and the rural setting is outstanding. The affable hosts made us feel at home. After an hour or two, we felt we had known them for a long period of time. The full plantation breakfast was very special and filling." (A. Radi, Jr.)

"They sent us home with wonderful goodies. We got engaged on Friday night after our delicious dinner. The Linden House will always be very meaningful to us." (C.Smith)

"The Linden House is a lovely place. Ken and Sandy are wonderful hosts. The food is great. The service good. The staff puts you at ease and make you feel comfortable. They go the extra mile for their guests." (P. Briggs)

Charles City

North Bend Plantation B&B
12200 Weyanoke Road
Charles City, VA 23030
(804) 829-5176 or (800) 841-1479
Innkeepers: George and Ridgely Copland

♛♛♛ Rating: A
Rates: Double/$95-120

General Sheridan used this historic plantation home on 250 acres as his headquarters during the Civil War. The home, built in 1819, is a historic landmark, and is located halfway between Williamsburg and Richmond in Virginia Plantation country, off Route 5. There are four guest rooms on the second floor and each has a private bath, family antiques, color TV, and lovely period decor. One suite offers two connecting bedrooms, one with queen-bed and the other with double bed. There's a modern bath between the bedrooms and this suite offers ideal privacy for three to four people. Several common rooms at the inn include summer porches with wicker furnishings, a billiard room, and parlor which boasts a collection of rare books and antique furnishings. Popular activities here include walks on the property, a refreshing swim in the pool, bike riding on country roads, plantation home tours, antique shops, a public golf course, and Colonial Williamsburg attractions. Full country breakfast. Restricted smoking to porches.

Guests write: *"This was only our second experience with a B & B, but this has convinced us to keep staying. The owners are so friendly and made us feel as 'family' guests. The room was decorated to suit the time-frame of the home. We were served a typical country breakfast: waffles, bacon, sausage, fruit, juice, tea."* (B. Pitzer)

"You are surrounded by antique family heirlooms and furniture that dates around the Civil War era. Our friendly host and hostess gave us a wonderful tour of the house, giving us historical insights into many of the pieces of furniture and decor. Most fascinating was General Sheridan's desk with the original pigeon-hole labels on it and the magnificent bed owned by Edmund Ruffin who fired the 'first shot' at Fort Sumter. My wife and I took a bicycle ride on the long stretches of dirt roads on a 'bicycle built for two' provided by our hosts. Last evening we watched in amazement as about a dozen deer playfully ran about in the fields. Breakfast was served on elegant china which had stampings of being made in 'occupied Japan.' " (R. Knapp)

"We would have preferred to stay several days more if it were possible so that we could enjoy the surrounding area at leisure and spend more hours exploring North Bend, browsing through the historical documents and admiring all the artifacts—and also just relaxing on the verandah or upstairs sun porch with a book." (S&J Stryker)

"Our stay was delightful! They walked us through history and served a delicious breakfast and we enjoyed the breakfast chats with George." (A. Southworth)

"The setting, the books, the room, the breakfast, and especially the Coplands was delightful." (W. Canup)

"It's wonderfully peaceful here. We really enjoyed traversing the field with Ridgely and looking at the Civil War trenches. The fox hunt was splendid!" (A. Bedwell)

"Our accommodations were historic and comfortable and the girls were right at home playing around the farm. Ridgley gave us a wonderful trip down to the river during which we met a herd of llamas. Both hosts are tireless in sharing their knowledge of the area and their enthusiasm for the history of their property and families. The hospitality of the Coplands is exceptional and privacy is a much appreciated option after a day of sightseeing." (N. Engeman)

Charlottesville/North Garden

Inn at the Crossroads
Route 2, Box 6
North Garden, VA 22959
(804) 979-6452
Innkeeper: Lynn Neville

♕♕♕   Rating: A-
Rates: Double/$59-69
Charge Card: MC, V

Historic landmark tavern built in 1820 is located 9 miles south of Charlottesville off Route 29 at Route 692. Named for different facets of art and literature, each of the five guest rooms are designed to be as close to what they might have been in the original days of the tavern. Take time to unwind with a book and explore the grounds which open to the foothills of the Blue Ridge. The inn is ideally located near Monticello, Ash Lawn, Michie Tavern, and Montpelier. Full breakfast. Small meeting facilities available. Restricted smoking.

Guests write: *"As we entered the Squire Room, our home away from home for two nights, it was like stepping back into yesteryear. With familiar objects of years ago; fireplace, rough plastered walls, variable sized floorboards fastened with handmade nails, one could easily visualize the activities of time past when travelers and families congregated to tell their stories of experience and hope. The food prepared could only be classified as excellent cuisine."* (D. Fellers)

"The hot breakfasts were excellent, imaginative, delicious, and beautifully presented. The rooms were cozy, cheerful, and tastefully appointed. The proprietor was friendly, gracious and helpful." (W. Shen)

"If you are looking for a friendly host, wonderful food, comfortable rooms, and a relaxed countryside location all wrapped up in an historic building, this is the place to go! I've never had such a wonderful time, nor felt so driven to return again and again. Don't miss this stop if you're in Charlottesville." (E. Gerller)

"Since it was Valentine's Day, we were treated with heart-shaped cookies waiting for us in our room and fresh flowers for breakfast. Lyn, who is also the sous chef at a popular restaurant in Charlottesville, served cinnamon pears and baked herb eggs one morning, and French toast with blueberry sauce the second morning. The inn is in the country with wonderful country roads all around. We enjoyed the king-size bed, electric blanket, and terrycloth robes. " (M. Alexander)

Charlottesville/Scottsville

Chester Bed & Breakfast
Route 4, Box 57
Scottsville, VA 24590
(804) 286-3960
Innkeepers: Dick Shaffer
and Gordon Anderson

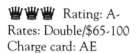 Rating: A-
Rates: Double/$65-100
Charge card: AE

Historic Greek Revival home built in 1847 is located 17 miles south of
Charlottesville near Routes 726, 20, and 6. There are four second-floor guest
rooms with shared baths or a downstairs guest room with four-poster bed and
private bath. The entire inn is air-conditioned and each guest room features a
woodburning fireplace. The first floor living room has a fireplace and fine art
collection and the second-floor library offers informal seating and an interesting selection of books. The extensive grounds include an unusually large
number of tree specimens, including the largest white pine in Virginia.
Bicycles and a kennel for pets are available. Area attractions include
Monticello, Ashlawn, University of Virginia, winery tours, canoeing and
tubing on the James River, skiing, and golf. Full breakfast. A four-course
dinner, with complimentary wine, is available with advance reservation at $24
per person.

Guests write:*"We have enjoyed staying at Chester twice. It is a beautiful drive from
Charlottesville and our daughter is at University of Virginia. The downstairs room
with the private bath is particularly comfortable. Love the conversation and great full-
size breakfasts!" (T. Ingram)*

*"Wonderful place! Large rooms are nicely furnished. Well-planned and beautifully
prepared breakfasts. It's located in a lovely quiet Virginian countryside. The owners
breed dogs but they are quiet and well-mannered (and outside). Smoking is
permitted. Recommended for anyone who finds other B&Bs a bit dull!" (W. Piez)*

*"The best B&B we stayed at due to the hospitality of Dick and Gordon. The
beautiful and immaculate house, the fine cuisine, and the roaring cheery fireplaces.
They create a warm and lively social environment for a group of people who arrive,
but don't remain, strangers. " (J. Marx)*

*"Beautiful surroundings, warm and hospitable hosts — this is an extremely relaxing
ambiance and ideal place for a weekend getaway. " (D. Schwartz)*

Chincoteague

The Watson House Bed & Breakfast
4240 Main Street, P.O. Box 905
Chincoteague, VA 23336
(804) 336-1564 or (800) 336-6787
Innkeeper: Tom Watson

♛♛♛ Rating: A
Rates: Single/65-95; Double/$75-105
Auto club, senior, government,
and corporate discount
Credit Cards: MC, V

1898 two-story Victorian country home is located 100 miles north of Virginia
Beach and Norfolk on Virginia's Eastern Shore. Gabled roofs, wrap-around
porch and gingerbread accents highlight the inn which is located near the
heart of town in a residential section across the street from the Chincoteague
Bay. Choose from six guest rooms, each with private bath, that are individually decorated with Victorian and country furnishings and nostalgia pieces. All
have air conditioning and ceiling fans. The parlor has the same decor, making
it romantic yet comfortable, perfect for mingling with other guests or reading a
good book. Borrow bicycles from the inn to tour the island and refuge.
Chincoteague Island is the gateway to the Assateague National Wildlife
Refuge and is famous for its wild ponies that roam the Assateague seashore.
Shops, galleries, and restaurants are within walking distance. Activities
include boating, fishing, crabbing, beachcombing, and bird watching. Full
breakfast, served inside or on the veranda. Meeting facilities available.
Restricted smoking.

Guests write: *"Our room was furnished with an antique dresser, washstand, and a
bed with a massive headboard and footboard. Our room and bath, the whole house
in fact, was spotless, simply immaculate. The breakfasts and tea desserts that Jo
Anne and Jacque prepared and served each day were so good that I went back for
seconds and thirds. Their egg dishes and baked goods are too tempting to resist."* (J.
Gunnels)

*"They offer a delightful afternoon tea, fabulous breakfasts, and beautiful rooms.
There are so many extras, suggestions for supper including menus, beach towels,
bicycles, beach chairs, and interesting reading material."* (M. Keating)

*"Obviously a great deal of thought has gone into the plans for decorating this
property. The wrap around verandah and carefully chosen decor give this B&B inn a
very rustic and pleasant atmosphere."* (S. Ahmad)

Locust Dale

The Inn at Meander Plantation
HCR 5, Box 460 A
Locust Dale, VA 22948
(703) 672-4912
Fax: (703) 672-4912
Innkeepers: Suzie Blanchard and Suzanne Thomas

♛♛♛ Rating: A-
Rates: Double/$95-$155

Three-story 1766 Georgian mansion with early Classical Revival front portico, columned front porch, and two-level wrap-around porches sits on top of a hill in the middle of 80-acres of rolling pasture and woodlands. Six guest rooms, some with views of the Blue Ridge mountains and five with private baths, are furnished with varying antiques including a carved rice four-poster bed, Chinese red Oriental area rug, oak washstand, antique side tables, and trunks. A small, one bedroom cottage is found near the stables and includes a kitchenette, private courtyard, and sitting room. The historic reception room features a baby grand piano, wing back chairs before a colonial fireplace, and original chestnut floors and paneling. Relax in the large living room where Thomas Jefferson sat and had tea in front of the detailed and pilastered fireplace or explore the surrounding grounds with formal boxwood gardens and walking trails that lead to the Robinson River. Enjoy afternoon tea, walk to the historical family cemetery with graves dating to the 1700s or go horseback riding from on-site stables. Area attractions: Montpelier (home of James Madison); Monticello, Ashlawn, and Michie Tavern; Civil War battlefields; wineries; University of Virginia, and many antique shops. A Plantation breakfast menu often includes hot, fresh orange and cranberry compote, spicy upside down sausage-oregano cornbread, cheese grits, eggs with chives, and bacon is served on the antique cherry dining table in the formal dining room with its black slate floors and fireplace. Weddings and meeting facilities available. No smoking.

Guests write: *"This feels like being immersed in another century while having the luxuries and amenities available today. The careful attention to historical accuracy in colors, furniture reproductions, and other furnishings was a particular delight for the historian in me."* (S. Schmidt)

"The inn provides a close and convenient location and launching pad to the path of history in this location, one of the prime sites for such exploration. The inn offers a conspicuously clean and comfortable setting, a treat to Southern hospitality and style." (E&R Kolb)

Middleburg

The Middleburg Country Inn
209 East Washington Ave
Middleburg, VA 22117
(703) 687-6082 or (800) 262-6082
Fax: (703) 687-5603
Innkeepers: John and Susan Pettibone

♛♛♛ Rating: A
Rates: Single or Double/$145-195; Suites/$225-275
Breakfast and dinner included in daily rate
Senior, corporate, and auto club discounts
Credit Cards: AE, MC, V

Federal Colonial built in 1820 originally served as the Episcopal rectory in this small town found 40 miles west of Washington DC on Route 50. The three story brick building has six guest rooms, all with private baths, and each featuring Colonial furnishings, four-poster, canopy beds, a fireplace, and cable television with VCR. Relax in the parlor with complimentary coffee, tea, and baked goods at guest's disposal or on the veranda when the weather is pleasant. Walk through the quaint, Colonial town with designer boutiques, jewelry shops, antique dealers, and art galleries. Order a picnic basket from the nearby Hidden Horse Tavern or visit area attractions: wineries, horse racing, historic buildings, the Shennandoah Valley, Skyline Drive, Manassas Battlefield, and Harper's Ferry. A full breakfast offers such specialties as blueberry muffins, eggs any style, and Country Inn waffles. Wedding and meeting facilities.

Guests write: *"We reserved all eight rooms for the weekend of our daughter's wedding. We were told by our hostess that we could feel as if it were our very own home and indeed we did. Each room was comfortable furnished in colonial style and had a working fireplace. Our hostess supplies wine and hors d'oeuvres for the guests at arrival and served a delicious breakfast (not the usual continental style) with choices of eggs any style muffins, coffee cake, waffles, quiches, fresh fruit, and coffee. Warm hospitality abounded and every effort was made to make us feel comfortable. I would highly recommend this inn located in this very beautiful part of Virginia."* (D&L Wilkins)

New Church

The Garden & The Sea Inn
4188 Nelson Road, PO Box 275
New Church, VA 23415
(804) 824-0672
Innkeepers: Tom and Sara Baker

♛♛♛ Rating: A
Rates: Double/$85-150
Credit Cards: AE, MC, V

Farmland and a small village surround this large Victorian home with wrap-around porches, gabled roofs, dormers, stained glass, and gingerbread details. Just 12 miles from Chincoteague Island and Assateague Island National Seashore, the multi-colored, "painted lady" style inn boasts five guest rooms with private baths, with two rooms in the main house and three in the newly renovated Victorian Garden House. Each guest room has been individually detailed with Oriental rugs, imported fabrics, and a mix of antiques. Read, relax, and enjoy refreshments in the Garden House parlor. Sitting room with its 19th century decorated "drawing-room" style or in the parlor with oriental rugs, custom satin and lace window treatments, and antiques. There is a work-study area and kitchenette for guest's use. Enjoy the area's water recreation facilities, fishing, crab digging, or canoeing or take the back roads to see the historic towns and buildings of the Eastern Shore. Visit Assateague and Chincoteague, just 20 minutes away, or go shopping at the nearby shops and galleries. Continental-plus breakfast is served on china and silver and includes warm croissants, cereals, local fruit and berries, and freshly squeezed citrus juices. A candlelight gourmet dinner, prepared by the chef/owner, is available in the 30-seat dining room. Small meeting facilities available. Families welcome. Restricted smoking.

Guests write: *"The beautiful Victorian decor reflects exquisite taste, and all the amenities, including whirlpool baths, were designed for the comfort and enjoyment of guests. The meals were outstanding. Also, we were provided with brochures and directions as to how to reach points of interest in the area."* (M. Herron)

"We attended the musical weekend which was very special. The quality of the performance was high, and I would certainly like to attend another. Our room had delightful Victorian period decor, but the bathroom was 20th Century efficient, well-lit, and spotless. The hosts were most helpful with information on scenic drives, back roads, and restaurants we never would have found on our own." (M. Fox)

New Market

Cross Roads Inn B&B
9222 John Sevier Road
New Market, VA 22844
(703) 740-4157
Innkeeper: Mary-Lloyd Freisitzer

♛♛   Rating: B+
Rates: Single or Double/$55-90
Charge card: MC, V

White clapboard Victorian with black and white awnings is located on 1 1/2 acres of landscaped gardens, 2 hours southwest of Washington DC. on Route 211 in New Market. Boasting a view of the Shenandoah Mountains and New Market Gap, the inn has five guest rooms, all with private baths. Each room features English floral wallpapers, antiques, canopy or four-poster beds, and down comforters. Relax in the guest parlor with brick fireplace and antique silver service or in the living room with its toy box for children, antique rocking horse, and television with VCR. The breakfast room has windows on three sides looking out into the manicured garden. Guests are welcome to fruit and beverage found in the pantry. Walk to antique and book shops or to nearby restaurants and churches. Rich in history, the area's main attractions include the Battle of New Market Museums, Calvery Museum, Shennandoah and Luray Caverns, Shennandoah National Park, and the Skyline Drive. Enjoy the innkeeper's Austrian traditional of the in-room, first cup of coffee as well as afternoon coffee or tea with strudel. A typical full breakfast, served on Blue Danube china, includes homemade apricot pecan muffins, Bismarks (oven-puffed pancakes), and country sausage served with imported Austrian coffee and home baked breads. No smoking. Weddings and meeting facilities available. Families welcome. Wheelchair access.

Stanley

Jordan Hollow Farm Inn
Route 2, Box 375
Stanley, VA 22851
(703) 778-2285 or 778-2209
Innkeepers: Jetze and Marley Beers

♛♛♛   Rating: A+
Rates: Double/$140-180
Charge card: MC, V

Restored Colonial horse farm nestled on 145 acres of rolling hills and meadows and surrounded by the Shenandoah National Park is located six miles south of Luray. Two separate lodges on the property offer twenty-one guest rooms with private bath, handmade furniture, and family heirlooms. The top priced rooms are spacious with whirlpool tubs, and working fireplaces. There is a mini-barnyard with farm animals, and pony rides for children are available by appointment. Horseback riding for beginners and experienced riders is available daily. Carriage rides and lessons are available by special reservation. Popular activities here include swimming, hiking mountain trails, relaxing on the porch, and nearby fishing, skiing, and golfing. Area attractions: Luray Caverns, Skyline Drive, and the New Market Battlefield Museum. The rates include breakfast and dinner for two. Function rooms for weddings and meetings are offered. Families welcome.

Guests write: *"We stayed in the Mare Meadow Cottages, and they were decorated with a cabin-like atmosphere but a little more elegant with a gas fireplace that actually heated the room. You can walk all over the property and pet the horses. They have hammocks and chairs in the woods that you can relax on after you walk through the pasture and through the woods. Breakfast was buffet style and the fruits and juices were fresh along with an egg dish."* (M&K Weber)

"Jordan Hollow Farm Inn is a beautiful horse farm with a breathtaking view of the Shenandoah Valley. The room in the Mare Meadow lodge was furnished with beautiful quilts and horse memorabilia. The room has a large whirlpool tub and a gas fireplace for those romantic evenings. There is also a reading room in the lodge for those quiet times with a good book. We enjoyed relaxing on our private porch and watching the horses in the pastures. We had a wonderful view of the horses and the ducks from our window during dinner. Jordan Hollow offers horse rides for various stages of riders. I being a first time rider, was given a horse that was very gentle during the ride along the trails." (R&K Munch)

Staunton

The Sampson Eagon Inn
238 East Beverley Street
Staunton, VA 24401
(800) 579-9722 or (703) 886-8200
Innkeepers: Laura and Frank Mattingly

♕♕♕ Rating: A+
Rates: Double/$80-95

Circa 1840 Greek Revival mansion with some Italianate and Victorian touches has been restored and is located in Staunton's Historic Landmark District of Gospel Hill which is 150 miles southwest of Washington DC and 120 miles west of Richmond. Four guest rooms have been furnished with period antiques and feature a private bath, air conditioning, queen-size canopy bed, sitting area, and TV equipped with VCR. Relax in the living room or out on the porch overlooking a side garden. Stroll through the neighborhood with its historic architecture or walk one block to downtown for specialty and antique shops. Nearby attractions include the Woodrow Wilson Birthplace and Museum, Museum of American Frontier Culture, Mary Baldwin College, Skyline Drive and the Blue Ridge Mountains. Grand Marnier soufflé pancakes, Kaluha pecan Belgium waffles, or eggs Benedict are full breakfast specialties. Restricted smoking.

Guests write: *"The innkeepers take a special interest in their guest's comfort. We especially appreciated their extensive knowledge of the history of the house. Each of the guest rooms has been named after a previous owner and decorated in the appropriate time period. This was an especially good value for B&B travel. The warmth and enthusiasm of our hosts is unsurpassed and the food great." (S. Cruse)*

Strasburg

Hotel Strasburg
201 South Holliday Street
Strasburg, VA 22657
(703) 465-9191 or (800) 348-8327
Innkeeper: Gary Rutherford

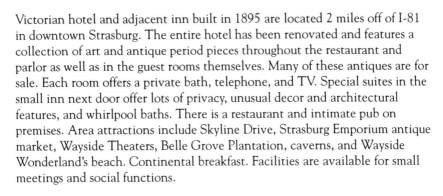

♛♛♛   Rating: A-
Rates: Double/$69-149
Auto club, senior discounts and business travel discount
Charge card: AE, MC, V

Victorian hotel and adjacent inn built in 1895 are located 2 miles off of I-81 in downtown Strasburg. The entire hotel has been renovated and features a collection of art and antique period pieces throughout the restaurant and parlor as well as in the guest rooms themselves. Many of these antiques are for sale. Each room offers a private bath, telephone, and TV. Special suites in the small inn next door offer lots of privacy, unusual decor and architectural features, and whirlpool baths. There is a restaurant and intimate pub on premises. Area attractions include Skyline Drive, Strasburg Emporium antique market, Wayside Theaters, Belle Grove Plantation, caverns, and Wayside Wonderland's beach. Continental breakfast. Facilities are available for small meetings and social functions.

Guests write: *"Walking down the long stairway from our beautiful second-story room, reminds me of breakfast at grandmother's. From the well-appointed lobby to meeting rooms next door, the Hotel Strasburg offers the finest in rooms, meeting areas, meals and hospitality."* (R&H Johnston)

Williamsburg

Newport House
710 South Henry Street
Williamsburg, VA 23185-4113
(804) 229-1775
Innkeeper: John Fitzhugh Millar

♛♛♛   Rating: A-
Rates: Double/$100-125

Newport House is a careful reproduction of an original 1756 house and it is located within a five minute walk of Colonial Williamsburg. There are two spacious guest rooms with private bath, four-poster bed, period American antiques and reproduction furnishings. There is a large parlor on the main floor with fireplace and a collection of books. Guests are invited to stroll through the flower, herb, and vegetable gardens or join in a Colonial dance in the upstairs ballroom on Tuesday evenings. Hostess is a registered nurse who enjoys making eighteenth-century clothing. Host is former captain of an historic full-rigged ship and is now an author and publisher of history books. Area attractions include historic sites in Jamestown and Yorktown, the James River Plantations, and Busch Gardens. Full breakfast specialties often include apple-cinnamon waffles, specialty breads, baked apples, and authentic Colonial recipes. Families welcome.

Guests write: *"John and Cathy Millar have created an establishment which truly enhances a visit to Williamsburg. The house and the beautiful furnishings perfectly combine 20th-Century comfort with 18th-Century elegance and taste. The facilities are superb, the breakfasts delightful, and the conversation uncommonly pleasant."* (B. Smith)

"The two rooms that are set aside for guests, the Philadelphia Room, and the Newport Room, make other accommodations in Williamsburg look shabby. Each morning, breakfast is enlivened by delightful conversation and the antics of Sassafras, the rabbit, and Ian, the Millar's little boy. For those visitors who wish to be close to the center of the restored area, but far from the maddening crowd, Newport House is perfectly located. It is but a short walk from Duke of Gloucester Street, but the quiet that surrounds it is always welcomed." (C. Potter)

Woolwine

Mountain Rose Bed & Breakfast
Rt. 1, Box 280
Woolwine, VA 24185
(703) 930-1057
Innkeeper: Hermien Ankersmit

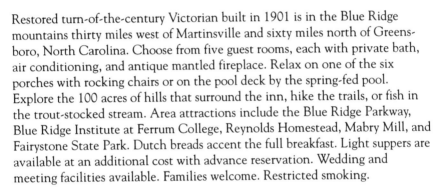

 Rating: B+
Rates: Single/$60-70; Double/$60-85
Charge card: MC, V

Restored turn-of-the-century Victorian built in 1901 is in the Blue Ridge mountains thirty miles west of Martinsville and sixty miles north of Greensboro, North Carolina. Choose from five guest rooms, each with private bath, air conditioning, and antique mantled fireplace. Relax on one of the six porches with rocking chairs or on the pool deck by the spring-fed pool. Explore the 100 acres of hills that surround the inn, hike the trails, or fish in the trout-stocked stream. Area attractions include the Blue Ridge Parkway, Blue Ridge Institute at Ferrum College, Reynolds Homestead, Mabry Mill, and Fairystone State Park. Dutch breads accent the full breakfast. Light suppers are available at an additional cost with advance reservation. Wedding and meeting facilities available. Families welcome. Restricted smoking.

Guests write: "*Mountain Rose is terrific. Hermien and Maarten are warm, friendly, and welcoming. Our room was attractive, as was the entire house— comfortable and very clean. The breakfast was delicious with homemade jams and jellies, a variety of home made breads, and fresh fruits all attractively served. The main dish was also delicious. Upon our arrival we were warmly greeted with refreshments. We really enjoyed our stay. "* (J. Lanford)

Leavenworth

Haus Rohrbach Pension
12882 Ranger Road
Leavenworth, WA 98826
(509) 548-7024 or (800) 548-4477
Innkeepers: Robert and Kathryn Harrild

♛♛♛   Rating: A-
Rates: Single/$55-140; Double/$65-160.
Senior discount
Credit Cards: AE, MC, V

European-style Alpine inn is at the foothills of the Washington Cascades, 25 miles from Wenatchee and 100 miles east of Seattle. Choose from twelve guest rooms, eight with private bath. Three modern suites offer spacious accommodations, fireplace, and whirlpool tub overlooking the valley below. The main inn has a large gathering room with wood-stove and deck with comfortable chairs to enjoy the mountain and valley views. The property maintains an in-ground swimming pool. Go hiking, rafting, fishing, windsurfing, biking, or skiing. Visit the Bavarian village of Leavenworth, just two minutes away, with its many shops and restaurants. The full breakfast is served out on the deck in warmer weather and may include sourdough pancakes, "Dutch Babies", and home-made cinnamon rolls. Meeting facilities available. Families welcome. Wheelchair access. No smoking.

Guests write: *"Haus Rohrbach Pension is a delightful mountain chalet tucked into a hillside that overlooks the Leavenworth valley and the town below. We generally come to Haus Rohrbach in the winter for some quiet solace after the holiday crush of the city. The silent snow draped landscape viewed from our balcony room invites long walks that are gentle tonic to hyper-stimulated nervous systems. After a day outdoors in the snow, my favorite spot is the long settee behind the wood stove in the large common room. This is a great place to visit with our fellow guests and hear of their day's adventures. More often than not, we hear of a restaurant, bakery, brewery, shop or park that we have not yet explored. Breakfasts at the main chalet are served family style, and Bob's 'Dutch Babies' are an annual treat for us. Deserts are served until 10 p.m.; and if you should stop by in the afternoon, you may catch the enticing aroma of deep dish apple pie wafting its' way from the kitchen." (T&L Scott)*

"Our family has stayed at Haus Rohrback at least once a year for the past ten years. We open the door and instantly relax." (L. Tanz)

"We have been staying at Haus Rohrbach Pension, in Leavenworth, Washington, for the past 10 years! It is a delightfully resting place, with a European flavor. All the

breakfasts are special, and beautifully served; but we especially love the homemade cinnamon rolls and sourdough pancakes. Bob and Katharine maintain very high standards of cleanliness, comfort, and convenience. The hot tub under the stars on a snowy winter night is terrific, and the grounds during the summer are lovely."
(E&R Braman)

"Imagine yourself sitting in a cozy living area around a warm woodburning stove, chatting with old friends or meeting new, looking out over a quaint village refurbished in the German motif. This is one of the warm scenes conjured up at Haus Rohrbach in Leavenworth, Washington. Nestled at the foot of a mountain at the edge of town, the inn is tastefully decorated in NW country—complete with handmade quilts and flower arrangements everywhere right down to the hearty country breakfast served each morning—sourdough pancakes, homemade cinnamon rolls, Dutch babies, ham sausage, etc. In the winter there is a multitude of cross-country ski trails close by and downhill slopes within an hour. An excellent sledding slope is right out the front door and a hot tub where you can enjoy snowflakes as well as the warmth of the spa." (K. Peters)

Port Townsend

Bishop Victorian Guest Suites
714 Washington Street
Port Townsend, WA 98368
(206) 385-6122 or (800) 824-4738
Innkeepers: Lloyd and Marlene Cahoon

♕♕   Rating: B
Rates: Single/$54-79; Double/$68-98.
Senior discount
Credit Cards: AE, MC, V

Victorian hotel built in 1890 has been completely restored and is located right in the heart of downtown Port Townsend near the ferry terminal. The lower floor of the building is used as a storefront and a flight of steps leads to the inn's lobby. Thirteen guest suites are furnished with some period pieces and offer private bath, sitting area, full kitchen, and one or two bedrooms. Walk to area shops, restaurants, and the ferry terminal. Area attractions include Olympic National Park (40 minutes by car), Mt. Baker, the Cascades, Admiralty Bay, and Fort Worden State Park, known for its use in the movie, "An Officer and A Gentleman". Continental breakfast. Families welcome. Restricted smoking.

Yakima

37 House
4002 Englewood Avenue
Yakima, WA 98908
(509) 965-5537 or 965-4705
Innkeeper: Andrea Price

♛♛♛   Rating: A
Rates: Single or Double/$65-120.
Corporate discount
Credit Cards: AE, MC, V

37 House is a lovely 7,500 square-foot mansion built in the 1930s that has been completely restored and is situated in a quiet residential area overlooking the city located 140 miles east of Seattle. There are six guest rooms with shuttered window panes, custom Waverly curtains and bedspreads, window seats under the eaves, and fully tiled private baths. One suite on the second floor offers two bedrooms, a sitting room, and full bath. The main floor consists of a knotty-pine paneled library with fireplace, a fireplaced living room, and a formal dining room. A lower level recreation room is more informal and offers TV and fireplace with chairs and a sofa. The grounds of the estate include a tennis court and English garden. Area attractions include Yakima Valley wineries and the Sun dome. Full breakfast includes fresh-baked muffins, fresh fruits, and a special hot entree. Function rooms for meetings and weddings are available. Families welcome. No smoking.

Guests write: *"The breakfast of eggs Benedict was cooked to order and we've never tasted better. I can't say enough about the 37 House. It is what I always thought B&Bs should be like but never experienced."* (D. Williamson)

"This was my husband's first experience at a B&B and he was surprised he liked it so well. I have stayed in B&Bs before but this one is first rate. We thoroughly enjoyed ourselves. I think perhaps we shall make it an annual Anniversary event and I'm so glad they saved this wonderful house from the wrecker's ball." (F. Webb)

"This was a home I had often admired during my growing-up years in Yakima and it was fun staying there as a guest. The manager graciously moved us to another room when we expressed a concern about noise from the traffic during the night. We were given the master suite at no added expense and appreciated this courtesy very much. Our breakfast was delicious and attractively presented." (S. Parkhill)

Petersburg

Smoke Hole Lodge
P.O. Box 953
Petersburg, WV 26847
(304) 242-8377
(winter phone only,
no phone in summer)
Innkeeper: Edward W. Stifel, III

♛♛♛   Rating: A
Rates: Single/$95; Double/$175.

Spacious newly-rebuilt mountain lodge and ranch on 1,600 remote wilderness acres is 12 miles south of Petersburg, close to Monongahela National Forest. Choose from five comfortable and pleasant guest rooms with pine furnishings on the second floor. There are also two dormitory rooms on this level that together can sleep nine. Each room offers a private, modern bath with shower. The ranch runs on kerosene, wood, and bottled gas as it has neither electricity nor phone. This makes for a fascinating turn-of-the-century experience. The ranch is an Angus cattle operation, and many other animals live there as well. The property abounds with deer and on occasion a bear is sighted. This is a relaxing, get-away-from-it-all spot for the whole family. Enjoy bass fishing on the river, swimming, inner-tubing, and hiking on the property. Hearty full breakfast, lunch, and dinner are included in the rates, as is round-trip transportation from Petersburg where hosts will meet you for the hour-and-a-half trip up the mountain by four-wheel drive. Families and supervised pets welcome. Open May through October.

Guests write: *"Yes, there is a heaven on earth and it's in West Virginia at Smoke Hole Lodge. Anyone from the Washington, DC area (and anywhere else for that matter) should plan on staying at least two nights — it takes a day to unwind and leave behind the stress of the city. But the hammock, porch chairs, fireplaced living room, and good home cooking contribute to a sense of well-being. What to do? Ask to hike part of the way into the lodge — you may beat the four-wheel drive truck with luggage. There is more nature here than some folks would think existed. My teenagers and I had a lunch packed for us and we took off hiking, fording the river several times and got soaked but loved every minute of it. My family left appreciating the good earth and Ed's important stewardship of this pristine environment."* (S. Sonke)

Baraboo

Pinehaven Bed & Breakfast
E13083 Highway 33
Baraboo, WI 53913
(608) 356-3489
Innkeepers: Lyle and Marge Getschman

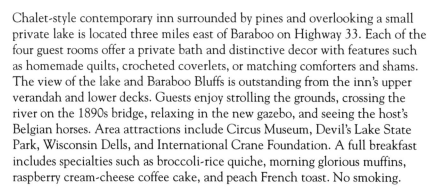

♛♛♛   Rating: A
Rates: Single/$60-70; Double/$65-75
Credit Cards: MC, V

Chalet-style contemporary inn surrounded by pines and overlooking a small private lake is located three miles east of Baraboo on Highway 33. Each of the four guest rooms offer a private bath and distinctive decor with features such as homemade quilts, crocheted coverlets, or matching comforters and shams. The view of the lake and Baraboo Bluffs is outstanding from the inn's upper verandah and lower decks. Guests enjoy strolling the grounds, crossing the river on the 1890s bridge, relaxing in the new gazebo, and seeing the host's Belgian horses. Area attractions include Circus Museum, Devil's Lake State Park, Wisconsin Dells, and International Crane Foundation. A full breakfast includes specialties such as broccoli-rice quiche, morning glorious muffins, raspberry cream-cheese coffee cake, and peach French toast. No smoking.

Guests write: "*Country tranquillity, a beautiful setting, and all possible creature comforts—perfection! Tastefully decorated, each room was sparkling clean, as were the well-appointed, modern bathrooms. The home was lovely and offered several porches that looked out on a small private lake. Breakfast each morning was delicious and imaginative—served on beautiful china and crystal, it was a treat for the eye as well as the tastebuds.*" (J&D Sorden)

Burlington

Hillcrest Bed & Breakfast
540 Storle Avenue
Burlington, WI 53105
(414) 763-4706
Innkeepers: Dick and Karen Granholm

♛♛♛   Rating: A
Rates: Single or Double/$60-75; higher for suites.

Edwardian home built in 1908 is situated on the crest of a hill with panoramic view of the valley and waterways below and is located off Highway 11 West. There are three guest rooms with individual decor and one offers a private bath. Special features of the room include queen-size carved oak or walnut beds, river views, period antique furnishings, lace curtains, and Oriental rugs. A converted carriage house offers three new deluxe guest accommodations. Two offer a fireplace and Jacuzzi and one is a large suite that runs the length of the second-floor with two bedrooms and Jacuzzi tub. The lower porch on the main house offers antique wicker furniture and views of the surrounding lakes and rivers. Guest enjoy exploring the landscaped grounds and restored gardens. Area attractions include antique shopping, golfing, skiing, swimming, and boating. Full breakfast. No smoking.

Cedarburg

Washington House Inn
W62N573 Washington Avenue
Cedarburg, WI 53012
(414) 375-3550 or (800) 554-4717
Innkeeper: James Pape

♛♛♛ Rating: A
Rates: Single or Double/$59-159.
Senior and auto club discounts
Credit Cards: AE, MC, V

Historic Victorian urban inn is centrally located in the town's Historic District, 3 miles west of I-43, exit 17. There are twenty-nine guest rooms throughout the complex and each features a private bath, antiques, cozy down quilts, fireplaces, and fresh flowers. Deluxe suites offer Jacuzzi tubs and unique architectural features. Area attractions include Historic Cedar Creek Settlement, antique shops, and Pioneer Village. Continental breakfast includes fresh-baked muffins and fresh-squeezed juices. Function rooms are available for weddings and meetings. Families welcome. Wheelchair access.

Guests write: *"Some of the features we enjoyed at the 'gathering room': afternoon hour for local wine sampling, veggies and dip and assorted cheeses, the uncluttered and well considered mixture of tasteful furnishings and efficient workings (whirlpool bath, gas fireplaces, excellent bathrooms). And, oh yes, the town at Cedarburg is super too—great coffee shop, wonderful browsing bookstore, waterfall, some good eateries, and lots of shopping."* (D. Hobson)

Chetek

Canoe Bay
W16065 Hogback Road
Chetek, WI 54728
(800) 568-1995
Innkeepers: Dan and Lisa Dobrowolski

♛♛♛   Rating: A
Rates: Single or Double/$89-179
Senior and auto club discounts
Credit Cards: MC, V

A-Frame country inn is situated on 280-acres of wooded land surrounding a 50-acre lake in northern Wisconsin, 90 miles east of the Twin Cities. Four guest suites feature a two-person whirlpool tub, separate shower, original murals, and sitting area. Four additional rooms are available with private baths and decks, fireplaces, and wet bars. Gather with other guests around the massive fieldstone fireplace in the great room with soaring cathedral ceiling. A TV room offers comfortable furnishings and cable stations. Fine art is displayed throughout the inn with original pottery, oil paintings, and lithographs. Relax in the private whirlpools, or go cross country skiing, ice-skating, boating, swimming, fishing, and bicycling on the grounds. This area offers a very private and quiet retreat with nature, a spring fed lake, and oak and aspen forest. Full breakfast specialties may include Canoe Bay egg soufflé, orange French toast, or baked apple oatmeal. Dinner is available by advance reservation and features northern Wisconsin cuisine with fresh ingredients, wild rice, fresh-baked breads, and fruit pies. Wheelchair access. No smoking.

Guests write: *"Since discovering Canoe Bay in July, 1993, we have enjoyed three seasonal experiences and the activities which Canoe Bay has to offer in each: summer (canoeing, swimming on two very secluded private lakes), fall (hiking through spectacular wooded trails) and winter (cross country skiing, ice skating and warming up with mulled sangria in front of the great room's natural stone fireplace). Canoe Bay is a unique opportunity to enjoy intimacy with each other intertwined among an extremely beautiful natural setting. The surroundings are only a part of the Canoe Bay experience. Gourmet dinners and desserts prepared on site. The plush accommodations which you can't wait to indulge in, including whirlpool tubs for two, top off your stay." (D. DuPont)*

"Our first favorable impression was the acreage with a beautiful, winding, wooded road leading to the lodge. Next, our warm greeting from our hosts, Dan and Lisa. We immediately felt welcome. Each suite is completely different. Ours was the Cedar Suite. The dust ruffle, sheets, comforter and many pillows done in a southwest flavor

makes it so inviting. The art work in our suite is varied and done in great taste as is the art work throughout the lodge." (E&T Mizen)

"From the moment you walk into "The Lodge at Canoe Bay' you are quickly transported into an environment of art and beauty, nature's solitude, and new friends who treat you as valued guests. Then there is the 25-foot high field stone fireplace, surrounded by a large comfortable room, appointed with chairs and sofas, overstuffed for your comfort, and at your finger tips, numerous magazines to peruse, and the daily paper to read if you need or ignore if you wish to perpetuate your sense of quiet, set apart from the world." (W. Watson)

Kenosha

The Manor House
6536 3rd Avenue
Kenosha, WI 53143
(414) 658-0014
Owner: Clifton Peterson

♛♛♛   Rating: A
Rates: Single or Double/$100-140.
Corporate discounts
Credit Cards: AE, MC, V

Historic Georgian manor house built in the 1920's is in the heart of the Lakeshore Historical District of Kenosha and overlooks Lake Michigan, yet is only four miles from I-94. There are four second-floor guest rooms with private bath, cable TV, rich fabrics, Oriental carpets, and 18th-Century antiques. A small sitting area found between two bedroom wings offers a private corner for relishing breakfast or viewing the lake. The first floor common rooms are spacious with unusually fine antiques and appointments. A lower level offers special conference facilities. The grounds include a fountain, rose garden, gazebo, and many varieties of trees. Area attractions include the nearby Historic District, museums, beaches, golf courses, and county parks. Continental breakfast includes seasonal fruits. Restricted smoking.

Guests write: *"This was the best place to enjoy our 11th Anniversary. It was truly relaxing with super, gracious hosts." (B. Mooney)*

"The Manor House is very pretty and comfortable, elegant, and cozy - a relaxing weekend get-away and wonderful one-year wedding anniversary." (A. Kelman)

Wyoming

Additional information on B&Bs in Wyoming is available from the following B&B reservation agency: B&B Western Adventure (406) 259-7993.

Ontario, Canada

Additional information on B&B in Ontario is available from the following B&B reservation agency: Toronto Bed & Breakfast (416) 588-8800

Toronto/Mississauga

By the Creek Bed & Breakfast
1716 Lincolnshire Blvd.
Mississauga, Toronto, Canada L5E2S7
(905) 891-0337 or (905) 278-5937
Innkeeper: Edith Dew

♛♛   Rating: B
Rates: Single/$35-40; Double/$55-60.
Senior and corporate discounts
Credit Cards: MC

Built in 1958, this split-level home overlooks the Etobicoke Creek on the border of Metropolitan Toronto. Each of the three guest rooms have been individually decorated and are air conditioned; two offer a private bath. One of the rooms is a large suite which encompasses the entire lower (garden walkout) level of the home and is perfect for families and groups. A large living room is a favorite gathering place for guests and it showcases the host's paintings and art collection. A large sunroom with comfortable furnishings overlooks the spacious backyard. Relax in front of one of the two fireplaces or the patio decks overlooking the creek. Walk to public golf course and the shopping mall. Visit the nearby Canadian National Exhibition, International Centre, and Stage West or take the QEW to Niagara Falls. Toronto sights are within 20 minutes. A full breakfast consists of fresh fruit, cereal, and a hot dish. Families welcome. Wheelchair access. No smoking. No Pets.

Guests write: *"As a regular guest I can highly recommend this B&B. Surroundings are warm, comfortable, very clean, and tastefully decorated with many artifacts and antiques. I particularly enjoyed the relaxing evenings and great fruit salads for breakfast. The hosts have extensive knowledge of the area's history and are most helpful in suggesting the the best travel routes and methods." (D. Gidley)*

Quebec, Canada

Montreal

Manior Ambrose
3422 Stanley
Montreal, QC, Canada H3A 1R8
(514) 288-6922; Fax: (514) 288-5757
Innkeeper: Lucie Seguin

♛♛   Rating: B-
Rates: Single/$30-65; Double/$40-70
Credit Cards: MC, V

Turn-of-the-century Victorian brownstone is located in the heart of the city.
There are twenty-two guest rooms between the two buildings that are joined
in the center. While there is a wide variety in the size, decor, and quality of
the rooms, each offers a TV, radio, and telephone; fifteen have a private bath.
A breakfast room on the lower level is a pleasant area where guests help
themselves to a continental breakfast and beverages. From the inn, its only a
short walk to restaurants, theaters, shopping, and convenient public transportation. There is limited off-street parking behind the inn.

Trinidad

Port of Spain/Maraval

Carnetta's House
28 Scotland Terrace
Anadalusia, Maraval,
Trinidad , West Indies
(809) 628-2732; Fax: (809) 628-7717
Innkeepers: Carnetta and Winston Borrell

♛♛   Rating: B+
Rates: Single/$46; Double/$66
Credit Cards: AE, MC, V

Carnetta's House is a large contemporary home built in 1974 that is located on
the bank of the Maraval River in an up-scale neighborhood suburb of Port of
Spain. The surroundings offer a tropical paradise of lush plants, tropical fruit
trees, mountain views, and colorful wildlife. There are five ground floor guest

rooms with floral themes which feature air-conditioning, direct dial telephones, TV, and private baths with shower. Guests relax in a second floor
living room with cable television and a dining patio with vistas of the mountains and rain forest. Area attractions: St. Andrew's golf course, hiking in the
rain forest, theaters, nightlife with calypso and steel bands, bird sanctuary,
botanical garden, art galleries, swimming beaches. Full breakfast includes fruit
juice, fruit plate with choice of three local fruits, breakfast meat, and eggs any
style. Lunch and dinner are available upon request and advance reservation.
Rental cars, babysitting, and tours available. Families welcome.

Guests write: *"We must cross over from neighboring Tobago monthly or more often
in connection with our business and we have experienced every level of
accommodation available before discovering Carnetta's House. The personal
attention of Winston and Carnetta have ended our search for a place to stay. As long
as the space is available, Carnetta's House will be our permanent home away from
home."* (E. & H. Louis)

*"Accurate directions were given to personal places of interest, a wake-up call was
requested and given on time and pleasantly. Breakfasts were served with a smile and
good conversation and the food was well prepared and available on request. The
house is within a half hour drive from the best beach on the island."* (M. Shaw)

Port of Spain/Maraval

Monique's Guest House
114 Saddle Road
Maraval, Trinidad, West Indies
(809) 628-3334 or FAX (809) 622-3232
Owner/Manager: Michael & Monica Charbonne

♛♛   Rating: B-
Rates: Single/$46-51; Double/$57-62
Credit Cards: AE, MC, V

Contemporary two-story situated in the Maraval Valley, surrounded by tropical
green hills and a variety of flowers and plants. Twenty guest rooms with
private baths offer queen size beds, small kitchenettes, telephones, television
and balconies. Relax in the television room or common room. Walk to a
small, tropical zoo, botanical gardens, historic buildings, shopping, and a small
museum. Area attractions: Bird Sanctuary, Pitch Lake, Blue Basin Waterfall,
and the city of Port-of-Spain. Full breakfast includes eggs, breakfast meats,
pancakes, and juice. Families welcome.

Alabama -- (See Mississippi)

Alaska

Alaska Private Lodgings, Stay With a Friend
P.O. Box 200047
Anchorage, AK 99520-0047
(907) 258-1717
Fax: (907) 258-6613
Owner: Mercy Dennis

Despite Anchorage's 5,000 hotel rooms, 500 B&B rooms and 80 hostel rooms, accommodations are very tight during the summer months and advance reservations are strongly suggested. B&B accommodations range from guest rooms and suites in a variety of rural or in-town locations. Private unhosted apartments are also available with fully furnished kitchens. Geographic area represented is Southcentral Alaska.
Office hours: Daily 9 am to 6 pm in-season; off-season office hours are flexible with an answering machine for after hours.
Inspections of B&Bs: Annual.
Deposit: A personal check covering one night's lodging must be paid in advance or a credit card guarantee can also be accepted.
Payment: AE, MC, V, cash, personal checks. There is a discount for cash or check payments. 5% travel agent commission available.

Arizona

Mi Casa Su Casa
P.O. Box 950
Tempe, AZ 85280-0950
(602) 990-0682 or (800) 456-0682
Fax: (602) 990-3390
Owner: Ruth Young

Geographic area represented includes Arizona, New Mexico, Utah, and Nevada.
Office hours: Daily 8 a.m. to 8 p.m.
Inspections of B&Bs: Annually.
Deposit: A first night's deposit is required for stays under one week. For one-night stays, payment includes an extra $5.00 charge. For stays over seven nights, 20% of the total amount is required as a deposit..
Payment: Cash or traveler's checks only.   (Continued)

Guests write: *"My wife and I are frequent traveler's to the American desert Southwest. Our vacations often return us to the Arizona and New Mexico area. We have come to rely on Mi Casa, Su Casa reservation service to assist us during our travelers. We relate our travel plans, the type of accommodations we are looking for, any special features (tennis, etc) and our budget limitations and she comes up with the rest."* (W. Dickson)

"We wanted to stay up for hours visiting with our lovely hosts. In the morning I was asked if we'd like to try their grapefruit. So our host went out to his tree, picked a grapefruit and we ate it. Now that was fresh! We're from the Midwest so this was very special. The smell of orange blossoms is heavenly. We trust Mi Casa Su Casa to find us a place to stay where we feel welcome and comfortable. They have never let us down." (A. Bush)

California

Eye Openers Bed & Breakfast Reservations
P.O. Box 694
Altadena, CA 91003
(213) 684-4428 or (818) 797-2055
Fax: (818) 798-3640
Owner: Ruth Judkins

Eye Opener's strives to match traveler's requests with a wide range of B&B homes and inns throughout the entire state of California.
Office hours: Weekdays 10 a.m. to 6 pm.
Deposit: A $25 deposit is required to confirm reservations
Payment: MC, V, checks, traveler's checks. Travel agent commission available.

Guests write: *"Arrangements were made on our behalf for a stay in San Francisco. We were delighted with our accommodations. The host could not have been more helpful and hospitable and we were very happy with our room in their house. We hope to return to the USA before long and will certainly be using Eye Openers B&B again."* (S. de Brett)

"The little thumb nail sketch of each home was most appreciated and helpful in choosing the B&B most to our liking. Our hosts made us feel at home in their home and we spent a time each day together. So much nicer then being by ourselves in a motel." (M. Friedlander)

"We were particularly pleased with the B&B accommodations that were made for us by Eye Openers B&B Reservations. Our hostess was delightful and gracious in sharing her home with us." (B. Pincince)

Florida

Bed & Breakfast Scenic Florida
P.O. Box 3385
Tallahassee, FL 32315-3385
(904) 386-8196
Owner: Dianne Mahlert

Choose from 27 B&B hosts throughout the north and central Florida area including Tampa, Orlando, and Ft. Lauderdale.
Office hours: Weekdays 9 am to 5 pm; Saturday 9 am to 2 pm. Closed Sunday.
Inspections of B&Bs: Annually.
Deposit: A deposit equal to one night's stay is required to confirm reservations.
Payment: MC, V, Personal checks.

Georgia

Bed & Breakfast Atlanta
1801 Piedmont Avenue, #208
Atlanta, GA 30324
(404) 875-0525, 875-9672
(800) 96-PEACH; Fax: (404) 875-9672
Madalyne Eplan

Established in 1979, this agency covers the geographic area of metropolitan Atlanta (site for the 1996 Olympics) and selected sites around Georgia.
Office hours: Weekdays 9 am to 5 pm.
Inspections of B&Bs: Annually.
Deposit: A deposit equal to one night's stay is required to confirm reservations.
Payment: AE, CB, D, MC, V, and Personal checks.

Guests write: *"I was impressed with the ease and efficiency of the reservation service. Much was accomplished with one brief phone call."* (B. Wilson)

"Our hosts were very gracious. Their home was everything as described and more. I would emphasize how very helpful the staff person was at B&B Atlanta. She not only knew the available inventory, but knew what made each home different and this helped us made a choice." (A. Farley)

Hawaii

Bed & Breakfast Honolulu (Statewide)
3242 Kaohinani Drive
Honolulu, HI 96817
(808) 595-7533; (800) 288-4666 (USA & Canada)
Fax: (808) 595-2030
Owner: Gene Bridges

B&B accommodations are available throughout all islands. Car and inter-island air coupons are available at low rates.
Office hours: Weekdays 8 am to 5 pm and Saturday 8 am to noon.
Deposit: 50% deposit for stays more than 3 days. Full payment is required in advance for stays of three days or less.
Payment: MC, V, Cash, Traveler's checks.

Guests write: *We have used Hawaii's Best B&B twice, both times on short notice and in one case during the height of the Christmas season. Both times we were fixed up with ideal cottages matched to our taste. They provided exceptional service right down to arranging rental cards and hotel accommodations. We have stayed at several of their cottages and all were up to the very high standards advertised."* (T. Kendrick)

"The reservations, directions, descriptions were all managed most professionally and made our Hawaii vacation a delightful experience." (E. Griswold)

"Barbara Campbell has done a wonderful job choosing accommodations that truly convey the aloha spirit. All of our facilities were very clean and well tended. She leaves the impression of being a gracious and caring person and we felt she strives to bring those characteristics forward in choosing accommodations to represent." (J. Mahoney)

Hawaii's Best Bed & Breakfasts
P.O. Box 563
Kamuela, HI 96743
(800) 262-9912 or (808) 885-4550
Fax: (808) 885-0550
Owner: Barbara Campbell

Accommodations are available throughout all islands. A detailed itinerary can be specifically tailored to a guest's personal travel requirements. Rental cars available.
Geographic area: All Hawaiian islands.

Office hours: Weekdays 9 am to 5 pm; Saturday 8 am to noon.
Inspections of B&Bs: Annually.
Deposit: A deposit equal to one night's stay at each location is required to confirm reservations.
Payment: Personal checks or cash.

Massachusetts

Bed & Breakfast Associates Bay Colony, Ltd.
P.O. Box 57166, Babson Park
Boston, MA 02157
(617) 449-5302 or (800) 347-5088
Fax: (617) 449-5958
Director: Marilyn Mitchell

This reservation agency was established in 1981 and represents over 170 B&B accommodations in Eastern Massachusetts including greater Boston, Cambridge, North and South Shore areas, Cape Cod, Martha's Vineyard, and Nantucket.
Inspections of B&Bs: Annually.
Deposits: $25 per night stay is required to confirm the reservation.
Payment: AE, MC, V. 5% travel agency commission available.

Guests write: *"B&B Associates asked me the right questions which allowed them to find me convenient, lovely, comfortable, and affordable accommodations for a week in Boston — something my travel agent was unable to do! Staying in Charlestown in spacious accommodations with a view of the Bunker Hill monument, minutes away from Back Bay, not to mention Quincy Market and Filene's Basement — is one of the best ways to spend a week in Boston. This is a top-notch organization."* (V. Jennings)

"We stayed on Beacon Hill central to downtown in a beautifully furnished two-room apartment. A beautiful breakfast was served in the sitting room and included fresh fruit, juice, coffee, and muffins. This was one of the best B&Bs we've stayed in anywhere in the world." (S. Loyrey)

Massachusetts

Bed & Breakfast Cape Cod
P.O. Box 341
West Hyannisport, MA 02672
(508) 775-2772; Fax: (508) 775-2884
Owner: Clark Diehl

Select from 90 B&B homes, country inns and historic homes on Cape Cod, Nantucket, Martha's Vineyard, Gloucester at Cape Ann and south of Boston in Cohasset, Scituate, and Marshfield.
Deposit: A deposit of 25% of total room rate plus a $10 booking charge is required to confirm reservations.
Payment: AE, D, MC, V accepted for deposit and full payment.

Guests write: *"Thanks to B&B Cape Cod for assistance in finding a lovely B&B. Hosts were gregarious, easy-going, informative, efficient, and cheerful." (R. Hage)*

"Thanks to B&B Cape Cod for a fabulous recommendation. This B&B is going to be a place we shall return to. Spotlessly clean, totally engrossing ambiance with every detail accounted for." (A. Vinci)

"I thank them so much for their advice and guidance in my choice of accommodations. They operate an excellent service with efficiency and expertise." (M. Merkley)

"Our B&B in Scitutate Harbor was an unforgettable experience — one that I could replicate neither before nor since. The house is beautiful and wonderfully situated. The hosts congenial and they know just how much to host and yet give you lots of privacy." (A. Tonello)

Golden Slumber Accommodations
640 Revere Beach Boulevard
Revere, MA 02151
(617) 289-1053 or (800) 892-3231 (outside MA)
Owner: Leah Schmidt

A wide variety of accommodations are available throughout Boston, North and South Shores, and specializing in Cape Cod. Many locations welcome families with children and several have handicapped accessible accommodations. Limousine service is available to address guests' transportation needs. A

complete host home directory is available. No reservation fee charged.
Office hours: Monday through Saturday 8 am to 9 pm; Sunday noon to 6 pm.
Inspections of B&Bs: Annually.
Deposit: One third total room rate must be paid in advance.
Payment: MC, V, Traveler's checks, Money orders.

Mississippi

Lincoln Ltd, Bed & Breakfast
Mississippi Reservation Service
P.O. Box 3479
Meridian, MS 39303
(601) 482-5483; Fax: (601) 693-7447
Owner: Barbara Lincoln Hall

Select from a variety of B&Bs located throughout Mississippi, Natchez to
Memphis, eastern Louisiana, and selected areas of Alabama.
Inspections of B&Bs: Annually.
Deposit: A deposit equal to one night's stay is required to confirm reservations.
Payment: AE, MC, V. Travel agent commission available.

Guests write: *"Their accommodations helped make our trip memorable. We had a
wonderful glance of the South and learned many new things; travel by bike may be
slow, but affords opportunity to see lots!"* (J. Buerklin)

Montana

Bed & Breakfast Western Adventure
P.O. Box 20972
Billings, MT 59104-0972
(406) 259-7993; Fax: (406) 248-5683
Owner: Paula Deigert

Geographic area represented includes Montana, Wyoming, Black Hills of
South Dakota, and Eastern Idaho.
Office hours: May through September, weekdays 9 am to 5 pm and Saturday 9
am to 1 pm. Winter hours are weekdays 9 am to 1 pm.
Deposit: A deposit equal to one night's stay is required to confirm reservations.
5% travel agency commission available on bookings of at least two nights.

Guests write: *"I'm a business traveler who prefers B&B to hotels/motels. All my comments come not as a vacationer but regarding a place to stay on business. I find B&Bs gearing up for people like me who like comfort and pampering. As a single, professional woman, B&Bs are the answer. There was a lovely selection of rooms to choose from. Hostess was very warm and friendly." (T. Elliott)*

"The reservation process was prompt with excellent courtesy, assistance, and directions. Wonderful room and food. The town is lovely and the surroundings give you many things to do. (F. Thatcher)

"We always use B&Bs whenever we can and we have used B&B Western Adventure numerous times. We know we can always count on a home which has been inspected and we have always found the hosts most congenial and the accommodations most comfortable." (M. Thorndal)

Nevada -- (See Mi Casa, Su Casa under Arizona)

New York

Abode Bed & Breakfast
P.O. Box 20022
New York, NY 10028
(212) 472-2000
Owner: Shelli Leifer

Reservations may be made for over 100 B&B accommodations throughout Manhattan. Also available are unhosted, fully equipped apartments in owner-occupied brownstones. Guests have total privacy in their own apartment and still enjoy the benefits of having hosts on hand for questions, information, and advice.
Office house: Weekdays 9 am to 5 pm and Saturday 11 am to 2 pm.
Inspections of B&Bs: Annually.
Deposit: A deposit of approximately 25% of the stay is required to confirm reservations.
Payment: AE is accepted for deposit and full payment.
Restrictions: Minimum stay is two nights.

Guests write: *"I was greeted by a spotlessly clean facility, tastefully decorated, comfortably furnished, a cup of coffee in the waiting and a dozen roses that lasted during my entire stay. The location was ideal. My host offered us a tour — it was a nice and welcoming thing to do." (V. LaFrance)*

Bed & Breakfast & Books
35 West 92nd Street
New York, NY 10025
(212) 865-8740
Owner: Judith Goldbert

Reservations can be made for over 60 B&B accommodations located throughout Manhattan, Upper West and East sides, Chelsea, Gremercy Park, Greenwich Village, and Soho.
Deposits: A deposit equal to one night's stay is required to confirm reservations. 5% travel agent commission available.

Ohio

Private Lodgings, Inc.
P.O. Box 18590
Cleveland, OH 44118
(216) 321-3213
Owner: Jean Stanley

Reservations can be made for more than 40 B&B homes and inns located throughout the Cleveland metropolitan area.
Office hours: Weekdays 9 am to noon, 3 to 5 pm. Closed Wednesdays.
Inspections of B&Bs: Annually.
Deposit: A deposit of 50% is required to confirm reservations.
Payment: Cash and traveler's checks are accepted for full payment.

Pennsylvania

Hershey B&B Reservations
P.O. Box 208
Hershey, PA 17033
(717) 533-2928
Owner: Renee Deutel

Choose from a variety of B&Bs located throughout the south-central section of Pennsylvania. Personalized service is offered in matching guests to just the right B&B whether the trip is for a family vacation, a farm experience, a long stay when transferring into the area, a romantic honeymoon, a for a business retreat in a relaxing setting.
Office hours: Weekdays 10 am to 4 pm. (Continued)

Inspections of B&Bs: Annually.
Deposit: A 25% deposit is required to confirm reservations.
Payment: AE, MC, V accepted for full payment. 5% travel agent commission available.

Guests write: *"When our whole family decided to get together for a vacation in Lancaster County, we knew that we wanted to stay at a B&B but we were unfamiliar with the area. I contacted Hershey B&B Reservation Service who were immediately able to recommend the perfect place. This beautiful farm turned out to be everything they promised. Their services didn't end at finding us the perfect B&B. She kept in close contact to give us helpful information and tips on things to do in the area complete with restaurant menus, easy-to-follow directions and coupons."* (C. Schindewolf)

Bed & Breakfast Connections
Bed & Breakfast of Philadelphia
P.O. Box 21
Devon, PA 19333
(610) 687-3565 or (800) 448-3619 (Outside PA)
Fax: (610) 995-9524
Owners: Peggy Gregg and Lucy Scribner

Choose from a number of accommodations in the metropolitan Philadelphia area including Main Line suburbs, Chestnut Hill, Germantown, Mt. Airy, Valley Forge, Brandywine Valley, and Amish communities.
Office hours: Weekdays 9 am to 7 pm and Saturday 9 am to 5 pm.
Inspections: Annually.
Deposits: A deposit equal to one night's stay is required to confirm reservations.
Payment: AE, MC, V accepted for full payment. 5% travel agency commission available.

Rest and Repast B&B Reservation Service
P.O. Box 126
Pine Grove Mills, PA 16868
(814) 238-1484
Owner: Linda Feltman

Select from over 60 B&B homes and inns located throughout Central Pennsylvania including the Penn State area.
Office hours: Weekdays 8:30-11:30 am. Closed weekends except during peak times.

Inspections of B&Bs: Annually.
Deposit: A $25-50 deposit per night is required to confirm reservations.
Payment: Cash only.

Guests write: "My B&B needs have changed dramatically in the 10 years since I left college. Yet every year, Rest & Repast places me with the perfect host. From my 'every penny counts' years when they saved me $70 off the cheapest hotel room, to my years when a crib and a host close to the action counted most. Rest & Repast comes through with flying colors!" (D. Painter)

"Our Rest & Repast hosts always prepare salt-free breakfasts for me which are exceptional. On those occasions when we were unable to obtain tickets for a football game, our host is often able to get them for us from some of her many friends. We are always made to feel at home." (B. Sacks)

"My son loved the Penn State bedroom at our host's home. Our breakfast of fresh fruit, oven French toast, sausage, juice, and coffee was great. We felt as though we were staying with family. I was able to bring home some recipes from Pennsylvania that a lot of people in New Hampshire enjoy." (S. Kamitian)

South Carolina

Historic Charleston B&B
60 Broad Street
Charleston, SC 29401
(803) 722-6606 or (800) 743-3583
Fax: (803) 722-9773
Owner: Douglas B. Lee

Reservations can be made for over 60 private homes and carriage houses in and around Charleston's historic district.
Office hours: Weekdays 9 am to 5 pm.
Inspections of B&Bs: Annually.
Deposits: A deposit equal to one night's stay is required to confirm reservations during low season. A two night deposit is required during high season.
Payment: AE, MC, V, Personal checks accepted for full payment.

Guests write: "Our son had just returned to Charleston after seven months with the Navy in the Middle East. We were looking for a touch of home for Christmas Eve and Christmas Day and found it! Our hosts placed a small, decorated tree in the living room of the carriage house — a lovely touch which was great appreciated." (B. DeCarolis)

South Dakota -- See Montana

Utah -- See Arizona

Virginia

Guesthouses Bed & Breakfast
P.O. Box 5737
Charlottesville, VA 22905
(804) 979-7264;   Fax: (804) 293-7791
Owner: Mary Hill Caperton

Guesthouses has matched guests with B&B hosts since 1976. Select from
B&Bs located throughout Charlottesville, Albemarle County, and Nelson
County. The variety of B&Bs available includes distinctive private homes and
guest cottages.

Office hours: Weekdays noon to 5 pm.

Inspections: Each B&B is inspected annually by Guesthouses and certified by
the Virginia Health Department.

Deposits: 25% deposit plus tax is required to confirm reservations and may be
charged to AE, MC, V. Payment to hosts on arrival must be cash or personal
check only.

Guests write: *"The Guesthouses services were prompt and courteous." (S.
Beddingfield)*

*"We loved our hostess and her B&B. A great find! Country charm and her warmth
made for a great stay." (B. Messerly)*

*"The match between host and guest was perfect! My friend who was in a wheelchair
found the house perfectly accessible, even more than her own home. She needed an
escape for a few days and this was it. She went into the guest room and you should
have seen her face brighten and her whole demeanor change for the better." (J.
Brown)*

*"Guesthouses arranged our first B&B experience. Because of the warmth and
hospitality shared, I am sure it will not be my last. I would not hesitate a moment to
recommend our hosts. My traveling companion, who is an experienced B&B
traveler agrees with me 100%." (M. Cress)*

Princely Bed & Breakfast, Ltd.
819 Prince Street
Alexandria, VA 22314
(703) 683-2159
Owners: E.J. and Trish Mansmann

This agency represents B&Bs in the Alexandria Old Town historic district which is conveniently located only 8 miles from either Washington, DC or Mount Vernon, Virginia. A new metro subway can whisk visitors into Washington within 15 minutes. Accommodations are all in distinctive homes dating between 1770 and 1900.
Office hours: Weekdays 10 am to 6 pm.
Inspections of B&Bs: Annually.
Deposit: A deposit equal to one night's stay is required for reservations.
Payment: Full payment upon arrival must be by check or cash. Ask about cancellation policy.

Guests write: *"I was most impressed with E.J. Mansmann and the professionalism he showed. It is likely we will use his services again. We love our charming cottage and first-class hospitality. We have made a fine friendship and are thankful for the introduction. The restaurants are superb!"*

Wyoming -- See Montana

Canada

Toronto Bed & Breakfast
Box 269, 253 College Street
Toronto, Ontario, Canada M5T 1R5
(416) 588-8800;   Fax: (416) 964-1756
Owner: Larry Page

Reservations are available for more than 20 B&Bs throughout the metropolitan Toronto area. While the agency specializes in the Toronto area, it is also part of a network referral system serving Niagara Falls, Kingston, and Ottawa.
Office hours: Weekdays 9 am to 7 pm.
Inspections of B&Bs: Annually.
Deposits: A one night's deposit is required to guarantee your reservation. In the event you are making a deposit by personal check, it must reach the agency within 7 days prior to your arrival date.
Payment: AE, MC, C, Traveler's checks and cash.